Narrative an of US National Security

Dominant narratives – from the Cold War consensus to the War on Terror – have often served as the foundation for debates over national security. Weaving current challenges, past failures and triumphs, and potential futures into a coherent tale, with well-defined characters and plot lines, these narratives impart meaning to global events, define the boundaries of legitimate politics, and thereby shape national security policy. However, we know little about why or how such narratives rise and fall. Drawing on insights from diverse fields, *Narrative and the Making of US National Security* offers novel arguments about where these dominant narratives come from, how they become dominant, and when they collapse. It evaluates these arguments carefully against evidence drawn from US debates over national security from the 1930s to the 2000s, and shows how these narrative dynamics have shaped the policies pursued by the United States.

RONALD R. KREBS is Associate Professor in the Department of Political Science at the University of Minnesota. He is the author of *Fighting for Rights: Military Service and the Politics of Citizenship* (2006), and co-editor of *In War's Wake: International Conflict and the Fate of Liberal Democracy* (Cambridge University Press, 2010). His articles on a wide range of topics in international relations have appeared in leading scholarly journals, including *International Organization, International Security*, the *European Journal of International Relations*, and *Security Studies*, as well as in outlets like *Foreign Affairs*, ForeignPolicy.com, *Slate*, and the *Washington Post*.

Cambridge Studies in International Relations: 138

Narrative and the Making of US National Security

Cambridge Studies in International Relations

Series list continues after index.

1, 2, pg 145
5, (6), 8

Narrative and the Making of US National Security

RONALD R. KREBS

CAMBRIDGE
UNIVERSITY PRESS

CAMBRIDGE
UNIVERSITY PRESS

University Printing House, Cambridge CB2 8BS, United Kingdom

Cambridge University Press is part of the University of Cambridge.

It furthers the University's mission by disseminating knowledge in the pursuit of education, learning and research at the highest international levels of excellence.

www.cambridge.org
Information on this title: www.cambridge.org/9781107503991

© Ronald R. Krebs 2015

First published 2015

Printed in the United States of America by Sheridan Books, Inc.

A catalogue record for this publication is available from the British Library

Library of Congress Cataloguing in Publication data
Krebs, Ronald R., 1974–
Narrative and the making of US national security / Ronald R. Krebs.
    pages cm. – (Cambridge studies in international relations ; 138)
ISBN 978-1-107-10395-5 (hardback)
1. National security – United States – History. I. Title.
UA23.K7757 2015
355'.033573–dc23

                                                2015008271

ISBN 978-1-107-10395-5 Hardback
ISBN 978-1-107-50399-1 Paperback

To my children – our future

Contents

Figures

Tables

Acknowledgments

I've been at work on this book a very long time. I didn't know it at first. It began as correspondence in *International Security* (2004), in response to Chaim Kaufmann's provocative piece, and then as an article in *Security Studies* (2007) on how the meaning of 9/11 became fixed and how that shaped the debate over the Iraq War. Colleagues and friends urged me to consider a larger project, but I was eager to get to work on another book entirely. They eventually wore me down, with the promise that I could write it quickly. Were they ever wrong.

But they were right to insist that I rethink the arc of my research – if you will, to revise the narrative of my scholarship. In the course of this long, long haul, I've accumulated an extraordinary number of debts. For comments on earlier versions of various chapters and on articles drawn from this book, I am most grateful to so many colleagues that I cannot possibly list them here – and, if I tried to list them, I would likely omit someone in error. You know who you are, and you have my deepest gratitude. I also received helpful feedback from audiences at presentations I gave at American University, Bar Ilan University, Brown University, Darmstadt Technical University, the Hebrew University, Northwestern University, the University of California at Berkeley, the University of Chicago (both PISP and PIPES), the University of Haifa, the University of Minnesota (I imposed on the MIRC family more than once!), the University of Southern California, the University of Texas at Austin, and the University of Virginia, as well as at meetings of the American Political Science Association, the International Studies Association, and the Interuniversity Seminar on Armed Forces and Society, and at a workshop on "The Politics of Talk in International Relations," held at the University of Bremen.

For the last thirteen years, I have had the privilege of being a member of an extraordinary intellectual community at the University of Minnesota. It is safe to say that I would never have written a book on narrative and national security had I not been a part of it. This book has its origins in conversations springing out of MIRC and out of graduate seminars, with fellow faculty and Ph.D. candidates alike. My IR colleagues at the University of Minnesota – Ben Ansell, Mike Barnett, Dara Cohen, John Freeman, Colin Kahl, Jim Ron, Martin Sampson, Kathryn Sikkink, and especially Bud Duvall, and more recently Ben Bagozzi and Dan Berliner – not only shaped my thinking, but even more importantly built this supportive yet critical community of scholarship and ideas. As for my students at the University of Minnesota, I owe them more than they realize: without them, I wouldn't even have *asked* the questions that animate this book. I am also grateful for the careful comments I received from students in graduate seminars I taught at the Hebrew University and the University of Minnesota. Finally, this project could not have been completed without the assistance of many students: I thank Kathryn Chylla, Lindsey Cunneen, Giovanni Mantilla, Ashley Nord, Aaron Rapport, Molla Reda, Rob Thompson, and especially Geoff Dancy for their superlative research assistance. For providing me with both time and resources to work on this project, I must acknowledge the University of Texas at Austin's Harrington Fellowship, the University of Minnesota's McKnight Land-Grant Professorship and various other programs, and the US-Israel Educational Foundation, which awarded me a Fulbright Senior Scholarship.

I'm especially grateful to those colleagues and friends who read an early draft of the entire manuscript in the summer of 2012. Their incisive comments led to a large-scale revision and reframing of the manuscript over the next year. As with all of the readers, for the many flaws that remain, I'd love to be able to hold responsible Bob Jervis, Brian Rathbun, and Jack Snyder – but I'm afraid I cannot. They tried to save me from errors of reasoning and fact, and if I failed to follow their advice, they can be blamed only for being insufficiently persuasive. Do feel free, however, to hold David Edelstein and Stacie Goddard accountable. My oldest friend in the world of scholarship, and as always a bit of a bulldog, Stacie read these chapters more times than anyone – and more times than anyone should have to. Since our days sharing an office at the Belfer Center, where we waited on tenterhooks to hear what sorry university would employ us and come to regret it, David has lent me his wise counsel. He read chapters from this book repeatedly, from the first draft to the last. Just before it went to press, he did so again – and I look forward to repaying that debt.

John Haslam of Cambridge University Press first heard of this project well before I was prepared to show him much of anything. I am grateful for his patience and encouragement. The anonymous reviewers of Cambridge University Press, who later revealed themselves to be Roland Bleiker and Jennifer Mitzen, were remarkably thoughtful and thorough, and their constructive critical comments, along with guidance from the series editors, especially Chris Reus-Smit, proved crucial in the book's final stages. Thanks, too, to the many fine folks at Cambridge University Press – especially Joanna Breeze and Sophie Rosinke – who have helped to bring the book into print, and to Diana Witt for the fine index.

Portions of this book have, in modified form, appeared in other outlets. Parts of Chapters 4 and 8 appeared in an essay, "The Rise, Persistence, and Fall of the War on Terror," in James Burk (ed.), *How 9/11 Changed Our Ways of War* (Stanford University Press, 2013). I drew on parts of Chapters 1 to 4 for "Tell Me a Story: FDR, Narrative, and the Making of the Second World War," *Security Studies* (2015) 24 (1): 131–170, and on parts of Chapters 5 to 8 for "How Dominant Narratives Rise and Fall: Military Conflict, Politics, and the Cold War Consensus," *International Organization* (2015) 69(4).

My family, thankfully, does not believe that it is their job to write my books for me. They do, thankfully, seem to believe that it is their job to prevent me from writing my books. And I don't know what I would do without them: the disruptor-in-chief, my wife Shira, and our four wonderful diversions – Yonit, Dahlia, Avital, and Eytan. The older two distracted me as I tried to finish my last book. The younger two came along to distract me from this one.

This book is dedicated to them, to our future. Yonit was born just two weeks before 9/11. She and her siblings do not know a world unmarked by the Terror narrative. By the time Eytan was born, a year into the Obama presidency, that narrative's dominance was finally waning. But we see its legacy everywhere – in our political institutions, in our expectations regarding liberty and privacy, in our understanding of history, in the private sector where homeland security is big business, and in our universities. The next generation cannot undo the past, but we hope they can learn from it.

But they cannot challenge dominant narratives if they are not even aware of how they structure our politics, how they rise to dominance, and how they fall from that exalted position. That's where this book comes in.

1 | *Narrating national security*

In the winter of 2007, as Americans grew increasingly weary of a protracted and seemingly unwinnable war in Iraq, President George W. Bush bucked the political winds and, rather than bring the troops home, called for dispatching more forces, a "surge." This would be a last-ditch effort to bring order to Iraq, which had known little peace since US forces had invaded the country and toppled Saddam Hussein's regime four years before. But, while the military struggled to dominate the battlefield in Iraq, Bush faced a rhetorical insurgency at home. This was not a surge, many Democrats warned, but a dangerous "escalation." Failing to back the surge was tantamount to capitulating to "Jihadist Joe," one Republican congressman memorably charged. Democratic opponents countered that resisting the surge was the surest way to save "GI Joe." Where the administration saw controllable "sectarian strife," many Democrats saw an unmanageable "civil war."[1] There was a lot at stake in these rhetorical battles. Both sides believed that, with their patience wearing thin, Americans wanted nothing to do with someone else's "civil war." Sectarian or civil "strife," though, seemed like a law-and-order problem, just the sort of thing that well-meaning outsiders could help to quash.

Such familiar rhetorical contests shape the course of politics, even in matters of national security. That is hardly news to politicians the world over, who spend untold sums on staff and consultants to help them craft their messages. It would not surprise generations of scholars across the humanities and social sciences who have labored to reveal language's inner workings and contradictions, its relationship to human cognition and experience, and its deep structures, and to catalog the techniques of rhetorical mastery. Yet, it would come as news to many scholars of politics, especially of foreign policy and international

---

[1] Indeed, so did the CIA, in a classified November 2006 report: see Gordon and Trainor 2012, 295.

1

relations, who often dismiss "mere" rhetoric as posturing and as unworthy of analysis. This book sides with the politicians – not because the world of politics is a genteel debating society, whose participants politely puzzle over the central issues of the day, but because it is not. In politics, language is a crucial medium, means, locus, and object of contest. It neither competes with nor complements power politics: it *is* power politics.[2] Through language, actors exercise influence over others' behavior. Through language, political subjects are produced and social relations defined.[3]

This book rests on three related premises. First, that the largest questions of national security require leaders to engage public audiences and thus to legitimate, or provide public justification for, the policies they prefer. Second, that not all conceivable policies can be legitimated in the public sphere, and that which cannot be legitimated cannot be pursued over the long haul. Third, that international developments are a key ground for legitimation, but that those events do not speak for themselves; much of the politics of national security revolves around a competition over their meaning. From these premises, it follows that students of security affairs should devote attention to how debate is structured, to how the bases and boundaries of legitimation are set and reworked, and to the impact on the policies states pursue.

That intellectual agenda leads to the concept of "narrative." It is through narrative that human beings order disordered experience and impart meaning to themselves and their world. Insofar as any grand strategy rests on a coherent portrait of the global environment, it rests on narrative. Most students of national security and foreign affairs would acknowledge narratives' existence and even their ubiquity, but far fewer would grant that these narratives matter – in the sense of having a substantial impact on policy. They would argue that states have little choice but to adapt themselves to the dictates of an unforgiving international system, that narratives are the product of events whose meaning is clear to all, or that a narrative's dominance simply reflects the interests of powerful groups and leaders. While there are exceptions, hailing especially from the critical wing of the discipline,

---

[2] Bially Mattern 2009.
[3] On interactive and constitutive forms of power, see Barnett and Duvall 2005.

the putative mainstream generally denies that narrative is a powerful force shaping either national security debate or policy outcomes.

This book challenges that commonly held view. Debates over national security are in fact often underpinned by dominant narratives that weave present challenges, past failures and triumphs, and potential futures into a coherent tale, with well-defined characters and plot lines. It is thanks to these powerful narratives that the implications of global events seem clear. It is thanks to these powerful narratives that the international system seems to issue dictates. The Cold War consensus that allegedly gripped US foreign policy from the late 1940s through the Vietnam War was a dominant narrative that made sense of the world for Americans and arguably led to missed opportunities to moderate superpower rivalry. The War on Terror was more than a slogan: it was shorthand for a post-9/11 narrative that not only placed that day's horrific events in a meaningful context, but also set the terms of national security debate in the United States for the next decade. Critics who wished to be taken seriously beyond niche audiences had to ground their arguments in these narratives, which had given rise to the policies they found objectionable. Dominant narratives of national security establish the common-sense givens of debate, set the boundaries of the legitimate, limit what political actors inside and outside the halls of power can publicly justify, and resist efforts to remake the landscape of legitimation.[4] Dominant narratives thereby shape the national security policies that states pursue.

Two questions follow. First, how and when have particular narratives of national security become dominant, and how and when have these dominant narratives come undone? Second, what impact has the emergence of narratives as dominant, and their subsequent fall from that powerful perch, had on national security policy? The first question is this book's primary focus, but some will understandably wonder why they should pay much attention to the rise and fall of dominant narratives. They observe the narrative to and fro, but they see the chief drivers of policy lying elsewhere. Attention to the second question should relieve some of their skepticism.

---

[4] The phenomenon of contest within relatively settled narratives, and of the politics entailed in patrolling those sacrosanct boundaries, has been well explored. I have done so myself in Krebs 2006. Within international relations, see, among many others, Barnett 1998; Campbell 1998; Kornprobst 2008; Weldes 1999.

There are two intuitive answers to the first question – the puzzle of narrative dominance – but both are unsatisfying. First, untrammeled agency: charismatic, well-funded, or institutionally empowered individuals are well positioned to shape the nation's security narratives. Such individuals, especially politicians, know all too well the power of dominant narratives, sometimes because they have fallen victim to them. Consequently, and despite politicians' reputation for short time horizons, they often devote substantial resources to what Stuart Hall termed "hegemonic projects," which aspire to "the remaking of common sense."[5] The Republican Tea Party darling Senator Ted Cruz has declared that "the essential battle is the meta-battle of framing the narrative," because, as he summarizes Sun Tzu, battles are won by "choosing the terrain on which [they] will be fought."[6] No surprise then that the purveyors of rhetorical silver bullets have long done a fast business inside the halls of power.[7] But this agent-centered account captures only a very partial truth. Politicians know how rarely their hegemonic projects come to fruition. Even holders of the presidential "bully pulpit" in the United States have learned, through bitter experience, of its limits. Equally important, elites, even brilliant and authoritative orators, do not stand outside or transcend social structures that they then manipulate at will.

Second, international events' plain, unmediated meaning: some interpretations just make sense, others simply do not fit the facts. But the seeming "brute facts" of the domestic and international environment – material resources, geographical assets, demographic trends, sedimented social constructions – seem less fixed if one takes the long view. Moreover, such an account has things backwards: alleged facts acquire meaning only when people weave them into coherent stories. Nor can we confidently ascribe narrative dominance simply to the speaker's fortunate place in historical time, to her good luck in facing a favorable configuration of forces. Stephen Skowronek suggests that this is what makes even otherwise ordinary politicians seem like great orators and

---

[5] Hall 1988, 8. Scholars across subfields have sometimes recognized this. In American politics, see Green 1987; Skowronek 2008, ch. 1; Smith 2007b. In comparative politics, see Scott 1990; Wedeen 1999. In international relations, see Barnett 1999; Ish-Shalom 2011; Williams 2007, and, from a very different perspective, Kaufmann 2004.

[6] Jeffrey Toobin, "The Absolutist," *The New Yorker*, 30 June 2014.

[7] In the United States, see, for instance, from the Left, Lakoff 2004; from the Right, Luntz 2006.

leaders.[8] But rhetorical brilliance cannot be a product of structure alone: many an opportunity goes unseized.

This book's answer to the puzzle of narrative dominance knits together three elements: the rhetorical demands of the environment; the material, normative, and institutional power speakers bring to bear; and the rhetorical modes they adopt. A dominant narrative of national security is a realized hegemonic project. It is a social fact, not an object of active political challenge. During such routine times, there is political contest, sometimes even intense, but it usually takes place within the terms of the dominant narrative. Occasional efforts to shape the nation's security narrative are then likely to fall short. During unsettled times, in contrast, multiple narratives legitimately circulate in the public sphere, and political contest is less bounded. Such critical junctures are openings for narrative projects that aim to lay the foundation for subsequent argumentation. When authoritative speakers – notably, the president in the US context – seize that opportunity and express themselves in the rhetoric of storytelling, they shift debate back into a relatively settled narrative zone. In this account, developed theoretically and explored empirically in Part I, structural openings intersect with both authority (derived from institutional position) and human agency (via rhetorical mode) to shape the narrative landscape.

To explain when dominant narratives endure and when they collapse, I turn to this same basket of factors – structural context, narrative authority, and rhetorical strategy. A common view is that entrenched institutions, ideas, and discourses persist, even in the face of evidence that they are inefficient or unwarranted; they give way only after a shocking failure, which overwhelms the forces of inertia. In Part II, I argue, against this conventional wisdom, that even substantial failures work against narrative change in the security arena: a faltering military campaign impedes challenge to the dominant security narrative, while encouraging narrow policy criticism that reproduces the narrative. Equally surprising, victory in war and coercive diplomacy makes narrative change possible. These counterintuitive conclusions follow from the dynamics of narrative authority, in combination with political incentives and identity: battlefield setbacks erode presidential authority, creating an opening for the

---

[8] Skowronek 1997.

political opposition, while notable successes bolster the authority of their "owners," within and outside government. Although potentially applicable beyond the United States, the theoretical framework is tailored to the US context, and the book's empirical focus, reviewed in greater detail at the end of this chapter, is on major debates in US national security from the 1930s through the 2000s.

Consider once more the debate over the "surge" of US forces into Iraq. Lingering puzzles and previously occluded questions now glide into view. It becomes clear that supporters and opponents of the surge occupied some of the same narrative terrain: they agreed that the United States was engaged in a war not of its own choosing, but forced upon it by ideologically driven terrorists, who had struck without cause at America and its freedom on 9/11. Yet this was not the only way to understand what had transpired, who the protagonists were, and what moved them. As I show in Chapter 4, there were plausible competing narratives of the attacks and the post-9/11 world, and neither the ostensible facts of global politics nor the power of the bully pulpit can alone explain why this particular narrative triumphed over those alternatives. More persuasive is the conjuncture of an unsettled narrative situation, George W. Bush's presidential authority, and his predominantly storytelling rhetoric. This dominant Terror narrative shaped the policies pursued by the United States in the name of national security after 9/11 – from extraordinary rendition to Guantanamo to the Iraq War. Six years later, Bush again sought to exploit his bully pulpit, this time to silence contending accounts of the Iraq War's progress and prospects. However, during this more routine time in which the Terror narrative structured political debate, the administration's characterization of recent events in Iraq as "civil strife" did not become an accepted common sense, and "civil war" was equally common and legitimate in public discourse. Yet, the Iraq War's shortcomings did not fatally undermine the underlying Terror narrative. Just the opposite: when the Democrats launched an assault on the Iraq War – as a distraction from the War on Terror properly understood – they shored up the legitimating narrative.

Dominant national security narratives are hardly a peculiarly American phenomenon. Consider the civilizing mission of liberal empire, the Nazi obsession with "living space," the Gaullist vision of restoring French grandeur, the Communist faith in capitalist aggression and imperialism, the Iranian Revolutionary regime's Great and Little Satans, and the Israelis' conviction that they have "no partner for peace." These shorthand expressions encapsulate rich narratives that offer portraits of the protagonists, scene, and action of a global drama and that, at least for a time, constituted the nearly unquestioned foundation for policy deliberations in their respective nations. Scholars have devoted the lion's share of their attention to the more routine, explicitly debated instrumental and normative considerations that enter into the making of national security policy. Policy's often unspoken narrative underpinnings have received far less attention. Yet, they are arguably more important.

This book is not the first word on these under-explored questions. Nor will it be the last. It builds on an earlier linguistic turn in the study of foreign policy and threat construction,[9] on work in the field of international relations that has placed narrative at its analytical center,[10] and on theorizing about rhetoric and narrative from far-removed disciplines. It is part of a growing and vibrant literature on legitimation and the making of foreign policy.[11] But it makes a unique contribution – in its synthetic theoretical framework, its conceptualization of rhetorical mode and specifically storytelling, the diversity of its methods, and the breadth of its empirics, exploring the dynamics of national security narrative in the United States over 70 years.

Language, narrative, and the politics of national security

There is no shortage of claims about politics' essence. It is often said that power, interests, or ideas – to invoke a common scheme – are the stuff of politics. Yet, language, too, Aristotle suggested, lies at its core. Man's nature as a political animal is deeply intertwined with his distinctive capacity for speech, which "serves to indicate what is useful and what is harmful, and so also what is just and what is unjust." Other animals communicate. Many species act in accord with basic ethical principles. But only humans give voice to the moral sense; only they

[9] Among many others, see Campbell 1998; Doty 1996; Fierke 1998; Weldes 1999.

[10] See, most notably, Banerjee 1998; Barnett 1999; Bially Mattern 2005; Edkins 2003; Kaufman 2009; Lynch 1999a; Ringmar 1996; Snyder 2015; Williams 2007, ch. 4. See also, on narratives of war's origins, Suganami 1996, 1997a, 1997b, 1999.

[11] Although they do not all use the term, see especially Barnett 1998; Bukovansky 2002; Goddard 2009; Goddard and Krebs 2015; Jackson 2006; Nexon 2009; Williams 2007. For a related sociological text, see Smith 2005b.

articulate, reason about, and debate good and evil, noble and ignoble, beneficial and harmful.[12] Human beings express ideas through language and other forms of symbolic communication. They cannot recognize their common and competing interests, and they cannot forge coalitions, except through the articulation of ideas. They cannot direct power, nor can they interpret its exercise, in the absence of language. It is true that habit governs vast zones of social life, including to some extent the political realm.[13] But, as Nelson Goodman observes: "We can have words without a world, but no world without words or other symbols."[14]

Contestation is the lifeblood of politics, but it is never unstructured. As Jenny Edkins notes: "For language to work at a particular time and in a particular context . . . [t]here has to be some provisional agreement, accepted ideology or central authority structure that will halt the fluidity of terms and make language meaningful."[15] Some premises are unquestioned. They often go unspoken because they strike participants and observers as common sense. But they are the product of human agency.[16] Roland Barthes was especially aware, and resentful, "of the 'naturalness' with which newspapers, art and common sense constantly dress up a reality which, even though it is the one we live in, is undoubtedly determined by history," and he devoted himself to demystifying this naturalness, to revealing the history and politics that lie beneath.[17] Whether one calls it myth (like Barthes) or ideology, the effect is the same: to produce the social order as inevitable and timeless, to conceal its contingent origins, and to replace fundamental political contest with a technology of governance.[18] Disputed propositions are most powerful when they become indisputable norms.

---

[12] Aristotle, *The Politics*, 1253a7, as interpreted by and cited in Chilton 2004, 5.
[13] Hopf 2010, and relatedly, Pouliot 2008.   [14] Goodman 1978, 6.
[15] Edkins 2003, 7.
[16] A wide range of scholarly traditions, despite differences in epistemological orientation and substantive concern, would endorse this proposition, including Schattschneider's classic insights into agenda-setting, sociological accounts of political competition over the "definition of the situation," Bourdieu's *habitus* that structures the everyday cultural forms through which subjects express themselves, Laclau's writings on the establishment and disruption of *doxa*, Foucault's genealogies of institutional and disciplinary discourses, and so on. This is also a point of intersection with research on the impact of elite framing and cuing on mass political attitudes.
[17] Barthes 1972, 11 and passim. See also McAlister 2005.
[18] Edkins 1999, 5–11.

"Truths," Nietzsche wrote, "are illusions which one has forgotten *are* illusions."[19] What strikes people as undoubtedly true shapes both what ends they pursue in the political sphere and how they pursue those ends.

No wonder, then, that political actors do not seek merely to purchase or compel others' assent to specific policies. They also aim to shape the linguistic axes that define the scope and substance of political debate. They seek not only to fit their programs into the prevailing language, but to fix the terms in which debate is conducted, policy legitimated, and events interpreted. How political actors attain discursive dominance was the central concern of Antonio Gramsci, who saw the advantage it bequeathed. Michel Foucault similarly observed that "discourse is not simply that which translates struggles or systems of domination, but is the thing for which and by which there is struggle, discourse is the power which is to be seized." Or, on a lighter note, Lewis Carroll has Humpty Dumpty insist to Alice that the essential question is not "whether you can make words mean different things," but rather "which is to be master."[20]

Political discourse is not just the realm of cost-benefit analysis or even dueling values. It is also, and I would venture to say more deeply, the realm of narrative. Narrative is a scholarly mode of analysis and presentation.[21] But it is also ubiquitous in the real world of politics.[22] Politicians tell stories, expertly or clumsily, to evoke an emotional response – to unsettle and confuse or to restore order and reassure. They may relate stories in great detail, with all the trimmings, or they may tell radically truncated stories, alluding to them via code.[23] People are "storytelling animal[s]."[24]

---

[19] Quoted in Stern 1978, 70.

[20] Gramsci 1992; Foucault 1984, 110; Carroll 1954, 185.

[21] See, for instance, Bates *et al.* 1998; George and Bennett 2005; Klotz and Lynch 2007, 45–51; Mahoney and Rueschemeyer 2003.

[22] See Bially Mattern 2005; Patterson and Monroe 1998; Ringmar 1996; Shenhav 2005, 2006; Somers and Gibson 1994. See also Snyder 2015.

[23] I use the terms "story" and "narrative" interchangeably. Some use "narrative" for those tales that purport to represent facts and reserve "story" for those that are openly fictional (e.g. Gabriel 2000, 28–29). Others decompose all narratives into *what* is depicted – content or "story" – and *how* it is depicted – form or "discourse" (e.g. Chatman 1975, 295).

[24] MacIntyre 1981, 201. On *homo narrans*, see Fisher 1984.

The impulse to narrative is universal, across humankind and human history. Narratives are essential to how human beings make meaning, to how they make sense of, and order, messy experience.[25] Scientists have documented how little the human mind tolerates disorder and how readily it imposes an interpretive and specifically a narrative framework on disparate pieces of data.[26] Children very early, perhaps even naturally, organize their life experiences into narratives. There is now much evidence that narratives shape how people group ideas, what they remember, and what solutions they find most attractive.[27] Narratives also help us cope with the uncertain and unexpected, for, as Jerome Bruner puts it, they even "conventionalize the common forms of human mishap into genres."[28] By defining reality, narratives do not stand opposed to reason, but rather make rational decision-making possible. They are the vehicle through which human beings formulate understandings of self and other (identity) and of what self and other want (interest). And because narratives are always composed for some audience – because they are "irreducibly social" – so too are interests, which are not the stable properties of atomistic actors, but vary according to the story being told.[29] This is not some abstruse scholarly insight: as David Brooks has written in the *New York Times*, "unlike other animals, people do have a drive to seek coherence and meaning. We have a need to tell ourselves stories that explain it all. We use these stories to supply the metaphysics, without which life seems pointless and empty."[30] Stories are powerful both when they seem absurd to outsiders – as in tales of alien abduction[31] – and when they seem

---

[25] On narrative as "a panglobal fact of culture," see White 1981, 1. See also Barthes 1975, 237; Hutto 2007; Kermode 1981, 79–80; Nash 1990; Turner 1980, 167.

[26] On the human penchant for imposing cognitive order, see Gilovich 1991, esp. 9–28; Kruglanski 2004; Perlovsky 2009; Sorrentino and Roney 2000. Thanks to Chris Federico and Jason Plaks for guidance.

[27] For relevant psychological findings, see Bruner 1990; Gerrig and Egidi 2003; László 2008, 37–38; Schank and Abelson 1995. For experimental evidence from other fields, see, among others, Berinsky and Kinder 2006; Jones and Song 2013; Shanahan, Jones, and McBeth 2011; Shanahan, McBeth, and Hathaway 2011. For a review, see Hammack and Pilecki 2012.

[28] Bruner 2002, 31.

[29] McGee and Nelson 1985; Ringmar 1996, ch. 3. See also Charland 1987; Habermas 1984, 136.

[30] Brooks, "The Rush to Therapy," *New York Times*, 10 November 2009. See also Lakoff 2008.

[31] Clancy 2005.

perfectly plausible. And all stories are necessarily fictional, in the sense that they level out the jagged discontinuities of human experience in favor of coherence.[32]

Literary theorists, followed by historians and social scientists, have defined narrative more precisely. The elements to which they point do not draw a bright line between the narrative and the non-narrative; rather, they establish the criteria for inclusion in a narrative "fuzzy set."[33] First, narratives are necessarily *selective* in their presentation of events. No narrative can sustain its thread without erecting boundaries that leave some events outside the story. Second, narratives represent these select events as *temporally* ordered – one event occurring earlier in time, another later. Third, narratives cast that temporal ordering as *meaningfully structured*: the first event did not merely occur before the second, but was a cause of the second.[34] As Frank Kermode vividly puts it, narrative "goes nowhere without his doppelganger or shadow, causality." Or, as Erving Goffman similarly observes, storytelling emphasizes "the causal fabric of experience" and downplays the accidental.[35] Together, these three elements express the idea that narrative revolves in part around *plot*, and the imposition of coherence on messy reality involves *emplotment*. Fit to a narrative, events are not discrete and disconnected, one damn thing after another, but tightly linked to each other via the familiar form of a causal sequence.[36] Finally, narratives are also populated by characters, by agents who act, who are acted upon, and who react to the world around them. Whether these characters shape the course of events varies according to the type of narrative: classic tragedies are stories of overwhelming structure, in which human beings struggle with little effect against forces greater than themselves, while romances are inhabited by heroes capable of overcoming whatever obstacles history and society place in their way.[37] Skeletal narratives are constituted by both plot and protagonist.[38]

---

[32] Edkins 2003, 88. [33] Ryan 2007, 28–30.
[34] The seminal work is Ricoeur 1984–1988.
[35] Goffman 1974, 503; Kermode 1981, 79–80. See also Mishler 1995, 91.
[36] White 1987. [37] On these literary genres, see Frye 1957.
[38] In addition to previously cited works, see, on narrative, Franzosi 1998; Griffin 1993; Mitchell 1981; Patterson and Monroe 1998; Polkinghorne 1988; Somers and Gibson 1994; Stone 1979. For an incisive and integrative analysis, see Shenhav 2005.

Much energy has gone into formulating a fixed typology of narratives. Folklorists have debated how many foundational tales there are, while Northrop Frye famously arranged all literature into five modes.[39] Regardless of what one thinks of such efforts,[40] they suggest that the narratives people deploy are not entirely of their own choosing. In David Brooks' view, people are autonomous beings who "have a conscious say in selecting the narrative [they] use to make sense of the world."[41] But we live in a world that is always already narrated, in which most of us, most of the time, are readers and speakers, not writers. Brooks hints at this, perhaps unconsciously, when he writes of "selecting" narratives, as if from an existing menu, rather than composing narratives. Most of us, most of the time, are hardly even aware of the narratives that underpin our political commonplaces, of the stories to which we allude, of the ways they define the political agenda and the universe of legitimate policy alternatives.

This book concerns not public or even political narratives in general, but specifically those regarding national security. Fully drawn narratives flesh out Kenneth Burke's dramatic "pentad": act (what is happening?), scene (where is the action taking place? what is the background to action?), agent (who is acting?), agency (what means or instruments do agents employ?), and purpose (what are agents' motives or reasons for action?).[42] Adapting Burke's pentad, narratives of national security answer the following questions. *Agent*: Who are the key actors in global politics, specifically with reference to national security? How unified are they? What resources do they possess, and how great a threat, or useful an ally, are they? *Purpose*: What is the character, and what are the interests, of the self? What is the character, and what are the interests, of the other(s)? Is the resulting relationship best characterized as zero-sum, mixed-motive, or positive-sum? *Act* and *Agency*: What evidence supports this portrait of the relationship? What have self and other done in the

[39] For applications to American politics, see King and Langston 2008, and to war mobilization, Smith 2005b.
[40] Skeptics include Barthes 1975, 237; Polkinghorne 1988, 168–169.
[41] Brooks, "The Rush to Therapy."
[42] Burke 1969 [1945]. For a similar breakdown of narrative's structural elements – into setting, plot, characters, and moral lesson – see Jones and McBeth 2010.

past? *Scene*: Are national and global security divisible, or do they constitute a seamless whole?[43] Different answers to these questions yield different narratives. Whereas many narratives focus entirely on the past – as in conventional historical writing[44] – national security narratives weave together past, present, and future, offering a forecast based on the lessons they draw from signal past events.

Such a narrative is constitutive of grand strategy. Grand strategy is, in Barry Posen's definition, "a state's theory about how it can best 'cause' security for itself."[45] That theory requires that strategists define a national interest, identify threats and prioritize among them, and fashion appropriate policy responses – so as to bring the nation's resources into alignment with its ends abroad.[46] That theory, in other words, rests on a national security narrative.[47] That narrative is akin to what Ernest May once termed the "axiomatic" dimension of strategy – "the broad formulation that fixes priorities and provides standards by which the appropriate choices among alternatives may be made" – as opposed to its "calculated" dimension – the level of effort states expend, the scope of targets against which they direct efforts, and the means they employ.[48] Like grand strategy, a national security narrative sets out the broad contours for policy. Whether explicitly articulated or left implicit, it is the reason that some beliefs regarding how to advance state goals in the international arena seem naïve and that others seem realistic. But it also can sustain contentious debate over contending policy options that are equally true to the core elements in the dramatic pentad.

Not all national security narratives are sustainable, in a given context. Even in times of crisis, leaders cannot deploy just any story before public audiences. Those stories must be faithful to deeper identity narratives, which are fairly stable and only occasionally challenged. For instance, American exceptionalism, asserting a unique

---

[43] See, relatedly, Doyle 1997, 22; Weldes 1999, 13–16.

[44] Robert Scholes insists that "narrative is past, always past." "To speak of the future," he asserts, "is to prophesy or predict or speculate – never to narrate." Scholes 1980, 206.

[45] Posen 1984, 13.   [46] Kennedy 1991, 1–2.

[47] Elsewhere I argue, with Stacie Goddard, that legitimation is essential to the process through which grand strategy's constituent elements take shape and thus through which strategy is both formulated and executed. See Goddard and Krebs 2015.

[48] May 1962, 659.

and uniquely moral national mission, has shaped debates over foreign affairs since the nation's founding. To challenge its premises is, in US politics, to relegate oneself to the margins – like the Vietnam-era New Left, which alleged that America was corrupt and oppressive rather than a beacon of and force for freedom. It has long hindered realist arguments, for a foreign policy governed by power politics, from gaining traction in the public sphere.[49] At the same time, American exceptionalism has been sufficiently flexible to have sustained policies that are diametrically opposed – from George Washington's valedictory warning against "artificial ties" and foreign entanglements, legitimated with reference to European moral corruption and the priority of maintaining America's purity, to Woodrow Wilson's crusade to remake world order, similarly legitimated with reference to America's superiority, but now confident that values would stream only east across the Atlantic.[50] Americans debate *how* they should advance their national mission of spreading freedom and democracy, but not *whether* they are so obligated. Publicly sustainable narratives of national security rest on enduring identity narratives.

Dominant narratives of national security are the terrain on which politicians, pundits, and activists battle.[51] Those narratives do not smother political contest. They channel it, privileging particular courses of action and impeding the legitimation of others. Legitimation – the articulation before key publics of publicly acceptable reasons for concrete actions and policy positions – is typically an imperative, not a mere nicety, of politics, both domestic and foreign.[52] It is not to be invoked only when outcomes seem puzzling: it is politics as usual. An individual who does not legitimate his claims "is quickly regarded as a fanatic, the prey of interior demons, rather than as a reasonable person seeking to share his convictions."[53] While political actors are free in principle to say anything they like, the dominant narrative is, according to James Scott, nearly always "the only plausible

---

[49] Dueck 2006.
[50] On the flexibility of American ideals in informing the nation's foreign policy, see Osgood 1953.
[51] On the narrative basis of policy debate, see Roe 1994.
[52] On legitimation in general, see Elster 1995, 244–252; Suchman 1995.
[53] Perelman 1982, 16. On the importance of audiences in shaping communication, see also Perelman and Olbrechts-Tyteca 1969 [1958]; Sawyer 2001, ch. 3. This conception differs from how political theorists normally treat "justification," in which reasons are universal and audiences abstractions: see Garsten 2006, 5–6.

arena of struggle."[54] Policies at odds with underlying narratives strike audiences as illegitimate: they have few public advocates, and their few advocates are ignored or treated as beyond the pale. Even those who do not privately subscribe to the dominant narrative normally pay public fealty to it and abstain from open challenge – a phenomenon that Elisabeth Noelle-Neumann famously called "the spiral of silence."[55]

There are few social settings in which legitimation does not prominently feature. Although exasperated parents may eventually command their children to "do as I say!", at even a fairly young age children resist parental orders they think morally wrong or otherwise illegitimate; parental authority holds sway only in the domain of convention, which shrinks over time.[56] In hierarchical societies, the dominated – whether on the basis of class, ethnicity, caste, religion, or gender – refuse to grant legitimacy to their subordination.[57] Superiors in a bureaucracy do at times issue orders without explaining themselves, but they, too, typically justify their decisions, to secure their underlings' buy-in. Certainly, the powerful, more than the weak, can say patently absurd or contradictory things and still get their way. But, in most circumstances, even they must explain themselves in terms that others find acceptable. That is why decision-makers sometimes opt for covert action: because they cannot conceive of justifications that domestic and/or international audiences would deem legitimate. Legitimation is necessary whenever publics must be mobilized, and it lurks in the background wherever there is a reasonable chance that the glare of public attention will turn. While much escapes public scrutiny in large-scale, bureaucratic nation-states, policies must be, at least, *capable* of public legitimation.

This is not to deny that political actors deploy language strategically. Of course they do. They carefully construct arguments to persuade or compel. They frame their preferred policies in what they believe to be the most attractive light. But whether actors actually mean what they say is not crucial to effective legitimation.[58] Speakers who are seen as

---

[54] Scott 1990, 102.   [55] Noelle-Neumann 1993.

[56] Perkins and Turiel 2007; Turiel 2002, esp. 107–118; 2015.

[57] See Scott 1985, and, from a psychological perspective, Turiel 2002, esp. 67–93.

[58] A legitimation perspective thus need not take a strong stance on whether we can ascertain the sincerely held motives that are the "real" drivers of action. The faith that we can – or at least that we can come sufficiently close – underpins

credible have an advantage in legitimating policy, but credibility is not a matter of taking on costs that separate the sincere from the fake. That behavior, born of strategic reflection, undermines the claim to authenticity. "An authentic person," Jeffrey Alexander observes, "seems to act without artifice, without self-consciousness, without reference to some laboriously thought-out plan or text, without concern for manipulating the context of her actions, and without worries about that action's audience or its effects."[59] Perceived authenticity derives from effective performance,[60] and performance is about cultivating appearances, including the appearance of not cultivating appearances. Effective performance does not lie in actually baring one's soul. "Appearances have real consequences," notes Edwin Black, and that premise lies at the heart of the study of rhetoric.[61]

Whether legitimation requirements extend to international politics has been the subject of much debate, but there is little question that they are a critical feature of domestic politics. And national security policy, while responsive to international pressures, is made first and foremost in the domestic sphere.[62] How certain narratives of national security become dominant, how they become a crucial component in states' "security software,"[63] demands explanation.

Narratives of national security and IR theory

It is curious that mainstream scholarship on international relations (IR) has had little to say about nations' security narratives. It is curious because how states identify and assess threats has long stood at the center of international relations, and threat assessment is, at its heart, a form of storytelling.[64] It is also curious because the discipline of international relations, often accused of slavishly serving power, has in this case displayed a tin ear: Washington insiders are obsessed with "the narrative" and want desperately to learn the secret of how to control it. Yet, the field's reigning paradigms tend to discount

many accounts. However, motives are unobservable, which is why rationalists prefer to assume or deduce preferences. For a rationalist discussion, see Frieden 1999, 39–45, 53–66. For criticism of motive-based social science, from non-rationalist perspectives, see Jackson 2006, 22–24; Ringmar 1996, 88. See relatedly also Alexander 2010, 283; Tilly 1998.

[59] Alexander 2004, 548.   [60] Alexander 2010, 17–38.   [61] Black 1992, 10.
[62] On domestic legitimation and foreign policy, see Trout 1975.
[63] Azar and Moon 1988, 77.   [64] Alker *et al.* 1980.

narratives, and they offer strikingly different answers to this book's two core questions. To the puzzle of narrative dominance, realists and liberals, for all their other differences, would agree that there is no puzzle: they generally see the implications of the global environment as clear, adopt an impoverished view of leadership, and overlook the politics of meaning-making. To the puzzle of national security policy, they advance a range of classic contending arguments, from international structural imperatives to the domestic distribution of power. They suggest that narratives of national security are far more product than cause and are thus not relevant to policy outcomes.[65] After laying out these foils and their alternative arguments, which reappear throughout the empirical chapters, I turn to closer interlocutors to lay bare my intellectual debts and to clarify this book's contribution.

Realists have long argued that systemic pressures, derived from the distribution of material power and geography, constitute an objective national interest that must (or should) be the chief driver of foreign policy. When states disregard these pressures, they will eventually suffer punishment for their imprudence. While structural realists put little stock in narrative as an explanation of policy, they would argue that the security narrative that best corresponds to objective reality must eventually vanquish its competitors.[66] So-called neoclassical realists also generally believe that the system yields clear dictates and that states would obey, if not for domestic or individual deformities that prevent them from perceiving or following those systemic imperatives.[67] Leadership, from a realist perspective, consists primarily of correctly recognizing and seizing structural opportunities and respecting structural constraints.[68] As Bismarck reportedly put it,

---

[65] This was not, however, true of classical realists or liberals – in contrast to the modern scientific variants examined here. On the classical realists, see, especially with regard to rhetorical leadership, Tjalve and Williams 2015. On the classical liberal tradition, see Doyle 1997, 205–311; Reus-Smit 2001.

[66] Miller 2010a, 2010b. See also Mearsheimer 1994/95, 43.

[67] This is a point of disagreement among self-declared neoclassical realists. The formulation here is based on Rathbun 2008. For a less structural version of neoclassical realism, see Taliaferro *et al.* 2009.

[68] This is true as well of neoclassical realists whose structuralist commitments extend to domestic politics. For instance, Schweller's sophisticated account of "underbalancing" centers on domestic constraints, which he treats as largely fixed. See Schweller 2006, and also the essays in Lobell *et al.* 2009.

"the statesman ... must wait and listen until he hears the steps of God sounding through events; then leap up and grasp the hem of his garment."[69]

Realists' lack of attention to narrative is ironic because they have often seen themselves as the victims of dominant narratives. Railing against US foreign policy, they have frequently blamed such narratives for other Americans' refusal to endorse their understanding of global threats and opportunities. Hans Morgenthau and George Kennan were among the prominent critics of the Cold War logic that gave rise to the Vietnam War. Their contemporary counterparts offered an alternative reading of the September 11 attacks that was very much at odds with the reigning consensus.[70] John Mearsheimer and Stephen Walt, condemning "the Israel Lobby" for skewing US policy in the Middle East, are but the latest in a long line of frustrated realists to accuse parochial domestic interest groups of hijacking policy.[71] If realists' views are often at variance with the dominant narrative, even when the resulting policies are disastrous and costly – as realists argue they were with regard to the wars in Vietnam and Iraq – then it seems likely that, *pace* realists, more than one line can fit the scattered data points. In an international system marked by complexity, even clear-eyed observers might disagree about systemic pressures, and more than one narrative could plausibly organize experience.

Modern IR liberals share the view that narratives have no real impact on foreign policy. For them, policy is the product of bargaining among societal groups seeking to further their material or ideational well-being, mediated by institutions of representation, and "the demands of individuals and societal groups are treated as analytically prior to politics."[72] For one stream of liberalism, narratives exist, but there are as many as there are interests. If state policy conforms to a particular narrative, it is a reflection of the power of its advocates. The notion that a broadly shared narrative might structure political contest is

---

[69] Quoted in Taylor 1955, 115.

[70] See, for instance, Nicholas Lemann, "The War on What?," *The New Yorker*, 16 September 2002.

[71] Mearsheimer and Walt 2007.

[72] Moravcsik 1997, 517. Key liberal accounts of grand strategy include Fordham 1998; Narizny 2007; Trubowitz 1998, 2011; as well as much of the voluminous literature on the democratic peace.

antithetical to this atomistic version of liberalism.[73] For another stream, well-designed institutions can thwart power and its corrosive effects in narrative competition: an open marketplace of ideas allows the best narrative – that is, that most closely capturing objective reality – to triumph, or at least ensures the defeat of dangerous narratives.[74] Putting these two streams together, liberal leadership consists of strategic choice based on an accurate assessment of the objective "slack" inherent in the international environment and of the economic interests of one's coalition.[75] Yet, if politics entails merely exchange among actors with fixed preferences, why would leaders bother to seek to cultivate assent? If geopolitical slack were given, why would politicians offer audiences contending narratives of national security? Such efforts presume that policy must be rendered socially sustainable and that sustainability is not pre-determined by the configuration of material interests. Such efforts imply a politics in which meaning can be the object of contestation.

Even mainstream constructivists have devoted little attention to dominant narratives, generally focusing their analysis instead on the origins and consequences of ideas, identity, and norms. But this is an incidental, not a necessary, omission. This book shares the core constructivist insight that structures of meaning and competition over meaning are central to social (including political) life. It builds on constructivists' explorations of how particular contested understandings become shared and settled in global politics.[76] Yet, the catalog of mechanisms remains incomplete,[77] and the conditions under which they are most likely to operate are still to be identified. And, in contrast to most constructivist work, this book recognizes that these processes are inherently public and linguistic,[78] that narrative is central to

---

[73] This is ironic because of the relative dominance of liberalism in the American academy. But it also makes sense: liberalism, as an ideology, works to hide from view, and therefore preserve, its dominant standing.

[74] See, for instance, Snyder and Ballentine 1996; Snyder 1991.

[75] See especially Trubowitz 2011.

[76] See, among others, Crawford 2002; Finnemore 2003; Finnemore and Sikkink 1998; Keck and Sikkink 1998; Price 2003; Tannenwald 2007.

[77] For an important catalog, see Finnemore 2003, 146–161.

[78] On language and the constitution of order in international relations, see Onuf 1989 and, for a recent application, Weber and Kowert 2007. See also Crawford 2009. Some have characterized the emphasis on language as characteristic of post-positivist constructivism: see Walter and Helmig 2008.

meaning-making, and that the processes through which situations are defined, standards determined, and relevant institutions and experts identified are inherently power-laden.[79]

This book is inspired by certain strands of critical theory. Critical approaches, notably those whose roots lie in Gramsci and Foucault, seek to reveal dominant articulations for what they are, to explore how they are configured and reproduced and how they silence alternatives, and thereby to deprive them of their privileged status. As Karin Fierke explains, the "intent is to denaturalize what has come to be assumed in order to open a space for alternatives."[80] This book shares that aspiration. It demonstrates how international events might have been interpreted differently, traces the prevailing interpretations to their (intermediate) origins, and explores the silencing of dissent. It builds on critical approaches' recognition that social reality is *narratively* constituted. Critical scholars have devoted attention to deconstructing narratives and exposing their assumptions, metaphors, and contradictions.[81] Their insight that language in general, and narrative in particular, are central to the construction of meaning and the politics of identity serves as my starting point.[82] This book's diverse methods are largely put to causal analysis, but they serve more critical ends, too, liberating readers from the bonds of common-sense narratives and helping them envision a different, and hopefully more appealing, world.

Just as the field's putative mainstream, allergic to rhetoric and narrative, will not feel entirely comfortable with this book, neither

---

[79] By my reading, much constructivist literature remains beholden to a liberal worldview, in which power relations and coercion are absent from normative change. This is true of approaches inspired by Habermas, thanks to his focus on deliberation, and by social psychology, thanks to that discipline's core assumptions. On persuasion's centrality to constructivism, see Crawford 2002; Finnemore 1996, 141 and passim; Finnemore and Sikkink 1998, 914; Payne 2001. Drawing on Habermas are, among others, Lynch 1999b, 2002; Müller 2001; Risse 2000.

[80] Fierke 2007, 102.

[81] Although few engage with theories of narrative or explore storytelling as a pragmatic activity. Key texts include Campbell 1998; Edkins 2003; Steele 2010. Other examples include Bleiker 2001; Devetak 2009; Jarvis and Holland 2014; Manjikian 2008.

[82] On language in general, see Der Derian and Shapiro 1989; Shapiro 1981. For examples of engagement with narrative, see, among others, Berenskoetter 2014; Hancock 2011; Homolar 2011; Senn and Elhardt 2014; Strömbom 2014.

will many critical scholars – for two reasons. First, many, especially those close to the post-structuralist end of the spectrum, deny that any narrative achieves, or even really approaches, dominance. They would thus take issue with my central analytical questions. As Jenny Edkins writes: "The story is never finished: the scripting of memory by those in power can always be challenged, and such challenges are very often found at moments and in places where the very foundations of the imagined community are laid out."[83] It is true that no narrative is classically hegemonic, in the sense of rendering resistance impossible. It is true that narratives are not nearly as coherent as they claim. They are necessarily fragile, and any narrative stability is relative and temporary. But that does not mean that the social world is one of continuous or even regular flux. Thus, Edkins, in her powerful work on the memorialization of national trauma, admits that, "despite attempts by scholars to question what representations were appropriate, it came to be accepted that there was one narrative history of the Holocaust and that it had to be told."[84] Maja Zehfuss asserts that continual contest has marked German memory of the Second World War, but her careful history reveals that the myth of the *Wehrmacht* and the average German's innocence has been stable and widespread.[85] Students of American politics, meanwhile, have been surprised by the stability of issue-frames,[86] which reflects deeper narrative structures. It is true that, in large-scale polities, even in a regime like Stalin's Soviet Union, there are always advocates and adherents of dissenting narratives. Some elements may even penetrate popular culture.[87] But a dominant narrative, which excludes others from the zone of the respectable and legitimate, is compatible with diversity and dissent at the margins.

Second, many will be skeptical of my commitment to conventional causality and generalizable mechanisms and relationships. They would prefer to speak of the "conditions of possibility" for narrative dominance.[88] Critical scholarship has thus identified common

---

[83] Edkins 2003, 18–19, and generally ch. 3. See also Edkins 1999, 54.

[84] Edkins 2003, 17.   [85] Zehfuss 2007.

[86] Baumgartner *et al.* 2009, 176; Wood and Vedlitz 2007, 553.

[87] Hopf 2012.

[88] Post-positivist causality does not strike me as very distant from the concept of a necessary condition – although post-positivists would insist that no condition is truly necessary, that there are multiple background conditions that would make X possible. But the identified causes seem to do their causal work in very similar ways.

discursive moves – presenting narrow interests as universal, representing the status quo as natural and inevitable, neutralizing radical dissent
by presenting it as a difference within the mainstream.[89] It has also laid
out abstract linguistic processes, such as articulation and interpella-
tion, through which chains of associations are constructed and subject
positions created.[90] But these moves should in principle be available
to all contestants. No surprise, then, that critical scholars, when
confronted with discursive dominance, have ascribed it to the absence
of competition. This is Ernesto Laclau's answer to the puzzle of
fascism's triumph, and Stuart Hall's to that of Thatcherite discourse.[91]
Michael Williams does not discuss whether or how neoconservatives'
opponents countered their representational strategies, nor does Stuart
Croft explain why the "decisive intervention" proved decisive after
9/11 and why alternatives were "silenced by the noise of the successful
interpretation."[92] A satisfactory account would display a more dialogic
sensibility: it would explain why some narratives acquire the status of
common sense at the expense of competitors, while others remain
contested, and while still others are ignored or consigned to the realm
of the damned. Such an account will necessarily move away from static
discourses to contending speakers' concrete articulations, to those
speakers' social and political positionality, and to the constitution of
key audiences.[93]

   Within the critical orbit, my closest interlocutors are members of
the Copenhagen School, who have highlighted the importance of
"securitization": how rhetorical deployments locate issues within the
realm of security and beyond the purview of politics.[94] They build on

[89] Giddens 1979, 188–196; Jessop 1982, 241–247; Laclau 1977; Laclau and
   Mouffe 2001. See also Hajer 1989, 1997.
[90] For IR work in this tradition, see Campbell 1998; Doty 1996; Weldes 1999.
[91] Hall 1988, 154; Laclau 1977, 124–134. For a related critique of Laclau, see
   Miller 2004. This problem is also reflected in Laclau-inspired work in IR: see,
   e.g., Nabers 2009.
[92] Croft 2006, 8; Williams 2007, ch. 5. For another otherwise excellent work that
   also suffers from this problem, see Kornprobst 2008.
[93] Many sympathetic scholars have similarly criticized critical and post-modern
   accounts on this basis. See, in the literature on international relations, Banta
   2013, 393–395; Bially Mattern 2005, 12, 93; Fiaz 2014, 493; Neumann 2002;
   and, relatedly, Berenskoetter 2014, 280.
[94] The Copenhagen School's relationship to critical theory has been ambiguous.
   Although Fierke (2007, 102–114), for instance, treats it as within the critical
   sphere, she contrasts securitization to "more critical" approaches.

J. L. Austin's theory of speech acts, which points out that some utterances – such as saying "I do" at a wedding or making a promise – are themselves actions, and which argues that the key to their productive effect is their conformity to linguistic rules.[95] Following Austin, scholars of securitization ascribe security rhetoric's productive power partly to the field's internal grammar. But, recognizing that compliance with the rules of a given domain cannot adequately account for variation, a seminal programmatic statement also briefly mentions non-linguistic factors, such as the securitizing actor's social capital and the threat's referent.[96] Expanding on this too-succinct sketch, Holger Stritzel suggests that a fully fledged theory of securitization would focus on features of the text, on the context that renders a text resonant, and on the social and political structures that ground speakers' authority.[97] The theoretical arguments of this book, in Chapters 2 and 5, map onto that abstract scaffolding and advance that agenda.

Among conventional constructivists, my closest interlocutor is Jeffrey Legro, who has explored when states alter their approach to international society.[98] Legro argues that policymakers embrace new ideas only when exogenous shocks challenge social expectations and discredit old ideas, and when a small number of viable alternatives are present, permitting for the consolidation of a new orthodoxy. However, Legro's (overly) parsimonious framework treats three crucial elements as exogenous. First, he seeks to explain the rise and fall of collective causal beliefs regarding the effective *means* for advancing state goals in the international arena.[99] Yet, how actors construe that arena, which affects what means they see as efficacious, is not theorized. Second, crucial to Legro's account is that there is only one

---

[95] Austin 1975.   [96] Buzan *et al.* 1998, esp. 31–41.

[97] Stritzel 2007, 368–376. See, similarly, Balzacq 2005, 2011.

[98] I am also indebted to Ian Lustick's work on hegemony and the politics of empire, Cecelia Lynch's research on peace movements, and Janice Bially Mattern's work on representation and international order. The first two are stronger, however, on demonstrating that shifts in axiomatic assumptions (Lustick) and constructions of narratives (Lynch) shape politics than on accounting for those axioms and narratives. Bially Mattern powerfully argues that coercive rhetoric repairs a dissolved identity by re-imposing the pre-crisis order, but her account is thus one always of continuity, never change. See Bially Mattern 2005; Lustick 1993; Lynch 1999a.

[99] Or, as Legro (2005, 7) puts it, "beliefs about effective means for achieving interests or how states think about achieving their ends ('instrumentality')."

feasible alternative.[100] He does not explore theoretically how the universe of policy alternatives is constituted at any given time. Third, Legro attributes the unsettling of the regnant orthodoxy to an objectively sizable shock, with the twist that only those who run counter to social expectations impel change.[101] But while events are exogenous, "shocks" are not.[102] Legro does not explain why political violence and economic dislocation are sometimes experienced as challenging but manageable problems and sometimes as unmanageable shocks. This book speaks to these three silences. National security narratives include a portrait of the international arena, define the range of legitimate policy options, and set the standards that sort troubling events into the categories of problem and shock. Accounting for how dominant narratives of national security coalesce and collapse is important in its own right, but it also sheds light on one of the central questions of international relations: major foreign-policy change.

Plan of the book

This book explores the life-cycle of narratives of national security: their rise to dominance and their fall from that perch, sometimes wholesale and sometimes piecemeal, sometimes precipitously and sometimes gradually. It focuses on the making of national security in just one,

---

[100] Legro 2005, 35–36. This is somewhat plausible only because Legro's typology limits the number of approaches to three, one of which has just been delegitimized. However, what counts as a true alternative, rather than a variant on a common theme, is less clear in the empirical cases. For instance, Legro suggests that, despite elite consensus on the need for change, Americans returned to separatism after the Great War because there were two competing versions of internationalism (balance of power vs. multilateralism) in the public arena (63–64). Yet, two internationalisms (great power condominium *realpolitik* vs. multilateral containment) competed after the Second World War, and the United States, as Legro demonstrates, did not return to the interwar orthodoxy of separation.

[101] At times, Legro suggests that one cannot specify a priori how great a failure is needed to drive change, as he argues regarding the impact of Germany's total defeat in the Second World War (111). But at other times he seems to employ such "an undefined threshold" in defining what constitutes a (sufficient) shock. Thus, for instance, he maintains that Admiral Perry's visits to Japan in 1853–54 were not shocking because death and destruction did not follow in their wake – even though they were clearly unwelcome and at odds with dominant social expectations (133).

[102] Widmaier *et al.* 2007.

albeit important, country, the United States. This has the regrettable consequence of reproducing the traditional great-power- and US-centric biases of the discipline of international relations. It leaves readers understandably unsure about whether and how the book's arguments travel beyond the United States, to the dynamics of narrative contestation elsewhere. But limiting the theoretical and empirical analysis to the United States has distinct advantages. One must be especially sensitive to geographic, cultural, and institutional settings when thinking about narrative and discourse, and these are kept relatively stable in a single-country longitudinal research design.[103] Moreover, as the United States was unusually powerful throughout the period under study – from the 1930s through the first decade of the twenty-first century – and as it was confronted with a series of major security challenges, from Hitler's Germany to the Soviet superpower to Al Qaeda,[104] it might be seen as an especially "hard" case for an approach that takes narrative seriously.

Parts I and II focus on different sequential stages of the narrative life-cycle. Part I investigates why politicians' narrative projects – their efforts to install their preferred narratives of national security as common sense – succeed or fail. Part II examines why dominant narratives endure (remain dominant) or collapse (lose their dominant status). Any speech act, broadly conceived, involves a speaker, content, technique, context, and audience – that is, (1) who may legitimately speak, (2) what they say, (3) how they say it, (4) where/when they say it, and (5) to whom they say it. The two parts' respective theoretical frameworks, laid out in Chapters 2 and 5, draw on these five factors to different degrees and in different ways. While this book focuses primarily on accounting for the rise, persistence, and fall of dominant narratives, it always keeps an eye on these narratives' impact – on how they shaped what the United States actually did to further its national security.

In Part I, Chapter 2 theorizes narrative dominance as emerging out of a specific conjuncture of moment (narrative crisis), authority (linked to the institution of the presidency), and rhetorical mode (storytelling,

---

[103] Put differently, a single-country study makes it easier to carry off a "most similar" research design. See George and Bennett 2005, 164–167, 252.

[104] The last was only debatably a major or even substantial security threat. Yet, it was certainly seen as such – thanks to a successful narrative project.

rather than argument). Chapters 3 and 4 put that theory to work in examining four efforts by presidents to shape narratives of national security, with varied outcomes. With the presidency as a constant across the cases, the emphasis lies with moment and mode, crisis and storytelling. Chapter 3 examines two cases of presidential failures to provide crucial shape to the national debate on security – because the president did not engage in adequate storytelling when he should have (in an unsettled narrative situation) and because the president relied heavily on storytelling when he should not have (under conditions of relative narrative stability). First, before December 1941, Franklin Roosevelt often made his case for intervention in the European crisis in instrumental terms, and when he did deploy storytelling rhetoric, that narrative was inadequately drawn, especially with regard to the scene of global politics. The result, in the unsettled narrative situation of the early 1940s, was a powerful non-interventionist coalition that retained legitimacy and frustrated Roosevelt's ability to see through his favored policies. Second, Ronald Reagan's brief for combating Communist advances in Central America relied heavily on a storytelling rhetoric. The result, in the context of a renewed Cold War, was a persistent alternative narrative among both congressional Democrats and activists – countering Reagan's characterization of the protagonists and suggesting that assistance and advisers would enmesh the United States in "another Vietnam."

Chapter 4 explains the emergence of dominant narratives – during the Second World War and amidst the War on Terror – as the product of both particular moments, in which public demand for narrative was elevated, and presidents' rhetorical choices, to express themselves predominantly in the storytelling mode. It also explores what difference the stabilization of narrative made to subsequent debate and policy: how the settled portrait of the adversary during the Second World War, as the Nazi regime rather than the German people, placed a harsh peace beyond the pale, and how the Terror narrative quieted leading Democrats who might otherwise have opposed the 2003 Iraq War. The key alternative argument in both cases is not just that an important event, specifically an attack on the United States (Pearl Harbor, 9/11), was key to the stabilization of narrative, but that that event spoke for itself – that is, its meaning was given and clear. I have not included one important and obvious case since the Second World War – the consolidation of the Cold War consensus – because I discuss it in detail in Part II.

With Part II, the discussion shifts from the rise of dominant public narratives to their persistence and possible fall. War and significant episodes of coercive diplomacy are the crucibles in which the mettle of national security narrative is tested. Yet, their effects are not straightforward. It seems intuitive that substantial battlefield setbacks, culminating in defeat, would delegitimize the narrative on whose basis the mission had been justified and that victory would impede narrative change. Chapter 5 turns this conventional wisdom on its head. It shows how disappointing military performance in protracted and uncertain wars gives both opponents and supporters of war in the political opposition incentives to criticize the government while reaffirming the military campaign's underlying rationale – that is, while bolstering the underlying narrative of national security. Furthermore, it argues that victory in war and in coercive diplomacy creates a political opening for its owners to advance an alternative narrative. In short, significant military setbacks promote the consolidation or persistence of dominant narratives, while victory opens space for and makes possible narrative challenge.

This counterintuitive argument is sustained in Chapters 6 and 7 by a careful study of the dynamics of the Cold War consensus – based in part on a large-scale content analysis of foreign affairs editorials in two leading newspapers and in part on process-tracing of crucial episodes. After explaining the rationale and elucidating the method, Chapter 6 reports the four novel findings of the content analysis: there was a dominant Cold War narrative (or consensus) in the 1950s, but it was narrower than conventional historical accounts have suggested, revolving only around representations of the Communist threat and the interconnectedness of global politics; that narrow narrative achieved dominance in the early to mid 1950s, rather than the late 1940s; that dominant narrative began to erode in the early 1960s, long before Americans turned against the Vietnam War, which is often credited with unraveling the consensus; and a new zone of consensus emerged in the 1970s, around an amalgam of exceptionalism and internationalism. Neither exogenous shocks, nor alleged global realities, nor change in presidential administration can account for this pattern. It is, however, consistent with the theoretical framework of Chapter 5. Chapter 7 delves deeply into the history, politics, and rhetoric of Cold War America to show why the Cold War narrative rose and fell as it did. It zeroes in on what would be key moments in any history of the Cold War – the Korean

War, the Cuban Missile Crisis, the Vietnam War – and shows how these remain causally crucial, but in ways that, although expected by my theory, are unexpected by conventional theory and history. Chapter 8 concludes Part II with a twofold mission: to clarify what light this revisionist history of the Cold War narrative sheds on important puzzles of US policy, at home and abroad, during the Cold War; and to demonstrate the theory's relevance to the more recent past, the politics of the War on Terror.

The book's conclusion, in Chapter 9, considers the present and future of public narrative and the making of national security. We live in a rapidly changing communications environment. Whereas classical writings on rhetoric presumed a well-ordered public sphere, the internet is more like a cacophonous assembly in which everyone is speaking at once. Many believe that finding a forum has become easier, but acquiring anything beyond a niche audience has become harder, and leadership has become well-nigh impossible. Audiences have become so fractured that the very notion of a dominant national narrative strikes some as illusory, if not farcical. But the new media environment, I argue, has not eliminated the demand for rhetorical leadership. There is even reason to think that the public's desire for a simplifying narrative that can cut through the dizzying complexity of global affairs will only grow. Moreover, there is reason to celebrate the endurance of public narratives of national security: for making leadership possible, for providing the grounds for holding leaders accountable, and for helping people transcend endemic ontological insecurity. Powerful narratives are not without their perils, but the alternative – a world of anomic individuals, adrift without political community or identity – is not only unrealistic, but unappealing. The politics of narrative will continue to be central to US national security – to ongoing debates over policy and strategy, to whether particular strategic approaches succeed and endure, and to how Americans make sense of the world emerging around them.

PART I

Crisis, authority, and rhetorical mode: the fate of narrative projects, from the battle against isolationism to the War on Terror

2 | Domination and the art of storytelling

Aristotle believed that the production of meaning is fundamentally a rhetorical process. He objected to the common definition of rhetoric as the art of persuasion: its "function is not persuasion," he insisted, ". . . [but] rather the *detection of the persuasive aspects of each matter.*"[1] The stylistic questions to which professional orators devoted themselves were secondary, in his view.[2] Rhetorical skill, he concluded, does not exert its effects by changing listeners' minds.[3] Rather, rhetoric has its greatest impact by defining the situation in such a fashion as to make the speaker's conclusions seem *naturally* right, so that the listener feels that she has discovered for herself something that should have been obvious all along. In other words, Aristotle conceived of rhetoric as a tool for producing common sense.

However, how particular narratives become dominant, triumphing over their competitors on the field of narrative play, is not well understood. Dominant narratives are not the straightforward product either of events or of the desires of powerful interests and individuals. Aristotle alerted us to what actors say and how they say it and to what effects their articulations produce. In an astute study, Bruce Lincoln suggests that authority is located in "the conjuncture of the right speaker, the right speech and delivery, the right staging and props, the right time and place, and an audience whose historically and culturally conditioned expectations establish the parameters of what is judged 'right' in all these instances."[4] According to Lincoln, that conjuncture is so contextually contingent that specifying any general features is impossible. And he is of course right in a way: there are no rhetorical surefire winners that always strike one's opponents dumb, and there can be no theory of

---

[1] Aristotle 1991, 69–70.

[2] Despite Aristotle's dismissive attitude toward the tricks of the orator's trade, however, his *Rhetoric* devotes much attention to precisely such techniques. This apparent contradiction has led to much commentary.

[3] Garver 1996, 185.   [4] Lincoln 1994, 11.

31

dominant narratives that generates point predictions extending across all time and space. But that does not mean that we cannot identify at least some conjunctural elements that transcend the episode.

This chapter develops a theory of narrative dominance, focusing on the interplay of text, context, and authority. It begins by unpacking two concepts: narrative situation (context) and rhetorical mode (text). It then sets these ideal-types into motion to generate four distinct political dynamics. Not all participants in public debate, however, are equally socially empowered (authority), which affects both how they speak and how audiences respond. With the conjuncture complete, the theoretical discussion closes with reflections on the nature of leadership and the content of storytelling. The chapter then turns to a series of methodological matters: the standards by which the theory is to be evaluated, the operationalization of narrative situations and rhetorical modes, and the place of counterfactual analysis.

When and how we speak

Public rhetoric is designed to make an impression on and evoke a response from an audience. Speakers can express themselves however they like, but they are also both social beings and strategic actors, and thus sensitive to what audiences expect and deem legitimate.[5] Speakers are not puppet-masters, pulling the strings of a dutifully dancing public, nor are they the puppets, prancing this way and that as the public's mood dictates. A speaker is the leader in a *pas de deux* who can inspire his partner to elegance or reduce her to clumsiness, encourage collaboration or prompt combativeness. Rhetorical skill is not just, or not primarily, having a way with words, the knack for an elegant turn of phrase or a fresh metaphor. It is less abstract and more socially grounded. It is, first and foremost, about recognizing social circumstances and grasping what the audience expects. Rhetorical skill is a matter of *embedded* agency.

Narrative situations: two contexts for speaking

Structures vary in their degree of slack: they can be very tight, reducing choice so dramatically that individuals feel suffocated, or they can be

---

[5] Benoit 2000; Perelman and Olbrechts-Tyteca 1969 [1958]. See also Jamieson 1973; Miller 1984.

very loose, as in those moments in which individuals perceive a world of possibility. Narrative structures are no different. In routine, or settled, narrative situations,[6] there is a dominant narrative, and elites generally legitimate their preferred policies with reference to it and thereby reproduce it. This common foundation for legitimation limits the scope of policy debate, but does not generate complete policy consensus. Dominant narratives do not abolish political difference or render exchange trivial or superficial, but they do support only a limited range of legitimate stances. Although alternative narratives are conceivable and may even be deployed on the margins, they lack legitimate standing and are therefore not in wide circulation. Those who nevertheless invoke such narratives – either by explicitly articulating them or by legitimating policies with reference to them – meet with a rude reception. Leading elites and mainstream media normally ignore them. When that is not possible – perhaps because the speaker is unusually prominent – or when attention serves political purposes, such arguments not only fail to resonate, but become the target of fierce attacks denying their legitimacy, as opposed to merely their wisdom.

In contrast, when narrative situations are unsettled, debates over national security are comparatively unstructured. During these periods of narrative disorder, there is no single storyline that serves as the regnant common sense. Multiple narratives swirl about the public sphere with more or less equal legitimacy. These are the moments that historical institutionalists have identified as "critical junctures" – when the scope of legitimate choice is wide, when those choices are consequential, when political actors exercise meaningful and expansive agency.[7] The scope of debate is thus broader than during settled times: politicians and activists legitimately, and without penalty, advance a wide range of policy stances, grounded in a variety of narratives.

To illustrate the difference narrative situation makes, consider once again the case with which this book began – the debate in 2006 to 2007 over the prospect of surging US forces into Iraq, and then over the surge's achievements, which took place in the shadow of the dominant Terror narrative. Proponents of increasing temporarily the US presence

---

[6] On settled and unsettled times, see Swidler 1986. See, similarly, drawing on the Marxist theorist Nicos Poulantzas' distinction between "normal" and "exceptional" states, Jessop 1982, 167–169.

[7] Capoccia and Kelemen 2007, 343. See also Soifer 2012.

in Iraq, located largely in the White House, hoped it would, along with a shift in tactics, bring stability to that war-torn nation, suppress the ongoing insurgency, and thereby advance the War on Terror. They averred that Iraq had become a magnet for jihadists and had become the leading edge of that larger war. As the surge floundered that spring, that link to the War on Terror gave it a new lease of life, when invoked by the politically astute and much-lionized commanding general, David Petraeus.[8] As expected in a settled narrative situation, the surge's opponents also generally legitimated their opposition with reference to the dominant narrative. In light of Iraq's full-blown sectarian civil war, they doubted that the surge would have much positive impact, on security on the ground and certainly on a political accord. Casting Afghanistan and Pakistan as the real frontline of the War on Terror, they further argued that the surge would tie down US forces in Iraq and thus prevent the United States from taking on Al Qaeda more directly.[9] These arguments were designed with an eye to narrative fidelity: they either, in their pure cost-benefit analysis, left the Terror narrative untouched or, in invoking that narrative, bolstered its grip.[10] When more radical critics flung arguments from less safe ground, implicitly or explicitly questioning the Terror narrative itself, the mainstream response was predictable. These were the beyond-the-pale "hyper-ventilating left-liberals," whom Roger Cohen charged with "America-hating, over-the-top ranting."[11] These were the illegitimate dissenters, from whom mainstream liberals, both defenders and detractors of the Iraq War, were desperate to distance themselves.[12]

---

[8] Gordon and Trainor 2012, 413.

[9] On the debate over the surge, see Gordon and Trainor 2012, 429–437; Ricks 2009, 188, 243–251; Woodward 2008, 226, 315–316, 338–350. On the Democrats' call in fall 2006 to focus on Afghanistan, see also Gates 2014, 13, 17; and on this theme subsequently among Democratic presidential candidates, Krebs 2013, 65–71.

[10] Leading Democrats did not, however, take more concrete action against the surge because they wanted it to remain Bush's war in the 2008 campaign: see Gordon and Trainor 2012, 332, 410; Ricks 2009, 79, 150.

[11] Cohen, "Globalist: A Manifesto From the Left Too Sensible to Ignore," *International Herald Tribune*, 30 December 2006. See also Eric Alterman, "Iraq and the Sin of Good Judgment," *The Nation*, 29 January 2007.

[12] With justification, since the right was eager to paint all with the same illegitimate brush: see Sidney Blumenthal, "Operation Iraq Betrayal," *Salon*, 26 July 2007. On liberals' embrace of the War on Terror, see Tony Judt, "Bush's Useful Idiots," *London Review of Books*, 21 September 2006.

To distinguish between settled and unsettled narrative situations is to assert that social life is not always and everywhere equally contested. This should not be a controversial proposition, for it guides much social theory. Less clear is what accounts for change. Some suggest that hegemonic ideas are so well grounded that only large exogenous shocks – wars, natural disasters, economic recessions – can uproot them.[13] But shocks are clearer in retrospect than in prospect. The same events might seem to be manageable problems, which leave established narratives intact, or unmanageable crises, which established narratives cannot effectively assimilate.[14] Because dominant narratives always contain contradictions that disputants can exploit, small fissures that can widen into unbridgeable chasms, maintaining a narrative's dominance requires "ceaseless work" by its spokesmen.[15] Yet, paradoxically, their efforts to shield the dominant narrative from disruption cannot but create vulnerabilities. They, more than marginalized critics, identify the crucial tests that permit developments to "dislocate" a dominant narrative.[16] Crises are, in this sense, constructed and endogenous.[17]

Even settled social systems are thus fragile: the stability we observe is always temporary, relative, and partial. The corollary is that change, though often narrated as radical discontinuity, is rarely dramatic. This follows from the nested nature of language. As Nelson Goodman observes, "world-making as we know it always starts from worlds already on hand."[18] Those who seek to legitimate new projects must overcome the "liability of newness."[19] New narratives of national security must demonstrate fidelity to more stable, still-accepted foundational identity narratives. The trick is to project fidelity and novelty at the same time. Thus, the dominant post-9/11 narrative departed from statist presuppositions, but conformed to the broad contours of American exceptionalism – in its portrait of America as an innocent abroad, its Manichaean attitude, and its crusading liberal spirit. The Bush administration's 2002 *National Security Strategy* occasioned a

[13] Hall 1993; Krasner 1984; Somit and Peterson 1992.
[14] Edelman 1971, 1988.
[15] Hall 1988, 133. On the incoherence of discourse and the opportunities for resistance, see, in addition to Gramsci, Derrida 1981; Dirks *et al.* 1994; Williams 1977.
[16] Torfing 2005, 16. See similarly Burke 1991, 842.
[17] Hay 1996; Widmaier *et al.* 2007.   [18] Goodman 1978, 6.
[19] For this expression, see Stinchcombe 1965, 586.

vigorous debate over whether the document had sharply broken, or was of a piece, with the past. Yet, it was both.

Rhetorical mode: two ways of speaking

Public speakers make many choices – from the metaphors, figures of speech, and tone they employ[20] to how closely they conform to rhetorical conventions.[21] Yet, the former are too fine-grained, and the latter too contextually specific, for my purposes. Broadly, as Jerome Bruner suggests, we can productively distinguish between two rhetorical modes: argument and storytelling.[22] Of course, real speakers do not express themselves consistently in only a single mode: they do not just argue or tell stories all the time. But analysis of these ideal types does not just serve heuristic purposes: one or the other does often seem to predominate in political speech.

"A good story and a well-formed argument are different natural kinds," Bruner observes.[23] They differ in their *purpose*: arguments seek to persuade the audience of the correctness of a course of action, while stories seek to explain a series of events to an audience that either knows itself to be confused or whom the speaker believes to be confused. They differ in their *structure*: arguments deduce the recommended course of action from general principles, and thus take the form of "X fits into category Y, therefore policy A follows," while stories focus on the particular features of chain of events X, emphasizing less what makes it another instance of Y than what makes it distinct from every other Y. They also differ in the *depth of their presumptions*. Arguments presume, or at least pretend, that the interlocutors and audience share certain understandings – metrics by which to weigh costs and benefits, norms by which to assess conformity or violation – and an effective argumentative brief fits these shared understandings. In contrast, storytelling, as the primary way in which human beings impart order to inherently messy reality, provides the basis for those

[20] Hart *et al.* 2013; Lakoff and Johnson 1980.
[21] On genres, see Fairclough 2003, chs. 4–6. For good examples of genre analysis, see Campbell and Jamieson 1990, 2008.
[22] Befitting his disciplinary home of psychology, Bruner calls these two "modes of thought," but I am more interested in them as modes of public expression. See Bruner 1986, esp. 1–14.
[23] Bruner 1986, 11.

shared understandings. It fixes the terms of argument. Storytelling is at a further remove from particular courses of action, but it is more powerful, in sculpting the terrain of argumentation.

Argument comes in at least two varieties. *Instrumental* argument is perhaps the most familiar, with its language of costs and benefits, advantages and harms. These legitimating appeals invoke the logic of instrumental rationality: follow policy A because it will come closer to achieving the objectives at less cost than the alternatives. Political contest conducted on the ground of instrumental argument thus revolves around disputed means. *Normative* argument calls for behavior in line with putatively accepted values. Its legitimating appeals invoke the logic of appropriateness: follow policy A because it is most consistent with the rules of proper behavior. Both instrumental and normative arguments are prevalent in debates over US security policy – and not only on one side of the ledger. Arguments for and against US assistance to Israel, for example, sometimes take an instrumental form: some claim that Israel's oppression of the Palestinians fosters antipathy toward the United States, increasing the costs of alliance, while others maintain that terminating assistance to Israel would adversely affect the United States' strategic capabilities and reputation for trustworthiness, increasing the costs of abandonment. Both pro- and anti-aid camps advance normative arguments as well: some call on the United States to halt assistance to Israel because it is an apartheid regime, while others respond that the United States has a moral obligation to support the only true democracy in the region.

Most importantly, both instrumental and normative arguments presume a settled system of political language. In both, contestants strive to establish that the proposed policy "promotes societal welfare, as defined by the audience's socially constructed value system."[24] Such claims, if they are to resonate, must draw on or project a value system that is not itself the object of contest and on a relatively stable array of underlying narratives. This is obviously true of normative argument, but it is equally true of instrumental argument: to invoke costs and benefits suggests a common scale upon which value is measured.[25] Both normative and instrumental arguments work best to the extent that

---

[24] Suchman 1995, 579.
[25] On shared "yardsticks" making possible meaningful argumentation, see Panke 2010.

they invoke and attach themselves to rhetorical tropes that are beyond question. Effective framing thus consists of fitting one's preferred policy into broadly accepted values and "grafting" new issues onto well-established ones.[26] But neither form of argumentation on its own normally leads opponents to concede defeat. Both sides can usually marshal legitimate arguments in their defense. On the one hand, even stable normative systems are diverse, permitting opposed projects to appeal to equally sacred social values – as in the debate over abortion, featuring an individual's (the fetus') right to life versus an individual's (the woman's) right to choose. On the other hand, the consequences of policy are always uncertain, and estimating the net costs of alternative courses of action is always contestable.

Storytelling is not about making the case for a particular policy, at least not directly. Rather, by setting the scene, organizing events into a causal sequence, identifying and characterizing protagonists, and depicting the exchange among them, storytelling transports audiences into a world of meaning. Placed into stories, events no longer seem random. The more successful storytelling is, the more natural its way of situating events appears. It works "to fix and consign an event, to articulate a common interpretation of it, so to fashion a public memory of it that it can hardly thereafter be remembered in any other way."[27] George W. Bush's rhetoric after 9/11 epitomized this mode. As Chapter 4 records, he had little interest in argument: he did not compare the costs and benefits of the War on Terror to those of less militarized alternatives. Rather, he sought to make sense of the seemingly incomprehensible horror and to provide the nation with a narrative around which it could come together.

Storytelling can be put to either radical or conservative purposes. Some stories aim to unsettle audiences, to challenge the narratives that constitute their social worlds.[28] These stories disturb us and make us cringe. But narrative chaos is not the normal state of affairs. Most people experience narrative disorder as disorienting and disconcerting. They crave an environment that facilitates the unreflective action of everyday life. As a general rule, they seek to limit uncertainty, and thus

---

[26] A vast literature concludes that claims resonate when they fit with widely accepted linguistic structures. On framing, see Benford and Snow 2000; Goffman 1974. See, from the literature on transnational activism, Crawford 2002; Price 1998, 2003; Tarrow 1998.

[27] Black 1994, 29.   [28] Thanks to Nick Onuf for reminding me of this.

they desire "non-specific cognitive closure"; they often prefer any answer to no answer or an ambiguous one.[29] They yearn for "ontological security," or security of the self,[30] and ontological security rests on narrative order. When confronted by troubling or confusing events, persons, or objects, audiences look to authoritative speakers to tell stories that "resolve the imbalance or uncertainty of the problem and … restore equilibrium," providing "a sense of purpose and place."[31] Storytelling grounds social life, weaves community together, and makes possible participation in politics.[32] Public storytelling is constitutive of political identity.

Public storytelling is powerful because it structures the field of political play, not because it leads ineluctably to a particular policy outcome. Yet, full-blown storytelling is rare.[33] Normally, it surfaces at ritualized moments, such as holidays, in which communal identity is performed and re-inscribed.[34] More common are allusions to taken-for-granted narratives, snippets that evoke in listeners the entire story.[35] These truncated versions reproduce dominant narratives and cement their common-sense status. Storytelling typically becomes the *focus* of rhetorical performance during times of crisis, when underlying narratives no longer seem like common sense.

An extended example can help to clarify the nature of storytelling. Consider a signal moment in the early Cold War: President Harry Truman's 1947 address to Congress requesting assistance for Greece and Turkey and announcing the so-called Truman Doctrine. The contours of the postwar world had not yet come into focus, many Americans still thought of Soviet premier Joseph Stalin as an avuncular figure, and what would become known as the Cold War consensus was anything but. Truman began with what he represented as the bare facts

[29] The need for non-specific closure, however, varies with personal predilections, circumstances, and culture. See Kruglanski 2004; Webster and Kruglanski 1994.

[30] Giddens 1991, 35–63. For an application to international relations, see Mitzen 2006.

[31] Patterson and Monroe 1998, 320–321.

[32] Condit 1985, 288. See also Perelman and Olbrechts-Tyteca 1969 [1958], 51–55.

[33] Smith 1981, 228. See, relatedly, Hansen 2006, 44.

[34] Storytelling overlaps in routine times with the ceremonial genre that Aristotle labeled "epideictic." On this genre, see Charland 1987; Condit 1985; Gaines 2000; Hauser 1999; Leff 1993.

[35] On "terse stories" in organizational storytelling, see Boje 1991.

of the situation. Britain, which had previously extended aid to both states, no longer had the financial wherewithal to do so, and only the United States was "willing and able" to provide the military materiel that would enable Greece to beat back its Communist rebels and Turkey to maintain its national integrity. Even in this spare setting of scene, Truman did crucial narrative work. He cast the United States as the defender of last resort, as the reluctant savior of not only two vulnerable nations, but higher principles: national self-determination and freedom. He cast the United States as a responsible global leader that would not abandon its duties. He implicitly contrasted trustworthy postwar American statesmen with irresponsible interwar isolationists who had permitted Nazi Germany's rise and whose postwar brothers-in-arms would repeat those errors. With these "facts" in place, how could the United States not come to Greece and Turkey's aid?

Easily, Truman apparently thought. He might have advanced an instrumental argument for aid – detailing the benefits that would accrue from the Greek Government's victory and Turkey's stability, comparing those gains to the cost of assistance, and weighing all this against alternative policies – but he did not.[36] At the time, some advisers, notably George Kennan, believed that he should have made the case this way. They worried that a broad framing and high emotional pitch would be too provocative to the Soviet Union; in retrospect, they blamed the speech for having paved the way for an overly ideological policy and a too unselective form of containment.[37] But opponents, Truman presumably feared, might then have argued that the stakes were not that high, that the costs of aid exceeded the benefits, or that Greece and Turkey could fend for themselves.[38] The rest of Truman's address thus focused on situating the events of the eastern Mediterranean in a larger narrative, on telling their story. "At the present moment in world history nearly every nation must

[36] For a careful analysis of the speech's crafting, see Bostdorff 2008, 91–109.
[37] Acheson 1969, 221; Jones 1989, 45; Jones 1955, 154–155.
[38] By some accounts, Secretary of State George Marshall had presented the case in such "dry and economical terms" to the congressional leadership, to disappointing results. His undersecretary, Dean Acheson, then intervened, placing the situation in this broader narrative. Sen. Arthur Vandenberg, a leading Republican, reportedly offered his support, if the president would make the case in public as Acheson had in private. See Jones 1955, 139–144. Whether this is really what happened is debatable: see Bostdorff 2008, 69–71.

choose between alternative ways of life," he declared. "One way of life," he explained, "is based upon the will of the majority ... The second way of life is based upon the will of the minority forcibly imposed upon the majority."[39] Truman thereby hailed the United States and its unnamed adversary into stylized roles, one democratic and free, the other authoritarian and coercive. Greece and Turkey were, in Truman's tale, lacking in agency; they were passive, acted-upon – as victims of predation and subversion or as prospective beneficiaries of US protection and largesse. So too were the protagonists. The United States and its unidentified rival appeared not as nation-states exercising independent will, but as the embodiments of larger historical forces, "ways of life" that acted through and upon them.

If one assented to this narrative, much more was at stake than the fate of two small nations. Opposing aid to Greece and Turkey amounted to throwing in the towel in a global struggle and even to bucking history. Truman sought to cut through the murkiness of the postwar world, to fix the meaning of a global environment that had, since the defeat of the Third Reich and imperial Japan, resisted clear definition, and to lay the foundation for subsequent debates over foreign policy. In the end, this narrative did not silence its leading competitors, which either shared its portrait of US interests but challenged its view of the Soviet Union, or shared its view of the Soviets but challenged its portrait of global politics as tightly interconnected. No consensus formed around the narrative to which Truman gave voice in March 1947. To understand why, we need a theory that puts these concepts – narrative situations and rhetorical modes – into motion.

A conjunctural theory of dominant narratives

In combination, these dimensions of social life – narrative situations, divided into settled and unsettled, and rhetorical modes, divided into argument and storytelling – generate four ideal-typical political dynamics (see Figure 2.1). In the two "matched" cases, the speaker's

[39] Special Message to the Congress on Greece and Turkey: The Truman Doctrine, 12 March 1947, available at *The Public Papers of the President*, American Presidency Project, www.presidency.ucsb.edu/ws/. Unless otherwise indicated, all further references to presidential speeches come from this source.

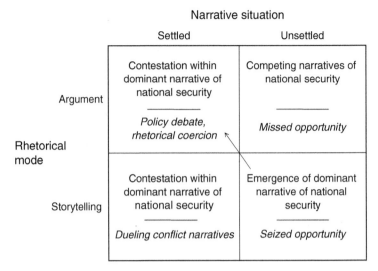

Figure 2.1 Dynamics of contestation.

rhetorical mode is properly aligned with the narrative situation: when the narrative situation is relatively settled and speakers employ argument, and when that situation is relatively unsettled and speakers employ storytelling. While speakers have incentives to match their rhetorical mode to the narrative situation, they also sometimes deploy an inappropriate, or "mismatched," rhetorical mode – due to stylistic preferences, the uncertainty endemic to political and social life, and simple error. These are Figure 2.1's lower-left and upper-right cells: when the narrative situation is relatively unsettled and speakers turn to argument, and when the situation is relatively settled and speakers nevertheless focus on storytelling. This model embodying elements of structure (narrative situation) and agency (rhetorical mode) is a useful first-cut, but it does not take into account *who* is speaking (authority) or *what* they say (content). After laying out the dynamics of the sparer model, I explore both authority and content to generate more specific claims.

1. *Contestation within dominant narrative: policy debate, rhetorical coercion.* When the narrative situation is relatively settled and speakers employ argument, political contestation may be vigorous, but it is constrained: only those policies that can be legitimated *within* the terms of the prevailing narrative are sustainable. Chiefly concerned

with advancing resonant claims, both those in control of the reins of government and their opponents operate within well-defined limits. Consider the politics of national security in the United States after 9/11: once the War on Terror had become well established, numerous projects were legitimated in its name, but few questioned the war itself, as opposed to how it might be waged.

The power of relatively settled narratives to channel debate is most apparent in those rare moments when prominent figures transgress their boundaries. Until recently in Turkey, for instance, anyone who questioned the decades-old denial of Kurdish identity, even leading Turkish politicians with established nationalist credentials, was widely denounced. Prime Minister Suleyman Demirel acknowledged Turkey's "Kurdish reality" upon ascending to office in 1991, but swiftly abandoned that phrase when bombarded with criticism.[40] Turgut Özal, Turkey's long-time prime minister and then president, reversed his fidelity to the Kemalist narrative in the early 1990s, maintaining that "since 1984 the main issue was the Kurdish question" and averring that "we must discuss everything, including the issue of a unitary state."[41] When parties across the spectrum howled in protest, Özal backtracked.[42]

When the narrative situation is relatively settled, "rhetorical coercion" is possible. Actors can, in principle, employ rhetorical strategies that deprive others of the materials out of which they might construct a sustainable counterargument.[43] The rhetoric of human rights, for instance, has been an essential arrow in activists' quivers, sometimes forcing recalcitrant state leaders to talk the talk and even ultimately to walk the walk. The impact of rhetorical maneuver is most clear when the weak use it to overwhelm the strong.[44] But the victims of rhetorical coercion are most often those out of power. In 2002 to 2003, leading Democrats generally shied away from challenging the Bush administration's central claims regarding Iraq. As Chapter 4 suggests, one way

[40] MacDowall 2004, 433, 446.
[41] "Özal on Election, Terrorism, Madrid Peace Talks," *Tercuman*, 1 November 1991 (FBIS-WEU-91213).
[42] "Özal Interview on Kurdish Question, Party Issues," *Hurriyet*, 19 August 1992 (FBIS-WEU-92–165); "Özal Interview on Kurdish Issue, Violence," *Milliyet*, 23 August 1992 (FBIS-WEU-92–172).
[43] Krebs and Jackson 2007. Relatedly, see Bially Mattern 2005; Schimmelfenig 2001.
[44] As I have shown in Krebs 2006.

to understand their relative silence is through a rhetorical prism: the dominance of the post-9/11 Terror narrative narrowed the scope for sustainable argument over Iraq, so that the Democrats had difficulty advancing arguments against the war.

2. *Emergence of dominant narrative: opportunity seized.* When the narrative situation is unsettled, audiences are well disposed to speakers who express themselves predominantly in the storytelling mode. As discussed above, most people crave the stability that narrative order provides and the rational decision-making and habitual behavior that it makes possible. According to Nabers, Ernesto Laclau even asserts that people care less about the nature of order than its mere existence.[45] Laclau exaggerates: the fact of order does not fully trump its content, for narratives of national security cannot run afoul of deeper identity narratives. But people *are* eager for a rhetoric that would help return them to that ordered narrative state. Psychologists have termed this "seizing" – seizing on whatever promises closure.[46] Storytelling is a key means through which orators stabilize their polities.[47]

Speakers who focus their rhetorical efforts on storytelling in times of narrative crisis find audiences unusually attentive and receptive, and their narrative projects are most likely to meet with success in shifting contestation from the relatively unsettled right side of Figure 2.1 to the relatively settled left side. Concretely, this leads to the expectation that major media outlets and leading political figures and talking heads reproduce the emerging story-line. Debate narrows, and policy options that lack narrative grounding are not merely rejected after due consideration, but treated as illegitimate, either ignored or condemned. Storytelling need not reproduce the old order, however. When people "seize," they are open to novel ideas.[48] When the narrative situation is unsettled, debate has slipped its moorings, and rhetorical work must be done either way – to reattach it to the old narrative pier or to attach it to a new one. The storytelling mode can be "a language of transformations."[49]

Periods of narrative disorder are not all born equal, however, and the strength of public demand for storytelling varies accordingly. Success, in its own way, can be as unsettling as failure: the end of the Cold War,

---

[45] Per Nabers 2009, 204. See also Edkins 2003, 13–14; Holland 2009, 289.
[46] Kruglanski 2004, 14–17.   [47] See, relatedly, Burke 1969 [1950], 187–197.
[48] Kruglanski 2004, 14–17.   [49] Too 2001, 252.

though a great triumph for the United States, also ushered in uncertainty regarding both the US role in, and the future of, global politics. But the uncertainty that follows victory is a challenge that past performance promises can be overcome; success increases the public's tolerance for ontological insecurity. Psychological research has found that individuals' need for closure is lower when the costs of its absence are lower; as those costs rise, and as the benefits of closure rise, so does the felt need.[50] For a nation confident that it will ultimately make its way in a changed world, forging a new narrative consensus may then not seem a priority. The result is a protracted phase in which no narrative emerges as dominant. Rather than a story of continuity – if it ain't broke, don't fix it – an adaptation of that aphorism seems more apt: it's broke, but it ain't worth fixin' yet.[51] During the 1990s, Americans could not reach agreement on the emerging global order, but that also did not seem urgent. Bill Clinton's forays into narrating the post-Cold War world were bumpy due less to his focus on domestic affairs or to flaws in his rhetorical strategy than to a context in which public demand for narrative was muted. This may explain why the debate in the United States over the 1999 Kosovo intervention was relatively unstructured.[52] Only once the lack of narrative direction comes to seem costly does the public's demand for order rise. Only then does wide-ranging deliberation figure as passivity, aimlessness, or incoherence. This casts moments like 9/11 in a different light: it was a catalyzing event that highlighted the dangers of drift. No wonder then that the presiding president, George W. Bush, was hailed for his rhetorical leadership.

When the public demand for meaning-making is elevated, multiple suppliers have incentives to ply their stories in the political marketplace. It seems likely that there are substantial first-mover advantages, entrenching early entrants at the expense of competitors.[53] Audiences are receptive to storytelling rhetoric because it restores ontological security and facilitates action. It follows that they should stick with a narrative that has gained traction rather than continually reconsider its

---

[50] Kruglanski 2004, 7–13.
[51] Playing off of, and contrasting with, Legro 2005, 34.
[52] For analysis of that debate's contending metaphors, see Paris 2002.
[53] From an institutionalist perspective, see Mahoney 2000; Pierson 2004. Psychologists refer to this as "freezing" on an existing closure: see Kruglanski 2004, 14–15.

validity. Moreover, narratives are often self-reinforcing: as they make sense of events, they come to seem unquestionably true. Finally, a dominant narrative may empower material and ideological interests in its reproduction – from the military-industrial complex of the Cold War to the "terror industry" that sprang up after 2001.

3. *Competing narratives: opportunity missed.* Unsettled narrative situations present an opportunity for fixing meaning, not merely fitting it to established expressive conventions, but political contestants may not always seize it. They may conclude that silence is the better part of valor, to give themselves greater room for maneuver while public attention lies elsewhere. They may employ an inappropriate rhetorical mode because they misread the narrative situation or because they are, for reasons of personal style, more comfortable in that mode.[54] Ronald Reagan, for instance, was notoriously inattentive to detail and prone to sweeping abstractions, regardless of the circumstances. His successor, George H. W. Bush, was his rhetorical opposite; deeply uncomfortable with what he derided as "the vision thing," Bush had, as one aide put it, an "anti-grandness gene."[55] Leading politicians are more skilled than the average person at discerning audiences' rhetorical expectations. But the political system selects candidates for many reasons unrelated to rhetorical ability, and, as Barack Obama would attest, effective campaign rhetoric does not translate smoothly into the rhetoric of governance. Over time, politicians' skill in matching mode to situation may improve, but learning is limited by the number of opportunities, by the difficulty of tracing undesirable consequences to rhetorical choices, and by consistency constraints that prevent speakers from continuously reinventing themselves.

When, in unsettled narrative situations, leaders are either silent or express themselves predominantly in argument, they miss an opportunity to advance a narrative project. Since, in these circumstances, argument is comparatively unstructured, policy may be legitimated with reference to mutually inconsistent narratives, and rhetorical coercion is rare. National leaders are stymied, unable to marginalize their opponents. Silence can be even more dangerous, as it allows others to supply the meaning and order for which audiences are so eager. FDR's

---

[54] For evidence that personal style matters to leaders' rhetorical choices, see Wood 2007.

[55] On Reagan, see Erickson 1985; Ritter and Henry 1992. Bush official Richard Haass, quoted in Chollet and Goldgeier 2008, 8–9.

campaign to shunt non-interventionism aside before the Second World War, Chapter 3 argues, fell flat partly because of his failure to articulate a well-drawn narrative regarding the emerging global situation.

4. *Contestation within dominant narrative: dueling conflict narratives.* The other "mismatched" case regards the employment of storytelling rhetoric during a relatively settled narrative situation. This can take two forms. First, speakers may openly challenge the dominant narrative. These are the brave dissenters, who recognize how the dominant narrative confines politics and who wish to undo its constraints. Although they are consigned to the margins in the moment and are sometimes persecuted, their efforts help keep alive an alternative should the dominant narrative collapse. For instance, with McCarthyism's wounds still raw and with the Cold War narrative ascendant, challengers were few and far between in the mid 1950s. However, their writings, published in obscure outlets and ignored at the time, may have had substantial impact later, when some on the Left were prepared to break with the Cold War. Dissenters sacrifice in the present to make possible narrative reformulation in the future. Actors well positioned to take on dominant narratives directly are rare, partly because the political system picks out rebels: those who rise to political heights are those who readily grasp and comfortably operate within the regnant narrative. And, as the earlier example of Turkish leaders suggests, even should such well-positioned dissenters arise, they are not immune from punishment.

Second, and more commonly, in a relatively settled narrative situation, actors may employ storytelling rhetoric to fold a specific case into the dominant narrative. This may be a reasonable choice, given the menu of available legitimation strategies, but it hardly shuts down debate – just the opposite. Consider, for instance, how officials justified US military assistance during the Cold War. A typical instrumental argument – that it is cheaper to build up foreign forces than to dispatch US troops – presumed that the Cold War narrative was pertinent; it invited criticism that aid was wasteful or counterproductive, but the relevance of the underlying narrative was not the focus of contest. At times, however, they downplayed the costs and benefits of assistance in favor of storytelling. Thus, US officials justified military aid by depicting the prospective recipient as a beacon of freedom under assault by the malignant cancer of global Communism. Such an account devoted effort to establishing the circumstances, while presuming there to be little debate over the means. This invited response not just to the proposed policy, but to the speaker's narrative, especially because, in settled times, there is little demand for storytelling. Thus, in a relatively settled narrative situation, storytelling rhetoric leads to stalemate, as both sides maintain their legitimacy. Chapter 3 shows how Reagan's storytelling rhetoric regarding the Nicaraguan civil war gave rise to a counter-narrative among both prominent Democrats and peace activists and left the Great Communicator greatly frustrated.

A missing piece: authority

This model, interacting rhetorical mode with narrative situation, rests on the assumption that all speakers are equal. But all speakers are not equal. They are not equal in the communications resources they can deploy or in the level of public and media attention they draw. They are also not equal in their authority – in whether and how they can legitimately express themselves in public forums. Not everyone "can 'do' or 'speak' security successfully," and, in specific contexts, some are "more or less privileged in articulating security."[56] Authority is sometimes a product of personal credibility. It is also sometimes the product of unique access to information, whether technical expertise or classified intelligence. But authority is fundamentally a social relationship,[57] which varies by policy domain and institutional setting. In the United States, in the security arena, presidents possess unusual authority. They have never quite commanded the national stage as we once thought they did. They can, by their actions and their record, squander their authority. But the bully pulpit still has merit, for the president's power to speak for the nation in times of crisis remains unparalleled.

Once upon a time, observers of American politics held an exaggerated view of the bully pulpit. As Woodrow Wilson pointed out, "there is but one national voice in the country, and that is the voice of the President."[58] Holder of the premier nationally elected office, capable of mobilizing coalitions across party lines, and commander-in-chief of the military, possessed of classified information, the president was thought

---

[56] Buzan *et al.* 1998, 27, 32. See also, relatedly, Williams 2007, 64–66.
[57] See especially Lincoln 1994.   [58] Pestritto 2005, 192.

to be a "director" of mass opinion.[59] This proved an easy target for rigorous research. Now scholars typically see the president as but a "facilitator" who reflects widely held views.[60] His bully pulpit has withered thanks to the explosion of alternative media outlets and the contraction of the audience for hard news.[61] Media coverage of the president's public activities is no longer uniformly favorable, even during the "rally" after US military interventions.[62] Presidents have adapted by focusing less on the public at large than on niche audiences.[63] In short, scholars now believe that presidents were never able to engineer large-scale shifts in mass opinion, and even if they once could, they no longer can.

But the pendulum has swung too far in the direction of presidential powerlessness. Presidents are not just *prima inter pares*, first among equals. Occupying a unique space in the American symbolic universe, the president serves as the nation's narrator-in-chief. As the journalist Richard Reeves puts it, simply if inelegantly, the president is the nation's "first explainer."[64] Or as Michael Novak elaborates, the US president is:

king – king in the sense of symbolic, decisive focal point of our power and destiny. He is *prophet* – prophet in the sense of chief interpreter of our national self-understanding, establishing the terms of our national discourse. He is *priest* – priest in the sense of incarnating our self-image, our values, our aspirations, and expressing those through every action he selects, every action he avoids.[65]

---

[59] Hailing the power of the bully pulpit are Cornog 2004; Greenberg 2009. For important studies in this tradition, see Campbell and Jamieson 1990, 2008; Hinckley 1990; Stuckey 1991, 2004. For sympathetic criticism of these bold claims about presidential rhetoric's causal impact, see Beasley 2009, 589–590; Hart 2008, 246; Zarefsky 2009, 451.

[60] Edwards III 2003, 2009. Also skeptical of the power of presidential speech to mold opinion are Jacobs and Shapiro 2000; Sobel 2001; Wood 2009b, 120–156. There is some suggestive evidence that *popular* presidents can lead public opinion and that other voices then have little impact, but the measured effects have been modest, even under the best of conditions. See Brace and Hinckley 1992; Canes-Wrone 2005; Page and Shapiro 1985, 34; Ragsdale 1984.

[61] Baum and Kernell 1999; Cohen 2008.

[62] Baum and Groeling 2010b; see also Entman 2004.   [63] Cohen 2008, 2010.

[64] Quoted in Brewer 2009, 7. See also, relatedly, Campbell and Jamieson 2008, 13–14; James 2009, 59–62; Rossiter 1956, 103.

[65] Novak 1974, 52.

Americans look to the president not to tell them what to think about specific proposals for the welfare system or the tax code. They look to him to make sense of developments at home and abroad, to exercise "interpretive leadership."[66] Reflecting on his first term, Barack Obama identified as his major mistake "thinking that this job was just about getting the policy right. And that's important. But the nature of this office is also to tell a story to the American people that gives them a sense of unity and purpose and optimism, especially during tough times."[67] Narrative performance, not policy advocacy, lies at the heart of "the rhetorical presidency."[68]

That authority, however, varies by both policy domain and narrative situation. Modern states are replete with producers of culture, who by no means look always to official sources for their cues as to the boundaries of the legitimate. But unsettled times are different, especially when they involve narratives of national security. In that arena, the stakes are higher – sometimes in reality, certainly in how they are culturally construed. Not only are publics then most receptive to rhetorical efforts to introduce narrative order, but they are also then least likely to tolerate competing narratives and most likely to look to official sources for the production of meaning. In the United States, that is the president.[69] Crisis heightens the president's narrative authority. Only a limited number of speakers are authorized to serve as the community's designated agents of narrative production. Having many speakers rhetorically weaving the social fabric would undermine the very purpose for which they had been authorized: to unify the community and to stabilize the narrative. Whereas instrumental policy debate revels in difference and division, in moments of narrative disorder, writes one scholar of rhetoric, "such a focus on partial interests is anathema. When speakers violate this rule … audience members feel a sense of misuse of an occasion."[70] For others to offer a competing narrative would not only work at cross-purposes with the impulse for stability, but would also challenge the president's authority to speak on the

---

[66] Widmaier 2007.

[67] Lindsey Boerma, "Obama Reflects on his Biggest Mistake as President," 12 July 2012, www.cbsnews.com.

[68] Tulis 1987. See also Medhurst 2008.

[69] This is the proposition at the heart of the two-presidencies thesis. See Canes-Wrone *et al.* 2008; Wildavsky 1966; and for supporting evidence Bennett *et al.* 2007. However, see Eshbaugh-Soha and Peake 2011.

[70] Condit 1985, 289. See also Perelman and Olbrechts-Tyteca 1969 [1958], 53.

nation's behalf. It would, moreover, assert that the speaker occupied that authorized position – a tall order.[71] This is consistent with psychological research finding that when individuals' "need for closure" is elevated, they are drawn to and less apt to deviate from official pronouncements and definitions, and discussions tend to be less egalitarian, dominated by particular speakers.[72]

Finally, the president's narrative authority is rooted in the public's trust. It is normally granted by default, but misdeeds and missteps can fritter it away. Presidents who engage in deception and abuse that trust, or who make poor decisions and demonstrate incompetence, create openings for opponents to shape the contours of public debate.[73] Even George W. Bush, the legitimacy of whose election opposed partisans had questioned from the start, enjoyed the presumption of credibility. Yet, Bush's, and more generally the Republicans', narrative authority eroded as evidence mounted that key administration figures had, in making the case for the Iraq War, exaggerated the evidence, if not lied, and that the occupation of Iraq was proving far more challenging and costly than they had promised.[74] By the 2006 midterm electoral campaign, Democrats and independents were no longer willing to toe the president's story-line as they had after 9/11. When the administration began openly to characterize the adversary as "Islamo-fascism," it met with intense resistance. Although this language was consistent with the thrust of the dominant Terror narrative, opponents claimed that this portrait of the enemy was an irresponsible escalation. The erosion of the president's narrative credibility shifts authority to the opposition. Whether they seize that opportunity is another matter, as Part II explores in detail.

The entire conjuncture – narrative situation, rhetorical mode, and authority – has now come together. Unsettled narrative situations present politicians with an opportunity to advance narrative projects. Presidents are, in such moments, in an especially advantageous position. They can realize the potential of the bully pulpit by properly gauging the audience's demands and expectations and by speaking in the right way – that is, by seizing the national rostrum relatively promptly, and by expressing themselves disproportionately in the

[71] Murphy 1992, 72–74.   [72] Kruglanski 2004, 112–113, 124–126.
[73] Simon 2009, 141–147; Skowronek 2008, 13.
[74] For related evidence, see Goble and Holm 2009.

storytelling mode. When they do, they are more likely to move politics from the right to the left side of Figure 2.1, from unsettled to settled narrative circumstances. The bully pulpit thus works, under particular conditions, and in subtle but still powerful ways – by shaping the presuppositions of national debate and the policy menu.[75] No wonder that scholarship examining the effects of presidential rhetoric on mass opinion overlooks "the peculiar rationality of presidential communication."[76]

Another missing piece? The content of national security narratives

This chapter places its theoretical bets on the match between rhetorical mode and narrative situation, in combination with institutionally grounded authority. Yet, presumably, some narratives of national security are better than others. Perhaps we can predict which narrative will triumph on the basis of its content. Some may fit better with underlying identity narratives. Some may better satisfy individual psychological needs. Some may be more consistent with gendered norms. Some may tell stories that use more emotionally resonant images and metaphors or otherwise conform more to rules of good storytelling. Each of these approaches has value, and can be productively layered onto my core framework, but each also has limits.

Good storytelling has identifiable elements. It requires impeccable timing (telling a story when the audience wants to hear it), resonance (whose relevance to their lives the audience can immediately appreciate), interest (whose topic piques their curiosity), rich detail, memorable images, a dramatic but believable setting, a gripping plot, characters about whom one develops strong feelings (especially empathy), dramatic tension, and appropriate pacing.[77] Leaving substantial room for interpretation, it invites the reader to participate in its writing.[78] Yet, such a list reveals little: how much detail is too little or too much? What

---

[75] Hart 2008, 244–246. This is per the suggestion also of Edwards III 2009, 191.
[76] Ryfe 2005, 7. See also Cohen and Hamman 2005, 142–143; Edwards III 2009, 191–192; Graber 2005, 9; Peake and Eshbaugh-Soha 2008, 130–131. Important exceptions include Cohen 2008, 2010; Eshbaugh-Soha and Peake 2011; Rottinghaus 2010; Wood 2009a.
[77] Drawn from Schank and Berman 2002. See also Snyder 2015.
[78] Bruner 1986, 24–37.

makes images memorable? How do you know when the time is right? How much scope for interpretation is just enough? Kenneth Burke suggests that good stories start with an imbalance (Trouble) among the elements of his dramatic pentad and conclude with more balanced ratios.[79] Yet, he provides no criteria to ascertain whether the pentad is in balance. Good stories typically begin with a canonical breach, with tension between the audience's expectations and what actually happened; as Bruner puts it: "Something goes awry, otherwise there's nothing to tell about."[80] Yet, many good stories involve events in line with our expectations: the public's appetite for tales of wealthy celebrities behaving badly and for heart-warming stories of self-sacrificing saints seems never to be sated.

If we are interested in how stories are received and in the effects they produce, we should focus less on stories as cultural objects than on storytelling as a practice. "Any narrative," Roland Barthes writes in his foundational work, "is contingent upon a … body of protocols according to which the narrative is 'consumed.'"[81] Some of these protocols vary by culture, such as whether the author must resolve the original tension for the audience to find the story compelling. But much also appears to depend on things as fickle as the audience's mood. One student of storytelling observes that "any story can be good or bad depending on who is hearing it, and what they are thinking about or caring about at the time."[82] We might complicate matters further: metaphors, figures of speech, style (for example, high mimetic, comedic, ironic), and visual images may all affect the outcome of narrative competition. But the more deeply we drill down into these fine-grained elements, the more difficult it becomes to identify general processes – even if we limit the analysis by arena (national security), national context (United States), and temporal scope. Better, in my view, to see how far a theoretical framework built on narrative situation, rhetorical mode, and authority takes us and to use that as a baseline from which to measure how contingent factors shape the dynamics of particular cases.

It is plausible that there are general features of powerful stories of national security, based on social norms or human psychology. For instance, norms of gender. Perhaps narratives of national security that

---

[79] Burke 1969 [1945].   [80] Bruner 2002, 17.   [81] Barthes 1975, 265.
[82] Schank and Berman 2002, 308. See also Smith 1981.

project manly strength always trump those that project feminine weakness.[83] It is women, as Beautiful Souls, whom male Just Warriors are to protect; it is the hearth, of which women are the pre-eminent symbol, that men are to secure.[84] Such gendered norms are nearly universal: with few exceptions, men are raised to valorize the warrior ideal.[85] Yet, such gender norms do not crucially tilt the narrative playing field. Even manly sorts can make mistakes; to admit error can be a sign of strength and self-confidence, and to refuse to do so a sign of stubbornness and foolish pride. "Real men," it is often said, do not need to remind others of their manhood through public displays of aggression, for manliness is also about self-discipline, in contrast to feminine hysterics. Even withdrawal from the field of battle can be narrated in terms of manly virtue: thus, Charles de Gaulle, the epitome of the warrior, successfully cast France's withdrawal from Algeria as a painful necessity for his nation to return to (manly) grandeur. If manliness is a requisite for any narrative of national security, then being open to cooperation and refraining from aggression are as consistent with masculinity as is conflict. That war is traditionally and discursively a male affair does not mean that the only male affair is war.

Alternatively, one might mine social psychology for hypotheses regarding what frames are most likely to resonate.[86] People tend to attribute their own "bad" (unwelcome or undesirable) behavior to circumstances and others' "bad" behavior to their character. Fear makes individuals more favorably inclined to those whom they perceive to be like them and who share their beliefs, and makes them more hostile to those who are different. The need for closure is associated with conservative policy preferences.[87] No surprise then if, when they feel threatened, individuals are more receptive to simplistic appeals that demonize the other – and hawks win.[88]

Psychological research has yielded powerful insights into individual cognition and behavior. In these first two chapters, I have drawn on experimental findings regarding why and when individuals find order

---

[83] Thanks to Michael Barnett for raising this point.
[84] Elshtain 1987; Tickner 2001, 51–64.   [85] Goldstein 2001.
[86] Thanks to Brian Rathbun for pressing me to address this. For a general statement, see Kaufman 2012.
[87] For discussion of relevant psychological literature, see Huddy *et al.* 2005; Kruglanski 2004, 146–154; Merolla and Zechmeister 2009; Rathbun 2012, esp. 212–214.
[88] Kahneman and Renshon 2007. See also Johnson 1994; Mueller 2005.

and stability appealing and how narrative proves indispensable to human reasoning. Yet, such research, because it is built on individualist foundations, can shed only limited light on the process by which any particular narrative emerges as dominant. When psychologists prime subjects to "fear" in the laboratory, and then explore how that shapes subjects' receptivity to particular framings, the real-world analogue is a dominant narrative that precedes and structures the episode. How a narrative becomes dominant is beyond psychology's gaze.[89] This is not just because it is part of the experiment's set-up. It is also because, contrary to the psychologist's conception, collectives must be more than aggregations of individuals, and collective identity must be more than the sum of individuals' beliefs and perceptions.[90] There need not be a necessary relationship between collective patterns and individuals' responses to stimuli, between public standards for legitimation and what people personally find legitimate.[91] Psychology thus yields greater insight into how dominant narratives shape individuals' attitudes and behaviors than it does into how those narratives become dominant in the first place.

I have argued that, as a general rule, we cannot look to the content of narratives of national security to identify the winners of narrative competition. However, the specific content of storytelling is crucial to understanding how dominant narratives shape subsequent exchange: what they establish to be the contours of legitimate debate and how those contours structure argumentation and policy outcomes. The chapters that follow thus pay close attention to the content of the security narratives that both leaders and would-be competitors advance.

The limits of leadership

Do speakers jump only through already open narrative windows? Or can they fling closed windows open, or even carve out new windows

---

[89] Psychologists might alternatively treat elevated fear as an objective fact, rather than as the product of contingent political contestation, but then they do not share constructivist premises and cannot be drawn upon to fill in the gaps in constructivist accounts.

[90] See, for instance, Sperber 1990; Theiss-Morse 2009.

[91] These comments are directed to mainstream social psychology, especially cognitive psychology. Even narrative psychologists generally focus on narratives as the mental representations of individuals. There have, however, been exceptions: see László 2008; Wagner and Hayes 2005.

where none had previously existed?[92] The first question implies that
agents play little role in defining the situations they confront. The
second suggests that it is within the power of transcendent leaders,
and it is the mark of their transcendence, to make routine events into
transformative moments. Neither of these extreme positions seems
right. On the one hand, crises are constructed. Societies have historically viewed poverty as divine punishment for the unworthy, as an
unexceptional if unfortunate condition of human life, as a problem
that demands attention, and only very occasionally as a crisis
that requires immediate redress. Which view has prevailed has not
correlated with the objective incidence or intensity of poverty.[93] On
the other hand, structures have more than a little bite. If leaders could
destabilize narratives at their pleasure, they would exercise no structuring effects, and extraordinary leaders would never feel powerless
in the face of their constraints. Yet, they do. FDR, for instance,
always ranks at or near the top of the list of greatest US presidents,[94]
but he was acutely conscious of the hurdles he faced in bringing the
nation to war.

This chapter rests on a conception of leadership that dances between
these two extremes. It presumes that, in the context of a settled narrative situation, leadership lies in setting out the standards by which
the dominant narrative is to be judged. These articulated standards
determine whether real-world developments constitute normal fric-
tion, problems, or crises, and thus whether they give rise to narrative
disorder. Leaders do not, via their rhetorical interventions, unbolt the
windows, break the glass, or punch a hole in the wall. Rhetorical
leadership is more akin to being the chair of the facilities committee,
which writes the manual dictating the conditions under which
the building's residents might be exposed to fresh air.[95] Leadership
subsequently consists of grasping what the moment demands – what
scholars of rhetoric call its exigence – and delivering. Structural
openings are forgotten unless agents stream through them. In the

[92] Thanks to Michael Barnett and David Edelstein for challenging me on this point.
[93] Edelman 1988.
[94] See Landy and Milkis 2000. For numerous surveys of elite and mass opinion,
see the relevant Wikipedia entry: http://en.wikipedia.org/wiki/Historical_
rankings_of_Presidents_of_the_United_States.
[95] I thus split the difference between so-called rhetorical realists and postmodernists.
See Aune 2009.

absence of such openings, narrative innovation strikes audiences as quixotic. Oratorical brilliance is a matter not of agency or structure alone, but of their conjoining.

There are two other ways, though, in which leaders might evade the constraints of dominant narratives, intentionally but indirectly flinging the windows open. First, they can play fast and loose with facts.[96] Leaders in totalitarian regimes write their own fantasies, of course. But even democratic leaders have often knowingly lied, especially when mobilizing their countries for war.[97] In October 1941, Roosevelt, for instance, told the nation that he had learned of secret Nazi plans to establish an empire in Central and South America and to abolish all religions there – a claim for which there was no authentic evidence, as Roosevelt well knew. Leaders lie because they are rarely caught; because even when they are caught, they may bear few costs, as setting the record straight has the paradoxical effect of giving myths new life;[98] and because their credibility is resilient, as proving that manipulation occurred, rather than mere error in a complex environment, is difficult. Second, they can seek to manipulate the course of events. FDR again provides a notable example: his orders to escort Lend-Lease ships increasingly far across the Atlantic sought to create a situation in which US military forces would appear the victims of German aggression, thereby fomenting popular outrage and finally silencing the isolationists.[99]

But such deception and manipulation are harder than they look. It is true that leaders can, at little cost, lie about "facts" that cannot be verified, but many events relevant to narratives of national security are broadly accessible and widely observed. Although narratives, like scientific paradigms, are capable of assimilating or explaining away discrepant evidence, narratives may eventually fail to make even adequate sense of those patterns.[100] When Sino–Soviet spats gave way to large-scale military mobilization and armed border conflicts in the mid 1960s, even ardent Cold Warriors had to concede that the

---

[96] Thanks to Marty Finnemore for discussion on these points.

[97] Mearsheimer 2011.

[98] See the research summarized in Shankar Vedantam, "Persistence of Myths Could Alter Public Policy Approach," *Washington Post*, 4 September 2007.

[99] See Schuessler 2010; Trachtenberg 2006. For a critique, see Reiter 2012. See also H-Diplo/ISSF Roundtable 5:4 (2013), www.h-net.org/~diplo/ISSF/PDF/ISSF-Roundtable-5-4.pdf.

[100] See also Baum and Groeling 2010a, 2010b.

Communist world really was no longer monolithic. American hawks had remained skeptical of the Soviet Union even after Mikhail Gorbachev let Eastern Europe go its own way, but when the USSR collapsed, even they had to admit that the Cold War was over. And, in an international system marked by unintended consequences, leaders are rightly cautious about trying to game it. When they do try, they often find they cannot mold it as they wish. Roosevelt's example is again instructive. Despite several incidents that he sought to represent as German belligerence and that he used as pretexts for ordering US vessels to shoot at German submarines on sight and for arming the merchant marine, none seemed sufficient – until the German declaration of war after Pearl Harbor.

I cannot disprove the counterfactual: it is always possible that a more brilliant presidential orator could have cast events in a new light that shone so clearly that old narratives seemed irrelevant. A leader's failure to transform the narrative situation may always be explained as a sign of her insufficient skill. We cannot know, because we do not have good ways of measuring oratorical brilliance, or incompetence, apart from the outcome. There is always an element of faith to our social ontologies. But it should not be too much to ask that we construct accounts with sufficient specificity that we can find evidence of their dynamics at work, or not.

Evaluating the theory

This chapter has laid out a framework to account for why and how particular narratives of national security have become relatively dominant in the United States in the twentieth and early twenty-first centuries. Later, in Part II and specifically Chapter 5, I develop an accompanying bookend on the erosion of dominant narratives of national security. Together, they offer a theoretical account of the lifecycle of national security narratives. They suggest generalizable mechanisms and causal relationships, but they do not and cannot make point predictions. This is not because rhetorical choices are a product partly of personal style – although they are – or because the framework has little to say about actors' motives for advancing particular narrative projects – although it does not. These are red herrings: derived via assumption or observation, both could safely be treated as exogenous inputs into a predictive model. There are at least two real obstacles to prediction. First, that rhetorical deployments are injected into streams of conversation among audiences with contingent and ever-fluctuating configurations of composition, mood, and expectations. Second, and still more important, that conceivable national security narratives are limited only by the human imagination. These are necessary concessions to the complex reality of social life. They require abandoning a strict covering-law model of social science, but they do not require abandoning either causality or generalization.

This book has a second, albeit secondary, goal: to show that the rise and fall of dominant narratives of national security have had an impact on US policy. Even if the argument is persuasive on its own terms, some will question whether even dominant narratives have mattered much. Perhaps narratives of national security reflect and shift with global realities or domestic material interests. Perhaps national security policy is made entirely behind closed doors, eliminating the need for legitimation. Perhaps, when legitimation is required, where there's a will, there's a rhetorical way, and other factors are therefore far more important drivers of policy choice. The empirical chapters address these alternative arguments in showing how a dominant narrative and its erosion have shaped the boundaries of legitimate argument over national security in the United States and in turn the policies pursued by the US Government. Given this book's novel concepts, the place of public rhetoric at its analytical center, and its departure from strict neo-positivism, it is even more important than usual to be clear about the relationship between theory and evidence and about the operationalization of key concepts.

The framework's propositions are not covering laws, but they are falsifiable, in that there are conceivable dynamics and outcomes that would challenge their expectations. Consider the two matched cells of Figure 2.1. In the upper-left cell, the narrative situation is relatively settled, and speakers predominantly deploy arguments, whether instrumental or normative. Policy debate then proceeds within the terms of the dominant national security narrative. At least two outcomes would pose a severe challenge. First, if policy arguments rooted in the dominant narrative were not effectively legitimated – that is, if they were cast by critics as beyond the pale and not just as, say, too costly. Second, if speakers were able to escape narrative constraints – that is, if they could openly advance arguments grounded in an alternative narrative and if those policy stances were recognized as legitimate by fellow elites.

In the lower-right cell, the narrative situation is unsettled, and speakers principally employ the storytelling mode. I have argued that their narrative projects are most likely to meet with success – shifting the narrative situation into the settled zone and laying the foundation of policy debate – either if competing narratives are absent from the public sphere or if they are especially authoritative speakers on national security affairs. As politics moves toward the settled zone, one should observe a concomitant narrowing of debate, as only arguments consistent with the emerging dominant narrative are recognized as legitimate. Again, two circumstances would pose a challenge. First, if the boundaries of legitimate politics were to narrow, and narrative competition were to abate, in the absence of a prominent rhetoric of storytelling. Second, if presidents did not enjoy any advantage in times of narrative crisis – if other leading political figures were to show little deference to the president, offer their own competing narrative, and bear few costs for so doing. Some contemporary observers of American politics believe that this is increasingly the case, that whatever authority presidents once had is rapidly eroding.

Identifying challenging outcomes in theory is one thing, identifying them in practice is another. That depends on having some reasonably rigorous way of distinguishing settled and unsettled narrative situations as well as the rhetorical modes of argument and storytelling. Regarding the narrative situation, I rely on several sources of evidence to aid in classification. First, content analysis. It has substantial limitations as a method, in part because it focuses on what is said and what is written. When a narrative becomes common sense, it recedes into the background; if it becomes the subject of argumentation, it has lost its privileged position. As two analysts of narrative write: "What is ordinary and right is discussed as a matter of fact. The unusual and exceptional are what is remarked on. Narrative thus provides data for analysis not only in spoken responses but also in the spaces and silences."[101] Nevertheless, content analysis can reveal when narrative elements are discussed with frequency, when new strands are introduced, and when others fall out of the conversation. It cannot explain these trends, but it provides essential data. Such data lie at the heart of Part II, on the Cold War consensus. However, as I discuss in

---

[101]   Patterson and Monroe 1998, 316. See also Perelman and Olbrechts-Tyteca 1969 [1958], 67–68.

Appendix A, computerized content analysis tools so far remain inappropriate for analyzing complex discursive structures like narrative. Human coding is thus necessary, but it is expensive and time consuming. Conducting a content analysis of this sort on a large corpus of materials is not always practical. As a result, I turn to other data sources as well.

Second, public opinion polls – the answers respondents provide and the questions pollsters ask. Surveyors' professional mission and interests require them to operate within the bounds of the respectable and acceptable. What questions are asked, what questions are not posed, what once-asked questions are no longer posed reveal what is assumed and what is contested.

Third, when available, contemporary observers' assessments, and those of historians, of whether a particular narrative is dominant. Political elites, who generally operate comfortably within the boundaries of the dominant narrative, are less likely to note its constraints than are those on the outside, acutely aware of the obstacles they face.

Fourth, and perhaps most revealing, how audiences respond to particular arguments and storylines allows analysts both to identify the nature of the narrative situation and to map the boundaries of legitimation. Are arguments rooted in different national security narratives treated as legitimate by public officials and the mainstream media? Are they given more or less equivalent attention, taking into account the material resources and social prominence of their advocates? If so, we are in the presence of an unsettled narrative situation. Or, rather, are some arguments and accounts castigated as beyond the pale, un-American, bordering on the treasonous, not just imprudent and unwise? If so, we are in the presence of a settled narrative situation. Moreover, in unsettled situations, there should be evidence of ontological insecurity, of public anxiety over the lack of narrative order. Such data feature prominently in the cases explored in Part I, Chapters 3 and 4.

Regarding rhetorical mode, because speakers employ both argument and storytelling to some degree, the analyst needs a method of ascertaining which, if any, mode was unusually prevalent in a given episode or period. Computerized content analysis programs are generally crude counters of words. Yet, there is also reason to think that certain words should appear disproportionately in texts in which the storytelling mode prevails. Roderick Hart has developed a content-analysis program, Diction, for the analysis of political rhetoric.[102] He has calculated the "narrative style" in speech as an additive measure of Diction's dictionaries for spatial awareness, temporal awareness, motion, and human interest.[103] This has face validity: narratives contain protagonists (human interest), involve action (motion), and take place in particular locations in time and space (spatial and temporal awareness). In Chapters 3 and 4, I use Diction to measure the relative degree of storytelling in major presidential addresses.[104]

Finally, what impact does greater or lesser narrative contestation have on national security *policy*, and how would one know? Available narratives, I have argued, sustain a limited menu of policy options, and policymakers can legitimate only policies on that menu. The impact of narrative is perceived in what does and what does not make it onto the menu, in the policies not discussed and the paths *not* pursued. Factors highlighted by conventional theorizing – from the international strategic situation to party politics to bureaucratic maneuvering – figure in which policy option is selected from that narrative-constituted menu. Demonstrating the power of narrative requires evaluating alternative explanations for silence, and evidence regarding options that receive little consideration is always sparse. The case for narrative's power rests on a counterfactual: had the dominant narrative been otherwise, and permitted now-marginalized stances to be legitimated, policy might have been different as well. When dominant narratives erode, and as the range of narrative possibilities expands, so too should the scope of policy debate; when a narrative becomes newly dominant, debate narrows. These shifts in narrative situation should render some previously (il)legitimate policy options more (less) controversial and easier (more difficult) to oppose openly.

The persuasiveness of the theoretical argument thus rests in part on counterfactuals. We can never escape counterfactuals, but this is especially true of theories that highlight contingency.[105] Both the matched and mismatched cases imply counterfactuals, and I try to be clear about the counterfactual antecedents and consequents in the chapters that follow.[106] Beyond that, the rules for the construction of

---

[102] See www.dictionsoftware.com/index.php.
[103] Hart and Childers 2005. On the Diction dictionaries, see Hart 2000.
[104] For further details on Diction, see Appendix A. For descriptive data on presidents' storytelling, see Appendix C.
[105] Capoccia and Kelemen 2007, 355–357.   [106] Levy 2008, 631, 633.

plausible counterfactuals fall into two broad categories. First, theoretical consistency – that is, the asserted path is one that, according to the analyst's preferred theory, should have been adopted. This is not a terribly demanding criterion, and the resulting counterfactual will be persuasive only to the extent that the reader accepts the driving theoretical logic and the weight of the observable empirical evidence.

Second, historical consistency. This entails, at a minimum, that "plausible-world counterfactuals ... [not] violate [readers'] understanding of what was technologically, culturally, temporally, or otherwise possible." It also suggests a "minimal-rewrite rule" – that is, the introduction of only a small number of historical changes, close in time to both antecedent and consequent. These changes must not themselves hinge on implausible counterfactual conditions.[107] It would, for instance, be implausible to consider how the Second World War, and especially the Holocaust, would have played out if the Allies had had precision-guided munitions: consider what other weapons would have had to be at their disposal, and what larger societal changes would undoubtedly have had to take place, were this technology – and all antecedent technologies – to be within their grasp. For this book, these guidelines suggest that counterfactuals premised on a different narrative situation or on actors occupying different institutional positions should be avoided. These counterfactuals require relatively grand historical changes, in the sense that they hinge on further unspecified counterfactual chains. More defensible and sustainable are the limited counterfactuals I employ: regarding choice of rhetorical mode or of particular representational strategy.

Even narrowly framed counterfactuals, however, raise a key second-order question: how do we know what is plausible or possible in a given set of circumstances? If a leader's decision to shy away from storytelling rhetoric rests on a judgment call, rooted in his estimate of what the public wants or will tolerate, why should one trust the analyst's assessment over that of the experienced politician? One should not. But nor should one defer to the judgment of a single politician, no matter how skilled. One should look rather for evidence as to whether

---

[107] Lebow 2000, 565, 568; Levy 2008, 634–638. Among a large literature, see especially Fearon 1991; Tetlock and Belkin 1996. For a summary of the challenges, see George and Bennett 2005, 167–169.

an alternative approach was possible. Were alternative rhetorics explicitly considered, but then rejected for other reasons? Had a given rhetoric proved sustainable or dominant in sufficiently similar circumstances in the past? Crucially, did other politicians at the time advocate for other approaches, and/or were they critical of the choice or thought it mistaken? All these are signs that there may have been room for maneuver. Such evidence is not always available, of course, but I deploy it when appropriate and feasible to bolster the implied counterfactual claims.

But the proof of the pudding really lies in the eating – in effectively addressing the most likely alternative explanations for the scope of debate and the policies not pursued. While any particular case must address idiosyncratic explanations drawn from histories and journalistic accounts, each must also confront general alternative explanations. For this book's first, and primary, question – why dominant narratives rise and fall – the chief alternatives are that narratives of national security: (1) reflect and shift with global realities; (2) reflect and shift with the distribution of domestic interests and power; (3) reflect the wishes of charismatic, institutionally empowered, or committed speakers; and, for Part II, (4) are jettisoned when they prove wanting and are bolstered when they prove successful. For the book's second, and secondary, question – whether and how dominant national security narratives shape policy – the chief general alternatives are that even dominant narratives: (1) are irrelevant, because legitimation is unnecessary; and (2) sustain a nearly infinite range of policies, imposing little constraint on the menu. Equally important, the empirical chapters show the explanatory limits of the factors commonly cited by realist and liberal analysts of these episodes.

The next two chapters range widely across the history of US national security debate between the late 1930s and the first decade of the twenty-first century. The cases maximize variation on the crucial elements of the conjunctural theoretical framework, and they present the full range of hypothesized dynamics – as Figure 2.2 indicates. The cases establish the plausibility of the framework and illustrate its dynamics, not provide a crucial test. Nevertheless, the breadth of the empirics should dispel concerns that I have picked only the ripest cherries off the tree.

The selected cases are also "hard" for this chapter's theory and "easy" for the most likely alternatives. Some would argue that

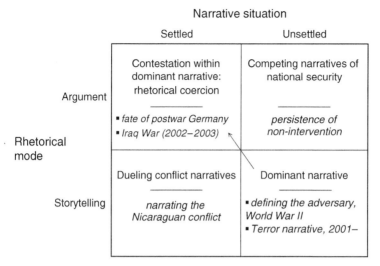

Figure 2.2 Placing the cases.

presidents, by virtue of their institutional authority, set the narrative foundation of political debate, and certainly that should be true of the most skilled presidential orators, like FDR and Reagan – the key actors in Chapter 3. Some would argue that international events normally have a clear meaning, and that should certainly be true of shocking attacks on the homeland, like Pearl Harbor and 9/11 – the subjects of Chapter 4. Narrative dominance, I argue in contrast, lies in the conjuncture of who speaks, when they speak, and how they speak: the dynamics of authority (in which presidents have advantages, at least at the start), the possibilities of the historical moment (in which events undercut or reinforce narrative claims), and the choice of rhetorical mode (in which storytelling can be powerful, when aligned with authority and moment). The next two chapters show, first, that events, even big and important events, are consistent with multiple narratives; if a narrative emerges as dominant, it is not because events alone have spoken so eloquently. Second, even presidents who are masters of "going public" cannot impose their will on public debate: even they must speak in the right way at the right time – or bear the consequences.

3 | Narrative lost: missed and mistaken opportunities

President Franklin Delano Roosevelt was, by all accounts, a master orator.[1] His Fireside Chats are cited as paradigmatic moments of presidential rhetorical leadership.[2] Nearly half a century later, Ronald Reagan entered the Oval Office, known as the "Great Communicator" for his capacity to connect with and inspire mass audiences.[3] If any presidents should have been able to impose their will on the nation's security narratives, they should have. Yet, Roosevelt could not shunt aside the non-interventionist alternative before Pearl Harbor, and Reagan could not persuade Americans of the danger that Nicaragua's governing Sandinistas posed to US national security, nor could he silence his, and the Nicaraguan rebels', critics. Rhetorical skill is not, on its own, enough to ensure narrative dominance – as these masters of the bully pulpit would attest.

Perhaps Roosevelt and Reagan failed because "going public" is simply not effective. That inference would be warranted if presidents' interventions did not sometimes profoundly shape the contours of US political debate – but they do. One might argue that presidents fall short when they are not skilled orators, when they are not deeply committed to the cause, and when they are reluctant to expend resources and to risk political capital – but the examples of Roosevelt and Reagan suggest otherwise. The theoretical framework of the preceding chapter offers four possible explanations. First, presidents can misread the narrative situation. They may wrongly believe that they are facing an unsettled period in which public demand for story-telling is high, and so they may traffic heavily in that rhetorical mode.

---

[1] See, among historians, Burns 1956, 203–205, 402; Smith 2007a, 487 and passim. Among scholars of rhetoric, see Beasley and Smith-Howell 2006; Ryan 1988.

[2] Buhite and Levy 2010. Some attribute the Fireside Chats' impact more to the medium (radio) than to FDR's message or skill: see Edwards III 2009, 29; Lim 2003.

[3] Carpenter 1987; Erickson 1985; Ritter and Henry 1992; Stuckey 1990.

In short, a mistaken opportunity. Second, presidents can err in thinking the political structure highly constrained, shy away from storytelling even when it might be well received, and opt for argument to legitimate their policies. In short, a missed opportunity. Third, presidents can remain silent and fail to seize the rhetorical initiative, allowing others to fill the narrative vacuum – another missed opportunity. Both missed and mistaken opportunities permit narrative alternatives to flourish and channel opposition to leaders' programs. Fourth, presidents can be dealt a bad rhetorical hand – the absence of opportunity. When public demand for storytelling is low, whether because the narrative situation is settled or because they are operating in the wake of foreign policy triumph, presidents can do little to rewrite the nation's security narrative.

This chapter explores in detail Roosevelt and Reagan's immense frustration with what they perceived as their fellow citizens' obdurate refusal to see clearly. Both were talented public speakers, both were desperate to reshape the national debate, but both found their path blocked by political opposition that they could not shake and whose narrative they could not silence. The reasons lay in all four of these causes. Roosevelt's failure began with the absence of opportunity, but became over time a missed opportunity: as the narrative situation became unsettled, he was slow to react, and his subsequently impoverished storytelling allowed the non-interventionist narrative, and especially its distinctive representation of the global scene, to remain a legitimate strand in public debate. Reagan's was both a mistaken and an absent opportunity: in the context of a fairly settled narrative situation, his storied rhetoric about Nicaragua did not silence his opponents, but rather encouraged congressional Democrats, as well as human-rights and peace activists, to offer a very different narrative. The case studies also devote attention to the implicit counterfactuals: FDR might have profited from more forthright storytelling, as his own advisers urged, but Reagan's prospects to win the narrative contest over Central America were weak, no matter the rhetorical mode he adopted.

The case studies, in this chapter and the next, follow a common five-part structure. I begin by establishing the narrative situation, the content of the dominant narrative, and/or the various contenders at the start of the episode. Second, I explore whether, to what extent, and in what mode the president rhetorically intervened. Third, I examine the effects of that intervention, for both narrative and policy, and whether they correspond to theoretical expectations. Fourth, I evaluate crucial counterfactuals, specifically whether the president might have expressed himself differently, with regard to either mode or content, and whether different rhetorical choices would have resulted in a different outcome. Finally, I close each case study by addressing the most persuasive alternative explanations for the failure (and, in the next chapter, the success) of the president's narrative project and for the resulting policy. These include explanations particular to the case as well more general explanations – notably, that the meaning of the events was given, and that the chief alternatives were politically or psychologically implausible.

FDR and the persistence of non-interventionism

By the fall of 1937, President Franklin D. Roosevelt had concluded that he could no longer remain silent. The interwar order was crumbling, and he worried that his fellow citizens were complacent, naïve, or both. So, in the heartland's capital, Chicago, he launched a rhetorical broadside against the nation's prevailing outlook on the world, which its advocates called non-interventionism and which he would later deride as isolationism.[4] In the "Quarantine" address, FDR gave voice to a different narrative of national security. He did not anticipate the vehement and widespread criticism that greeted this initial storytelling foray into global affairs. He was chastened. In the late 1930s, David Kennedy observes, "just as the president's internationalist convictions began to deepen, the isolationist mood of his countrymen started to congeal all the more stubbornly."[5] FDR learned the hard way that he confronted a settled narrative situation, in which the dominant narrative was not to his liking.

Over the next three years, the non-interventionist narrative's supremacy eroded. The claims for which Roosevelt had been vilified in 1937 came to be expressed within the mainstream. But, as the scope of legitimate national security debate broadened, the erstwhile dominant narrative did not itself fall beyond the pale. Until December 1941, FDR

[4] On why the non-interventionist label was also more accurate, see Braumoeller 2010.
[5] Kennedy 1999, 393.

faced persistent challenge from a diverse non-interventionist coalition that shared a very different narrative, a very different logic, and very different policies. A large gap often lay between what Roosevelt wanted and what he felt was politically viable, and non-interventionists remained a potent and legitimate force. As a result, the United States supported the Allies far less vigorously and aggressively and entered the war far later than the president would have liked. Roosevelt's speechwriter, Samuel Rosenman, retrospectively declared that by 1940 his boss's campaign to persuade Congress and the American people of the country's stake in the intensifying conflict had caused Americans' "attitude of sympathetic aloofness ... to drop away."[6] This loyal aide not only overstated the magnitude of the interventionist narrative's victory, but gave the president too much credit.

Why were FDR's efforts to thrust aside non-interventionism and its underlying narrative unsuccessful? Why did that narrative retain legitimacy as late as Pearl Harbor? The explanation cannot lie in inferior rhetorical skill (FDR was unmatched), in weak institutional prerogatives (he remained a powerful and popular president), in the balance of domestic economic forces (which had favored internationalism since the early 1930s), in a secure international situation (most agree that the Axis threatened vital interests),[7] or in the appeal of strategic buck-passing (which realists argue evaporated with the fall of France in June 1940). A common view is that Americans gradually overcame their isolationist predilections as "the sheer force of events" brought proof of Axis power and perfidy. Public opinion "flow[ed] from the facts of international life themselves, from the very real menaces."[8] In praising FDR's political perspicacity, Rosenman made the same point: the president "had to wait until the facts of war impressed themselves upon the people's thinking."[9] But events do not speak for themselves. If the fall of France had finally made clear that the United States could not stand aside, Roosevelt should not have moved so cautiously afterwards to

---

[6] Rosenman 1952, 194, 265. See, similarly, Green 1987, 153–155.
[7] For exceptions, see Nordlinger 1995; Russett 1972.
[8] Casey 2001, 26; Heinrichs 1988, 16. See also, among historians, Burns 1956, 399–400; Cole 1983; Dallek 1979, 227, 267, and passim; Kimball 1997, 59 and passim. Among political scientists, see Braumoeller 2010; Mearsheimer 2001, 255–256.
[9] Rosenman 1952, 266.

help Britain. Events alone explain little. What matters is how they are narrated.

Roosevelt has often been portrayed as a cautious internationalist who marched with, more than he pointed the way forward for, the American public. When it came to "the sentiments and habits of his constituents," John Morton Blum notes, this deeply political animal operated "within the limits that his political antennae instructed him to respect ... [H]e accepted the culture as it was and as it was becoming."[10] As FDR told the writer Upton Sinclair, he could not "go any faster than the people will let me."[11] The problem was less that his internationalist commitments were shallow, as some suspected, or that he rarely addressed national audiences about European developments. The problem rather was *how* he sought to foster a sense of urgency, what rhetorical mode he adopted in seeking to persuade Americans to overlook their disgust with European power politics and their regret over intervention in the Great War. As the European crisis intensified, the ever-cautious Roosevelt was reluctant to embrace fully a story-telling rhetoric and failed to make sense of the emerging crisis for the nation. As a result, the non-interventionist narrative of national security filled the void. He failed to perform the pre-eminent task of leadership in uncertain times, and his difficulties were in part of his own making.

A president quarantined

The prevailing national security narrative in October 1937, when Roosevelt bravely delivered the Quarantine address, rested on several premises: that other nations either were basically peaceful or were justified in seeking to undo the injustices perpetrated at Versailles; that international law and institutions could, and would, maintain global order; that the liberal European powers could handle their continent's problems on their own; and crucially that, regardless, the American homeland, surrounded by its oceanic moats, was invulnerable to large-scale attack. In terms of the Burkean pentad, this narrative

---

[10] Blum 1976, 6. Among those defending FDR's reading of the political tea leaves are Cole 1983; Dallek 1979; Edwards III 2009, 26–34; Heinrichs 1988; Hofstadter 1973, 316; Kimball 1991; Zelizer 2010, 43, 47, 50–51.

[11] Quoted in Schlesinger Jr. 1958, 558. On FDR's philosophy of leadership, see Milkis 1998.

ascribed agency not only to European powers, but to the League of Nations, represented states as committed to the interwar order and as demanding only revisions consistent with its spirit (such as modifying borders in accord with national self-determination),[12] and cast the global security scene as divisible. Rooted in popular disillusion with the US role in the Great War, which had not made the world safe for democracy and which many believed had served the interests only of arms manufacturers, this narrative underpinned Americans' commitment to neutrality and support for military preparedness.[13]

Americans did not look upon European goings-on with a neutral eye. In general, they detested the suppression of the Nazis' political opponents, were skeptical of Hitler's insistence that his territorial ambitions were limited, and found the regime's anti-Semitism repugnant. By the end of the decade, even the *Chicago Tribune* refused to defend the Nazis, averring that "it would be a strange American indeed who could stomach their creed and their attitudes."[14] Most leading non-interventionists, like Senator Burton Wheeler, ritualistically declared their dislike for "Hitler and all that he symbolizes."[15] But the fact that Americans found the Nazis vile did not gainsay the dominant narrative's key tenets. It proved resilient as the 1930s wore on, despite Germany's remilitarization of the Rhineland, expansion of the army and reconstitution of the General Staff, and *Anschluss* with Austria. It permitted the many Americans who doubted the Nazis' motives to remain at relative ease, despite Germany's growing strength and territorial reach and despite the League's failings. It was why every German move to undo the interwar order "intensified the American desire to sever all ties with a Europe about to go up in flames."[16]

The Quarantine address was carefully designed to confront the established narrative, and thus cast its key pillars in sharp relief.[17]

[12] On this in the British context, see Goddard 2015.

[13] On the dominant axes of US debate over global affairs in the 1930s, see Casey 2001, 23–24; Divine 1965; Doenecke 2000, 9–17, 325–327; Jonas 1966, 273–274.

[14] Quoted in Schneider 1989, 12.   [15] Quoted in Cole 1983, 343.

[16] Divine 1965, 30.

[17] Unless otherwise indicated, quotes are from FDR, Address at Chicago, 5 October 1937, available at *The Public Papers of the President*, American Presidency Project, www.presidency.ucsb.edu/ws/. Unless otherwise indicated, all further references to Roosevelt's (and later in this chapter Ronald Reagan's) speeches come from this source.

Contra pacifists and liberal internationalists, FDR insisted that not all were "peace-loving nations" that cherished freedom, respected law, and focused on commerce. "Ten percent" of the world was "threatening a breakdown of all international order and law," "piling armament on armament for purposes of aggression." Contra nationalists, the United States could not seal itself off from "the epidemic of world lawlessness." Globalization rendered America vulnerable: in a highly interconnected world, "war … can engulf states and peoples remote from the original scene of hostilities."[18] As FDR put it, in a Fireside Chat after the war's outbreak, "when peace has been broken anywhere, peace of all countries everywhere is in danger … [E]very word that comes through the air, every ship that sails the sea, every battle that is fought does affect America's future."[19] The Quarantine address was not a wonkish speech. Roosevelt did not weigh the costs and benefits of various responses to this epidemic. He did not even call for the repeal of neutrality. His policy recommendations were vague: "Those who cherish their freedom … must work together for the triumph of law and moral principles." He concluded with rhetorical boilerplate: "America hates war. America hopes for peace. Therefore, America actively engages in the search for peace."[20] The Quarantine address did not advocate any particular policy because its purpose was more fundamental. Roosevelt was throwing down the narrative gauntlet. He was seeking to rewrite the story into which Americans fit world events, to fix the meaning of the emerging global situation. The speech was

[18] On this theme, see, in *Peace and War: United States Foreign Policy, 1931–1941* (Washington, DC: US Government Printing Office, 1943) (hereinafter, *PaW*), 524–525, 527–528, 601–602, 665–667. This argument was repeated by the nation's propaganda apparatus; see Brewer 2009, 128–130.

[19] Radio Address, 3 September 1939, *PaW*, 383–387, 484. Secretary of State Cordell Hull often echoed these core arguments: for examples, see *PaW*, 370–371, 407–419, 432–439, 588, 616, 650–651.

[20] The next day, reporters pressed Roosevelt to elaborate on the address' practical import, and he repeatedly dodged: "I can't tell you what the methods will be … There are a lot of methods in the world that have never been tried yet." All this was not anodyne enough, however, for some, who questioned whether it was America's place to "actively engage" in the quest for international peace. Roosevelt's vagueness, which he presumably hoped would blunt criticism, backfired, since it also allowed opponents to attribute to him a most interventionist policy. See Press Conference, 6 October 1937. However, see Borg 1957, 422–424.

unusually "storied" – about 25 percent more than the average FDR major foreign affairs address between 1935 and 1939.[21]

But the dominant interwar narrative handily met Roosevelt's challenge, displaying its strength and subduing the president. In a settled narrative situation, media and political elites either ignore alternative narratives or treat them as beyond the pale. The first of these options was not available: defenders of the dominant perspective could not ignore a sitting president, especially when he had so audaciously pressed his narrative assault on their home turf, the non-interventionist stronghold of Chicago. But the second was. They responded to FDR's less-than-clarion call for action with a firestorm of criticism, whose severity and intensity surprised the president and his closest advisers.[22] They refused to rebut directly the president's alternative storyline and thereby accord it legitimacy. They generally, rather, replied with argument rooted in the prevailing common sense: a more engaged US policy, they warned, would inevitably lead the country into a costly war for limited gains. Such a policy had drawn the United States just two decades before into a bloody and pointless European war. "Entangling America in foreign quarrels," opined the *Chicago Tribune*, would inexorably leave Roosevelt, like Wilson before him, "with no alternative but resort to arms." Even sanctions, to give teeth to Western condemnation, would set the United States down that path.[23] This instrumental argument rested on a tacit nationalist narrative that depicted global security as divisible. Only that premise made it seem obvious that war was not worth the candle. The narrative situation, as far as other elites were generally concerned, remained settled.

Taken aback by the vehemence of his critics, Roosevelt abandoned his campaign to shift the foundations of national security debate. Rosenman thought FDR had the Quarantine Address in mind when he remarked that "it's a terrible thing to look over your shoulder when

---

[21] For Diction calculations, see Appendix C, Table C.5.
[22] For the shocked surprise among FDR and his aides, see Hull 1948, vol. 1, 545; Ickes 1954a, 226–227; Rosenman 1952, 166; Welles 1951, 13.
[23] "He, Too, Would Keep Us Out of War," 6 October 1937; "Whatever It's Called, It's War," 8 October 1937; "The Consequences of Boycott," 17 October 1937 – all in *Chicago Tribune*. For other press reaction, see "Nation-Wide Press Comment on President Roosevelt's Address," *New York Times*, 6 October 1937. However, see also Borg 1957, 426–433.

you are trying to lead – and to find no one there."[24] He accommodated himself to the interwar narrative's continued dominance and shied away from testing the boundaries of publicly sustainable argument. This is surprising only because, in other arenas, Roosevelt did not hesitate to treat the presidency as a site and instrument of moral leadership. As a leading biographer claims, "probably no American politician has given so many speeches that were essentially sermons rather than statements of policy."[25] Between the Quarantine Address and the war's start, FDR's major foreign affairs speeches were, according to Diction's measures, 30 percent less storied than those of his Cold War successors.[26] Both government officials and prominent figures in civil society took note of Roosevelt's humbling experience. Even as committed an Atlanticist as the columnist Walter Lippmann would not call openly for all-out support of Britain and France, and he was careful to frame his arguments for repeal of the arms embargo in terms of preserving American neutrality – to the frustration of his many European friends.[27]

But these relatively crude quantitative measures do not fully reflect how stunted Roosevelt's storytelling was. When FDR did offer the nation a security narrative, he did not specify who the protagonists in the global drama were, what they had done, and what motivated them. Rather, he told a tale of abstract villains, engaged in unspecified crimes, and of equally abstract heroes who opposed them. After the Panay incident in December 1937, in which Japanese planes strafed a US gunboat patrolling the Yangtze River, FDR requested additional funds for combat ships, but was careful to point out that, "in speaking of my growing concern, I do not refer to any specific nation or to any specific threat against the United States."[28] In April 1938, he imposed on Harold Ickes, his outspoken and irascible Secretary of the Interior, to placate Secretary of State Cordell Hull and to remove all references to Nazism, current dictators, or even specific nations in a nationally broadcast speech.[29] As late as his 1939

---

[24] Rosenman 1952, 167.   [25] Burns 1956, 476.
[26] See Appendix C, Table C.5.   [27] Steel 1980, 375, 379–380.
[28] Letter to the House Appropriations Committee on National Defense, 28 December 1937.
[29] Ickes complied, but was annoyed with Hull whom he accused of becoming "so timid that he tries to walk without casting a shadow." Ickes 1954a, 347–352, 389, quote at 211.

State of the Union address – that is, even after Munich – FDR would only vaguely allude to events abroad in support of his preferred policies. In his memoirs, Rosenman identified those events as "the mutilation of Czechoslovakia, Mussolini's conquest of Ethiopia, and Japan's aggression in China,"[30] but FDR himself left them and their perpetrators unnamed. Roosevelt expected Americans to share his disgust, but he did not seem to wish that they know by whom and for what reason they were to be disgusted. In short, not only did Roosevelt rarely speak in the storytelling mode, but on those occasions when he did, he told a tale that was impoverished with regard to – in Burke's terms – act, agent, and purpose and thus did not help Americans situate themselves on the terrain of identity. Nor did other administration spokesmen compensate by offering a more fully elaborated narrative.[31] In Hull's many public addresses, for instance, his rhetoric was markedly even less storied, as the lawyerly Secretary of State constructed an airtight argument detailing the costs of inaction and the benefits of action.[32]

The cautious crusade[33]

Beginning in spring 1939, the dominance of the non-interventionist narrative gradually began to erode, and the scope of debate over US national security broadened. Roosevelt could take little credit, for, since October 1937, he had hardly even tried to tell Americans a different tale about global affairs. Rather, it was proponents of the interwar narrative who set the tests that it would have to pass. Regarding the agents of the global drama and their purposes, they had insisted that Hitler's designs were limited and defensive and that, if they were not, international institutions were resilient, and Britain and France could keep Germany in its place.[34] Even those Americans who believed global security indivisible might support non-intervention if

---

[30] Rosenman 1952, 182–183.
[31] Ickes was a notable exception, but, as Secretary of the Interior, his opportunities to speak publicly on foreign affairs were few. He then tended to address narrow, often Jewish, audiences.
[32] Hull addresses, 17 March 1938 (Washington, DC) and 1 November 1938 (New York), *PaW*, 438, 418, 436.
[33] This felicitous phrase comes from Casey 2001.
[34] For examples, see Doenecke 2000, 9–12, 15–17, 29–37, 83–84, 151–154, 184–202.

these planks had merit. The first plank – regarding Hitler's allegedly limited revisionism and defensive goals – was struck a blow in spring 1939, when Germany invaded what remained of Czechoslovakia, in violation of the Munich accords and at odds with the rhetoric of self-determination it had trumpeted during the Sudeten crisis. It became even less sustainable over time, as the air war over Britain in summer and fall 1940, and then the invasion of the Soviet Union the next year, suggested that Hitler would not be satisfied with continental Europe – and so non-interventionists steered clear of Hitler's intentions and focused on Germany's capabilities.[35] The war's start in September 1939 was fatal to the second plank: international institutions were clearly not capable of sustaining the interwar global order, as the dominant narrative had insisted. The fall of France undermined the third plank: if the combined strength of Britain and France could not defeat Germany, an isolated Britain, without a continental toehold, could hardly defeat the Nazi war machine.

As the formerly dominant narrative's portraits of act, agent, and purpose crumbled, space opened for alternative narratives. Into the breach stepped interventionist civil society – the Committee to Defend America by Aiding the Allies, the Fight for Freedom Committee, the Century Group, the Council for Democracy, and many others. These organizations were not marginal: they counted among their leaders some of the nation's most distinguished citizens, unimpeachable members of the establishment. They prompted a powerful response: the formation of the America First Committee, headquartered in Chicago but with branches across the nation, and led by A-list celebrities like Charles Lindbergh. Interventionist activists agreed that the Nazi threat lay in the realm of values, and they saw ideological appeals – à la the Four Freedoms – as essential to rousing and rallying the American public. But, by 1940, because few non-interventionists still defended the Nazi regime, the debate revolved around the last remaining, and most essential, element of the formerly dominant narrative: scene. With the League of Nations effectively defunct, and with Britain alone and on the ropes, interventionists in civil society sought to persuade Americans that Nazi dominion over continental Europe posed a direct threat to the well-being of the nation's economy and security and that American democracy could not survive if Britain went down to defeat.

[35] Schneider 1989, 48.

As the famous "Stop Hitler Now!" advertisement of June 1940, composed by the playwright Robert Sherwood and placed in newspapers across the nation, put it: "If Hitler wins in Europe . . . the United States will find itself alone in a barbaric world . . . . We shall have no other business, no other aim in life, but primitive self-defense." The vast oceans on either side of the United States would afford no protection against the Nazi agents who, as in now-conquered European nations, have "for many years . . . been effectively at work in Latin America, gaining ground by persuasion, bribery, and intimidation."[36] The narrative situation after September 1939 was unquestionably unsettled.[37]

Nevertheless, Roosevelt's rhetorical tack remained largely unchanged. He engaged in little storytelling, and the stories he did tell lacked identifiable characters. Between September 1939 and the May 1940 blitzkrieg that led to the fall of France, Roosevelt made no references to Hitler by name or even to Nazis or Nazism in his major foreign affairs addresses; "Germany" appeared merely once, which was one more time than the other Axis members or their leaders.[38] In a Fireside Chat just two days after the invasion of Poland, FDR did not declare Germany the aggressor, but only hinted obliquely: "I cannot ask that every American remain neutral in thought as well. Even a neutral has a right to take account of facts. Even a neutral cannot be asked to close his mind or his conscience." His message to Congress later that month delved into history to explain the dreadful events, but it had little to say about who was responsible, and it shifted almost entirely into instrumental argument as it focused on the perils of neutrality revision.[39] Graphical representations derived from Centering Resonance Analysis reinforce this point. Before May 1940, no particular aggressor – Germany, Japan, or Italy – was prominent in Roosevelt's rhetoric, nor were ideological terms – freedom, democracy, dictatorship, slavery (see Figure 3.1). "Belligerent" linked to "power" is located toward the bottom of the figure, as is "enemy," which indicates that these phrases were marginally central to his rhetoric. None is strongly linked (by a dark line) to the defining elements of

---

[36] Reprinted in Johnson 1944, 86, and see generally ch. 5.
[37] On civil society debate, see Chadwin 1968; Johnson 1944; Olson 2013.
[38] For details, see Appendix B, Table B.1.
[39] Radio Address, 3 September 1939; Address to Congress, 21 September 1939 – in *PaW*, 485, 486–488.

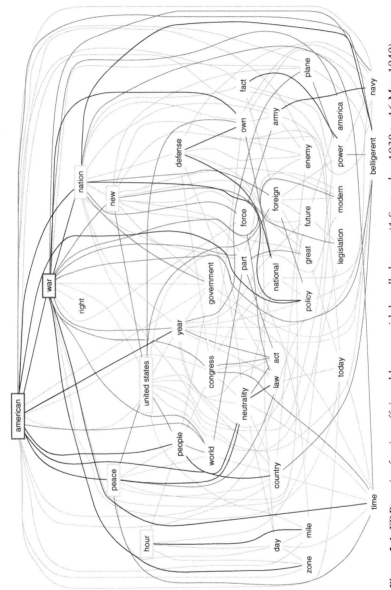

Figure 3.1 FDR, major foreign affairs addresses, with bundled terms (1 September 1939 to 16 May 1940).

FDR's rhetorical network – which revolved around national identity (American) and the global situation (war, peace).

This finally began to change only with the German invasion of Denmark and Norway in April 1940 and especially of France the next month.[40] After May, Roosevelt's foreign affairs speeches were nearly as storied, according to Diction's measures, as they would be after Pearl Harbor.[41] He began to represent America not just as another law-abiding country, but as a nation possessed of a distinctive history, mission, and values. The current crisis thus became part of the larger sweep of US history, a third foundational moment after the War of Independence and the Civil War.[42] He began to name names, finding occasions to demonize the Nazis and Hitler and to depict them as an existential threat, less to the physical security of the homeland, than to its values.[43] He increasingly narrated the war as a battle between democracy and dictatorship, freedom and slavery.[44] As Figure 3.2, derived from CRA data, shows, between May 1940 and December 1941, Hitler and Nazi were both central to the president's rhetoric, and they were strongly linked (by a dark line) to "United States" and separately to "American"; "freedom" was fairly prominent too, strongly linked to "defense" and to "American." When related phrases are bundled, as in Figure 3.3, "hitlernazienemy" and "ideological-terms" not only appear central to FDR's rhetoric, but important new linkages appear. Notably, the bundled ideological terms retain their tight connection to "American" and "defense," but also to "war" – suggesting even more strikingly that these terms became central to Roosevelt's narrative after the fall of France.

Yet, even after May 1940, Roosevelt's crusade remained, at its core, cautious. As a storyteller, he was treading ground that many, including the hawks in his cabinet, had trod before. Demonizing Hitler and the Nazis, portraying the United States as a beacon of freedom, casting the conflict in ideological terms: by this time,

---

[40] See, similarly, Casey 2001, 37–44.

[41] For details, see Appendix C, Table C.5.

[42] See Address, University of Virginia, 10 June 1940, *PaW*, 545–549.

[43] "Arsenal of Democracy" Fireside Chat, 29 December 1940, and Radio Address, 11 September 1941 (after the Greer incident) – both in *PaW*, 485–608, 737–743.

[44] A related transformation came over Hull's rhetoric as well: see, in *PaW*, Address, 20 June 1940 (Harvard University), 556–559; Address, 26 October 1940, 581–591.

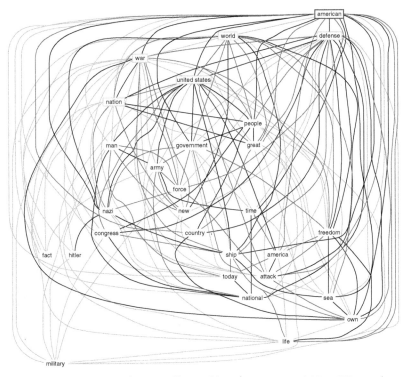

Figure 3.2 FDR, major foreign affairs addresses (26 May 1940 to 7 December 1941).

although the country remained on the war's sidelines, such rhetoric was mainstream.[45] The president's embrace of these well-traveled narrative elements could not decisively tilt the field. Thus, the promulgation of the Atlantic Charter, which drew a "sharp contrast . . . between the multilateral world vision of the democracies and the self-serving aims of the Axis," had little effect, according to Waldo Heinrichs, "because most people in the United States and Britain took for granted most of what it said."[46] Moreover, argument continued to feature very heavily in Roosevelt's rhetoric. The famous "Arsenal of Democracy" (December 1940) and Greer (September 1941) addresses revolved around instrumental and normative arguments – for assisting the Allies and arming the merchant

[45] For this point, see also Dallek 1979, 228–229.   [46] Heinrichs 1988, 152.

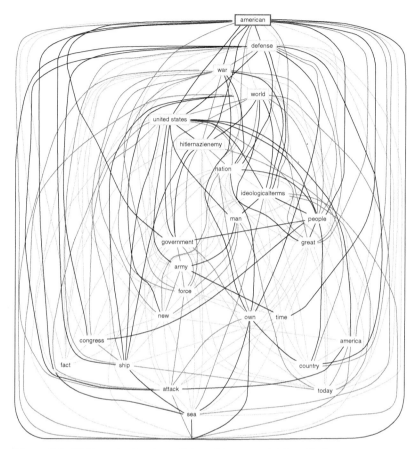

Figure 3.3 FDR, major foreign affairs addresses, with bundled terms (26 May 1940 to 7 December 1941).

marine – that did not follow from their hackneyed storytelling.[47] Strangely, FDR often still declined to identify America's adversaries by name. The 1941 State of the Union address, in which he articulated the Four Freedoms, made clear where his sympathies lay – with "the democratic way of life" against the "assault ... [on] the whole pattern of democratic life," which had begun 16 months before. Yet, Roosevelt did not name "the aggressor nations," nor did he invoke

---

[47] Radio Address, 29 December 1940, and Radio Address, 11 September 1941 – in *PaW*, 485–608, 737–743.

specific instances of aggression.[48] His narrative still often remained abstract, ahistorical, and bloodless.

Finally, and most importantly, Roosevelt's storytelling did not address a crucial element: scene. He devoted little attention to the interconnectedness of global politics – perhaps because he himself remained unsure whether Germany could threaten the homeland.[49] Yet, he thereby left a weak link in his brief. If the United States could remain prosperous and democratic in glorious isolation in its own hemisphere, it did not matter if Germany's regime was odious or if it had conquered Europe and Asia. A triumphant Germany, non-interventionists pointed out, would have its hands full coping with continental occupation, especially nationalist resistance.[50] Hitler's regime, they suggested, suffered from debilitating internal vulnerabilities, and projecting force over great distances would be beyond its capabilities. Finally, even if Germany could address its problems of domestic and imperial governance, the Atlantic and Pacific Oceans ensured America's safety: Germany would need military installations in the western hemisphere to engage in large-scale bombing or full-bore invasion, and a narrowly defined military effort could deny them those bases.[51] As FDR lamented in December 1939: "What worries me, especially, is that public opinion over here is patting itself on the back every morning and thanking God for the Atlantic Ocean (and the Pacific Ocean)."[52]

Non-interventionists narrated a world in which security was divisible. They foretold an unsullied America standing tall despite the death, devastation, and dictatorship surrounding it.[53] This depiction of the global scene had much intuitive appeal. The razor-thin House vote in summer 1941 on the renewal of the draft reflected its abiding power: "the American people were not convinced," Robert Divine infers from this episode, "that Germany and Japan truly endangered the security of

[48] Annual Message to the Congress on the State of the Union, 6 January 1941.
[49] On Roosevelt's ambivalence, see Casey 2001, 6–12.
[50] This argument would appear to have merit, based on the history of occupations. See Edelstein 2008.
[51] Students of military strategy might find this argument plausible, as they have observed the difficulty of projecting force – the "stopping power of water." See Mearsheimer 2001, 114–128.
[52] Quoted in Casey 2001, 24.
[53] For examples, see Cole 1983, 343–345; Doenecke 2000, 244–252; Schneider 1989, 48–49, 126.

the United States. The near-panic which followed the fall of France had subsided, and after the German invasion of Russia, many Americans felt that the immediate danger of a German thrust into the Western hemisphere had passed."[54] Roosevelt knew that global scene was his narrative Achilles' heel. Thus, in fall 1941, he occasionally engaged in scare tactics, claiming elaborate German plans to conquer the hemisphere and even presenting alleged Nazi maps (actually forged by British intelligence). But it remained hard to see how America's survival was threatened by the machinations of German agents in Latin America, who, whatever their ill designs, would have difficulty bringing the German military machine to bear over the watery expanse of the Atlantic Ocean.

Caution's consequences

Roosevelt's half-hearted embrace of storytelling, after the war's outbreak and even after the fall of France, left him ill-equipped to silence non-interventionist voices – or so I would expect, based on the theoretical logic of Chapter 2. And that was the case: both non-interventionism, and the narrative in which it was rooted, retained legitimacy on the American political scene. This was manifest in several ways. First, public opinion. On the most fundamental question – should the United States declare war? – non-interventionists retained majority support through Pearl Harbor. Not until after Japan's surprise attack did more than one-third of Americans ever answer that question in the affirmative. Consistent public opposition to declaring war reflected a steadfast popular faith in the homeland's invulnerability; even as Americans grew increasingly sure that they knew the identities of the good guys and the bad guys, they were unsure that the nation's interests in the Allies' victory warranted the ultimate sacrifice. Not surprisingly, non-interventionists sought to capitalize on the public's reluctance to enter the war. They denied the distinction between the administration's preference for "methods short of war" and war itself. They depicted assistance to the Allies as a slippery slope: as one memorably put it, during debates on the revision of neutrality legislation, "cash and carry" would become "clash and carry." Many later warned that US Navy escort of commercial shipping would draw the

---

[54] Divine 1965, 131. See also Heinrichs 1988, 160.

United States into the war. Senator Burton Wheeler, in a one-liner that particularly provoked FDR's ire, contended that Lend-Lease would "plough under every fourth American boy."[55] These assertions were troubling to the administration not only because they resonated, but because they struck uncomfortably close to the truth – as FDR tried to maneuver the nation into war in 1940 to 1941.[56]

Second, persistent debate over intervention hinging on deep differences over a key narrative pillar: scene. Non-interventionists explicitly articulated a view of global security as only loosely connected. This narrative foundation sustained two common instrumental arguments, which both pointed to substantial hidden costs of war involvement. These costs were not worth bearing because global security was, they argued, divisible. Non-interventionists thus maintained that shipping resources overseas would undermine national preparedness. Since 1939, Roosevelt had emphasized how unready the US military was for total war and how badly the nation needed to rearm.[57] Most non-interventionists were not pacifists, and they were quick to grant these requests for military materiel. But FDR had also claimed that the best way for the United States to escape war would be to keep the Allies solvent and strong, by serving as "the arsenal of democracy."[58] Non-interventionists highlighted a tension between these two claims. Should the United States be drawn into war, would not those same weapons made available via Lend-Lease have proved useful? Moreover, if Britain's condition was so dire, would not the shipments of aid prove a waste, and worse still bolster the German war machine, if Britain surrendered?[59] In short, non-interventionists argued, the United States could get more bang for its national-security buck by investing in its own military and industrial base. The risks of assistance might be warranted if the Allies' defeat ensured America's. But non-interventionists insisted that the United States could thrive even if Germany proved victorious on the continent.

---

[55] Cole 1983, 448, 298, 415; Doenecke 2000, 61–62.

[56] See Schuessler 2010; Trachtenberg 2006.

[57] In November 1941, after over two years of rearmament, far more Americans still thought the US Army, and to a lesser extent the air force, weaker than their German counterparts. See Cantril 1951, 17.

[58] FDR, "Arsenal of Democracy" Fireside Chat, 29 December 1940, *PaW*, 599–608, at 601.

[59] Doenecke 2000, 104–106, 117, 167–170.

In addition, non-interventionists argued that the administration's national security measures were undermining the democratic institutions they were supposed to protect. Most notably, they gave the executive branch too much discretion, threatening the four freedoms. Roosevelt, asserted the America First Committee's General Robert Wood, wanted "a blank check book with the power to write away your man power, our laws, and our liberties." During the debate over Lend-Lease, Senator Gerald Nye enumerated the bill's unusual executive powers and pointedly accused Roosevelt of aspiring to be a "dictator." This cost, too, was presumably worth bearing if the homeland were truly at risk. But such costs seemed excessive because the homeland was not at direct risk of attack, according to the non-interventionist narrative.[60]

Third, the fact that non-interventionists remained part of the mainstream debate over America's role. Cordell Hull later claimed that the 1939 contest over neutrality was "the last effective stand of the powerful isolation movement in the United States. The movement continued its fight by every means at hand and it remained a danger, but after war came in Europe it was never again able to thwart an Administration proposal."[61] Retrospective analysis of public opinion has found that non-interventionists had become a permanent minority by winter 1941. But, even after the fall of France, establishment America remained divided: for instance, campus leaders at Yale, not disaffected reactionaries, founded a campus chapter of the America First Committee in summer 1940, and nearly half of the university's undergraduates signed the campus AFC's petition against deeper American involvement in Europe's squabbles.[62]

That non-interventionists remained *within* the pale is paradoxically made clear by the ferocity of the administration's and its allies' campaign in 1941 to brand them *beyond* the pale. FDR regularly accused his opponents of delusion and wishful thinking, partisanship and profiteering. He caricatured their stance as an isolationism so extreme that the United States could not defend its interests.

---

[60] Cole 1983, 414–421, at 414, 420. See also Doenecke 2000, 43–44; Schneider 1989, 58–62, 137.

[61] Quoted in Cole 1983, 319. Cole exaggerates in depicting subsequent disputes as mere skirmishes. Neither the White House nor the non-interventionists saw them that way. See also Divine 1965, 86.

[62] Olson 2013, 220–227. See also Sarles 2003.

He employed the tried-and-true tactic of guilt-by-association: the isolationists, he alleged, abetted the Axis by weakening American morale
and giving comfort to the Nazis, and they were either traitors or dupes
and, in practice, a fifth column.[63] The pugnacious Ickes, who happily
did the president's rhetorical dirty work, labeled Lindbergh the "No. 1
Nazi fellow traveler," and a prominent pro-war group characterized
the America First Committee as a "Nazi Transmission Belt."[64] Radio
networks and Hollywood studios echoed the administration's allega-
tions or sought to smother the non-interventionists with silence.[65] So
too did leading interventionist groups in civil society, like Fight for
Freedom.[66] On the basis of little evidence, one historian asserts that, as
a consequence of this campaign, "isolationists were widely viewed as
narrow, self-serving, partisan, conservative, antidemocratic, anti-
Semitic, pro-Nazi, fifth columnist, and even treasonous."[67] Yet, if
this were true, why did the administration continue to pillory them?
If their position were so indefensible, of what use was further invective?
If they were so irrelevant, why did the president continue to feel
hamstrung throughout 1941, why was he still reluctant to call forthrightly for US intervention, and why was he still desperately searching
for an incident that would drag a reluctant nation to war?

Non-interventionists even remained politically relevant *after* Pearl
Harbor. As the US military suffered a series of crushing defeats in
the Pacific in 1942, non-interventionists made a comeback.[68] Late
that summer, the Office of War Information (OWI) noted that
"those Americans who, prior to Pearl Harbor, held views which were
commonly called 'isolationist[,]' show little embarrassment about
acknowledging them today. Either they remain convinced that they
were right in their earlier opinion or they believe that the errors demonstrated by hindsight are no cause for consternation." As for the coming

---

[63] *PaW*, 513, 527, 602–603, 664–670, 741, 769.

[64] Cole 1983, 461–463; Doenecke 2000, 1, 54–55, 257–258. On such tactics in
general, see Cole 1983; Doenecke 2000; Smith 1973; Steele 1979, 15–24,
29–30.

[65] Steele 1984, 1985.

[66] Chadwin 1968, 208–223. See also Schneider 1989, 143–145, 163–168,
184–188.

[67] Cole 1983, 411. See similarly Green 1987, 152–155.

[68] A historian of the Republican Party notes that "the aftermath of Pearl Harbor
intensified the disagreement between isolationists and interventionists." Gould
2003, 288.

mid-term congressional elections, the OWI predicted that neither past nor present criticism of the war would serve as much of an impediment to candidates.[69] The OWI was correct. Non-interventionist Republicans generally won their primaries, and, by the GOP's count, 110 out of 115 US representatives who had been "selected for purging by the 'interventionist' groups" were returned to office. A Democratic post mortem concluded that isolationism was as strong as ever in the Midwest, and a GOP analyst observed that "as an issue in the primaries or the final elections, 'isolationism' laid a very large egg" because "it was a direct attack on the patriotism . . . of the millions of citizens whose pre-Pearl Harbor attitude toward the Administration's foreign policy had been accurately mirrored by the congressmen who were now under attack."[70] Mid-war debates over US membership in prospective international institutions showed that nationalism was alive and well, and it persisted well into the postwar era.[71] Roosevelt himself opined during the war that "anybody who thinks that isolationism is dead in this country is crazy. As soon as this war is over, it may well be stronger than ever."[72]

Fourth, policy outcomes. The administration's legislative triumphs after 1939 are often cited as proof of the growing marginalization of non-interventionism – but they were just the opposite. FDR, always the clever tactician, asked only for what he thought politically achievable, and he repeatedly requested less than he wished.[73] In this respect, too, his was a cautious crusade. Time and again, Roosevelt avoided head-on conflict with his non-interventionist opponents. After the war's outbreak, he only gradually committed the country to selling scarce military supplies. In 1940, he hardly acknowledged his own peace initiatives, and he allowed others to take the lead on conscription. In spring 1941, to ensure Lend-Lease's passage, and recognizing that Senator Gerald Nye's call for "more Nathan Hales and fewer Caesars"

---

[69] Intelligence Report #37 (21 August 1942), Bureau of Intelligence, OWI, 8–10, quote at 8, in United States 1942–1944, vol. 1. For subsequent OWI concern about the vitality of "isolationism," see also Intelligence Report #57 (8 January 1943), in ibid.

[70] Quoted in Darilek 1976, 54–56.

[71] Divine 1965, 93–113; Rathbun 2012, 163–208.

[72] Quoted in Zelizer 2010, 59.

[73] On the problem with relying on "legislative scorecards" to assess congressional influence and on Congress' power to shape foreign policy through the executive branch's anticipated reactions, see Lindsay 1994.

was resonating, Roosevelt initially denied that he would ever use all the powers the bill granted him and ultimately sacrificed substantial executive discretion in the passed legislation.[74] Later that year, although he knew that Lend-Lease depended on goods reaching Britain safely, he moved slowly toward Navy escorts, and he accepted restrictions on conscripts serving outside the western hemisphere.

Roosevelt respected the non-interventionists' power in Congress and confronted them with care.[75] To an increasingly impatient Winston Churchill in summer 1941, FDR excused his glacial pace by invoking public opinion and by complaining that he was "skating on pretty thin ice in his relations with Congress." Clare Booth Luce acidly observed that "every great leader had his typical gesture – Hitler the upraised arm, Churchill the V sign. Roosevelt? She [Luce] wet her index finger and held it up," imitating Roosevelt testing the political winds.[76] It is worth recalling that the administration's triumphs were hardly foreordained: the final repeal of the Neutrality Act's key provisions passed narrowly, 50 to 37 in the Senate and 212 to 194 in the House, and the extension of Selective Service passed by only a single vote in July 1941.[77]

Counterfactual analysis

This argument rests on an implied counterfactual: had Roosevelt more fully embraced storytelling and had he done so earlier, he might have succeeded in casting non-interventionism to the illegitimate margins. FDR's reluctance had merit at first, and he had little opportunity to break the non-interventionist stranglehold. But as the dominant

[74] Cole 1983, 420.
[75] On the role of the congressional non-intervention bloc in shaping FDR's policies, see Burns 1956; Dallek 1979; Divine 1965; Kennedy 1999. For an alternative view, in which this was an excuse for FDR's hesitation, see Kimball 1991, esp. ch. 1.
[76] Quoted in Dallek 1979, 285, 336. See also Blum 1976, 6–7. On Churchill's frustration, see Clifford 1989, 220.
[77] As one might expect, given the tightness of the votes, the outcomes also turned on clever tactics. In 1939, for example, congressional interventionists succeeded in requiring a joint up-or-down vote on the arms embargo and cash-and-carry. The latter had more support than the former, and had the two been separated, the embargo might have been retained (Cole 1983, 329). Similarly, to ensure passage of Lend-Lease, Roosevelt forced Britain to sell key assets to demonstrate publicly how broke it was (Kennedy 1999, 473).

narrative collapsed under the weight of its own expectations – with regard to act, agent, and purpose – Roosevelt could have offered a true alternative to make sense of global events for Americans and restore interpretive order. The proposed counterfactual is the most minimal of "minimal rewrites": it requires changing nothing about the world except Franklin Roosevelt's rhetorical strategy.

One cannot take the retrospective analyst's word for it. Prominent contemporary observers, including FDR's own advisers, thought that the president was excessively cautious and that the opportunity structure was more open. These men – from Ickes to Henry Stimson (secretary of war) to Henry Morgenthau (secretary of the treasury) – were not political naïfs. Long active in party politics and national affairs, they recognized that there were distinct limits to what the president could articulate in public, and they at times endorsed his prudence.[78] But, looking out on the same political landscape as FDR, they reached very different conclusions about his capacity to exercise rhetorical initiative. So did the renowned Republican newspaper editor William Allen White, of Emporia, Kansas, presumed to have his finger on the heartland's pulse: White, who himself clashed repeatedly with more aggressive interventionists over his desire "to keep fairly abreast of public sentiment and not to get too far in front," fumed in December 1940 that Roosevelt was "the Great White Bottleneck."[79] They all pushed Roosevelt to speak more often and more openly about what was happening in Europe and how it would affect America. Frustrated by Roosevelt's over-caution, they were calling for rhetorical leadership, for storytelling that would sustain a more assertive policy. In the words of a biographer, FDR was "almost a caricature of cautiousness" on foreign policy, lacking "that burning and almost fanatic conviction that great leadership demands."[80]

Time and again Ickes called on Roosevelt to undertake a campaign of national education. In January 1939, he urged FDR "to educate our own people on the issues involved." The president, Ickes recorded in his diary, protested that "it would be absolutely impossible for him or for

---

[78] See, for instance, Ickes 1954a, 478, 481, 713.

[79] Quoted in Chadwin 1968, 156–157; quoted in Olson 2013, 266. On White's cautious inclinations, see also Johnson 1944, 84 and passim.

[80] Burns 1956, 398, 403. See also, on the arms embargo repeal, Donovan 1951, 314. And for numerous contemporary assessments to that effect, see Olson 2013, 266, 289–298, 305–307, 342–344.

me to go on the air and talk to the world as we were talking. The people simply would not believe him." Acknowledging FDR's point, Ickes firmly "insisted that ... we had to begin." He tried again that summer to persuade the president to put his advisers to work "to strengthen public sentiment in the country ... to face the people and talk to them about the issues that are involved." Again Roosevelt demurred. After the fall of France, Ickes thought FDR had blown a fantastic opportunity to "tak[e] the country into our confidence"; he blamed the president's "lack of aggressive leadership" for the surprising strength of "the appeasement spirit," despite all that had happened. As time passed, Ickes became increasingly despondent that this "inactive and uninspiring president" was in danger of losing the country. He complained in his diary as late as spring 1941 that "the President has not aroused the country; has not really sounded the bell ... does not furnish the motive power that is required."[81] And he found allies in the Cabinet and White House. Stimson, "the American Churchill" a biographer calls him, was "infuriated by Roosevelt's caution."[82] FDR's loyal aide Harry Hopkins was frustrated that his boss "would rather follow public opinion than lead it."[83]

Walter Lippmann became an open convert to intervention after the fall of France and, like Ickes and Stimson, assailed the president for his over-caution. An informal adviser to Wendell Willkie in 1940, Lippmann encouraged the Republican nominee to take a more forthright stance in favor of intervention; Willkie's reluctance, and then his embrace of non-intervention late in the campaign, soured Lippmann's view of him.[84] Nor did Lippmann keep his criticism of Roosevelt's (lack of) leadership to himself. An August 1940 column made Lippmann's feelings plain:

There is bewilderment; the people would like a President who is resolute and imperturbable. There is suspicion and division; the people would like a President who is boldly magnanimous and chivalrous. There is vast disorder in human affairs and there are tremendous tasks to be done; the people would like a President who will organize their energies and thereby give them that courage and confidence that can be reached these days only as

[81] Ickes 1954a, 572, 704, 721; 1954b, 289, 511, 526. See also Ickes 1954b, 75, 208, 232–233, 376, 458, 485–486, 506–513, 549–551. Also on FDR's advisers' impatience with the president in 1941, see Rosenman 1952, 279–285.
[82] Hodgson 1990, 220, 230–231. See also Schmitz 2001, 125, 127, 139–142.
[83] Quoted in Burns 1956, 458.   [84] Steel 1980, 389–390, 404–411.

men, ceasing to brood and worry impotently, are put to work doing efficiently some hard job they believe is necessary ... For when the leaders are frightened, soft, untruthful, so meanly ambitious that they stoop to conquer, there is no vision and the people perish.[85]

Lippmann was calling for storytelling or narrative, which supplies order, organization, and stability. He called upon Roosevelt to speak more plainly and passionately because he believed the American people wanted such leadership. When Lippmann met Charles de Gaulle in London in summer 1942, he could not help but contrast the French general's confidence, sense of history, grand vision, and most importantly imperviousness to the petty politics of the moment to Roosevelt's political timidity. De Gaulle was France, Lippmann believed, in a way that Roosevelt never was, and never could be, the embodiment of the United States. In de Gaulle, Lippmann found a leader he felt worthy of his admiration.[86]

Franklin Roosevelt was a political savant, but his judgment was hardly unerring. The court-packing episode of winter 1937 is but the best known of his political missteps. In the foreign affairs arena, in addition to the Quarantine address brouhaha, FDR had also been burned in 1935, when he had sought to have the United States join the World Court and the Senate had refused to ratify the protocols. Just because Roosevelt was not inclined to exercise rhetorical leadership in 1939 to 1941 does not mean it was impossible.[87] The individuals cited above were admittedly not Roosevelt's equals – he has had few across American history, let alone in his own day – but they were experienced and attentive observers of US politics. If they believed an opening for more forceful rhetorical leadership was politically sustainable, that should not be discounted.

Alternative explanations

Why did non-interventionism and its underlying narrative of national security persist so long? Why were both ultimately swept away? Why

---

[85] In retrospect, Lippmann suggested that there may not have been much Roosevelt could have done at that juncture: see Lippmann 1943, 43–45. But I put more weight on his assessment at the time. Later, Lippmann was engaged in mobilizing the masses behind the president and the war effort.
[86] Steel 1980, 381–384, 387–389, 398–400.
[87] For examples of Roosevelt's rhetorical failings, see Costigliola 2012, 229, 258.

was the United States so slow to enter the war? Throughout the years
after 1937, Franklin Roosevelt had the authority of the presidency
behind him, was blessed with rhetorical talent, and was deeply
concerned about the deepening European crisis. For good reason,
therefore, explanations for both narrative dynamics and policy outcomes in the United States in the late 1930s and early 1940s commonly
revolve around four other factors. All, however, are either inadequate
or can be subsumed within my account. The first three revolve around
the sources of individual and group preferences – sectional economic
interests, individual psychology, and ethnic background.

Sectional economic interests

Peter Trubowitz gives credit for the triumph of internationalism
to changes in the structure of domestic economic interests: export-
oriented Southern cotton-growers and rising Northern industrialists
were dependent on global trade, shared a common internationalist
perspective, and were thus in favor of greater American involvement
in global affairs and specifically of early intervention in the European
crisis; rural forces based in the west, whose primary markets were
domestic, tended to gravitate toward isolationism.[88] While Trubowitz
persuasively explains sectional economic interests and their relationship
to foreign policy preferences, his pluralist account falters with regard to
both narrative and policy. Trubowitz claims that the South and North
forged a dominant internationalist coalition in the first half of the 1930s.
Yet, FDR would not have agreed that internationalism was already
dominant in 1937, when he delivered the Quarantine Address, nor
even in 1940 to 1941, when he carefully danced around his congressional opponents. If sectional economic interests were the key, non-
interventionism should have been tossed aside far earlier. It should not
have become stronger in the late 1930s, nor should it have retained
legitimacy through Pearl Harbor. Nor can fairly stable, long-term
sectional interests explain why the narrative then shifted in 1942 – as
we will see in Chapter 4. Liberal accounts of grand strategy can be
persuasive as to individuals' preferences, but the politics of legitimacy
do not reduce to preferences: after all, we all recognize as legitimate some
stances with which we do not agree, and we all have, at one time or
another, refrained from expressing some view that we know others

[88] Trubowitz 1998, ch. 3.

would not see as acceptable. Liberal accounts are blind to the structuring of political debate.

Human psychology

In the face of severe threats, people are remarkably adept at fooling themselves into thinking that they are not facing any threats, especially when they are unsure how to avert the threat or when the cost of doing so is high. As a common mental defense against anxiety,[89] denial may explain the persistence of non-interventionism. A psychological perspective would further note that one can repress reality for only so long, and so non-interventionism eventually had to collapse. But, because individuals' capacity to explain away discrepant information varies, the argument goes, support for non-interventionism peeled off gradually, as contradictory data accumulated unevenly. While this account of non-intervention seems plausible, it suffers from three analytical problems. It is unfalsifiable: we lack direct measures of people's true perceptions, and one cannot specify a priori how much discrepant evidence needs to accumulate before the supposedly false beliefs must be jettisoned. It presumes that only one narrative – in this case, that of the interventionists – fits the assembled facts and thus that only the pathologies of human psychology can explain why so many people did not recognize its truth. Finally, while such dynamics may have been at work among individuals, it is unclear how they aggregate to generate a social phenomenon like the boundaries of legitimation.

Political and ethnic identity

Adam Berinsky has persuasively shown that pre-war partisan and ethnoreligious affiliation had a deep impact on public opinion in the run-up to the Second World War. In 1941, those whose parents had been born in Axis nations were more likely than either those with US-born parents or those with parents born in Allied countries to look askance at England's prospects, downplay the costs of a Germany-dominated world order, and believe Axis motives to be benign, and less likely to endorse various interventionist policies.[90] In short, one reason, it follows, that non-intervention was so enduring is that there

---

[89] On defensive avoidance and foreign policy, see Lebow 1984, 115–119; McDermott 2004, 72–73.

[90] Berinsky 2009, ch. 6. Berinsky also shows that ethnic affiliation continued to structure US public opinion even after Pearl Harbor.

were so many German- and Italian-Americans. Perhaps they were also especially likely to fall prey to the psychology of denial, as they would find it especially difficult to reconcile their love for their (or their parents') country of origin with their love for their adopted land or home country. There is clearly much to this. But pre-war attachments, in Berinsky's account, are an intervening variable. The core independent variable is the flow of elite discourse, from which individuals take their cues, and the mass opinion literature has little to say about how and why elites respond to global developments.[91] It is quite conceivable that how elites make public sense of events depends on existing narratives and social standards for legitimacy – per this book's theoretical framework.

Unmediated events

This final explanation is the most important one. Scholars most commonly argue that Americans gradually overcame interwar isolationism, and brought the nation's security narrative along, as the realities of global politics made clear "the very real menace" posed by the Axis.[92] After the fall of France, Americans recognized that they could no longer pass the buck to the European democracies.[93] In line with this view, public opinion shifted decisively by winter 1941: a stable majority thought it more important to help England than to keep out of the war.[94] I have already argued at length that we cannot speak of events as having a natural meaning, separate from the narrative context in which they take place. But even the events commonly cited as having woken Americans up to the very real threats posed by Nazi Germany – its rapid advance across the Low Countries and France and its campaign

---

[91]   As Berinsky admits (2009, 124–125). For elite-driven accounts of mass opinion, see Page and Shapiro 1992; Zaller 1992.

[92]   For this expression, see Heinrichs 1988, 16. Among historians, see Burns 1956, 399–400; Casey 2001, 26; Cole 1983; Dallek 1979, 227, 267; Kimball 1997, 59 and passim. Among political scientists, see Braumoeller 2010; Mearsheimer 2001, 255–256.

[93]   As claimed by Mearsheimer 2001, 252–257, 269–272. However, most historians agree that, even before 1940, FDR was *domestically* handcuffed in his response to the growing German menace. They do not generally attribute his approach to an *international* strategic logic.

[94]   For the original public opinion data, whose sampling techniques were flawed, see Cantril 1951, 201–202, 751, 950, 973–975. For revised data, using sophisticated methods to compensate for the sampling error, see Berinsky 2009, 45–52.

for air supremacy over Britain – did not resolve the fundamental narrative contest over scene. They gave evidence of Germany's character and Allied weakness, but they did not even speak to, let alone settle, whether a continentally dominant Germany would threaten the physical security of the American homeland.

No surprise, then, that, mirroring the continued narrative contest, public opinion remained fairly stable in summer 1940, even after the fall of France.[95] No surprise, then, that the non-interventionist opposition did not melt away, and Roosevelt did not believe himself politically unconstrained – as would have followed if the strategic situation had been clear. Thus, FDR in September 1940 believed he could provide the British with only obsolete destroyers and even then only in exchange for basing rights; the following winter and spring, he provided aid only through the pretense of Lend-Lease, whose passage by Congress was hardly certain; the next summer, he searched desperately for a pretext upon which to drag the nation into war. For nearly a year and a half after France fell, FDR tiptoed around the powerful non-interventionists in Congress. Non-intervention remained legitimate in public debate because a key element of its narrative – scene, specifically the degree of global interconnectedness – remained plausible.

This account casts in a new light Japan's attack on Pearl Harbor. It was unquestionably the trigger, or immediate, cause of the US entrance into the war. But many historians have portrayed it as but the final blow to a non-interventionist movement whose ultimate defeat had long been clear and which had already been consigned to the margins and perhaps even to the ranks of the illegitimate.[96] From the perspective of the politics of narrative, in contrast, Japan's attack on Pearl Harbor was a crucial turning point, marking a deep change in America's narrative terrain. This transformation, however, did not

---

[95] Berinsky 2009, 49. For this reason, Berinsky attributes the later shift in public opinion to the nomination of Willkie, which led to a shift in Republican elite discourse and to the erosion of non-interventionist views among Republican partisans. But Willkie turned dramatically away from intervention toward the end of the campaign, in a desperate attempt to shore up his base. The move even seems to have worked, helping Willkie cut into FDR's lead and compelling FDR to promise that he would not send "your boys ... into any foreign wars."

[96] Although historians often provide different dates for what marked the isolationists' last stand. See, for instance, Cole 1983, 12–13 and passim; Heinrichs 1988, 11 and passim.

take place because of the event's inherent meaning. That Japanese airplanes had succeeded in striking American territory did not, in itself, undermine the non-interventionist portrait of the global scene. That Japan had struck a naval base in the middle of the Pacific did not mean it could invade California, notwithstanding the fear that gripped the West Coast. Nor did it mean that the mainland United States would be vulnerable to attack if Britain and the Soviet Union fell and if Nazi Germany turned its industrial might and ideological fanaticism on the United States.[97] As the next chapter explores in detail, Pearl Harbor was crucial because of how, in its wake, Franklin Roosevelt gave voice to a clear and powerful story.

Roosevelt's difficulty in fixing the nation's security narrative was less a product of circumstance than of choice. His reluctance to embrace a storytelling rhetoric had merit through winter 1939. But as the dominant narrative broke down, Roosevelt had a substantial opening to "sound the bell," as Ickes put it. Yet, FDR did not satisfy the heightened demand for storytelling during unsettled times. He eventually called for a crusade for freedom, legitimating the war in ideological terms and demonizing America's adversaries. But instrumental argument often muddied these storytelling waters, and Roosevelt's focus on agents and their purposes left the non-interventionist portrait of the global scene untouched. An adequate narrative would have made clear how the nation would be physically vulnerable to Axis predation and why the United States could not remain a thriving city of liberty on its lonely hill. But Roosevelt's rhetorical strategy allowed non-intervention to remain legitimate and prominent. As a result, every administration move toward deeper involvement was contested, and the United States moved only very hesitantly in that direction – even though internationalist economic interests were pre-eminent, and even once it was clear that the Allies lacked the wherewithal to counter Germany. FDR insisted to an increasingly desperate Churchill that he was politically hamstrung. He was not lying. The irony is that Roosevelt had done a good part of the stringing himself.

---

[97] That is not the reason, however, that the United States declared war on Germany. Richard Hill has convincingly argued that the key lay not in the German declaration of war four days after the attack, but in Roosevelt's charge that Germany was, as the leader of the tightly coordinated Axis, to blame for Pearl Harbor. See Hill 2003.

The Reagan contra-revolution

Ronald Reagan entered the Oval Office in 1981 determined to reverse the errors of his predecessors. The United States had allowed its military capabilities to erode, lost sight of the inherent evil of the Soviet regime, and sat by while global Communism went on the offensive – so Reagan and his fellow neoconservatives charged. In retrospect, the USSR's decline was well under way even before Reagan's election, but at the time few thought an American victory in the Cold War inevitable. For Reagan, the United States sat at a critical juncture: if it reversed course now – rebuilt its hollowed-out military, negotiated only from strength, committed itself to rolling back Soviet influence, supported anti-Communist forces worldwide, and generally seized the initiative – victory would be within its grasp. Otherwise, its survival as a democracy was in doubt.[98] The test of these principles lay in America's "backyard": Central America. Both the festering insurgency in El Salvador and the Sandinista triumph in Nicaragua held out the terrifying prospect of "another Cuba" – a Marxist-Leninist puppet regime keen to spread revolution throughout the hemisphere. Securing assistance for the Salvadoran government and for the anti-Sandinista rebels, popularly known as the "contras," was among Reagan's highest priorities. Not surprisingly – given the administration's perception of the stakes, the Democratic House's opposition, and Reagan's confidence in his own talent for mass communication – contra aid became the centerpiece of an unusually intense rhetorical campaign: it was the focus of one-fifth of the nearly quarter-million words the president uttered in major foreign affairs addresses in his eight years in office.[99]

But, even though he repeatedly put his prestige on the line, the Great Communicator failed.[100] Americans were solidly, at times

---

[98] On Reagan's strategic approach, see Scott 1996. Hailing Reagan for his flexibility is Tucker 1988/1989, 12–21. Also praising the administration's pragmatism, but more critical of its inconsistency, is Zakaria 1990, esp. 389–390. See also Pach Jr. 2006; Wilentz 2008, 163–168. On Reagan's apocalyptic rhetoric, see Ritter and Henry 1992, 11–34, 39, 46, and passim.

[99] That does not even include those passages about Central America that appeared in broader-ranging addresses like the State of the Union. For detailed data, see Appendix C, Table C.7.

[100] On Reagan's commitment, see Pastor 1987, 250. However, others argue that Reagan was committed only to the general principle of rollback; he "more or less drifted into the commitment" to arm the Nicaraguan rebels because he

overwhelmingly, opposed to aiding the contras: on Nicaragua, as
one official put it, trying to change the public mood "was like trying
to push water uphill."[101] Reagan won some key votes, but Congress
also often resisted his entreaties. The chief problem, Thomas
Carothers concludes, was that Americans were simply "not per-
suaded that the Sandinista government presented a grave security
threat to the United States. Nor did they accept that the contras were
'freedom fighters.'"[102] Less than a decade after pulling US forces
out of Vietnam, Americans feared a repeat. To pre-empt parallels
between Central America and Southeast Asia, Reagan advanced a
narrative demonizing the Sandinistas and valorizing the contras. But
many publicly demurred. Their contrary characterizations of the
protagonists, the stakes, and thus likely futures – that is, their alternative storylines – remained very much within the mainstream and
had many adherents. In his memoirs, Reagan identified his "inability
to communicate to the American people and to Congress the serious-
ness of the threat we faced in Central America" as "one of my
greatest frustrations."[103] His was a failure of narrative.

Why did the Great Communicator fall far short of fixing the narrative foundation upon which the nation debated policy toward
Nicaragua? It cannot have been due to a shortage of effort or skill.
Nor can it have been due to the Vietnam Syndrome: Americans' general
reluctance after Vietnam to intervene militarily abroad. Americans
supported the use of force when its costs were low, as in Grenada. If
the Sandinistas were as unpopular as Reagan claimed, the Vietnam
Syndrome should have created little impediment. But Reagan's difficulties were predictable. Presidents enjoy advantages in storytelling,
but *only* when the narrative situation is unsettled and public demand
for stabilizing rhetoric is correspondingly high. A master storyteller,
Reagan characteristically tried to win support for the contras by telling
a starkly moralistic tale. But he operated during a time of relative
narrative stability. In the early and mid 1980s, the Cold War was
again ascendant, and mainstream elites, right and left, expressed little
doubt about America's identity, its role in the world, and the chief

permitted activists to set the government's agenda. See Gutman 1988, 23–57,
quote at 83.
[101] Quoted in LeoGrande 1998, 449. See also Edwards III 2003, 51–54; Lockerbie
and Borrelli 1990; Sobel 1993.
[102] Carothers 1991, 95–96.   [103] Reagan 1990, 471.

challenges it confronted. Under these circumstances, the theoretical logic expects that Reagan's efforts to narrate the Nicaraguan case within the Cold War pentad would not close off avenues of rebuttal, but would rather invite opponents to challenge his portraits of the agents, their purposes, and their acts. This opposed narrative sustained the contention that funding the contras would lead to another Vietnam. If the contras were not honorable freedom fighters, the United States would find itself again defending a venal, brutal, and unpopular regime at tremendous cost. If the Sandinistas were less than wholly evil, perhaps the United States could thrive even if their rule consolidated. On occasion, the Reagan administration cobbled together supportive coalitions in Congress, but it could not fashion the shared narrative underpinnings the president believed essential to more enduring support.

Reagan's rhetoric and the renewed Cold War

In electing Ronald Reagan, the American people chose the anti-Carter. Comedians had savagely caricatured Jimmy Carter as an engineer in the White House, obsessed with mind-numbing detail and incapable of delegation. Reagan was his rhetorical and administrative opposite. Reagan turned to stories (sometimes apocryphal), not mounds of statistics, when he reached for evidence. He preferred grand, if elusive, visions to technical argument. He focused rhetorically not on the pros and cons of policy, but on how Americans made sense of their world.[104] To a nation battered by economic recession, he proffered hope as a "faith healer." To a nation cowering in fear of nuclear holocaust, he promised safety through the Strategic Defense Initiative.[105] Even by presidential standards, Reagan was unusual in his "constant transformation of political material into stories."[106]

This special penchant for storytelling may have come naturally to Reagan, but it was also often politically useful. It allowed him to sidestep technical arguments and defang the experts who assailed him for playing fast and loose with facts. When he attacked the notion of a nuclear freeze in his March 1983 "evil empire" speech, he did not make

---

[104] Ritter and Henry 1992, 61–92.
[105] Crable and Vibbert 1983; Rushing 1986.
[106] Erickson 1985, 5 and passim.

his case by enumerating a freeze's costs, laying out the logic of deterrence, specifying appropriate force levels, or challenging his critics' spending priorities. Freeze advocates were disarmed, as "there was nothing to argue about."[107] When experts complained of Reagan's proclivity to oversimplification, they came off as pedants who lacked his "uncommon common sense."[108] Reagan's storytelling moved debates from the technical into the moral arena, where experts had no authority and where Star Wars' appealing vision of a future free of nuclear fears trumped doubts as to its feasibility.[109] Storytelling also freed the Teflon president from accountability, since there were few concrete benchmarks to which he could be held.

Reagan's rhetorical style was, however, a poor fit for the narrative situation of the early 1980s, which was more settled than we often realize. The Cold War consensus, which – I argue in Part II – had eroded even before the Vietnam War heated up, made a substantial comeback in the late 1970s, with the collapse of détente. Contrary to his reputation as a naïve human rights activist, Jimmy Carter was a passionate Cold Warrior, albeit one who denied that moral values needed to be sacrificed on the altar of realism.[110] By the end of his term, détente was dead, and his hawkish National Security Adviser Zbigniew Brzezinski had triumphed over his dovish Secretary of State Cyrus Vance. Carter's rhetoric had become so hard-line that there was little difference between how he and Reagan narrated the world. Americans across the spectrum saw the invasion of Afghanistan in 1979 as proof that the Soviet Union was irredeemably aggressive and that the premises underlying détente had been false.[111] In this period, the gap between the liberal flag-bearer, the *New York Times*, and its conservative counterpart, the *Chicago Tribune*, on representations of the Communist other narrowed sharply – as Chapter 6 shows. Moreover, while the Vietnam War had promoted challenges to American identity from the margins, elites on the right and left came together in the 1970s to beat back the radicals and insist on America's unique mission in global affairs. The nationalist Right in the 1950s had still questioned whether it was America's place to uphold liberal world order, but in the 1970s

---

[107] Goodnight 1986, 402–403. See, relatedly, Depoe 1988.
[108] Goodnight 2002, 216. See also Ivie 1984.   [109] Rushing 1986.
[110] On Carter as Cold Warrior, see Smith 1986; and, more recently, along similar lines, Mitchell 2010; Schmitz 2006, ch. 5.
[111] Garthoff 1994, chs. 26–27.

they came fully into the internationalist fold. As Chapters 6 and 7 show, there was after Vietnam, for the first time since the Second World War, a dominant narrative regarding America's role in the world.

The relatively stable narrative situation that then reigned may have made Reagan's foreign affairs rhetoric seem more storied than it actually was. Reagan had a reputation as a notable storyteller, but computerized content analysis finds that his major addresses on foreign affairs were about as narrative in style as those of the average Cold War president. Demand for storytelling is most intense when established narratives have been called into question and least intense when they have not. It comes as no surprise, then, that Dwight Eisenhower's foreign affairs rhetoric, at the height of the Cold War consensus, was light on narrative: over 13 percent less than the average Cold War president. Nor is it surprising that presidents most above the Cold War average – Lyndon Johnson, Richard Nixon, and Jimmy Carter – came during and after Vietnam, when American exceptionalism came under fire, and that the rhetoric of the post-Cold War presidents, Bill Clinton and George W. Bush, was substantially more storied than the postwar average. Given the settled narrative situation, Reagan's proclivity for the storytelling mode may have seemed especially striking.[112]

Storytelling was central to Reagan's rhetoric legitimating his opposition to the Sandinista government and support for the Nicaraguan rebels. As one historian, who worked on Capitol Hill in the 1980s, notes, Reagan "substitut[ed] broad appeals to standing up to communism and rallying around the flag for detailed arguments about what was happening in the region and how we might influence events there."[113] His strategy was to situate the Nicaraguan conflict in the Cold War drama. He represented the Sandinistas as unrepentant Communists who had made Nicaragua into a Soviet "satellite," so that it was an "advance base for furthering Soviet colonization of the Americas" and for transforming the Caribbean into "a Communist lake." It was part of "the Soviet-Cuban-Nicaraguan axis" arming insurgents around the region.[114] In line with the domino theory, he argued that Communist

[112] For the data on which this paragraph has drawn, see Appendix C, Tables C.2, C.3, and C.4.

[113] Arnson 1993, 114.

[114] Reagan 1990, 472–473; Remarks at a Cuban Independence Day Celebration in Miami, Florida, 20 May 1983; Remarks at a California Republican Party Fundraising Dinner in Long Beach, 30 June 1983.

success in Nicaragua would prompt the collapse of non-Communist governments across Latin America – because it would harm the US reputation for resolve and because Communism was a cancer that would spread in the absence of radical intervention.[115]

Over time, these themes became increasingly prominent in Reagan's rhetoric, according to Centering Resonance Analysis (CRA). As Figure 3.4 indicates, in his major addresses on Central America in 1983, "Communist" was not among the most prominent terms in his rhetorical network; Cuba was tightly linked to Nicaragua, but was peripheral to the network, as was Sandinista (per their location on the figure's edges); the Soviet Union appeared, but was not tightly linked to any other terms (via a dark line). According to Figure 3.5, by 1984, Communist, Sandinista, and Cuba were all among the most important elements in Reagan's rhetorical network (per their location further up the figure). Communist was particularly central, tightly linked (via a dark line) to democracy and guerilla, and moderately linked (via a light line) to Sandinista, and freedom was tightly linked to peace, democracy, and economic assistance – suggesting that in 1984 Reagan sought to narrate the Nicaraguan conflict as another battlefield in the ideologically defined Cold War.

Despite Reagan's ramped-up Cold War rhetoric, he encountered resistance from congressional Democrats, who placed legal restrictions on US activities in the region. After his re-election in 1984, Reagan shifted rhetorical tactics, embarking on a concerted campaign to paint the Sandinistas and the contras in stark moral colors. Officials admitted that they aimed "to slowly demonize the Sandinista government in order to turn it into a real enemy and threat in the minds of the American people."[116] The CIA officer in charge of the public diplomacy campaign based in the White House summarized his task as "gluing black hats on the Sandinistas and white hats on the [contras]."[117] Although the administration did not explicitly invoke Vietnam, for fear of awakening

[115] For domino rhetoric, see Remarks and a Question-and-Answer Session with Members of the Commonwealth Club of California, 4 March 1983; Address to Joint Session of Congress, 27 April 1983; Remarks at a Cuban Independence Day Celebration in Miami, Florida, 20 May 1983. Generally, on the Cold War frame for Central America, see Carothers 1991, 96–97; Kenworthy 1987b; Schroeder 2005.
[116] Quoted in Kornbluh 1987, 166. See also Carothers 1991, 96–97.
[117] Quoted in LeoGrande 1998, 690, n. 111. See, similarly, an NSC staffer quoted in Gutman 1988, 141.

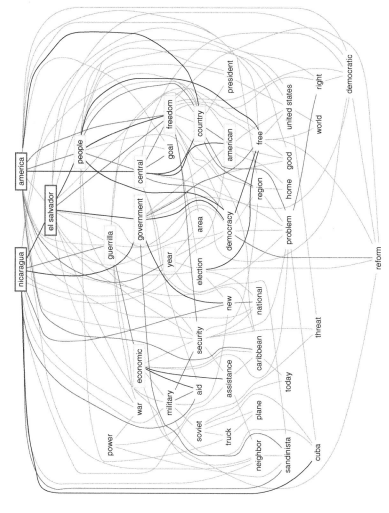

Figure 3.4 Reagan, major foreign affairs addresses on Central America, 1983.

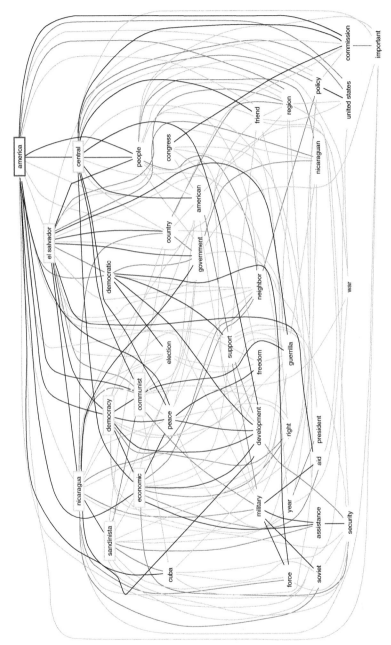

Figure 3.5 Reagan, major foreign affairs addresses on Central America, 1984.

traumatic memories of that war,[118] it sought to counter those who warned that arming the contras would lead the United States into "another Vietnam." Reagan implied that the Sandinistas were far worse, less popular, and more vulnerable than the run-of-the-mill Communists in Hanoi and that the contras were much better, more capable, and more deserving than America's corrupt and deceitful former South Vietnamese allies. Aid to the contras would, therefore, not lead to US troops on the ground. In the unlikely event that US forces were required, the venture would be less morally questionable and more likely to end in victory.

Reagan's demonization of the Sandinistas knew no bounds. Not only were they "a Marxist-Leninist clique," "eager puppets" of the USSR and Cuba, responsible for subverting freely elected governments throughout Latin America, but they were running drugs "to poison our youth," and their "brutal dictatorship" had undertaken a "reign of terror." He charged them with being viciously anti-Semitic and anti-Catholic and generally anti-religious, with conducting a genocidal campaign against the Miskito Indians, and with forcibly relocating defenseless peasants. With Americans sensitive to the threat of international terrorism, Reagan habitually contended that the Sandinistas were in bed with the Palestine Liberation Organization, the Irish Republican Army, and the rest of the international "terror network."[119] Even as he charged the Sandinistas with fomenting Communist revolution, Reagan denied that they purveyed *any* real vision (right or wrong) of the good

[118] Reagan's opponents, however, did not let him avoid talking about the parallels to Vietnam, and neither did the media. He was regularly asked how the logic of contra aid differed, and the shadow of Vietnam loomed whenever reporters asked for assurances that US troops would not be dispatched to Nicaragua.

[119] Some of these themes appeared even before the 1984 election, but only occasionally: see Address to Joint Session of Congress, 27 April 1983; Radio Address to the Nation on Central America, 14 April 1984; Address to the Nation on United States Policy in Central America, 9 May 1984. This rhetoric was ramped up in early 1985. For representative examples, see State of the Union Address, 6 February 1985; Radio Address to the Nation on Central America, 16 February 1985; Remarks at a White House Briefing for Central American Leaders, 25 March 1985; Remarks at a Fundraising Dinner for the Nicaragua Refugee Fund, 15 April 1985; Remarks at the Annual Convention of the American Bar Association, 8 July 1985; Address to the Nation on the Situation in Nicaragua, 16 March 1986; Address to the Nation on United States Assistance for the Nicaraguan Democratic Resistance, 24 June 1986. On the administration's demonization of the Sandinistas, see Kornbluh 1987, 160–181.

society: they were "the new mob, part of the 20th century's answer to Murder Incorporated," no more politically inclined than organized crime.[120] That Reagan so often repeated this litany of accusations belied his claim that these were well-known facts:[121] if they were, there would have been little reason to belabor them as he did.

Equally important, as the battle over aid intensified, Reagan valorized the rebels.[122] While the Sandinistas had betrayed their ideals, the rebels were, he often protested, not contras – the term, which the Sandinistas had originated and which he despised, meant "counter-revolutionaries" – but "freedom-fighters," "true revolutionaries," and "the Nicaraguan Democratic resistance." They were not Somocistas (backers of the deposed Anastasio Somoza Debayle), but "people of the land," "campesinos," "peasants, farmers, shopkeepers, and students," who had helped bring down the dictator.[123] Forty percent of the rebels, Reagan once insisted, had originally been Sandinistas.[124] However, they shared American values: they were "the moral equal of our Founding Fathers and the brave men and women of the French Resistance," "the moral descendants of men at Morristown and Valley Forge." As a result, Reagan concluded: "We cannot turn away from them, for the struggle here is ... right versus wrong."[125]

Meanwhile, the Cold War frame became even more central to Reagan's rhetoric. Per Figure 3.6, in 1985, Sandinista, tightly linked

---

[120] Remarks to Elected Officials During a White House Briefing on United States Assistance for the Nicaraguan Democratic Resistance, 14 March 1986.

[121] Remarks and an Informal Exchange with Reporters on United States Assistance for the Nicaraguan Democratic Resistance, 18 February 1986; Message to the Congress Transmitting a Request for Assistance for the Nicaraguan Democratic Resistance, 25 February 1986.

[122] This theme appeared occasionally earlier as well. See Address to Joint Session of Congress, 27 April 1983.

[123] There was some truth to the claim that it really was a peasant revolt. See Stoll 2005.

[124] Among many others, see Radio Address to the Nation on Central America, 16 February 1985; Remarks at a Fundraising Dinner for the Nicaragua Refugee Fund, 15 April 1985; Radio Address to the Nation on Grenada and Nicaragua, 22 February 1986; Address to the Nation on United States Assistance for the Nicaraguan Democratic Resistance, 24 June 1986.

[125] Remarks at the Annual Dinner of the Conservative Political Action Conference, 1 March 1985; Remarks to Jewish Leaders During a White House Briefing on United States Assistance for the Nicaraguan Democratic Resistance, 5 March 1986. See, similarly, Address to the Nation on United States Policy in Central America, 9 May 1984; Reagan 1990, 477.

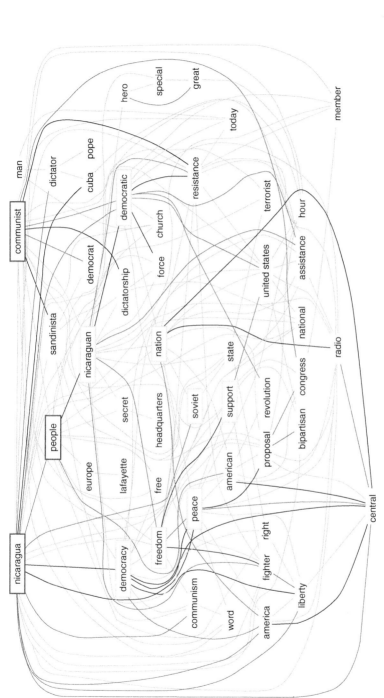

Figure 3.6 Reagan, major foreign affairs addresses on Central America, 1985.

to Communism (via a dark line), was higher up in the figure than the previous year, and the Soviet Union, relatively peripheral in 1984, became more pivotal and was moderately linked to Nicaragua (via a light line); Cuba was more important than ever, tightly linked to Nicaragua. But CRA also provides evidence of the shifting emphases of Reagan's rhetoric. Two rhetorical complexes – freedom-fighter and Nicaraguan-democratic-resistance – made their first appearance in his rhetorical network in 1985. Freedom-fighter lay at its center, tightly linked to US support. Terms of praise – hero, special, great – appeared in the same vicinity as, and loosely linked to, Nicaraguan-democratic-resistance. Meanwhile, dictatorship and dictator became newly prominent, as did terrorist. Analysis of pairs of years makes even clearer the intensification of both the Cold War frame and the focus on the contras. These themes continued to be deployed through 1987, although that year the Soviet Union fell out of the rhetorical network, perhaps because the Reagan administration did not wish to imperil warming relations with Gorbachev's USSR.[126]

Reagan and other officials offered numerous instrumental arguments in favor of assistance to the Nicaraguan rebels, pointing out how it would facilitate negotiations, undermine Sandinista subversion, prevent a refugee crisis, and limit Soviet military expansion into the hemisphere.[127] Always secondary, these arguments receded further as Reagan narrated an ever-more Manichaean tale. Normative argument became more prominent,[128] as officials cast the conflict as a struggle of contending moral principles. Resisting Soviet subversion, Reagan insisted, "is not only in our strategic interest; it is morally right.

---

[126] CRA graphical representations of pairs of years and of 1987 are not pictured here, due to space constraints.

[127] See Address to Joint Session of Congress, 27 April 1983; Address to the Nation on United States Policy in Central America, 9 May 1984; Radio Address to the Nation on the Situation in Central America, 30 March 1985; Remarks at a White House Meeting for Supporters of United States Assistance for the Nicaraguan Democratic Resistance, 3 March 1986. On Soviet bases, Address to the Nation on Defense and National Security, 23 March 1983; Address to the Nation on Recommendations of the National Bipartisan Commission on Central America, 14 January 1984. On the prospective refugee crisis, Radio Address to the Nation on Central America, 24 March 1984; Radio Address to the Nation on the Situation in Central America, 30 March 1985. On bargaining pressure, Remarks at a Fundraising Dinner for the Nicaragua Refugee Fund, 15 April 1985.

[128] See also Gutman 1988, 311–312.

It would be profoundly immoral to let peace-loving friends depending on our help be overwhelmed by brute force if we have any capacity to prevent it."[129] Or, as he related in his memoirs, "Based simply on the difference between right and wrong, it was clear that we should help the people of the region fight the bloodthirsty guerrillas bent on robbing them of freedom."[130] Officials even suggested that tallying the policy's costs and benefits was small-minded. Secretary of State George Shultz, who sometimes exceeded even the president in his moralism, saw at stake "a debate over what moral and political principles shall inspire the future of this hemisphere .... One vision – the vision of democrats throughout the Americas – calls for economic progress, free institutions, and the rule of law. The other is a vision of two, three, many Nicaraguas – a hemisphere of burning churches, suppressed newspapers, and crushed opposition."[131]

Storytelling and its discontents

A settled narrative situation prevents even talented and committed speakers, even when they reside in the Oval Office, from fixing the foundation and terms of debate. This helps to explain Ronald Reagan's frustration. As he recognized but could not understand, his efforts to dominate the national conversation on Nicaragua fell short – despite his personal popularity and his deep commitment to contra aid. If anything, his pollster Richard Wirthlin observed, Reagan's interventions polarized that debate – that is, they produced the very opposite of narrative dominance.[132] Although Reagan dismissed the fear that US aid to the contras would drag it into another Vietnam, and sought instead to foreground the Cuban analogy, Vietnam's shadow loomed over Nicaragua. The Democrats assented to Reagan's portrait of Nicaragua as a Cold War battlefield, but neither they nor their allies in civil society conceded his portrait of the contras. In other words, they assented to his representation of scene, but not to his representations of

---

[129] Address to the Nation on United States Policy in Central America, 9 May 1984. See, similarly, Message to the Congress Transmitting a Request for Assistance for the Nicaraguan Democratic Resistance, 25 February 1986.

[130] Reagan 1990, 479.

[131] Shultz, Nicaragua and the Future of Central America, Address before the Veterans of Foreign Wars of Washington, DC, 3 March 1986, reprinted in Kimmens 1987, 61–69.

[132] Storrs and Serafino 1993, 139.

the drama's protagonists, their acts, or their purposes. Refuting Reagan's depiction of the contras was crucial to making Vietnam seem relevant. And it had real consequences – restraining the administration's more hawkish elements, forcing it to take its program underground, and sustaining a mass mobilization that exceeded even the nuclear-freeze movement.

Reagan's success in situating the Sandinistas in the realm of unadulterated evil was limited. True, elected Democrats found it difficult to grant publicly that acknowledged Communists had any virtues, leading Assistant Secretary of State Elliott Abrams to gloat in 1986 that there was "complete consensus that the Sandinistas are really reprehensible people."[133] But non-governmental organizations regularly contradicted the administration's contentions about the Nicaraguan Government. No clear consensus emerged even on core charges against the Sandinistas: there was a vibrant debate over whether the Sandinistas undermined neighboring governments and whether their military build-up signaled aggressive intent. Even congressional committee staffs and the intelligence community failed to toe the line.[134] Reagan's insistence that "there can no longer be any legitimate doubt about the nature of [the Sandinistas'] regime" was belied by his own constant harping on their record and by his regular tirades against the "misinformation floating around about the true character of the Sandinista regime."[135] That said, prominent critics did not make defense of the Sandinistas the focus of their strategy, and even grass-roots protesters often prefaced their remarks by acknowledging the Sandinistas' failings.[136]

But Reagan's efforts to exalt the contras had even less traction. Opponents of aid had long highlighted contra misdeeds and accused

[133] Quoted by LeoGrande 1998, 442.
[134] Arnson and Brenner 1993, 196–197 and passim; Burns 1987, 34–43; Kornbluh 1987, 166–179.
[135] Message to the Congress Transmitting a Request for Assistance for the Nicaraguan Democratic Resistance, 25 February 1986; Remarks to Jewish Leaders During a White House Briefing on United States Assistance for the Nicaraguan Democratic Resistance, 5 March 1986; Remarks to the Georgetown University Center for Strategic and International Studies on United States Assistance for the Nicaraguan Democratic Resistance, 9 June 1986.
[136] Smith 1996, 231.

them of being thugs and thieves.[137] Reagan's over-the-top tributes to the "freedom-fighters" not only failed to silence aid opponents, but revitalized them.[138] Human rights groups detailed contra abuses, which were at least as great as those of the Sandinistas. The protest movement, which was largely associated with church groups and thus possessed a certain moral authority, brought further attention to contra crimes. While the contra rank-and-file was diverse, the leadership, many pointed out, was heavily Somocista. Aid critics brought to light evidence of contra corruption and drug-running.[139] As one scholar concludes: "No group of men could live up to [Reagan's] fanciful descriptions ... Such windy rhetoric invites ridicule."[140] Sensitive to the "disinformation" levied against "the democratic opposition," Reagan devoted much energy to combating the "orchestrated campaign to slander the freedom fighters." He regularly questioned his opponents' political biases, assailed their motives, and expressed doubt as to their patriotism.[141] But these attacks did little to silence the critics.

The power of Reagan's moral drama depended on its absolute clarity. This alternative narrative – so different in agent, act, and purpose, despite the shared scene – muddied matters. Secretary of State Shultz testified before the Senate Foreign Relations Committee: "I know which side I'm on; I know who the bad guys and the good guys are."[142] But, thanks to aid critics, even Republican legislators were unsure. As Senator Richard Lugar, then the committee's chairman, admitted: "It makes the whole problem a lot more ambiguous because you're trying to find out which guys are wearing the white hats and which guys are wearing the black hats."[143] To make the differences between Nicaragua and Vietnam seem less stark, administration opponents did not need to make the case that the Sandinistas wore

---

[137] See the 1983 House debate, as summarized in LeoGrande 1998, 320–321.

[138] Arnson 1993, 190–192; Smith 1996, 239–248.

[139] Burns 1987, 61–65, 71–79; Kornbluh 1987, 25–27, 32–34, 39–46; LeoGrande 1998, 413–417, 420–421, 455, 460–464; Smith 1996, 256–267; Smith 1987.

[140] Burns 1987, 78.

[141] See, among others, Remarks at a Fundraising Dinner for the Nicaragua Refugee Fund, 15 April 1985; Remarks to Elected Officials During a White House Briefing on United States Assistance for the Nicaraguan Democratic Resistance, 14 March 1986; Address to the Nation on United States Assistance for the Nicaraguan Democratic Resistance, 24 June 1986.

[142] Quoted in Kenworthy 1987a, 165.

[143] Quoted in LeoGrande 1998, 416–417.

white hats and the contras black hats. They just needed to show that the contras' hats were more gray than Reagan claimed.[144] Sullying the contras' reputation, providing evidence of their misdeeds, made the warning of "another Vietnam" seem apt. And it worked: dozens of opinion polls from the mid 1980s showed that the Vietnam analogy had a great deal of traction among Americans.[145]

Ironically, the Great Communicator's rhetoric bolstered the Vietnam analogy. On the one hand, when Reagan did speak of the Vietnam War, he characterized it as a "noble cause" that had been lost at home, not on the battlefield, and he lamented the withdrawal of US forces, not the original deployment.[146] On the other hand, Reagan regularly suggested that the threat posed by Communism's spread in Central America was great because it was located "in our backyard."[147] It was, he implied, greater than the threat posed by Communist governments in more distant lands and regions, such as Vietnam and Southeast Asia, where the United States had intervened to preserve its reputation for resolve. To legitimate his administration's activities in Central America, Reagan even frequently invoked the very domino logic that had under-pinned the Vietnam War.[148] In combination, Reagan's statements logically suggested that Nicaragua was on its way to becoming "another Vietnam." If the president thought more American blood should have been spilled to defend indirect US interests in Vietnam, would he not certainly call for Americans' blood to be spilled to defend interests in Central America that he thought more direct and substan-tial? Speaker of the House Tip O'Neill was characteristically pithy: the administration's request for military assistance to the contras was "the Central American equivalent of the Gulf of Tonkin Resolution."[149]

---

[144] Contra LeoGrande 1998, 475.   [145] Bennett 1989, 338.

[146] Bates 2011, 44–63; McMahon 1999.

[147] See, among others, the President's News Conference, 6 March 1981; Remarks and a Question-and-Answer Session with Members of the Commonwealth Club of California, 4 March 1983. On Central America's proximity, see Address Before a Join Session of the Congress on Central America, 27 April 1983; Address to the Nation on United States Policy in Central America, 9 May 1984; Radio Address to the Nation on Central America, 30 March 1985. For analysis of this imagery, see Kenworthy 1995.

[148] See, among others, Address to Joint Session of Congress, 27 April 1983; Radio Address to the Nation on Central America, 14 April 1984; Address to the Nation on United States Policy in Central America, 9 May 1984.

[149] Quoted in LeoGrande 1998, 455.

Operating in the relatively settled narrative world of the early and mid 1980s, Reagan's storytelling, rather than closing off avenues of opposition, invited opponents to offer an alternate narrative, and they could do so without violating the president's right to speak on the nation's behalf. The Democrats jumped through that open window on Nicaragua. They did not on Afghanistan, where the mujahedeen had been fighting Soviet forces since 1979.[150] There, they embraced the very story, of noble home-grown national resistance to Soviet aggression, that they had rejected in a region much closer to home. In Afghanistan, it seemed clear who wore which color hats. Charlie Wilson, the Democratic congressman from Texas who led the charge for aid, bragged, with only some exaggeration, that by 1984 "I had everyone in Congress convinced that the mujahedeen were a cause only slightly below Christianity." According to the CIA officer who ran the program, which at one time accounted for 70 percent of the agency's operations budget, it acquired the aura of a "holy cause – the one program everyone could be proud of and identify with."[151] Liberals largely ignored or quietly supported assistance for Afghanistan's freedom fighters,[152] whose battle White House and CIA leaders initially deemed of lesser import. At bipartisan congressional insistence, the CIA funneled huge sums to the mujahedeen through Pakistan's intelligence agency. It was, a historian has written, "without question, the ... least controversial

---

[150] On the contrast between Afghanistan and Nicaragua, see Crile 2003, 262–267, 339–340; Wilentz 2008, 216.

[151] Quoted in Crile 2003, 262, 340.

[152] This was not true, however, of the American public, which after the initial shock of the Soviet invasion did not generally endorse arming the Afghan rebels. This was true even when they viewed the Soviet occupation of Afghanistan as a "very serious problem" for the United States and even when pollsters did not identify the rebels as Muslims or mujahedeen. See ABC News/Harris Survey, January 1980; Gallup Poll, Jan. 1980; Time/Yankelovich, Skelly & White Poll, Jan. 1980; Cambridge Reports National Omnibus Survey, July 1980; Cambridge Reports National Omnibus Survey, Oct. 1980; Roper Report 81–5, April 1981; Roper Report 82–2, Jan. 1982; Roper Report 83–8, Aug. 1983; Roper Report 84–2, Jan. 1984; Roper Report 85–10, Oct. 1985; NBC News/Wall Street Journal Poll, Nov. 1985; Gallup/CCFR Survey of American Public Opinion and US Foreign Policy 1986, Oct. 1986; Gallup/CCFR Survey of American Public Opinion and US Foreign Policy 1986 – Followup, Jan. 1987 – all from iPoll, Roper Center Public Opinion Archives, generated via the search term: Afghanistan, 1/1/1980–1/1/1989.

application of the Reagan Doctrine."[153] Reagan's storytelling about Nicaragua met with a compelling, contrary narrative partly because there was much more penetration by US-based NGOs in Central America. But it was also because Reagan's high-profile campaign for aid had made Nicaragua a lightning rod, incensing and mobilizing its liberal opponents.

Alternative history: Reagan's rhetorical mastery and the Cold War

Sympathetic critics of the anti-aid campaign would dispute my characterization – and that of Reagan himself and many others – of the president's Nicaragua storytelling as a failure. By their account, Reagan and his aides, with their diabolical rhetorical cleverness and ruthless lies, wrote Nicaragua into the Cold War, cowed the pusillanimous congressional Democratic bloc into conceding the conflict's Cold War frame, doomed anti-aid activism, and created a sound and stable basis for contra funding.[154] By this account, Reagan's masterful rhetoric was responsible for both narrative and policy success: the dominant Cold War conflict frame and the contra aid program's resilience. Such histories of US debate on and policy toward Nicaragua are admirably, and unusually, sensitive to the power of rhetoric, and it is unquestionably true that contra aid had nine (or perhaps more) lives, despite the mass mobilization arrayed against it. But they inflate Reagan's rhetorical prowess, they misunderstand the consequences of the Cold War frame, they understate aid opponents' impact, and they misread why military aid resumed in 1986.

First, although Reagan's reputation as the Great Communicator was deserved, he could take little credit for successfully folding the Nicaragua conflict into the renewed Cold War. That process started under Jimmy Carter. After the 1979 revolution, Carter administration officials presumed that a Communist-led Nicaragua would tilt heavily toward the Soviets, and they sought to prevent the politically diverse, post-revolution government from turning "Castro-ite."[155] When General Wallace Nutting, head of the US military's Southern

---

[153] Scott 1996, 40, and generally, 40–81.
[154] Arnson 1993, 17, 149; Blachman and Sharpe 1987, 3. See also Schroeder 2005.
[155] Pastor 1987, 195, and generally chs. 10–11.

Command, tried – before Reagan's election – to persuade official Washington that "the tangle of problems afflicting Central America had primarily local roots" and that the Cold War was not relevant, he made little headway.[156] The Democrats had long seen the Sandinistas as dangerous Soviet agents. They saw no reason to challenge the Reagan administration's emplotment of the Nicaraguan conflict within the Cold War narrative – for they had done the same.[157] While aid critics might have liked leading Democrats to have protested that the conflict in Nicaragua had local origins, that the United States could lure the Sandinistas out of the Soviet orbit, or that hostile US policy was to blame for Sandinista enmity,[158] such positions, in the wake of détente's collapse, fell outside even what liberal internationalists could countenance. Such views would, moreover, have been bad politics in the conservative South, which the Democrats were then still trying, hopelessly, to retain.

Second, the Cold War setting for the Nicaragua conflict, though dominant, was not some rhetorical master-stroke: it did not guarantee contra aid's continued flow.[159] Although the Democrats generally echoed, and rarely gainsaid, the hawks' charge that the Sandinistas were Communist pawns, they were not quick to approve contra aid, and its renewal was always uncertain. Only after time did Congress grant the transfer of funds to the Nicaraguan rebels for humanitarian and especially military purposes. When the CIA's involvement in mining Nicaragua's harbors came to light in 1984, congressional Democrats furiously halted aid. A year later, Congress grudgingly approved a mere $27 million for only humanitarian ends – and only after Sandinista leader Daniel Ortega took an ill-timed trip to Moscow. A series of Nicaraguan Government military victories in the winter of 1985 to 1986 gave the aid lobby a boost, but even then Congress was wary of restarting military assistance. Approval finally came later that spring, after several aborted efforts and only at modest levels. Even then, the pro-aid coalition did not endure: contra aid suffered

---

[156] Gutman 1988, 121.

[157] On continuity between the Carter and Reagan administrations' views of Central American developments, see Pastor 1987, and also Gates 1996, 126–128, 242, 297.

[158] On the last, see Herring 1985; Lowenthal 1985.

[159] Pace Blachman and Sharpe 1987, 8–13; Brenner and LeoGrande 1991, 245–246; Kenworthy 1987b, 117–121; LeoGrande 1998.

aftershocks of the Iran-Contra affair, culminating in the House's 1988 rejection of even the small request the White House had dared to put forward. Calls to assist the Nicaraguan rebels met with cycles of resonance and resistance throughout the 1980s – despite the stable Cold War setting for the Nicaragua conflict.

The Cold War frame did not sweep away all opposition because it did not preclude critics from drawing parallels to the bloody war fought in Vietnam in the Cold War's name. Americans perceived Communist governments in Central America as a threat, but a majority consistently feared US entanglement in another quagmire even more. Worse than "another Cuba" would be another failed US intervention to prevent a Communist regime from taking root.[160] Henry Kissinger, who chaired the National Bipartisan Commission on Central America in 1984, put his finger on the administration's problem in beating back the Vietnam analogy: "It cannot be that [Nicaragua] is such a vital interest and [that] it can be solved with [merely] $100 million."[161] Reagan's overheated rhetoric on the stakes sustained critics, who discounted the administration's insistence that American involvement would stay limited and who warned that US military aid to the Nicaraguan rebels was a dangerously slippery slope. As Senator Edward Kennedy cautioned, contra aid was part of "a major effort to construct a vast military infrastructure that could support the deployment of American forces ... [O]ur people are becoming more and more directly involved in the conflict, and we are moving closer and closer to the fighting." He did not have to invoke Vietnam explicitly to land the coup de grace: "We do not want to wake up one morning to find American troops fighting and dying in Central America without the consent of the American people."[162] If the Cold War scene alone had decisively tilted the tables, the Reagan administration would not have vilified the Sandinistas so intensely that Communism came to seem like the least of their sins. In pulling out the rhetorical stops, much like FDR who sought to delegitimize the non-interventionists, Reagan confessed his failure.

---

[160] Although question framing was, as always, crucial. There is evidence that a plurality of Americans favored going to war to prevent Nicaragua from becoming another Cuba. See Sobel 1993, 50–52.
[161] Quoted in Kenworthy 1987a, 168.
[162] Kennedy, speech on the floor of the US Senate, 18 June 1984, reprinted in Kimmens 1987, 75–81, quotes at 75, 77, 78.

Third, the administration's success in 1986 in finally pushing aid to the Nicaraguan rebels through Congress did not follow inevitably from the Cold War scene. Had that been the case, one would have expected that shrill political attacks by the president and his aides on domestic opponents would have helped the cause – but they did not. Crude red-baiting backfired, even emboldening the opposition.[163] FBI harassment of anti-contra activists seems to have inspired rather than suppressed activism.[164] When the White House took a hard line, the House of Representatives initially rejected the aid package. The administration won only by changing its political tactics: by intensifying pressure on Republican holdouts, by offering moderate Democrats symbolic concessions, and by the president making extraordinary personal appeals. Even then, it took yet another Sandinista misstep – a March raid into Honduras in pursuit of the rebels[165] – for Congress to approve the full $100 million.[166] Aid did not resume thanks to the inexorable logic of the Cold War, but to the contingent construction of a narrow coalition.

The most important reason that Congress reinstated contra aid was member replacement: between 1984, when contra aid was canceled, and 1986, when it resumed, the legislature's composition changed substantially. For reasons largely unrelated to this issue, twenty-nine anti-aid House members were replaced by pro-contra votes. Since a number of these (Republican) pick-ups came in the South, the remaining Southern Democrats felt vulnerable and were ripe for conversion. For this critical swing bloc – more Democratic, more Southern, and more moderate than the House as a whole – contextual factors were crucial. The administration's conciliatory tone mattered perhaps most

---

[163] For examples of Reagan's efforts to delegitimize aid critics, see, for instance, Address to Joint Session of Congress, 27 April 1983; Address to the Nation on United States Policy in Central America, 9 May 1984; Radio Address to the Nation on the Situation in Central America, 30 March 1985. On these efforts and how they backfired, see also Arnson 1993, 190, 193–196, 207–208; Gutman 1988, 322; LeoGrande 1998, 411, 446–448. However, see Bennett 1989, 353–360; Kornbluh 1987, 192, 196, 205–211.

[164] Smith 1996, 319–324.

[165] Sandinista missteps of this nature were so common, and always so perfectly timed, that they prompted speculation as to whether they were intentional – since US hostility served Sandinista political purposes as well.

[166] Arnson 1993, 193–215; LeoGrande 1998, 439–475; Pastor 1987, ch. 13.

of all: the March 1986 appointment of the respected diplomat Philip
Habib as Reagan's special envoy to Central America seemed to suggest
that the administration was open to a diplomatic solution, and the
addition of an economic aid package for other Central American
countries seemed to hint that the administration understood that the
United States could not win friends in Latin America only by flexing its
muscle. Finally, Reagan himself reached out to these moderate
Democrats, displaying his famous charm.[167]

Fourth, Reagan's failure to dominate the narrative on Nicaragua
becomes clear when one considers both the consequences of that
failure and the counterfactual of narrative triumph. Had Reagan
met with the success he expected, there would have been little public
opposition to his policy of low-intensity warfare by proxy, and the
trumpeted warnings of "another Vietnam" would have been reduced
to a whisper. Had he succeeded, the opportunity structure facing
prospective protesters would have remained closed; there would
have been no "crusade of major proportions" that engaged over
100,000 Americans and that "mobilized more committed activists,
generated more political conflict, sustained itself over a longer period
of time, and made a greater political impact" than the anti-nuclear-
weapons movement.[168] Had he succeeded, the administration would
not have had to expend so much political capital on an enervating
political battle and would not have had to resort to a subterfuge that
nearly undid Reagan's presidency. The Iran-Contra affair – the reve-
lation in fall 1986 that senior White House officials had illegally
evaded a congressional arms embargo on Iran to secure the release
of American hostages in Lebanon and to provide funding for the
contras – was but the most extreme manifestation of the deception
that had surrounded US policy toward Nicaragua from the start.
Rather than admit their true objective of overthrowing the
Sandinistas, officials sold US operations in Nicaragua as a way of
interdicting arms traffic to the Salvadoran rebels. Leading officials
later admitted that such "sneak[ing] around" was an error.[169] Had

---

[167] Arnson 1993, 182–184, 197–202, 214–215; Gutman 1988, 334; LeoGrande
and Brenner 1993.
[168] Smith 1996, xvi–xvii, and on the political opportunity structure, 88–108.
[169] Quote of Robert McFarlane, then Deputy National Security Adviser, in
Gutman 1988, 117. See, similarly, Gates 1996, 294–295; LeoGrande 1998,
142–143, 304.

Reagan succeeded, he might even have fought the Vietnam War again, that "noble cause," this time in Nicaragua.[170] The Democrats may have failed to strangle contra aid fully and permanently, but that does not mean that Reagan was triumphant. He felt frustrated for good reason, and the failure of his narrative project had repercussions well beyond the realm of rhetoric.

Counterfactuals: structure, strategy, and Nicaragua

This case raises important questions about agency and structure. Would Reagan have been more successful if he had spent less time telling stories and more time advancing persuasive arguments? Would the Democrats in Congress have been a larger roadblock if they had conceded less of Reagan's Cold War definition of the situation? A tone of regret permeates retrospectives on both sides. All involved seem to think that, had they expressed themselves differently, the results might have been different. One Democratic House aide observed: "We got left in the dust on the big arguments. We lost the high road."[171] For administration officials, their dishonesty about their intentions in Nicaragua was "a major blunder."[172] Reagan himself, however, had no regrets. He attributed his failure to the Sandinistas' selling themselves as "a blend of Abe Lincoln and George Washington," to their "sophisticated program of propaganda that was the ultimate in hypocrisy," and to "a disinformation network that is beyond anything we can match." He blamed the US press, too, for not upholding journalistic standards when weighing Sandinista claims and for failing to tell the truth about the contras and US policy.[173]

---

[170] Kornbluh 1987, 159; Smith 1996, 370–371. Gutman, however, concludes that this was unlikely, because even the "war party" did not foresee coming to the contras' rescue militarily: Gutman 1988, 89, 145, and passim.

[171] Quoted in Arnson 1993, 210.

[172] Quote of L. Craig Johnstone, then Deputy Assistant Secretary of State for Latin American Affairs, in LeoGrande 1998, 287.

[173] Reagan 1990, 479–480; Reagan interview with *The Washington Post*, 1 April 1985. See also Radio Address to the Nation on Central America, 16 February 1985; Remarks and a Question-and-Answer Session with Regional Editors and Broadcasters on United States Assistance for the Nicaraguan Democratic Resistance, 11 March 1986; Reagan interview with *The New York Times*, 21 March 1986.

It is hard to imagine that Reagan would have met with less resistance had he focused more on instrumental argument. He would have had to enumerate the costs and benefits of a stable Sandinista regime in Nicaragua compared with the costs and benefits of revolution and the uncertainty of a contra regime – and such calculations did not necessarily work to his benefit. It is hard to imagine that the Democrats could have insisted that the Nicaragua conflict was distinct from the Cold War, especially because the previous Democratic administration had viewed the Sandinista regime through those lenses. It is hard to imagine that simply highlighting the "facts on the ground," rather than staging their own morality play, would have better advanced the critics' cause. This was the recommendation of the journalist Roy Gutman, whose reporting on US activities in Central America was a thorn in the administration's side and who believed that aid critics erred in "taking [Reagan's] bait."[174] But facts alone never win. The key is the storyline into which they fit. In 1984, the Democratic presidential candidate Walter Mondale tried to focus on the facts with Reagan, and he got nowhere.[175]

Given the settled narrative situation of the early 1980s, both Reagan and his aides, on the one hand, and contra-aid opponents inside and outside Congress, on the other, made the best of their bad rhetorical hands. The consequences of their narrative battles went well beyond aid for the Nicaraguan rebels. Nicaragua was the centerpiece of Reagan's campaign to revive America's belief in its own virtue and to set America back on the path toward greatness. The Reagan Doctrine promised Americans the moral clarity of the Cold War mission without the sacrifices that Vietnam had demanded. It stitched anti-Communism to democracy promotion and hitched both to the rhetoric of revolution. But this rickety structure collapsed under its own weight in Nicaragua, where combating the spread of Communism and fomenting global democratic revolution did not seem aligned. Reagan swept into office declaring that America had become wayward, but his administration ultimately fell prey to the same charge.

Their presidencies were separated by four decades, and animated by opposed ideologies, but Franklin Roosevelt and Ronald Reagan had

---

[174] Gutman 1988, 311–312.
[175] Debate Between the President and Former Vice President Walter F. Mondale in Kansas City, Missouri, 21 October 1984.

much in common: both were accomplished orators who rarely hesitated to take advantage of their bully pulpit; both felt deeply that they had to wake up their sleeping American brethren to the dangers around them; both sought to banish their opponents to the narrative tundra, and both were deeply committed to their respective causes. But both failed to set the narrative foundation of security debate in the United States – with very real consequences for the nation. They fell short for different reasons: Roosevelt, because he shied away from forthright storytelling when it might have proved productive, and Reagan, because there was really no effective way to counter the powerful truncated narrative implicit in "another Vietnam." Both would have profited from grasping the conjuncture of narrative situation, rhetorical mode, and authority: Roosevelt might have earlier and more fully embraced the storytelling that Americans craved, and Reagan might have avoided a fight that he could not win and that nearly destroyed his presidency via the Iran-Contra affair. But presidents' narrative projects are also not routinely doomed – as we will see in the next chapter.

4 | *Narrative won: opportunities seized*

If any events have unambiguous meaning, without need for intervening narration, attacks on the homeland – notably, that on Pearl Harbor in December 1941 and that on the World Trade Center and the Pentagon in September 2001 – would seem to fit the bill. At the very least, these events should have imparted such unimpeded narrative authority to the president that it hardly mattered how he expressed himself. It is true that these attacks marked turning points, that they gave birth to dominant narratives of national security, and that the president was crucial to those narratives' rise to dominance. Those narratives limned the full dramatic pentad: they identified the issues at stake, the protagonists, the sources of aggression, the setting of conflict, and the conditions for peace. But neither Pearl Harbor nor 9/11 had to yield the particular pentad that it did. There was more than one conceivable narrative configuration that might have become dominant. Moreover, that Franklin Delano Roosevelt's and George W. Bush's preferred narratives rose to the top depended not just on structural openings and institutional advantages, this chapter maintains, but on these authoritative speakers seizing the rhetorical opportunity and embracing the storytelling mode. Their rhetorical interventions shaped both the debates and the policy that followed.

Narrating the origins of German aggression

In Americans' collective memory, the Japanese attack on the US naval base at Pearl Harbor on 7 December 1941 was the key moment when Americans finally put "isolationism" and "divisionism" behind them. The attack resolved the narrative contest that had riven the nation in recent years. No one could any longer deny that the Axis threatened the survival of the United States and the American way of life. This was "the good war," and Americans swiftly united, in accord over both policy and its underlying narrative foundation.

122

Yet, US officials did not see things that way at the time. They did not think the Japanese attack had brushed aside all significant opposition. They noted how rapidly public indifference had set in. They fretted that Americans were not prepared for the long, hard slog they expected. Most worrisome of all, Americans still lacked a well-defined narrative of national security. Notwithstanding polls showing broad support for the war, officials believed the public's backing was shallow and brittle, because Americans remained ignorant of the nature, aims, and capabilities of the enemy, and they feared that support would collapse under the pressure of large-scale warfare. Not long after Pearl Harbor, the Committee on War Information, an interagency group tasked with coordinating propaganda efforts, charged Americans with complacency – the public "increasingly thinks of the war as something on the other side of the Atlantic and Pacific Oceans" – and provocatively compared their attitude to that of the French in 1939. Absent a sustained campaign to shape the public narrative, they forecast that isolationism was down but not out.[1] In short, US officials did not think that Pearl Harbor had spoken for itself and severely doubted that it had yielded a dominant narrative.

Pearl Harbor *was* a turning point of course. The United States, which had sat on the sidelines for over two years, finally entered the war, and a dominant narrative of national security took shape. But that narrative crystallized thanks not to the event itself, nor merely to the president's engagement, but to a marked change in FDR's approach to rhetorical leadership. The preceding chapter showed that prior to December 1941, Roosevelt had relied heavily on instrumental rhetoric and had presented, and then only occasionally, an impoverished story. After Pearl Harbor, he finally – and in the view of his more hawkish advisers in government and civil society, very belatedly – shifted to storytelling, as the case study traces next. His rhetorical efforts focused on defining the battlefield as global (rather than theater-specific), the war's core issue as ideological (rather than national), and the villains as Hitler and the Nazis (rather than the German people). FDR sought to help Americans make sense of disquieting events, and he found that national audience keen and receptive. The study's second and third sections show that his representations of scene, agent, and purpose became

---

[1] Casey 2001, 51–56, and passim, quote at 46.

dominant – as revealed by the silences and premises of public debate, by the reception of alternative narratives, and by the controversy over the Morgenthau Plan. The last is especially instructive, demonstrating what difference the dominant narrative made to postwar planning. Late in the war, Roosevelt sought to promote a postwar vision based on the German populace's guilt and to advocate a corresponding policy of mass punishment. But, although total war still raged and although he remained popular, the president was compelled to back away from the postwar policy he favored and to reaffirm the usual narrative. The study concludes by examining, and rebutting, alternative explanations for this narrative's rise to dominance.

Telling the story after Pearl Harbor

That Japan was able, and willing, to launch a strike on the Hawaiian islands came as a surprise, but it left much unresolved with regard to narrative. The basic facts did not, in and of themselves, settle the debate over the *scene* of global politics: non-interventionists might reasonably have distinguished between the vulnerability of an island outpost in the Pacific and of the continental United States, and between a one-time raid and conquest. Nor did the basic facts, in and of themselves, explain the war's *purpose*: were it a war of revenge, non-interventionists might reasonably have defined the Pacific and Atlantic campaigns as separate wars, rendering the latter more controversial and perhaps legitimating a limited military response. Nor did those facts, in and of themselves, identify the *agents* responsible for aggression: one might have made an equally reasonable case for the people as a whole, the political leadership, or the military. It was precisely with regard to these elements of the pentad – agent, purpose, and setting – that Roosevelt's storytelling before Pearl Harbor had been unsatisfying. It was precisely with regard to these elements that the attack on Pearl Harbor was inarticulate. And it was precisely with regard to these elements that Roosevelt launched a narrative offensive after Pearl Harbor.

The attack on Pearl Harbor, FDR seems to have believed, presented him with the moment for which he had long been waiting and toward which he had long been maneuvering – when Americans would look to him to make sense of the course of events, reaffirm their ideals, and gird them for a war (that seemed) suddenly thrust upon them. Accordingly, though long overdue according to many advisers, he not only spoke more often about foreign affairs after December 1941,[2] but embraced a more heavily storytelling rhetoric throughout the following year. Almost regardless of the subject at hand, he seized the opportunity to explain what was at stake, define the adversary, and proclaim American values, emphasizing how they differed from those of its adversaries: the "gangsters" and "dictators."[3] According to computerized content analysis, Roosevelt's major foreign affairs addresses were 34 percent more narrative in style between Pearl Harbor and his death than between 1935 and 1939 and over 14 percent more than between September 1939 and December 1941. His speech did not become more storied across the board, however, as his major domestic affairs addresses were unchanged in their storytelling quotient. Whereas FDR's major domestic and foreign affairs speeches were very similar in this respect between 1935 and 1939 (ratio: 0.95), they became markedly different in 1939 to 1941 (ratio: 0.76), falling off still further during the war years (ratio: 0.61).[4] The agencies charged with leading the government's "informational" initiatives – first, the Office of Facts and Figures (OFF), headed by the passionately anti-fascist poet Archibald MacLeish, and then, its more powerful successor, the Office of War Information, directed by the veteran newsman Elmer Davis – issued a steady stream of propaganda mirroring the president's line.[5]

The content of Roosevelt's addresses is even more revealing of how he rectified his past rhetorical failings and how he sought to foreclose limits of or alterations to the scope and focus of the war effort. First, whereas prior to Pearl Harbor, Roosevelt had often been reluctant to identify by name the forces of lawlessness, he regularly did so afterwards. Naming of a specific other – Hitler, Nazi, Germans, Germany, Japanese, Japan, etc. – occurred nearly three times more often in the

[2] After December 1941, FDR's major foreign affairs addresses averaged over 1,900 words/month, compared to over 1,200 words/month between September 1939 and December 1941, and just 160 words/month between January 1935 and August 1939. For details, see Appendix C, Table C.1.

[3] See countless prepared speeches, impromptu remarks, and press conferences in Rosenman 1950.

[4] See Appendix C, Tables C.4 and C.5, for more detailed data.

[5] Casey 2001, 54–56. For a less charitable assessment, see Winkler 1978, esp. 38–72.

two years after Pearl Harbor than in the two years between the war's outbreak and the Japanese attack.[6]

Second, rather than stoke the flames of national hatred, as the US propaganda apparatus had done during the First World War, FDR narrated the war as a battle of globe-spanning ideals. He linked the categories of civilized/barbaric and lawful/lawless that had featured in his pre-war rhetoric to free/slave and democratic/despotic. The barbarians were still "gangsters," but they were now also enemies of liberty and emblems of stifling conformism; the civilized were still "law-abiding," but they were now also defenders of freedom and democracy, paragons of individuality. Just a week after Pearl Harbor came the 150th anniversary of the ratification of the Bill of Rights. "The issue of the war in which we are engaged," Roosevelt told the nation on this occasion, "is the issue forced upon the decent, self-respecting peoples of the earth by the aggressive dogmas of this attempted revival of barbarism; this proposed return to tyranny; this effort to impose again upon the peoples of the world doctrines of absolute obedience, of dictatorial rule, of the suppression of truth, of the oppression of conscience, which the free Nations of the earth have long ago rejected."[7] This shift is reflected also in Centering Resonance Analysis (CRA) of Roosevelt's foreign affairs rhetoric. Although the bundled sets representing this ideological framing ("ideologicalterms") and the named adversary ("hitlernazienemy") were prominent in Roosevelt's rhetoric after May 1940 (per Figure 3.3), it was only after Pearl Harbor that the two became tightly and directly linked – as indicated by the dark line connecting them in Figure 4.1. FDR thus replaced the cold and substantively empty mission of upholding the rule of law with a passionate crusade for freedom, and thus with a narrative better suited to mobilizing the nation. As a war in defense of democracy – as both a universal ideal

---

[6] These figures take into account that Roosevelt spoke more often about foreign affairs after December 1941. Calculated based on the data in Appendix B, Table B.1, and Appendix C, Table C.1.

[7] Radio Address on the 150th Anniversary of the Ratification of the Bill of Rights, 15 December 1941; and, see also, among many others, Roosevelt, State of the Union Message to Congress, 11 January 1944 – both available at *The Public Papers of the President*, American Presidency Project, www.presidency.ucsb.edu/ws/. Unless otherwise indicated, all further references to Roosevelt's, and later in this chapter George W. Bush's, speeches come from this source.

Figure 4.1 FDR, major foreign affairs addresses, with bundled terms (8 December 1941 to 12 April 1945).

and a distinctively American set of institutions and practices[8] – it went beyond the instrumental calculation of costs and benefits.

Third, Roosevelt represented the war as a single conflict comprising interconnected battlefields, rather than two distinct wars, and he represented the adversary as a unified coalition, rather than three parties with distinct interests and methods. Even before Germany had declared

[8] In this way, Roosevelt linked global ideals to the protection of hearth and home. For incisive analysis, see Westbrook 2004; and for relevant survey results, see Cantril 1951, 1079.

war on the United States, Roosevelt, in his first post-Pearl Harbor fireside chat, averred that Japan, Germany, and Italy had embarked on a "collaboration so well calculated that all the continents of the world, and all the oceans, are now considered by the Axis strategists as one gigantic battlefield."[9] Equally important, he cast Japan as the junior partner, implementing plans that had been designed in Berlin.[10] The Japanese were dangerous – Pearl Harbor had proved that – but they did not represent the Axis' center of gravity: they, like the Italians, were mere "chessmen" (to Hitler's king) whose "dreams of empire ... were modest in comparison with the gargantuan aspirations of Hitler and his Nazis."[11] The implication was obvious: to wage war in the Pacific alone would leave the Axis' true animating force free to pursue its evil ends. A simple count of "Axis" in FDR's major foreign affairs addresses reinforces this point. In the two years after Pearl Harbor, he referenced the Axis over 50 percent more than he had since September 1939, when the war erupted.[12] Neither waging limited war, nor leaving Europe to Britain and the Soviet Union, matched the global scene faced by the United States.

Fourth, Roosevelt emphasized that German belligerence had its origins in the aims and methods of the Nazi Party and Adolf Hitler.[13] Rather than barbaric Huns or dangerous supermen, the German people were the regime's victims, like "all other peoples under the Nazi yoke."[14] "Slaves of the state" and "cannon fodder," downtrodden in "the mechanized hell of Hitler's new order," they were "dominated by their Nazi whipmasters." They did not follow Nazi commands willingly or out of robotic deference, like the Japanese. Their obedience

---

[9]   Fireside Chat, 9 December 1941. See similarly State of the Union Address, 6 January 1942; Fireside Chat on Progress of the War, 23 February 1942. See also Hill 2003, chs. 3–5.

[10] Message to Congress on the History of Relations between the United States and Japan, 15 December 1941. See similarly Address at Ottawa, Canada, 25 August 1943; Fireside Chat, 24 December 1943. See also Casey 2001, 66–69; Hill 2003, chs. 6–9. On public opinion on this point, see Berinsky 2009, 271–272, n. 41; Cantril 1951, 1078.

[11] State of the Union Address, 6 January 1942.

[12] This takes into account that Roosevelt spoke more often about foreign affairs after December 1941. For data, see Appendix B, Table B.1.

[13] For a different portrait of FDR, as consistently condemning all Germans, see Kimball 1976.

[14] Message to Congress on Refugees, 12 June 1944.

was "based, in great part, on direction, compulsion, and fear."[15] The problem lay not with the Germans' character, but with their leaders – "the Hitlerites, their subordinates and functionaries and satellites," "the Prussian military clique," the "fanatical militarists."[16] In FDR's telling, the Germans and Italians were not opposed to American values, and they would welcome those universal ideals if given the chance – reminiscent of the Bush administration's claims in the run-up to the 2003 Iraq War. From this representation of agent and purpose followed policy: "we mean no harm to the common people of the Axis Nations. But we do mean to impose punishment and retribution in full upon their guilty, barbaric leaders."[17] On this basis, Roosevelt rejected proposals to harass or arrest German resident aliens and German-Americans, and he refused to have much to do with German émigrés, like his old friend Emil Ludwig, who thought the administration's analysis naïve and who pronounced the average German guilty of aggression.[18]

Quantitative measures complement these observations. Over nearly six years of major foreign affairs addresses between the war's outbreak and his death, Roosevelt made reference to Hitler, Nazi, or some variant 253 times – nearly as often as he invoked Germany or Germans or Prussia. This compares strikingly to Japan, which FDR referenced in some form (including Japanese or Japs) 329 times – 33 times as often as he mentioned its leaders, whether Tojo or the emperor.[19] CRA makes the point still more clearly. Both Hitler and Nazi (indicated in Figure 4.2 by the bundled term "hitlernazienemy") were central to Roosevelt's rhetoric for two years after Pearl Harbor and were closely linked (via bold lines) to both "American" and "United States," which in turn were closely linked to the ideological cast of the war ("ideologicalterms"). German and Germany, even in combination ("germanenemy"), do not make the cut until 1944 to

---

[15] Radio Address on the President's Sixtieth Birthday, 30 January 1942; Radio Address on United Flag Day, 14 June 1942.

[16] Message to Congress on Refugees, 12 June 1944; Fireside Chat, 28 July 1943; Message to the Congress on the Progress of the War, 17 September 1943; Fireside Chat, 24 December 1943. See also Radio Address at a Dinner of the Foreign Policy Association, 21 October 1944.

[17] Address to the White House Correspondents' Association, 12 February 1943.

[18] Casey 2001, 57–58; Ludwig 1945, 128–137 and passim.

[19] For detailed data, see Appendix B, Table B.1.

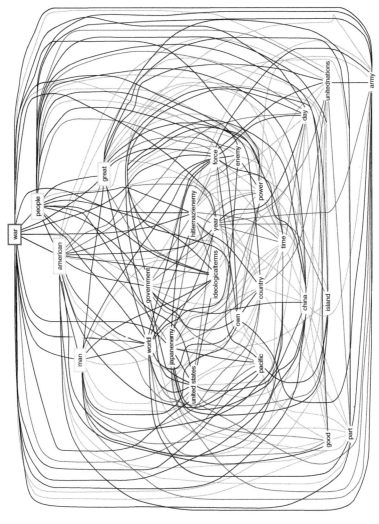

Figure 4.2 FDR, major foreign affairs addresses, with bundled terms (8 December 1941 to 23 December 1943).

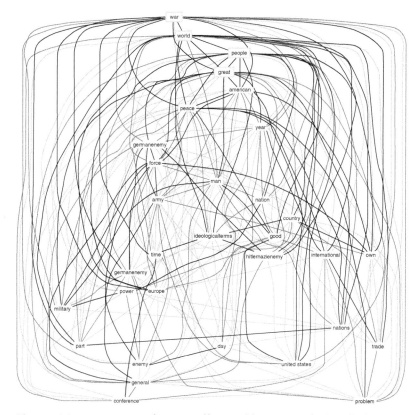

Figure 4.3 FDR, major foreign affairs addresses, with bundled terms (24 December 1943 to 12 April 1945).

1945, and even then are not closely linked to the ideological framing of the conflict, per Figure 4.3.

Where Roosevelt led, other government officials and agencies generally followed. In late spring and summer 1942, the OFF noted that most top officials consistently distinguished between the German people and the Nazi regime.[20] Although the White House issued no formal orders, OWI staff gleaned from the president's public remarks that the "enemy is not the German people ... but the militaristic and fascistic cliques," and pressed this message through radio programs, films, shorts, pamphlets, and formal speeches.[21] War posters

---

[20] Casey 2001, 57. See also Welles 1997, 333.
[21] Brewer 2009, 88–89, 104–107; Casey 2001, 60–63, quote at 61.

consistently portrayed the adversary on the European front as the Nazis or personified the threat in the figure of Hitler, but almost never referred to Germans.[22] Government-sponsored radio programs insisted that ordinary Germans were victims. A popular long-running series, broadcast weekly over all networks simultaneously during prime time from April 1942 through March 1943, was entitled, "This is War! You Can't Do Business with Hitler." Its episodes placed the dangers of Nazi rule at their center and relayed, didactically, the devastating consequences that the Nazis had brought upon Germans, who suffered nearly as much as had the peoples the Nazis had conquered.[23]

There were exceptions. Some of the president's advisers thought the distinction between Germans and Nazis both too subtle to focus the ignorant public and wrong as a matter of fact. It would, they believed, be more accurate and effective to depict the Nazis as a genuine reflection of the barbarism and aggression that lay deep within the German soul. Secretary of the Interior Harold Ickes protested in an April 1942 Cabinet meeting that "there was no difference between the German rulers and the German people ... The goose-step was a perfect expression of the German character." Secretary of the Treasury Henry Morgenthau argued that US propaganda efforts needed to promote blind popular hatred, and the pollsters Hadley Cantril and George Gallup agreed.[24] Ickes and Morgenthau's public rhetoric deviated from the presidential line, and thus a September 1942 OWI report expressed concern that official statements were not fully consistent on the question of war guilt.[25] Nevertheless, during this period, Steven Casey concludes, Germanophobes, inside and outside government, were "lonely, isolated voices."[26]

It is not clear why Roosevelt represented the German people as victims and the regime alone as villain. Before the war, American intellectuals typically indicted the masses in nations led by totalitarian regimes for voluntarily forming an obedient and "regimented" crowd.[27] Indeed, Roosevelt's own view of the relationship between the German people and their government may have been diametrically

[22] See www.library.northwestern.edu/govinfo/collections/wwii-posters/.
[23] Horten 2002, 55–59.
[24] Casey 2001, quote at 57; Hoenicke-Moore 2010, 139.
[25] "Intelligence Report: American Estimates of the Enemy," Bureau of Intelligence, OWI, 2 September 1942, in United States 1942–1944, vol. 7.
[26] Casey 2001, 57–58.   [27] Alpers 2003, esp. 94–128.

opposed to his public rhetoric.[28] One can nevertheless speculate on the reasons FDR might have opted for this public line. First, historical: ascribing guilt to the German masses might remind Americans of the crude propaganda of the First World War, which had come in for sharp criticism in the interwar years. Second, domestic political: exculpating the German people might court the German-American vote. Third, international strategic: exonerating the German masses might help spark an uprising against the Nazis.[29] Fourth, the postwar world: while blind hatred would help in fighting the war – thus War Department films, directed largely at soldiers, tended not to make any distinction between peoples and regimes[30] – it would complicate efforts to build a durable postwar order, because an enflamed public might tie Roosevelt's hands.[31]

Villainous Nazis, innocent Germans

After Pearl Harbor, Roosevelt's storytelling rhetoric matched the unsettled times and was, as expected, effective in establishing the background narrative upon which wartime debate proceeded. An attentive public tuned in to the president's radio broadcasts at a very high rate, national and local media gave prominent space to them, and OWI found a strong market for its various materials.[32] This did not reflect merely a general eagerness for information in wartime, since news could be gleaned from many sources. It reflected also demand for meaning and order, for a foundational story. When the president, the authoritative national spokesperson, gave voice to that story during unsettling and unsettled times, the media and public opinion followed his lead. Thus, most Americans believed that Germany had a hand in Pearl Harbor and, encouraged by administration evasiveness, that German forces were actively fighting in the Pacific.[33] Over the course of 1942, though few could name the Four Freedoms, Americans became increasingly confident that

---

[28] Beschloss 2002, 10–12; Hoenicke-Moore 2010, 116–118, 127–130.
[29] Skeptical of this speculation is Hoenicke-Moore 2010, 118, n. 49.
[30] These films had little impact on soldiers' views of the enemy. See
       Hoenicke-Moore 2010, 156–165.
[31] Blum 1976, 10. In general, this paragraph draws on Casey 2001, 58–63.
[32] On FDR and the media, see Winfield 1990. On OWI, see Casey 2001, 69–72.
[33] Hill 2003, chs. 3–5.

they knew why they were at war – for freedom, not just self-defense or revenge or the balance of power.[34] The impact of Roosevelt's narrative efforts is also clear in the silences of US political contest after December 1941. Neither a more limited military response nor a war on the Pacific front alone received serious consideration, as befits a war of ideals against an adversary tightly coordinated across fronts. Their impact is also clear in what Americans did argue about after Pearl Harbor. Debate periodically raged over whether to focus Allied military efforts on the European or Pacific front. Roosevelt was frustrated by the constant temptation to the latter,[35] but, equally important, that debate presumed that neither front could be abandoned. It was an argument over sequencing – when to fight on which front, not whether to fight on both.[36]

Finally, Roosevelt's storytelling had a profound impact on how Americans regarded the sources of aggression, especially in Germany, and thus on what should be done, in the wake of presumed Allied victory, to prevent Axis recidivism. Even dominant narratives, it should be recalled, do not literally silence all alternatives. This is especially true in a pluralistic society, in which one can nearly always discover multiple narrative streams.[37] While a government survey of newspaper and magazine editorials found in summer 1942 that under 1 percent cast the German people as the villain,[38] in 1944 no less a figure than Sumner Welles – former Under Secretary of State and Roosevelt confidant – made public his long-held private concerns about "militaristic pan-Germanism" in a best-selling book, *The Time for Decision*.[39] Hollywood generally pinned responsibility for the war and its atrocities on "the Hitler gang," as a 1944 film was titled in an echo of Roosevelt, and depicted the

[34] Cantril 1951, 1077–1079.

[35] To which he sometimes gave public voice. See State of the Union Address, 6 January 1945; and Press Conference Aboard the USS Quincy En Route From Yalta, 23 February 1945. See also Steele 1974, 214.

[36] On Germany-first vs. Japan-first, see Casey 2001, 48–79; Dallek 1979, 320–321, 348–349; Kennedy 1999, 523–525, 572–579, 585–587, 595–597, 612; Matloff 1986; Stoler 2000.

[37] One cannot therefore conclude, from the diversity of opinion alone, that "a consensus on how to assess the role of ordinary Germans" was "elusive" – as does Hoenicke-Moore 2010, 208 and passim. See also Alpers 2003, 208–218; Merritt 1995, 27–34; Olick 2005, 43.

[38] Casey 2001, 70.

[39] Welles 1944. For Welles' earlier privately expressed concerns, see Hearden 2002, 232.

German people as either dupes or innocent bystanders.[40] But popular novels, by one account, often elided the differences between Nazis and ordinary Germans, representing all as "unequivocal[ly] evil."[41] Nevertheless, even at the end of 1944, there were still "no widespread cries of outrage against the barbaric German 'Hun,' no strident and unanimous calls to impose a harsh peace on the nation as a whole."[42]

Although Roosevelt's storytelling did not completely crowd out alternative views, three pieces of evidence support the conclusion that his narrative achieved dominance. First, public opinion surveys – both their findings and their questions. Americans were periodically asked whether they believed "that our enemy is the German people [as a whole] or simply the Hitler [Nazi, German] government." While those identifying the people as the primary adversary doubled between 1942 and 1945 and those identifying both the government and the people increased – as one would expect over the course of a bloody war – no fewer than 64 percent ever named the government alone. Opinion on this question did not move much between fall 1943 and winter 1945, even after Allied forces directly confronted the German army on a large scale beginning in June 1944. Only with the liberation of the concentration camps in late spring 1945, where the cruelty on display was hard to square with ordinary Germans' innocence, did opinion begin to swing again.[43] Moreover, throughout the war, when pollsters asked about postwar plans, Americans were far less likely to endorse harsh handling when the object was "the German people" than when it was "the Nazis" or "the German Government" or "Germany as a nation": they were much less supportive of measures that directly impacted the German masses than of those that punished the elites and institutions that governed the German state and economy.[44] Even

---

[40] Alpers 2003, 190–203; Doherty 1993, 123–124; Koppes and Black 1987, 248–316. Alone among the Hollywood studios *before* 1941, Warner Bros. led a crusade against fascism and Nazism, but it was careful not to demonize the German people: see Birdwell 1999.

[41] Blum 1976, 49.   [42] Casey 2001, 174, and generally 171–174.

[43] On the latter surveys, see Casey 2001, 212–213.

[44] For relevant surveys, see Cantril 1951, 1112–1117, 1140. See also Berinsky 2009, 38, 47–48; Bruner 1944, 138–148. OWI, which foresaw popular hatred eventually taking over, found American sympathy for ordinary Germans surprising. See Intelligence Report #39 (4 September 1942), in United States 1942–1944, vol. 1. See also Intelligence Report, "Personal Identification with

during the war's final year, Americans continued to identify with the German masses, overwhelmingly supporting feeding the defeated even if it meant rationing at home.[45] Due to sampling flaws, these polling results are suspect, but nevertheless suggestive.

Polls' questions, however, are especially revealing of the presumptions and boundaries of legitimate discourse. After 1942, the American Institute of Public Opinion, led by George Gallup, rarely asked Americans explicitly whether they believed "that our enemy is the German people [as a whole] or simply the Hitler [Nazi, German] government," which suggests that this was not a matter seen as terribly controversial or on which mass opinion was in flux.[46] Polling on postwar plans, conducted regularly between 1942 and 1945, regularly distinguished between the German people and state elites, and thus presumed that ordinary Germans were not Nazis. In contrast, surveys normally drew no distinctions between the Japanese masses and the regime.[47]

Second, how alternative narratives are presented and received. A dominant narrative leaves its imprint on dissenting storylines. Thus, even those who cast the German people as willing supporters of the Nazis – the chief alternative – still had faith in the masses' potential for salvation, as Roosevelt's rhetoric suggested. A prevailing image was that the German people had been infected with a terrible disease, and analysts nearly always envisioned their eventual recovery. Michaela Hoenicke-Moore concludes that those who "held the Germans to be inherently and irredeemably aggressive present rare exceptions to the general American discourse and had no discernable impact on the Allied wartime debate."[48] In line with the dominant narrative, while the German people retained a core of reclaimable goodness, leading Nazis were generally thought to be beyond help. In contrast, the British drew less sharp distinctions between the German people and government and were accordingly more skeptical of the country's future peaceful integration.[49]

the War" (28 October 1942), in ibid., vol. 2; and "The Peace Settlement and the Post-war World, Survey #107" (23 March 1942), in ibid., vol. 11.
[45] Hoenicke-Moore 2010, 215, and generally on US public opinion, 211–216.
[46] Cantril 1951, 1075–1076, 1080–1081. See also Bruner 1944, 126–152.
[47] Generally, on wartime portraits of the Japanese, see Dower 1986, chs. 3–4.
[48] Hoenicke-Moore 2010, 208, 241, and passim.
[49] Goldman 1979; Olick 2005, 44–58.

Moreover, deep challenges to the dominant narrative were dismissed as illegitimate, not just imprudent. Robert Vansittart, a high-ranking British official before he retired to take up advocacy, was the most prominent spokesman for the view that the Nazis were the extension of Prussian militarism and that both aggression and racism were deeply embedded in German history, culture, and institutions. Famous in Britain from the end of 1940, he reached American shores a couple of years later. Running afoul of the dominant narrative, "Vansittartism" became a dirty word in American politics. Blatantly misquoted, or at least quoted out of context, he became associated with extreme positions, including mass extermination, which he had explicitly rejected. Vansittart's views were commonly rebuffed as Nazism inside-out, "an inverted form of Hitler's racial theories," according to a typical review.[50] This was harsh stuff in the midst of an ideological war, and historians have noted with consternation how Vansittart became reduced to a polemical label.[51] Yet, this misses the point. Vansittart challenged the dominant US narrative, and he paid the price. In Britain, in contrast, his over-heated rhetoric offended some as a violation of good taste, but his eventually became the official line of the British Government. Although Vanisttart was a lightning-rod for criticism in Britain, "he entrenched himself in the mainstream of public thought about Germany," according to his biographer.[52] At home, Vansittart was controversial. In the United States, he was a pariah.

Third, the dominance of the official narrative on the sources of German aggression is perhaps most clear in what followed when Roosevelt himself began to press at its boundaries. FDR seems to have been aware that demonization of the German people might constrain him, but he failed to anticipate how their exoneration might impose such bonds. By the Tehran conference in late fall 1943, he had begun to chafe privately at the public narrative he had earlier propounded – perhaps because he had harbored such views all along, perhaps because he had lost hope that the German people would rebel. Roosevelt went to Tehran committed to the postwar dismemberment and disarmament of Germany and to an aggressive program of

[50] On the debate over Vansittart, see Hoenicke-Moore 2010, 241–256, quote at 246.
[51] Alpers 2003, 208; Olick 2005, 44.
[52] Goldman 1979; Rose 1978, 244–265, quote at 262.

re-education to purge Germans of militarism and authoritarianism.[53] He informed Stalin that "fifty years ago, there had been a difference" between Germany's leaders and its people, "but since the last war it was no longer so."[54] He told his aides the same that summer, severely criticizing a draft "Handbook of Military Government" that Allied military headquarters in London had prepared. It was symptomatic of a deep problem, FDR observed to Secretary of War Henry Stimson: "too many people here and in England hold the view that the German people as a whole are not responsible for what has taken place – that only a few Nazi leaders are responsible. That unfortunately is not based on fact. The German people as a whole must have it driven home to them that the whole nation has been engaged in a lawless conspiracy against the decencies of modern civilization."[55] At the Second Quebec Conference in September 1944, Roosevelt finally departed openly from the official script – and learned that even contributing authors cannot easily rewrite dominant narratives.

As was his wont when his Cabinet split into warring camps,[56] Roosevelt had been cagey during the debate on postwar policy leading up to the Second Quebec Conference – with Treasury, led by Morgenthau and his aide Harry Dexter White on one side, lining up against the War Department, led by Stimson, on the other, and with Secretary of State Cordell Hull tacking with the winds. It was hard to reconcile Roosevelt's public portrait of cultured Germans enslaved by barbaric Nazis and militarist Prussian warlords with that of the outspoken Morgenthau. In Morgenthau's telling, the Depression had facilitated Hitler's rise, but neither was the root cause of German aggression: only because the Germans were "a people bent on war," marked by a "worship of force and [a] lust for war," had Hitler seemed an attractive solution to their problems. War was a mass obsession in Germany, he insisted: "desire for war has been as firmly planted in the German as desire for freedom in the American." More New Dealer than crusading avenger, Morgenthau pointed his finger at Germany's political economy, whose dominant interests profited from belligerence and promoted popular militarism. The German people were hardly

[53] On FDR's evolving views, see Casey 2001, 130–210; Dallek 1979, 472–476.
[54] *FRUS: Conference at Tehran*, 602. See also Kimball 1976, 15–19. On FDR's evolving views, see Casey 2001, 130–210; Dallek 1979, 472–476.
[55] Quoted in Dallek 1979, 472–473. See also Blum 1967, 342, 349.
[56] See, generally, on FDR's leadership style, Kimball 1991.

innocent, however, for they had welcomed their indoctrination.[57] The title of his 1945 manifesto, *Germany Is Our Problem*, implied, first, that *Germany* – not just the Nazi regime – is our problem, and, second, that Germany is *our* problem – from which Americans could not shrink as they had after the last war. Ridding Germany of Nazis and Junkers would not be enough. The reason, Morgenthau wrote in his inimitable style, was that "the German *people* had . . . [been] cultivated intensively for nearly two hundred years . . . [so that] they could produce those finest Nazi flowers – the gas chambers of Maidaneck and the massacre of Lidice."[58]

In Quebec, Roosevelt went beyond even Morgenthau's vision, pressing Churchill to support a deindustrialized, "pastoral" Germany. An initially reluctant Churchill came on board, perhaps encouraged by US concessions on Lend-Lease. Yet, Roosevelt's commitment to the collective guilt of the German people and mass punishment for their crimes swiftly withered. When the Quebec Conference agreement and Cabinet rift were leaked to the press at home, just five days after the conference's close, the response was uniformly negative. Criticism immediately poured in from across the political spectrum – from editorial pages and Capitol Hill, from Cabinet members whom Roosevelt had kept in the dark, from his Republican challenger for the presidency, Governor Thomas Dewey. Impractical and counterproductive, many argued. Others claimed it would impede Europe's postwar future, since a roaring German engine could power the whole continent. Many feared that retribution would lay the groundwork for Nazism's return.[59] Others alleged, without evidence, that the plan had contributed to recent battlefield setbacks, since German soldiers who expected harsh postwar treatment had every reason to fight on: it was as good as "ten fresh German divisions," Dewey claimed.[60] Far-reaching though

---

[57] Morgenthau Jr. 1945, 8, 144, 114.

[58] Morgenthau Jr. 1945, 105 (emphasis added), and more generally, 102–115, 144–154. Equally explicit is the September 1944 briefing book prepared by Treasury for FDR to take to Quebec, reprinted in *FRUS: The Conference at Quebec 1944*, 128–143, esp. 139–140. On the presumptions underpinning the Morgenthau Plan, see also Dorn 1957; Kimball 1976, 25–31.

[59] On Stimson's objections, see Blum 1967, 360–362; Hearden 2002, 248; Kimball 1976, 32, 111–114, 122–124. See also Memorandum by the Secretary of War, 9 September 1944, *FRUS: The Conference at Quebec 1944*, 123–126. On similar State Department views, see Kimball 1976, 7–12.

[60] Quoted in Blum 1967, 382.

Treasury's proposals were, however, they were not a "Carthaginian peace" or "super-Versailles" as so many charged, in an effort to delegitimize them. The Morgenthau Plan, and Roosevelt, got the same treatment Vansittart had the year before. They were treated as beyond the pale, with the twist that the Jewish Morgenthau was accused of acting not in the national interest, but out of a (natural) desire for vengeance on behalf of his co-religionists.[61]

Roosevelt was eager for the controversy to go away.[62] He denied to Hull that he had endorsed the Morgenthau Plan, he told Stimson that he had "no intention of turning Germany into an agrarian state," and he implausibly pretended that he did not know "how he could have initialed" those portions of the Quebec agreements dealing with post-war Germany.[63] Publicly, Roosevelt dealt with the matter by issuing a letter to the Foreign Economic Administration (FEA) suggesting that postwar planning remained unsettled. He instructed the FEA to "accelerate" its study "of what should be done after the surrender of Germany to control its power and capacity [so] . . . that Germany does not become a menace again to succeeding generations." Roosevelt did not explicitly reject the Morgenthau Plan, but he distanced himself from it by instructing FEA to conduct its work "under the guidance of the Department of State" – pointedly, not Treasury.[64]

Roosevelt's critics did not explicitly charge the president with inconsistency, with having endorsed a policy whose assumptions ran counter to his long-standing public narrative. Nor did they protest that his assignation of guilt to the German masses was misplaced. Rather, in addition to their use of delegitimizing rhetoric like "super-Versailles," they identified a host of negative consequences that would follow from the implementation of the Morgenthau Plan. These instrumental arguments derived their force from the dominant narrative. Fear of a revenge-inspired Nazi revival suggested that the German people were not inherently America's enemies, but that they could be made so.

---

[61]   In general, on the episode, see Blum 1967, 377–382; Casey 2001, 174–195; Hoenicke-Moore 2010, 293–321; Kimball 1976, 41–44.

[62]   Alliance politics may also have played a part. The Soviets' hunger for reparations was even greater than their hunger for revenge, and they thus found unappealing a weak, agricultural Germany, which would lack the wherewithal to feed their coffers.

[63]   Dallek 1979, 477.

[64]   Letter to the Foreign Economic Administration on Postwar Policies, 29 September 1944.

Anxiety that the plan would inspire frenzied German resistance imagined German soldiers as malleable, as neither committed Nazi ideologues nor wild militarists; the Allies could secure their cooperation with properly designed incentives. Concern that the plan would, by keeping Germany down, keep all of Europe down implied that a revived Germany was not necessarily a destabilizing force, that it was not German economic power or culture but Nazi ideology that threatened Europe and the world.

Roosevelt himself seems to have understood what had transpired as the dominant narrative coming home to roost. He concluded that only a public statement exhibiting fidelity to that narrative would quiet his critics. The following week, he thus reproduced the dominant narrative in a national radio address: while German resistance remained "as determined and as fanatical as ever," the blame lay with "the guns of Hitler's Gestapo" who were preventing sensible German officers from bringing the war to a conclusion. Two weeks later, he declared that "Hitler and the Nazis" – that is, not "the Germans" – "continue the fight, desperately." Roosevelt was careful to hold to account only those Germans "directly responsible for this agony of mankind."[65]

Sitting in the British Embassy in Washington, Isaiah Berlin wrote to the Foreign Office that "out of this brief storm" over the Morgenthau Plan "has come at least a lightning flash which has illuminated the public landscape."[66] It certainly taught Roosevelt the limits of his power. Stung, he returned to his usual strategy of attaining "consensus by postponement."[67] Humbled and frustrated, he avoided making decisions on postwar policy: "I dislike making detailed plans," he wrote Hull in October, "for a country which we do not yet occupy." He failed to issue clear guidance to Cabinet members, and he disengaged from the planning process for postwar Europe, allowing the bureaucracy to battle it out.[68] What ultimately emerged was a formal occupation plan that was in tone "the Morgenthau Plan lightly disguised,"[69] but that in practice – at the behest of Assistant Secretary of War John McCloy – gave military commanders great autonomy.[70]

---

[65] Radio Address from the White House, 5 October 1944; Radio Address at a Dinner of the Foreign Policy Association, 21 October 1944.

[66] Quoted in Nicholas 1981, 426.   [67] Kimball 1976, 44.

[68] Blum 1967, 383–414; Hearden 2002, 249–253, quote at 249; Kimball 1976, 44–57.

[69] Ziemke 1984, 58, 61. See also Blum 1967, 383–390.   [70] Olick 2005, 86.

Had FDR been free of these narrative constraints, he likely would have earlier and more consistently committed the United States to postwar punishment of the German people. It is less clear whether that would have made much difference to Germany's actual occupation. In the end, coping with chaos on the ground swiftly overtook formal plans. Democratization, re-education, and denazification were less urgent than the provision of basic supplies and the maintenance of order. US occupying forces had to rely on able local administrators, who normally had Nazi ties. US authorities did not announce a plan for democratic re-education until January 1947, and German procrastination then sidelined the program. Soon thereafter, mounting fear of the Soviet Union made reviving German industry a greater priority than social engineering.[71] Had he lived, FDR too would have had to confront these practical obstacles. He too would have had to take into account growing tensions with the Soviet Union and would have felt the same pressure to rehabilitate Germany.[72] Even the politically nimble and rhetorically talented Roosevelt could not have evaded these constraints.

Alternative explanations and counterfactuals

There was nothing natural about how Americans would tell the story of the Second World War. There was nothing natural about what postwar policies they would see as warranted and about how they would envision preventing future aggression. Japan's attack on Pearl Harbor did not foreclose the more limited military response that optimistic Japanese decision-makers hoped would follow, nor did it exclude a total war waged exclusively on the Pacific front. Sober analysts could (and sometimes did) note how the interests of the Axis powers diverged, cast the war as a struggle for power rather than a battle over ideals, and disagree over the popularity and stability of the Nazi regime. Yet, legitimate public debate did narrow: its boundaries were constituted by a foundational narrative that set the global scene, depicted the key protagonists, their motives, and their relationships, and explained the war's origins. According to that narrative, it was a

[71] Gimbel 1968; Herz 1948; Williamson 2001, 14–15.
[72] Presuming of course that Roosevelt would not have been able to avoid the Cold War. For an intriguing argument that he would have, see Costigliola 2012.

war of ideology, rather than a war fought for revenge or cold realist logic. It was a war of immense stakes, appropriately fought until unconditional surrender and decisive victory. And, as this case study has explored in detail, it was, at least in Europe, a war waged against a regime and its leadership, not a people. Legitimate public debate did not narrow because the facts spoke so clearly, because events themselves were articulate.

Legitimate public debate also did not narrow simply because of the power of the bully pulpit in a time of national crisis. Perhaps Roosevelt, as the nation rallied around him, could have said anything he wished, in whatever mode, and carried the day. Yet, Roosevelt understood that his narrative authority would not allow him to sweep away all opposition on policy. Consider, for instance, the crucial question of where the United States should devote its military energies. For Roosevelt, it was obvious that Germany was the existential threat and Japan a sideshow: the defeat of Japan would only marginally diminish the German threat, but the defeat of Germany would doom the Japanese war effort. But he was also aware that argument alone could not silence his opponents, whose Pacific-first stance could be legitimated in terms of the dominant narrative. Roosevelt worried that the American people would lose patience as the country's war machine only slowly generated sufficient materiel and placed it in position to confront Germany on the continent. Thus, over his generals' objection, he insisted on the invasion of North Africa in fall 1942, hoping to keep Americans engaged in the European conflict.[73] Nor did the conjuncture of bully pulpit and crisis allow Roosevelt to narrate the world whenever and however he wished. In summer 1944, the war's outcome was not a foregone conclusion: the Germans still had the capacity to launch a major offensive, as they would in the Battle of the Bulge, and the Japanese remained a tenacious foe, as huge naval and land battles lay ahead, in Leyte Gulf and Okinawa. Roosevelt remained immensely popular, with approval ratings above 70 percent – not as high as the immediate rally period after Pearl Harbor, but much higher than those he routinely received between 1937 and 1941.[74] Despite intense total wars on two fronts,

[73] Meyer 1959; Steele 1973; Stoler 2000. See also Casey 2001, 90–97; Dallek 1979, 321; Kimball 1997, 153.
[74] For Gallup data, see www.ropercenter.uconn.edu/CFIDE/roper/presidential/webroot/presidential_rating_detail.cfm?allRate=True&presidentName=Roosevelt.

and despite his popularity, Roosevelt found that, given the settled narrative situation, he could not recast the sources of German aggression and prepare the ground for his preferred postwar policy.

Legitimate public debate did not narrow because of the dictates of human psychology. In the anxious atmosphere after Pearl Harbor, one would have expected demonization of Germans, yet the dominant narrative treated the German people as the regime's victims. One might have expected the hawks to win once American forces were engaged in battle on the European continent, but just a few months after the invasion of Normandy in June 1944, the Morgenthau Plan was still not publicly defensible.

Perhaps Roosevelt was not leading public opinion, but simply following its dictates. Many Americans were of German descent, and they were naturally inclined to think of the average German as no different from the average American.[75] This accords with the common view of Roosevelt as a cautious politician, and, as we have already seen, he had before Pearl Harbor shown great sensitivity to what he believed public opinion would tolerate. Yet, Roosevelt apparently saw the Japanese attack as an opening sufficient to take the people to war, and afterwards he did not hesitate to narrate the war's fundamental stakes. It is hard to fathom why he would see public opinion as malleable on many deep-seated issues, yet as so settled on the nature of the German adversary that he could not have narrated it differently.

After Pearl Harbor, the long-standing narrative contest over national security came to a close. Japan's attack on the US naval base in Hawaii did not, in and of itself, resolve the public debate over agent, motive, and scene. It narrowed thanks to the success of Franklin Roosevelt's narrative project. Structural power and opportunity – the authority of the bully pulpit, an unsettled narrative situation – were surely important. But they were not sufficient. Agency is equally part of the conjuncture: Roosevelt needed to speak in the right way – in the rhetorical mode appropriate to the situation – if he was to shape the narrative that emerged. That narrative, defining the battlefield as global, the war as ideological, and the adversary as the Nazi regime, had real consequences. Most strikingly, it suggested that Germany could safely be reintegrated into the community of nations, once Hitler and the Nazis had been overthrown. Once installed as dominant,

---

[75] This is the view of Hoenicke-Moore 2010.

narratives confine even their authors. Late in the war, Roosevelt transgressed those boundaries: he sought to promote a very different vision of postwar peace, premised on Germans' aggressive character and their mass guilt. The short-lived experiment sent Roosevelt scurrying for political cover – much as he had seven years before, after the Quarantine Address.

Fixing the meaning of 9/11

Four planes were hijacked in the United States on September 11, 2001, in what was later discovered to be an operation designed and coordinated by Al Qaeda.[76] One crashed in Pennsylvania. One was flown into the Pentagon, home of the US Department of Defense. The remaining two barreled into the twin towers of the World Trade Center. Exceeding the hijackers' expectations, the buildings came crashing down, but only after hundreds of emergency workers had rushed to the scene. Excluding the 19 hijackers, nearly 3,000 people were killed that day in Pennsylvania, New York, and Washington. These facts are, conspiracy theorists aside, generally accepted, but these spare sentences on the drama's act are but the skeleton of a narrative: absent any portrait of the agent, the purpose, or the scene, they cannot make sense of that day's events. The Terror narrative imparted meaning to the shocking images by supplying a distinctive portrait of the drama's chief protagonists, their motives, and the historical setting. According to that narrative, the meaning of "9/11" – as the day came to be known in the United States – was, and is, clear: on that day, evil terrorists attacked a blameless America because they hate the values Americans hold dear and which America epitomizes; on that day, transnational terrorism showed itself to be the pre-eminent threat to the nation's security; that day marked a turning point in both America's history and global politics. The Terror narrative is often seen in the United States as

---

[76] This chapter revises Krebs and Lobasz 2007. Frank Harvey treats that article as an exemplar of "neoconism" – by which he means explanations for the Iraq War that emphasize leadership, ideology, and individual psychology. Yet, the analytical focus of both that article, and this revision and expansion, does not lie with the "first image." I am agnostic as to the motivations and psychology of key decision-makers, and I am critical of the tendency to reduce the Iraq War to a neoconservative cabal. Ironically, Stuart Kaufman takes me to task for not being *sufficiently* sensitive to the "first image." See Harvey 2012, 2–3 and passim; Kaufman 2012.

the "natural" interpretation. But that is a sign of the narrative project's relative success, not the day's and events' inherent meaning.[77] The Terror narrative's dominance hid from view that there were other conceivable and plausible narratives, revolving around different portraits of agent, purpose, and scene, and that these alternative narratives were swiftly marginalized after 9/11.

The conjuncture of narrative situation, institutional authority, and rhetorical mode again helps explain why and how the Terror narrative became dominant. In the wake of the US triumph in the Cold War, during the "long" decade of the 1990s – from the fall of the Berlin Wall to 9/11 – many narratives of national security swirled around the public sphere. That freewheeling atmosphere came to an abrupt halt on September 11, 2001. An already unsettled narrative situation was transformed into a moment of crisis, in which the narrative disorder that Americans had tolerated for a decade seemed suddenly intolerable. The public's demand for authoritative story-telling was elevated, and, after some initial fumbling, President George W. Bush satisfied it. Gravitating to the storytelling mode, he defined for his audience what had transpired, who the key actors were, what motivated them, and why America's ideals had with-stood, and would continue to withstand, the challenge. His call for a "War on Terror" followed from this narrative more than from any rational weighing of policy options.

The Bush administration's policy decisions naturally did not escape criticism. Yet, most critics rooted their arguments in the dominant Terror narrative – from those who maintained that the Iraq War was a distraction from the War on Terror, to those who characterized the 9/11 attacks as a heinous crime, rather than an act of war. True narrative alternatives, in contrast, offered divergent portraits of one or more dramatic elements: they suggested that the United States was hardly blameless, due to its heavy-handed behavior abroad, or that the attacks, though horrible, did not mark a rupture in the fabric of world politics, or that transnational terrorism, though capable of wreaking havoc, was but one threat among many. But these true alternatives generally garnered little attention. What response they did receive befitted claims that lay in the realm of the illegitimate – not

---

[77] On the contingency of the meaning of the attacks, see Croft 2006; Devetak 2009; Holland 2009, 2012.

reasoned argument, but deep hostility and charges of disloyalty. The Terror narrative constituted the terrain on which post-9/11 national security was debated and policy made. It foreclosed some stances, such as a deep reconsideration of US foreign policy, and it privileged others, including the tilting of the political field in favor of war with Iraq.

The story of US foreign policy after 9/11 is often told through the lens of the triumph of neoconservatism.[78] That plotline is appealing in its simplicity and its clear attribution of blame. It directs our attention to whether and why Bush became a convert to, or dupe of, the neoconservative cause and to how neoconservatives attained influence. But that account obscures the deeper changes in US national security discourse that affected the many who did not identify as either neoconservatives or liberal hawks, inside and outside the Republican Party, and that impacted US foreign policy even after the neoconservatives fell from grace. It masks the ways in which many critics of the Iraq War occupied the same narrative terrain as its defenders and assented to the logic of the War on Terror. This study focuses on two questions. First, why did the Terror narrative become dominant, while alternatives struggled to gain a hearing? Second, what impact did this dominant narrative have on debates over US national security and on the policies the United States pursued? I pick up the thread of the Terror narrative again later, in Part II, explaining why it remained dominant for so long and why it eventually eroded.

The case study is organized in three sections. The first establishes the unsettled nature of the narrative situation on the eve of the 9/11 attacks, traces how Bush gradually displayed greater rhetorical leadership, elucidates the features of his narrative, and shows that it became, and how it became, dominant. The second explores how else the events of 9/11 might plausibly (and implausibly) have been narrated, varying each element in the dominant pentad, and addresses alternative explanations for why a particular configuration became dominant. The third examines in detail the consequences of the Terror narrative's dominance: how it paved the way for the invasion of Iraq, by silencing the potential opposition among leading Democrats.

---

[78] See, for instance, Halper and Clarke 2007; Isikoff and Corn 2006; Mann 2004.

Making the Terror narrative

The conventional wisdom is that the 9/11 attacks "changed everything." Upon receiving word while flying over Detroit, Attorney
General John Ashcroft reportedly turned to an aide and said, "Our
world has changed forever." "History begins today," Deputy Secretary
of State Richard Armitage similarly recalled telling Pakistan's intelligence chief on September 11. George W. Bush reportedly informed his
National Security Council the next day: "this is a new world."[79] Bush,
Armitage, and Ashcroft were not right at first, but they would be
proved so over time: the attacks *did* change everything, and they *were*
a critical turning point in world history – because Americans narrated
them that way. The story of 9/11 as a moment of radical discontinuity,
ushering in a world transformed by transnational terrorism, was rarely
subject to challenge. Whether history had to have begun that day, it *did*
begin that day.[80]

To make sense of how 9/11 came to be a moment of historical
rupture requires locating 9/11 in history. For a decade, since the fall
of the Berlin Wall, numerous national security narratives had found
their way into the public sphere and occasionally even displayed staying power. The rivals came to be known by slogan-like shorthands:
the clash of civilizations, the coming anarchy, the China threat, the
unipolar moment, the indispensable nation. All had their advocates
among politicians and pundits, none swept away the competition.
Americans could agree on aspects of agent: the United States was the
"sole remaining superpower." But the other elements in the Burkean
pentad remained objects of continual contestation, and few stances
were expressly illegitimate in that permissive environment. The contours of the international order and threats to its viability remained
obscure in the post-Cold War mist. It was an unsettled narrative situation. But although the global atmosphere was uncertain, it seemed
benign enough. The mood in America was triumphalist during an era
that David Halberstam labeled "a time of trivial pursuits," and there
was little pressure to resolve those festering disagreements and stabilize
the national narrative.[81] America's victory in its decades-long struggle

---

[79] Eric Lichtblau, "Antiterror Campaign Made Ashcroft a Lightning Rod," *New
York Times*, 10 November 2004; www.pbs.org/wgbh/pages/frontline/taliban/
interviews/armitage.html; Woodward 2003, 62.
[80] See, relatedly, Jervis 2005, 52.   [81] Halberstam 2001, 500.

with the Soviet Union and global Communism had bred confidence both in the superiority of the liberal democratic model and in the capacity of the United States to overcome whatever challenges would eventually surface. The public looked upon the narrative disorder with little apprehension. As a result, the numerous efforts of President Bill Clinton, his advisers, and many journalists, activists, and intellectuals to narrate the world had little traction.[82]

Then came 9/11. The attacks shocked Americans. Not because of their sheer magnitude, for the physical damage the United States had suffered was, if not slight, then certainly manageable. Wall Street was quickly back up and running, so too was the Pentagon. The nation's sovereignty and political stability were intact. While the initial intense fear of another large-scale attack was understandable, vigorous counter-terrorist measures should have alleviated Americans' anxiety. Rather, the attacks brought on a *narrative crisis*, for they seemed to portend "the end of the end of history."[83] They punctured not only the myth of America's invulnerability, but its post-Cold War complacency. The attacks made clear that there were substantial costs to the nation's inability to settle on a clear picture of the threats it faced. As John Lewis Gaddis wrote afterward: "It was not just the Twin Towers that collapsed on that morning of September 11, 2001: so too did some of our most fundamental assumptions about international, national, and personal security."[84] How much of a superpower could America be if nearly 3,000 of its citizens, residents, and visitors had died in a single day? How crucial was US leadership to sustaining international order if it could not guarantee security at home? But, more than anything, the attacks reminded Americans that they had never sorted out the world after the Cold War, that they remained mired in narrative disorder. As Frank Rich noted just a few days later,

---

[82] For the best account of the era, and its endemic uncertainty, see Chollet and Goldgeier 2008. The authors ascribe the failure of these many narrative efforts to a reality so complex it defied simplification: "no single expression illuminated America's purpose after the Cold War. And it was folly to believe one could" (315). That claim is at odds with this book's constructivist premises.

[83] Fareed Zakaria, "The End of the End of History," *Newsweek*, 24 September 2001. But see Francis Fukuyama, "Their Target: The Modern World," *Newsweek*, 17 September 2001.

[84] Gaddis 2004, 80.

"This week's nightmare ... has awakened us from a frivolous if not decadent decade-long dream."[85]

Thrust into narrative crisis, Americans were eager for a stabilizing storytelling rhetoric that would make sense of what had happened, reaffirm national ideals, and imbue the nation with the sense of purpose that had been absent. The evolution of Bush's public addresses in the hours and days after the attacks are revealing, as, with each successive set of remarks, he more firmly embraced the storytelling mode and more competently fleshed out a satisfying narrative. At the beginning of the crisis, Bush offered little by way of story. He had been visiting a school in Florida at the time of the attacks, and he immediately took to the airwaves. But his brief statement, promising "the full resources of the Federal Government [to] go to help the victims and their families and to conduct a full-scale investigation to hunt down and to find those folks who committed this act," was widely seen as inadequate. Partly because its promises of action were vague. But mostly because he failed to offer a meaningful account to a public that felt desperately adrift. Bush told the nation what had transpired ("two airplanes have crashed into the World Trade Center in an apparent terrorist attack on our country"), but "act" is just one element in the pentad. Bush's brief references to "a national tragedy" and a "terrorist attack" did not explain who the perpetrators were, why they had done what they did, and why specifically "our country" had been targeted.[86] The president did not seem to recognize that the nation had been shaken to its narrative core. The brief address made so little impression that some recalled his initial response as "essentially private." The post-9/11 era had gotten off to a "shaky start," wrote one journalist, because Bush had failed to grasp the public's needs of the moment, because he did not "us[e] his bully pulpit to reassure or rally the nation."[87]

---

[85] Frank Rich, "The Day Before Tuesday," *New York Times*, 15 September 2001. See also Rich 2006, 21–23.

[86] Remarks in Sarasota, FL, on the Terrorist Attack on New York City's World Trade Center, 11 September 2001.

[87] Kenneth T. Walsh, "Now It's Bush's War," *US News & World Report*, 24 September 2001. Similar language pervaded much contemporary criticism of Bush's initial response: see Margaret Carlson, "A President Finds His Voice," *Time*, 24 September 2001; Helle Bering, "A Day of Infamy," *Washington Times*, 12 September 2001; Eric Pooley and Karen Tumulty, "Bush in the Crucible," *Time*, 24 September 2001.

Five hours later, Bush surfaced at a Louisiana air force base. He had finally landed, after having remained aloft in Air Force One on the advice of his security officials. Now he began to situate the day's events in the storyline that would become familiar: "Freedom, itself, was attacked this morning by a faceless coward, and freedom will be defended." More formally than before, Bush promised: "The United States will hunt down and punish those responsible for these cowardly acts."[88] Agent, purpose, and scene were still underdeveloped, but Bush began to tell the tale. The perpetrators were cowards, because they had attacked defenseless civilians. But they were also still unidentified, and their refusal to come forward and take responsibility, which rendered them "faceless," was perhaps also a sign of their cowardice. They were opponents of freedom, although it was not yet clear why. The United States was hailed into the opposing position of the free and the brave, whose innocence was presumed. This was a good start. Yet, the public wanted much more from the nation's authoritative spokesperson. Brief allusions to well-established war tropes would not be enough. This speech, too, was deemed "shaky."[89]

That evening, Bush again spoke to the nation, in a televised address that finally offered something approaching a satisfactory narrative. It started, like the Louisiana speech, by casting the attacks as a salvo in a battle against freedom: "Today our fellow citizens, our way of life, our very freedom came under attack in a series of deliberate and deadly terrorist acts." The perpetrators' target (our way of life, our very freedom) and motive (principled opposition to that way of life) were the same, but their character was markedly different: no longer cowards who might be dismissed as unworthy foes, they were now dangerous and calculating men, willing to violate sacred norms of combat, capable of planning death and destruction on a large scale. Bush went on to proclaim the victims' innocence ("the victims were in airplanes or in their offices: secretaries, business men and women, military and Federal workers, moms and dads, friends and neighbors"), and to contrast them with the distinctly un-innocent character of the perpetrators, for the first time labeled "evil" ("Thousands of lives were suddenly ended by evil, despicable acts of terror"). Much more than

---

[88] Remarks at Barksdale Air Force Base, LA, on the Terrorist Attacks, 11 September 2001.
[89] Pooley and Tumulty, "Bush in the Crucible."

in either of the previous addresses, Bush narrated the nation itself, giving voice to its "strength," its "greatness," its "resolve," and to its "quiet, unyielding anger." He dwelled on ordinary Americans' responses that, he said, reflected "the best of America": "the daring of our rescue-workers ... the caring for strangers and neighbors who came to give blood and help in any way they could." Within a day of the attacks, Bush articulated one of the striking themes of the Terror narrative – that "America was targeted for attack because we're the brightest beacon for freedom and opportunity in the world," because of what America is and what it represents, not because of what it had done. And he named what the nation was about to undertake: "the war against terrorism." Finally, Bush painted the day's horrors onto a larger historical canvas. They were, in his telling, neither of a piece with what had come before, nor were they merely discordant chords set against post-Cold War euphony. In the wake of the attacks, Bush told the nation, "night fell on a different world."[90]

Reeling from narrative crisis, Americans looked for rhetorical leadership that would make comprehensible and stable a world that had long been interpretively incomprehensible and unstable. Bush moved slowly but steadily to meet that challenge. The evening address was substantially more storied than the earlier speech at Barksdale Air Force Base – between 22 and 35 percent more.[91] Even more fully over the coming week, until he spoke with "perfect pitch" at the National Cathedral on 14 September and then to a joint session of Congress on 20 September,[92] Bush (along with lower-ranking officials) expended his rhetorical energies on constructing a narrative that would explain the day's horrendous events, articulate a vision of America and its values, and paint a portrait of those guilty of the horrific deed. They set the scene and defined the scope of the problem. They identified the agents, their nature, their means, and their motivation. Officials, especially Bush, devoted little effort to making the strategic or legal

[90] Address to the Nation on the Terrorist Attacks, 11 September 2001. Although even this speech failed fully to satisfy: according to some, it too "failed to meet either the magnitude of the day's events or the nature of the task ahead." See David E. Sanger and Don van Natta, Jr., "In Four Days, a National Crisis Changes Bush's Presidency," *New York Times*, 16 September 2001.

[91] Bush's first speech of the day was so short (well under 200 words) that I am reluctant to put much weight on the data Diction has generated regarding its storytelling.

[92] Pooley and Tumulty, "Bush in the Crucible."

case for a war on terror: they did not calculate for audiences the net costs of military action, compared to other policy instruments, nor did they identify which laws the terrorists had violated.[93] Their rhetoric reflected "symbolic reassurance," not a mastery of policy detail.[94] It was about telling the story, and fixing the meaning, of 9/11. To focus on these official storytellers is not to deny that opinion leaders outside government were sometimes crucial to the creation of the standard formulations and were always crucial to their dissemination. But only once government officials, especially the president, took them up did they become part of the standard narrative.

More formally, in terms of Burke's dramatic pentad, that standard narrative consisted of four key pillars.[95] First, and least controversially, *act*. The real target of the attacks on 9/11 was not the individual victims themselves, nor anything as abstract as global capitalism, but America. Second, fused *agent* and *agency*. The perpetrators, and thus the focus of America's righteous anger, were terrorists – not just Al Qaeda, but all those who would use violence against innocents. Third, *purpose*. These terrorists were not rational actors pursuing political ends, but ideologically driven, fascistic, evil forces with whom one could not negotiate. America was the attacks' blameless victim, targeted, even hated, because of its espousal of freedom and liberty. Fourth, *scene*, in two senses: (1) 9/11 was a moment of historical rupture, both novel and consequential; and (2) the threat of transnational terrorism was not just one problem among many for the United States in a disorderly world, but the pre-eminent menace to its national security, virtually on a par with the Soviet Union during the Cold War. This was the Terror narrative that Bush and other officials would fully articulate by the end of the week.

With Bush embracing his role as national storyteller, that narrative swiftly achieved dominance – as Chapter 2 would expect. Quantitative content analyses of the nation's reportage observed that national

---

[93] One could cite almost countless addresses. See, for instance, Proclamation 7462: National Day of Prayer and Remembrance for the Victims of the Terrorist Attacks on September 11, 2001, 13 September 2001; Speech to the Republican Party of Alaska, Anchorage (AK), 16 February 2002.

[94] Murphy 2003; Schudson 2002, 41; Smith 2005a.

[95] Because that standard narrative has been so carefully unpacked since 2001, I will not belabor the presentation with extensive quotation. I draw freely on Bostdorff 2003; Croft 2006, 69–73, 84–121; Devetak 2009, 804–808; Hodges 2011; Hutcheson *et al.* 2004; Jackson 2005; Silberstein 2004.

identity discourse, including the invocation of core American values and the demonization of the enemy, overshadowed all other framings in the weeks after the attacks.[96] Leading opposition politicians, who had before 9/11 exulted in Bush's blunders over China and in domestic politics, rallied behind both the president's policies and his narrative. "Save for a few criticisms of [Bush's] offhand remarks about a 'crusade' and wanting Osama bin Laden 'dead or alive,'" one scholar observes, "no significant domestic public criticism of [Bush's] discourse about evil was voiced." Once Bush overcame his early missteps after the Towers fell and "signaled that he was personally prepared to take charge," Samuel Kernell notes, "other Washingtonians quickly accepted his leadership."[97] With the nation's political elites speaking in narrative unison, dissenting storylines could barely penetrate the mainstream media.[98]

Both the results and design of public opinion surveys reinforce this conclusion. Americans overwhelmingly denied that US wrong-doing abroad had underlain the September 11 attacks. Only a small, highly committed minority subscribed to the view that US foreign policy was even somewhat culpable.[99] But polls are also social artifacts that reveal the concerns and presumptions of the moment. As Ian Lustick has noted, polls after 2001 normally asked not whether the United States should engage in a War on Terror, but rather how that war might be most effectively waged. They thus presumed not only the appropriateness of the "war," but also of the deeper narrative upon which it had been legitimated. "The War on Terror has ... achieved the status of a background narrative," Lustick rightly concludes.[100]

The more dominant a narrative, the less its spokespeople acknowl-edge, much less feel compelled to rebut, alternatives. Between September 2001 and March 2003, when the United States invaded Iraq, George W. Bush never, in his public addresses, allowed that there were other ways – right or wrong – of understanding what had transpired on 9/11. He did not expend rhetorical effort on combating alternatives, which would have acknowledged their existence and

---

[96] Coe *et al.* 2004; Hutcheson *et al.* 2004. See also Bligh *et al.* 2004a.
[97] Bostdorff 2003, 293; Kernell 2007, 186. See also Hess and Kalb 2003, 237.
[98] This is consistent with "indexing": see Bennett 1990; Zaller 1992; Zaller and Chiu 1996.
[99] Kohut *et al.* 2004.   [100] Lustick 2006, 15–18, quote at 17.

given them life.[101] To some, this was a sign of Bush's arrogance, his excessive faith in his own moral rectitude. More importantly, it revealed how dominant the Terror narrative was. By the time Bush began in earnest to build the case for war on Iraq, that shared foundation was so firmly established that it could be invoked in truncated form and merely alluded to – as in his fall 2002 speech at the United Nations. When it came to the Terror narrative, the mainstream media were government's "big helpers";[102] they rarely granted that there was any other way of narrating 9/11. On those infrequent occasions when marginalized narratives were acknowledged, they were derided and dismissed, treated as not merely misguided, but illegitimate. Members of the "reactionary left" who would blame in part US foreign policy for the attacks, one columnist wrote in *Newsweek* in October 2001, are simply "out to lunch" and engaged in "mindless moral equivalency," and "don't seem to understand: someone is trying to kill them."[103]

The dominance of a narrative is most clear when even critics adopt it. Advocates of *realpolitik*, such as former National Security Advisor Zbigniew Brzezinski, occasionally dissented from the portrait of terrorists as irrational evil-doers and asserted that they held a political agenda. But Brzezinski nevertheless felt compelled to reassure readers that he did believe terrorism to be morally reprehensible and, yes, even evil.[104] Former Vice President Al Gore, who had been a notable Iraq hawk, parted ways with fellow leading Democrats in aggressively criticizing the march to war with Iraq. Yet, he assailed the administration from the terrain of the dominant narrative: the war, he charged, would "seriously damage" the prosecution of the War on

---

[101] One could cite many speeches to substantiate this claim, but it would become tiresomely repetitive. At most, Bush alluded to "malicious lies and outrageous conspiracy theories concerning the attacks of September the 11th," which he called "the propaganda of terrorists" (President's Radio Address and Address to the United Nations General Assembly, both 10 November 2001). But these were cast as the narratives that *others* – non-Americans, terrorists – promoted, not as alternatives with any serious following among Americans.

[102] Nacos *et al.* 2011, 28–59, at 56.

[103] Jonathan Alter, "Blame America at Your Peril," *Newsweek*, 15 October 2001. See also Richard Lacayo *et al.*, "Antiwar Movement: Rapid Response," *Time*, 8 October 2001; Peter Beinart, "Fault Lines," *The New Republic*, 1 October 2001.

[104] Zbigniew Brzezinski, "Confronting Anti-American Grievances," *New York Times*, 1 September 2002.

Terror.[105] More than five years after 9/11, self-identified progressives continued to follow Gore's lead: insisting that the administration was fighting the War on Terror in the wrong place or the wrong way, that it had wrongly bound an unjust and illegitimate war in Iraq into the just and legitimate War on Terror, they too re-inscribed the defining narrative of the age.[106] This was true also of critics from the libertarian Cato Institute, who framed their traditional stance against US entanglement and intervention abroad within the Terror narrative.[107] The narrative even marked the most marginal of post-9/11 civil society: peace organizations. By rebutting directly the claims of officials, or "counter-framing," they were caught in a rhetorical vise, reproducing the very narrative they wished to challenge.[108] During the race for the 2008 Democratic presidential nomination, as candidates fell over each other in their rush to condemn and distance themselves from the Iraq War, it was clear that their differences with the Bush administration were over means, not ends. James Traub observed, as the campaign heated up: "Six years have passed since the terrorist attacks, but it seems that, psychologically" – I would say that "narratively" is more apt – "we remain inside their fearful penumbra."[109]

The Terror narrative even left its imprint on the line of argument that marked the far edge of legitimate criticism in post-9/11 America: that the declaration of a *War* on Terror had been misguided, that the United States instead needed to brand terrorism a crime, and terrorists criminals, and prosecute them accordingly. These critics, more often scholars and activists than elected politicians, charged that the administration, by framing its post-9/11 policy as a "war," had led the United States to embrace militarized means poorly matched to the threats it faced, mistakenly granted terrorist organizations legitimacy and the dignity of equality, and, by promoting a

---

[105] Gore, Iraq and the War on Terrorism, Commonwealth Club of California (San Francisco, CA), 23 September 2002, available at www.washingtonpost.com/wp-srv/politics/transcripts/gore_text092302.html.

[106] Beinart 2006; Marshall 2006. See also Tony Judt, "Bush's Useful Idiots," *London Review of Books*, 21 September 2006.

[107] See the brief essays from 2002 and 2004 reprinted in Carpenter 2008, esp. 84–90.

[108] For relevant data, see Maney *et al.* 2009, 307–310.

[109] Traub, "Is His Biography Our Destiny?" *New York Times Magazine*, 4 November 2007, 55.

crisis atmosphere, handed its terrorist adversaries a victory.[110] But the 9/11-as-crime model was still consistent with the Terror narrative.[111] It still represented the United States as a blameless victim, though of crime, not war. It left open the possibility that the perpetrators were consumed by evil; most presumed that those responsible for the 9/11 attacks could not be rehabilitated and would be either executed or permanently incarcerated. It did not challenge the portrait of terrorists around the globe as an undifferentiated mass. That it accepted, or could be reconciled with, much of the dominant narrative was central to its appeal.[112] It allowed critics to assail administration policies from the standpoint of the loyal opposition. Whereas Bush did not even bother addressing true alternative narratives, he did explicitly rebut the law-enforcement model, thus signaling that it was a legitimate, if wrong, way to think about the problem.[113] These dueling metaphors shared a common narrative foundation. As a result, when Attorney General Eric Holder in 2009 defended the Obama administration's decision to prosecute in civilian court the so-called 9/11 "mastermind," Khalid Shaikh Mohammed, and four others, he could do so by reaffirming that "we are at war" without seeming contradictory or absurd.[114]

---

[110] See, among others, Ackerman 2006, esp. ch. 1; Fallows 2006; Heymann 2003, ch. 2; Howard 2002; Lustick 2006; Mueller 2006; Pillar 2001, 1–10, 97–110. On the political challenges of framing terrorism as crime, see Winkler 2005, 203–206. By 2006, however, one of the early critics, the military historian Michael Howard, had conceded that, his objections aside, "it will go on being 'war' so far as the media are concerned, and so for the general public as well": see Howard 2006–2007, 9.

[111] For a contrasting interpretation, see Hodges 2011.

[112] This was true too of the alternative slogans periodically trotted out as replacements for the poisoned "War on Terror" – such as "a global struggle against violent extremism" and "a global struggle for security and progress." On these, see Eric Schmitt and Thom Shanker, "Washington Recasts Terror War as 'Struggle,'" *New York Times*, 27 July 2005; Detemri Sevastopulo, "Security Chief Decries 'War on Terror,'" *Financial Times*, 28 May 2008; Mike Nizza, "Thoughts on Tweaking the 'War on Terror' Message," *The Lede (New York Times Blogs)*, 29 May 2008.

[113] See, for instance, Bush, State of the Union Address, 20 January 2004.

[114] Charlie Savage, "Holder Defends Decision to Use U.S. Court for 9/11 Trial," *New York Times*, 19 November 2009.

Alternative narratives and explanations

The Terror narrative's dominance was a product of, in combination, an unsettled narrative situation, the president's narrative authority, and Bush's embrace of a storytelling rhetoric. Were there no other plausible ways of narrating the events of 9/11, this conjuncture could not be said to have mattered. But each of the elements in the pentad could have been represented differently, yielding different narratives.[115] The events of 9/11 did not speak for themselves.

Some representations were, of course, more plausible than others. For instance, with regard to *act*. Perhaps the attacks were directed not against America, but the global capitalist economic system.[116] The World Trade Center was located in the beating heart of the neoliberal empire, and the towers, with their worker bees from around the world, symbolized the borderless global economy. American military might, housed in the Pentagon, had long backed the system. Yet, the very fact that Americans had died in the largest numbers that September morning made the "attack against America" more credible. Moreover, this alternative representation became harder to sustain once Al Qaeda claimed responsibility, as it had not previously been much concerned with the inequities of global capitalism. The attacks might instead, or also, have been represented as a crime against humanity.[117] Constructing a satisfying narrative around this representation of act would have been challenging, however, as it rendered the agents' purposes mystifying. Such a representation is also often the perspective of the outsider: the Shoah and the Rwandan genocide were crimes against humanity in the eyes of the international community, but they were, as far as Jews and Tutsi were concerned, crimes perpetrated against their people.

A different understanding of the agents' *purpose* was more plausible, though it too faced an uphill battle. Perhaps "we" were attacked because of "what we have done" – and what that revealed about "who we are." Of what was the United States accused? Various voices, mostly from the Left,[118] charged the United States with a litany of

---

[115] As in America's closest allies: Britain and Australia. See Holland 2012; McDonald 2010; McDonald and Merefield 2010.

[116] Croft 2006, 113–115.

[117] Thanks to Bud Duvall for discussion on this point.

[118] From the religious Right, Jerry Falwell and Pat Robertson paralleled this rhetoric in blaming September 11 on their fellow Americans' moral corruption, specifically their embrace of a godless life and sexual deviance.

misdeeds. It had financially and politically assisted repressive regimes across the Arab and Muslim world. It had given Israel unquestioned support and implicitly sanctioned the occupation of Palestinian territory. It had, by spreading neoliberal economics, threatened traditional ways of life, generated dependency, and promoted a race to the environmental bottom.[119] In September 11 the United States reaped what it had sowed. The attacks were a wake-up call for Americans to change their ways of acting in the world. According to left-liberal critics, America had betrayed its noble values, and they called for a foreign policy of greater consistency, matching the nation's ideals. Realist critics saw the problem as a too-ideological, over-reaching foreign policy and called for retrenchment and for a focus on the nation's vital strategic interests.[120] Both shared the view that the United States had brought the tragedy upon itself.

Whereas the Terror narrative depoliticized the events of 9/11, this alternative attached the attacks to a substantive, political agenda. The Terror narrative's rhetoric of evil, rooted in the evangelical tradition,[121] placed events within a divine providential play: God, not human beings, made history.[122] When asked whether Osama bin Laden has political goals, Bush replied: "He has got evil goals. And it's hard to think in conventional terms about a man so dominated by evil."[123] But in the alternative narrative, the perpetrators were not evil automatons, but rational actors seeking to draw attention to and claim redress for grievances they traced to America's doorstep. In this tale, Americans' fate lay not with impersonal forces, with foot-soldiers of God or Satan, but partly with themselves and partly with those their nation had harmed.

Such a self-flagellating rhetoric faced psychological hurdles. It called for unflinching self-examination and suggested a dispositional

---

[119] For such arguments, see Barsamian 2001; Scraton 2002; Vanden Heuvel 2002.

[120] Bacevich 2008; Mearsheimer 2002. See also Nicholas Lemann, "The War on What?," *New Yorker*, 16 September 2002; Lemann, "How It Came to War," *New Yorker*, 31 March 2003; Benjamin Schwarz and Christopher Layne, "A New Grand Strategy," *Atlantic Monthly* (January 2002): 36–42; "War With Iraq is Not in America's National Interest," advertisement in *New York Times*, 26 September 2002, A29.

[121] On the centrality of evil in that tradition, see Fuller 1995; McGinn 1994. On religious imagery in Bush's rhetoric, see Domke 2004; Lincoln 2003, 29–32; Singer 2004.

[122] Appleby 2002.   [123] Quoted in Chang and Mehan 2006, 16.

explanation for the self's bad behavior. But we know that people are reluctant to reconsider their interpretive frameworks, except when contradictory evidence is overwhelming. They are partial toward their in-group and intolerant of difference, especially under conditions of threat, when mortality concerns are heightened. People like to think well of themselves, and thus they tend to explain their own less-savory actions situationally and others' dispositionally. National self-flagellation is thus unlikely in the best of times – let alone in the wake of an attack on the homeland.

Yet, this alternative representation of the other's purposes, and its implied criticism of the American self, might have enjoyed some psychological appeal after September 11. Belief change is most likely when discrepant information is strong and salient, when it presents itself en masse, and when the costs of maintaining the existing belief system seem excessive – conditions presumptively met by that day's events. Moreover, the "what we have done" account did not call for a radical rethinking of American identity, but for greater adherence to traditional values and interests; it demanded policy change, but did not challenge foundational identity narratives. Finally, there was no necessary contradiction between this alternative representation of the other's purpose and the dominant one. The national narrative might have recognized both that the extremists who had launched the 9/11 attacks were evil and that US misdeeds had fertilized the societal soil from which extremism sprang. Although the Bush administration was always at pains to distinguish between the mass of peaceful Muslims and the minority of violent Islamofascists, it denied legitimacy to ordinary Muslims' frustration by refusing to acknowledge America's past and present transgressions – which may be why Muslims around the world saw the War on Terror as a War on Islam.[124] Such a synthesis was very much available. It should also sound familiar from this chapter's first case study: many Americans claimed before and during the Second World War that the vengeful peace of Versailles, to which the United States had been (a reluctant) party, had rendered ordinary Germans easy prey for the Nazis. Even in times of elevated threat, there can be empathy for others and criticism of the self.

---

[124] Public unofficial discourse framing the War on Terror in terms of the crusades may have contributed as well: see Angstrom 2011, 231–233. For relevant polls, see Kull 2007, 5–6. Also relevant are findings from Esposito and Mogahed 2010, ch. 5.

Moreover, national self-criticism has hardly been unknown, on either the left or the right. In an intriguing study, William Callahan observes that, from the seventeenth century onward, deserved national humiliation has been an important strain in foreign policy debate: current challenges are traced to internal failings more than the perfidy of foreigners, and triumph over present adversity hinges on self-reflection and repentance.[125] In the interwar period, many British politicians, and occasionally their French counterparts, empathized with German moves to jettison Versailles and blamed themselves for Hitler's rise and Germany's assertiveness.[126] A self-flagellating narrative was prominent in Israel during the 1990s, as research by so-called "new historians" suggested that Israel's own leaders, some short-sighted and some rapacious, had missed opportunities to reach a *modus vivendi* with its Arab neighbors, to integrate the nation's Arab citizens, and to resolve the festering Palestinian problem.[127] Even hawks in the United States have sometimes argued that the challenges confronting the nation have been in part of America's own design – from the strategy document, NSC 68, whose logic underpinned the militarization of the Cold War, to Ronald Reagan and the New Right in the 1970s, to neoconservatives' calls for "a foreign policy of greatness" in the 1990s. All argued, in their jeremiads, that the United States had lost its way in foreign affairs, due to its failure to act with sufficient vigor.[128]

Most plausible of all were alternative representations of *agent*, *agency*, and *scene*. Regarding *agent* and *agency*, rather than all

---

[125] Callahan 2006.

[126] Adamthwaite 1977, 80, 109, 301; Adamthwaite 1995, 187–188; Gilbert 1966, 22–31, 56–67, 138–150; Jacobson 1972, 15 and passim.

[127] Arguments over the nation's founding, once restricted to scholars and intellectuals, burst onto the public scene in the mid 1990s. A television series celebrating the fiftieth anniversary of Israel's birth became a particular flashpoint. Many believed the series had given too much credence to the Palestinian narrative, and the host – a famous singer – resigned rather than be associated with an especially divisive episode. For a summary, see Silberstein 1999, 113–122 on the public controversy, and, from the Right, Hazony 2000, esp. 3–80.

[128] "NSC 68: United States Objectives and Programs for National Security," 14 April 1950, in Etzold and Gaddis 1978; Aune 2001, 123–126; Kristol and Kagan 1996. On jeremiads, both nostalgic and progressive, in contemporary American politics, see also Murphy 2009. On Reagan and the secular jeremiad, see Erickson 1985, 88–94; Ritter and Henry 1992, 35–60.

terrorists as purveyors of fear, a plausible alternative might have focused more narrowly on Al Qaeda alone. The evening of 9/11, before Bush addressed the nation, a Gallup poll found overwhelming support for military strikes against those "terrorist organizations responsible for today's attacks, even if it takes months to clearly identify them," rather than all "known terrorist organizations, even if it is unclear who caused today's attacks." Regarding *scene*, it is hard to imagine any US leader not giving transnational terrorism a higher profile after 9/11, but it was hardly necessary to treat terrorism as the defining feature of the new world disorder. Americans were, on the night of the attacks, evenly divided as to whether that day's events would lead them to change permanently how they lived their lives.[129] If terrorism was a greater problem than previously thought, but a manageable one for a great power, then 9/11 was not a moment in which everything changed. It had revealed the sophistication of Al Qaeda's operation. It had shown that globalization had a dark side. But it did not hasten or impede larger structural dynamics, notably the rise of China. It was on these dimensions that President Barack Obama eventually parted ways with the Terror narrative – narrowing US counterterrorist efforts to Al Qaeda and its affiliates and relegating terrorism to one among many challenges.[130]

There were then multiple ways in which one might have made sense of what transpired on September 11, 2001. The Terror narrative's rise was contingent, insofar as it rested on choices. But, once those choices were made, its triumph followed from the conjuncture of narrative situation, institutional authority, and rhetorical mode. Alternative explanations fall short. One cannot ascribe the Terror narrative's dominance to the "reality" of 9/11. Those supposedly most attuned to the realities of global politics – self-declared realists – interpreted the attacks as a response to hegemonic over-reach, saw terrorism as a serious but decidedly secondary concern, and preferred a narrowly circumscribed war on terror.[131] One cannot attribute the Terror narrative to the "terror industry" that stood to profit from mass anxiety,[132] for it gained prominence and its appeals held sway only after the narrative took hold. One cannot explain the Terror narrative's

---

[129] Hoenicke-Moore 2001. See also Saad 2001.
[130] For more extensive discussion, see Krebs 2013. See also King and Wells 2009.
[131] See Lemann, "The War on What?"; Mearsheimer 2002.
[132] On the Terror industry's rise and later influence, see Mueller 2006.

dominance by referencing the psychology of fear. Not only were there other psychologically plausible ways of narrating 9/11, but there was no reason that residents of Dubuque should feel afraid after attacks in New York and Washington – yet they did, because of the dominant Terror narrative.[133] Finally, one cannot credit the Terror narrative with greater rhetorical authenticity. The "what we have done" alternative was a jeremiad, a rhetorical form whose roots stretched back to colonial New England and whose secular variant had been invoked countless times over the centuries. Its always ongoing war between good and *internal* evil drew on evangelical eschatology and exceptionalism – long central to American discourse.[134] It was no less familiar rhetorically than the "prophetic dualist" tradition in foreign affairs, which represents global politics as an always ongoing war between good and *external* evil and from which the Terror narrative drew.[135]

Terror's impact: rhetorical coercion and the Iraq War

The Terror narrative did not make war with Iraq inevitable. Officials, activists, and pundits still had to forge links between that narrative and the long-festering conflict with Iraq. That is why much commentary has focused on the motives of key figures – on a neoconservative cabal and its dreams of falling autocratic dominoes, on George W. Bush and Dick Cheney's ties to the oil industry, on the sense of unfinished business that gnawed at veterans of the first Bush administration. That is why contrarians have asked whether a Gore administration would really have behaved differently.[136] The Terror narrative's dominance made it possible for hawks, inside and outside the administration, neoconservatives and liberals, to carry the nation to war. By narrowing the space for debate, it hindered a potential Democratic opposition, and it led many leading Democrats to hold their tongues: they became the victims of

---

[133] See, more generally, Mueller 2006, 1–28; Mueller and Stewart 2012, 83–95.

[134] On the jeremiad, see Bercovitch 1978; Carpenter 1978; Howard-Pitney 2005; Murphy 1990, 2009.

[135] On this tradition, see Wander 1984. See also Brands 1999; Campbell 1998, ch. 6; McDougall 1997.

[136] Harvey 2012, chs. 2–3 and passim.

rhetorical coercion.[137] Had the Terror narrative not constituted the foundation for post-9/11 national security debate, the Bush administration's war plans might well have run into far more formidable political obstacles.

The Bush administration's renewed emphasis on the promotion of freedom and democracy around the globe was neither novel nor controversial. There was little new in its affirmation of "freedom, democracy, and free enterprise" as the "single sustainable model for national success" and "the non-negotiable ... birthright of every person." These themes, and the absolute confidence in their rectitude, had long been central to the legitimation of US foreign policy. Nor were officials innovative in presuming that democracy held universal appeal and in justifying its promotion on normative, rather than material and strategic, grounds: "because these principles are right and true for all people everywhere."[138] Yet, how democracy was best promoted abroad – through the power of America's example or through the exercise of America's power – remained at issue.[139] And why, in a world of many autocracies, the United States should promote democracy in any particular location was always contestable.

What was novel was how Bush and other officials articulated, or linked, this traditional democracy promotion agenda to the War on Terror. In the dominant narrative, terrorists were represented not just as evil, but as a particular kind of evil: figures of repression and intolerance, of interwar fascism and Cold War totalitarianism in Islamist garb. Within days of the attacks, Bush contrasted the freedom that Americans prized with the despotism that her enemies represented, and he regularly returned to this theme. As he put it at West Point in June 2002, "our enemies are totalitarians, holding a creed of power with no place for human dignity. Now, as [during the Cold War], they seek to

---

[137] Harvey's meticulously researched evaluation of the Gore counterfactual regarding the Iraq War is less persuasive on whether Gore would have narrated 9/11 in the same way Bush did. See Harvey 2012, 185–187.

[138] Bush 2002, iv–vi; Bush, Graduation Speech at West Point, 1 June 2002. Generally, on the lack of novelty in the Bush administration's 2002 *National Security Strategy*, see Gaddis 2004; Hoff 2007; Leffler 2004, 22–24; McCartney 2004. See also David M. Kennedy, "What 'W' Owes to 'WW,'" *Atlantic Monthly* (March 2005): 36–40.

[139] On these debates over the sweep of American history, see Monten 2005; Tucker and Hendrickson 1992.

impose a joyless conformity, to control every life and all of life."[140] All terrorists, because they sow fear, were democracy's sworn enemies: "freedom and fear are at war."[141] Bush made the opposition of freedom and fear seem natural, but there was nothing natural about it. It required displacing a more natural opposite of freedom – slavery – and it required overlooking that democracies had frequently brutalized civilian populations in armed conflict. By positioning terrorism in the same realm as totalitarianism, Bush associated current threats with those recalled in the nation's collective memory as existential, linked the War on Terror to the unmitigated triumphs of the Second World War and the Cold War, and insinuated that critics were practitioners of appeasement.

Building a democratic Iraq did not lie at the core of the campaign legitimating the war, which focused instead on Iraq's continued quest for weapons of mass destruction (WMD).[142] But the association between terrorism and autocracy lurked in the background. It helped to explain why the prospect of a nuclear-armed Iraq was so dangerous and why the solution lay in regime change: Hussein's repressive rule served as prima facie evidence that Iraq was inclined to terrorism, that non-state terrorists were its natural allies, and that Iraq would likely share WMD with its terrorist friends. Even when officials focused on Iraq's WMD programs as the basis for war, they pointedly referred to Hussein as "the dictator" or "the tyrant" – labels that did substantial rhetorical work even though they served no logical or argumentative purpose. They highlighted Hussein's murder of Iraqi citizens, which had no necessary bearing on his responsiveness to deterrent threats or his rationality, but which spoke to his lack of respect for the rule of law and which implied that he, like the 9/11 terrorists, did not hold human life sacred. Per the Terror narrative, state terror cast Hussein in league with transnational terrorists who also purveyed fear.

---

[140] Bush, Graduation Speech at West Point.
[141] Bush, Address Before a Joint Session of Congress, 20 September 2001; Bush 2002, 7. On this score, the administration's rhetoric was remarkably consistent: see Bush 2006.
[142] It became a major feature of the war's post-facto legitimation, as evidence of Iraqi WMD programs failed to surface. But it featured centrally in only one of Bush's major addresses before the war. See Bush, Remarks to the American Enterprise Institute Annual Dinner, 26 February 2003.

Other elements in the administration's rhetoric also centered on creating durable bonds between Saddam Hussein, the Iraqi regime, and the War on Terror. Including Iraq as a charter member of the "axis of evil" suggested that the regime was on the same moral plane as Al Qaeda. Maintaining that the Iraqi regime had "something to hide from the civilized world" placed it in the realm of barbarism, where Al Qaeda resided. Asserting Hussein's hatred of the United States and its values hinted that he and Islamist terrorists had a common agenda. Continuously focusing on Hussein, rather than the nation of Iraq or its government, suggested a further parallel with Osama bin Laden; their organizations reflected their leaders' political programs and personal pathologies, in contrast to democracies in which law, not whim, ruled.[143] It is well known that the administration and its civil-society allies hinted, and sometimes outright charged, that the Hussein regime had operational links to Al Qaeda and was partly responsible for the 9/11 attacks.[144] These blunt tactics shaped mass opinion, but mostly among Republican partisans already inclined to war, and they never acquired the status of common sense.[145] But more subtle rhetorical deployments, capitalizing on the nation's post-9/11 narrative, were crucial in making Iraq into the "central front" of the War on Terror. If war was to be waged on terror, then war was also to be waged on Saddam Hussein's Iraq.[146]

These linkages were sustainable, and went largely uncontested, because of the enduring ways in which Saddam Hussein and Iraq had long been represented in US political discourse. First, as early as October 1990, President George H. W. Bush suggested that Hussein was "Hitler revisited," that the invasion of Kuwait was akin to

[143] This reconstruction of the administration's rhetoric draws on an extensive survey of the rhetoric of the president and leading administration figures. The particular quotes come from Bush, Address before a Joint Session of the Congress on the State of the Union, 29 January 2002. Also particularly useful are Bush, Address before a Joint Session of the Congress on the State of the Union, 28 January 2003, and Address to the Nation on Iraq, 17 March 2003; and Paul Wolfowitz, "On Iraq," 16 October 2002, available at www.defense.gov/speeches/speech.aspx?speechid=295.

[144] Freedman 2004; Kaufmann 2004.

[145] Harvey 2012, 147–151. Harvey focuses on whether Democrats echoed (or countered) that Iraq was involved in the 9/11 attacks, but this misses the point. As he also shows, they did not challenge the more fundamental claim that Iraq was central to the War on Terror.

[146] For a complementary analysis, see Hodges 2011, 64–83.

Hitler's invasion of Poland, and that the consequences of failing to resist Hussein's aggression would parallel those that followed appeasement at Munich.[147] Rhetoric equating Hussein with Hitler and Baathist Iraq with Nazi Germany did not taper off much during the 1990s.[148] Hussein's credentials as a figure of imposing evil were thus well established by the time George W. Bush included his regime in the "axis of evil." Opponents might have countered that he was a pathetic tyrant who lacked Hitler's competence or resources, but this flew in the face of over a decade of assertions to the contrary. Second, the Clinton administration repeatedly justified the containment of Iraq in terms of the regime's terrorism.[149] US newspapers speculated that Iraq had a hand in the 1993 World Trade Center bombing, and Iraq was blamed for other terrorist activity.[150] The image of Saddam Hussein as a terrorist had deep roots. Finally, over the course of the 1990s, a consensus had emerged that not only defined Saddam Hussein as a problem of the first order, but that identified his overthrow as the solution. The 1998 Iraq Liberation Act established regime change as official US policy, albeit with paltry financial support and the president's half-hearted commitment. In 2000, both parties' platforms called for Hussein's ouster, and both Bush and Gore pledged to work to that end.[151]

---

[147] See, among many others, George H. W. Bush, Remarks, Fundraising Luncheon for Gubernatorial Candidate Clayton Williams (Dallas, TX), 15 October 1990; Remarks, Republican Fundraising Breakfast (Burlington, VT), 23 October 1990; Remarks, Republican Party Fundraising Breakfast (Burlington, MA), 1 November 1990; and Remarks, Republican Campaign Rally (Albuquerque, NM), 3 November 1990.

[148] James Bennet, "Clinton Sets Out to Revive Support for Stand on Iraq," *New York Times*, 20 February 1998; Patrick O'Driscoll, "Administration Sticking to its Hard Line," *USA Today*, 20 February 1998.

[149] See, among others, Clinton, Address to the Nation on the Strike on Iraqi Intelligence Headquarters, 26 June 1993, and Remarks Announcing a Missile Strike on Iraq and an Exchange with Reporters, 3 September 1996.

[150] See William J. Broad and Judith Miller, "Germ Defense Plan in Peril as Its Flaws are Revealed," *New York Times*, 7 August 1998; Steven Erlanger, "Republicans Back Clinton on the Use of Force on Iraqis," *New York Times*, 27 January 1998; Charles M. Sennott, "Terrorism Specialists See Links to Iraq in Trade Center Bombing," *Boston Globe*, 17 January 1995; Sennott, "Blast Probers Say Trail Leading to Iraq," *Boston Globe*, 10 February 1995; Tim Weiner, "Attack Is Aimed at the Heart of Iraq's Spy Network," *New York Times*, 27 June 1993.

[151] Burgos 2008; Pollack 2002.

Open dissension from Democrats, especially party leaders, was rare as war neared in 2003, partly because they lacked an effective means of legitimating their opposition. Nearly all top Democrats, especially the front-runners for the presidential nomination, supported the war, even if some took issue with the details.[152] At the leadership level, there was "broad bipartisan support for ousting" Hussein by "a military invasion if other options fail": by summer 2002, the question of his removal was, even among Democrats, not if, but when and how.[153] Less prominent Democratic politicians and activists were less bound by these narrative constraints, and a "rift" reportedly emerged between the leadership and the rank-and-file. Party leaders made it "very hard," according to Senator Dianne Feinstein, for lower-ranking Democrats to speak out, and opponents of the war were placed "on the defensive."[154] As Nicholas Lemann observed, congressional Democrats had been forced into "cowed silence." They were neither doves nor hawks, but lambs, Tom Ricks quipped later. Center-left media outlets had similarly fallen prey to "a fearful conformism" as they "align[ed] their editorial stance with that of a Republican president bent on exemplary war."[155] As one Democratic foreign policymaker lamented, "Democrats have fallen into a 'soft neoconservatism' that has dulled the party's voice on foreign policy." "Liberalism in the United States today," Tony Judt charged, "is the politics that dare not speak its name."[156] The Terror narrative, in combination with the existing portrait of Saddam Hussein, deprived leading Democrats of sustainable alternatives upon which they might have relied to oppose the administration. They were left to raise questions about only the timing and circumstances of an invasion. No wonder that the

---

[152] Hess 2006, 106–111; Western 2005.

[153] James Dao, "Call in Congress for Full Airing of Iraq Policy," *New York Times*, 18 July 2002. See also Harvey 2012, 135–136.

[154] Jim VandeHei, "Louder War Talk, and Muffled Dissent: Party Leaders Make Opposition Difficult, Wary Democrats Say," *Washington Post*, 25 September 2002; James Traub, "The Things They Carry," *New York Times Magazine*, 4 January 2004; Jim VandeHei, "GOP Nominees Make Iraq a Political Weapon," *Washington Post*, 18 September 2002.

[155] Lemann, "How It Came to War"; Ricks 2006, 85, and generally 86–90; Judt, "Bush's Useful Idiots."

[156] Flynt Leverett, "Illusion and Reality," *American Prospect*, 12 September 2006; Judt, "Bush's Useful Idiots."

mainstream media followed suit and gave little coverage to domestic war opponents.[157]

What were the alternatives? First, Democrats might have argued that the status quo was tolerable, that containment remained an adequate response to an Iraq that had been weakened by a decade of sanctions – and indeed a small number did.[158] But if transnational terrorism was an evil that could not be tolerated – as Democrats had agreed by signing on to the War on Terror – and if Saddam Hussein was a terrorist – as Democrats had long argued – then there was little reason not to apply the same to Iraq. Second, Democrats might have argued that the costs of a war would be prohibitive and that the United States had higher priorities.[159] Not only, however, did the administration insist that the costs of invasion and reconstruction would be low,[160] but the embedding of the Iraq War within the War on Terror put critics in the uncomfortable position of having to argue that they would sacrifice national security for the sake of a few dollars. Third, perhaps Democrats could have adopted earlier what would become later their chief line of attack: that the Iraq War was a distraction from the War on Terror, against Al Qaeda and the Taliban. This was the view of Al Gore.[161] But attempts to insert space between Iraq and the War on Terror in fall 2002 failed to comprehend how firmly the two were linked. The media not only cast Gore as an exception among Democrats, but as inconsistent and thus not credible – since he, a

[157] Although, interestingly, there was substantial coverage of foreign critics: see Hayes and Guardino 2010. On the media and the Iraq War, see, among others, Bennett *et al.* 2007; Massing 2004; Nacos *et al.* 2011, 98–112. For a synthetic review, see Holsti 2011, 133–137.

[158] The most prominent among these opponents – Senators Robert Byrd, Carl Levin, and Ted Kennedy – are the exceptions that prove the rule: old lions of the party, they could speak freely because they held secure seats and no longer harbored aspirations for national office.

[159] See "Senate to Debate Iraq Resolution; Key Democrats Have Doubts, But Measure on Track for Passage," *Washington Post*, 4 October 2002; also Mark Dayton, "Go Slow on Iraq," *Washington Post*, 28 September 2002.

[160] Although there was much evidence that these projections were overly rosy. For a useful summary of contrary predictions regarding the war's likely costs, see Holsti 2011, 48–52.

[161] Gore, Iraq and the War on Terrorism, Commonwealth Club of California (San Francisco, CA), 23 September 2002, available at www.washingtonpost.com/wp-srv/politics/transcripts/gore_text092302.html. See, similarly, Senator Bob Graham, in David Johnston and Eric Lichtblau, "Little Headway in Terror War, Democrats Say," *New York Times*, 15 November 2002.

long-time Iraq hawk, had said just months before (in February) that the War on Terror would not be complete without a "final reckoning" with Saddam Hussein.[162]

In the post–9/11 rhetorical space, Democrats who might have vigorously opposed the invasion of Iraq held their tongues. Deprived of winning arguments, of socially sustainable avenues of reply, they fell prey to rhetorical coercion: they either jumped on the administration's war bandwagon or offered a more modest critique. They could, and did, argue that violating Iraq's national sovereignty required the imprimatur of the international community. This view in fact carried weight with the public: just a month before the invasion, a clear majority of Americans opposed going to war without United Nations sanction.[163] But this already conceded the administration's most fundamental points. Nor was it particularly constraining, as the administration co-opted selective multilateralism by recasting the issue: would the United Nations uphold its own commitment to shut down Iraqi WMD programs?[164] The administration correctly predicted that Americans' objections to unilateral action would fall away once the war began and that their long-term view would be shaped more by the success and/or the cost of the operation, not the lack of UN approval.

The consolidation of the Terror narrative heavily stacked the decks in favor of war with Iraq. With the Bush administration leading the charge, Democrats found their room for rhetorical maneuver severely constrained, and those with national political aspirations largely supported the war, to their later regret when the war proved a disaster.[165] A common alternative explanation is that Democrats went along with the Iraq War because they did not wish to be accused of being soft on national security – long an area of political vulnerability for the party. Many had opposed the first Gulf War a decade

---

[162] Dan Balz, "Gore: Bush's Iraq War Threatens Terror Battle," *Washington Post*, 24 September 2002.

[163] Holsti 2011, 36–38; Kull *et al.* 2003–04, 569–570.

[164] Western 2005, 201–206.

[165] Accounts of the Iraq War often emphasize the pre-war manipulation of intelligence, the quiescence of the media, the psychological impact of the 9/11 attacks, and the embrace of neoconservative foreign policy ideas. None of these speaks to the relative absence of political opposition or explores the mechanisms through which the opposition was silenced. I discuss these alternative accounts in greater detail in Krebs and Lobasz 2007.

before, and they had been left holding the political short end of the stick when the US-led coalition won an overwhelming victory.[166] Democrats' anxiety was real, but misguided, as the public's memory after the first Gulf War proved very short: most Americans could not recall Democrats' stance on the war just five months later,[167] few Democrats suffered at the polls, and George H. W. Bush's triumph on the Gulf battlefield did not pay off on the political battlefield, as he lost the presidency to Bill Clinton the following year. But Democrats' much-documented fear of seeming soft is more a complementary than competing explanation for their relative silence during the lead up to the Iraq War. Long at a disadvantage on national security, on which the public trusted Republicans more, Democrats had nevertheless not always rolled over. Why did leading Democrats so fear seeming soft in this particular case, and why did that fear seem to point only toward their quiescence? After all, they could have even displayed toughness by calling for a greater commitment to the war against Al Qaeda, as they would later. The answer was 9/11 – not the unmediated fact of the attacks, but how they had come to be narrated. As Tom Daschle, then Democratic Senate majority leader, recalled: "We had just experienced 9/11. Bush was telling me that Iraq had WMD and we had to move … The country expected us to work together. We [Americans] felt threatened."[168] Democrats fell into line out of political fear, but that fear reflected the dominance of the Terror narrative, the Bush administration's effective linking of political repression to terrorism, and the rhetorical hurdles that Democrats confronted.

September 11, 2001 was a tragic day. But tragedy is a genre, capable of supporting numerous narratives. From the array of conceivable narratives, one emerged as dominant. According to the Terror narrative, the attacks of 9/11 were directed against an innocent America, perpetrated by agents of terror, who were motivated by a hateful ideology that perverted Islam and valorized oppression; they marked the dawn of a new world in which transnational terrorism was the overriding threat to US national security. It was not the only plausible way to make sense of those events, but the importance of its triumph

---

[166] Jim VandeHei and Juliet Eilperin, "9/11 Changed Equation for Democrats; 1991's Doves Now Back War," *Washington Post*, 6 October 2002; Isikoff and Corn 2006, 127–128, 137–138; Ricks 2006, 62.
[167] Zaller 1994, 269.   [168] Quoted in Isikoff and Corn 2006, 151.

cannot be overstated. The Terror narrative's dominance for nearly a decade legitimated the extension at home of unchecked executive power, made possible the 2003 Iraq War, and precluded searching examination of US engagement with the Middle East. 9/11 did change everything. It just didn't have to.

Pearl Harbor. 9/11. The meaning of these pivotal episodes, their very standing as pivotal, seems obvious to us in retrospect. But if their meaning seems obvious, that is a sign of the success of the narrative project that has imparted meaning to them. As this chapter has shown, the narratives that became dominant in their wake did not reflect the objective meaning of these events, nor can their triumph be attributed solely to powerful ideologues or the bully pulpit. These particular narratives were also not required by human psychology. They were rather the product of an authoritative speaker (the president) speaking in the right way (the storytelling mode) at the right time (a long unsettled narrative situation transformed into a narrative crisis). But narrative dominance is always fleeting. Some narratives are more enduring. Some are more flexible, in making sense of a changing world. Some are more resilient to periodic challenges. But all eventually collapse, giving way to an era of greater narrative contestation, in which the shape of the world is less certain. Part II explores the second half of the narrative lifecycle.

Narrative at war: politics and rhetorical strategy in the military crucible, from Korea to Iraq

5 | *The narrative politics of the battlefield*

The Terror narrative served as the organizing axis of US debate on national security for a decade. One might have expected it to have met its end in the sands of Iraq. The Bush administration had sold the Iraq War by binding it tightly into the War on Terror, and setbacks in Iraq might have reflected poorly on, and perhaps even delegitimized, the Terror narrative. This outcome would have been consistent with the theoretical conventional wisdom. Because inertia is a powerful force in policy and in the institutions, discourses, and ideas that underlie it, we tend to think that only large-scale shocks produce change. Significant unexpected failures, as in Iraq, unsettle settled minds and discredit dominant ideas. In their absence, and certainly in the wake of success, change in policy, let alone in more foundational ideas and narratives, is highly unlikely.[1]

The conventional wisdom is intuitive, and it would seem to be backed by the historical record. Notably, it appears to fit the Cold War consensus. Broad agreement on ideology and policy supposedly so took hold in the United States by late 1947 or 1948 that alternatives to militarized global containment could not get a hearing. Pre-eminent for two decades, the consensus was blamed for numerous errors and tragedies of US policy – from military brinkmanship to imprudent intervention, most notably in Vietnam, to alliance with rapacious autocrats and brutal rebels to an inflated defense budget. According to the standard history, it finally unraveled only amidst the trauma of the Vietnam War: Americans lost faith in the Cold War as its military floundered in the jungles of Southeast Asia.[2]

---

[1] This logic informs accounts in many policy domains, as I discuss further below. For general discussions, see Capoccia and Kelemen 2007; Pierson 2004.

[2] This presentation of the standard view of the Cold War consensus draws on, among others, Allison 1970–1971; Gelb and Betts 1979, ch. 6; Halperin *et al.* 1974, 11–12; Hoffmann 1978, ch. 1; Hogan 1998, 10–17.

The Terror narrative took a seemingly different course: it survived public frustration with the failures of Iraq.[3] The usual theory supplies an explanation: those failures were not clear or great enough to shake the war's narrative foundation. However, this explanation does not specify a priori how substantial failure must be to drive change. Equally important, it presumes that events speak for themselves, that the fact, magnitude, and sources of failure are clear to all. Part II builds on Part I's account of the rise of dominant narratives of national security to advance a provocative theory of when they endure and when they fall. That theory starts from two premises: that events' purported lessons are the product of interpretation by political actors; and that the critical junctures in which narratives are reconfigured are not productively theorized as responses to exogenous shock.[4] From that more deeply political foundation, I argue that failure and success have effects quite the opposite from the expectations of existing theory. Rather than propelling change in the dominant narrative, the politics of protracted military failure impede it. Rather than necessarily reinforcing that narrative, victory on the battlefield and in high-stakes coercive diplomacy creates an opportunity for departure from it and for the erosion of its dominance. This theory suggests that the Terror narrative persisted not despite the US military's setbacks in Iraq, but because of them – or rather because of the politics surrounding them.

Dominant narratives of national security endure as long as leading political and cultural elites continue to reproduce them, and their dominance breaks down when elites publicly challenge key tenets. Presidents, we saw in Part I, have marked advantages as storytellers-in-chief in times of narrative disorder and crisis. Chapter 2 suggested

---

[3] Perceptions of the Iraq War have fluctuated over time, mediated by party identity. However, there is no question that the United States experienced unexpected battlefield setbacks after March 2003 and that the entrenched insurgency and civil war soured many Americans on the war. By early 2005, Americans were about evenly divided as to whether the decision to use force in Iraq had been right, and by mid 2006, a majority thought it had been a mistake. That remained the majority's judgment for five years, until mid 2011. See "More Now See Failure than Success in Iraq, Afghanistan," Pew Research Center for People and the Press, 30 January 2014, available at www.people-press.org/2014/01/30/more-now-see-failure-than-success-in-iraq-afghanistan/.

[4] See, similarly, Bially Mattern 2005, 56–60; Legro 2005, 28–35; Widmaier *et al.* 2007.

that two factors could detract from their capacity to fix the narrative foundation: first, diplomatic and military triumph, which would ease public demand for narrative order, and, second, the erosion of their credibility, due either to missteps or deception. The first suggests that there is an irony to victory: it can open new narrative possibilities, yet also impede new narratives from achieving dominance. The second draws attention to the choices of the political opposition: when do its members seize the opportunity to undermine the dominant narrative and broaden the contours of debate, and when do they criticize policy while remaining faithful to, and reproducing, that narrative?

Part II builds on these caveats to answer that question. The prevailing view – that substantial military failure serves as the impetus to fundamental change in the narrative in whose terms officials had legitimated the mission – makes sense when failure is extreme or sudden, when wars are short and defeat overwhelming. But the collective perception of military failure normally coalesces only after a series of battlefield setbacks. Early in an uncertain and protracted campaign, these setbacks give both doves (war opponents) and hawks (war supporters) in the political opposition incentives to criticize the war's conduct while reaffirming the underlying narrative. Opposition doves pull their rhetorical punches to avoid bearing the political costs of deep wartime criticism, while opposition hawks are moved by the prospect of gain, but the effect is the same. In contrast, success creates an opening for its "owners" to advance an alternative: riding a political high, they can argue that, as a result of their wise policies, the world has changed, that a different narrative is now more apposite. In short, when it comes to public narratives of national security, the conventional wisdom has it backwards.

To assess this argument's plausibility, Part II reconsiders the Cold War consensus. Although the consensus is a mainstay of Cold War history, scholars have not studied it rigorously. I do so by conceptualizing the Cold War consensus as a dominant public narrative of national security and by tracking that narrative via a content analysis of foreign affairs editorials, whose methods and findings are discussed in detail in Chapter 6. Conventional theory accords with the usual view that the consensus persisted until the Vietnam War and then collapsed amidst that harrowing conflict. It fits less comfortably, however, with the content analysis' findings, which show that the zone of narrative agreement was at first narrow; that this narrow Cold War narrative did not

achieve dominance – that is, the consensus did not coalesce – until well
into the 1950s, amidst the bloody Korean stalemate; that it fell from its
dominant perch even before the Americanization of the Vietnam War
in 1965; that no new consensus regarding the leading actors, their
purposes, and the nature of their relationship in the global drama
took its place in the 1960s; and that, when a new consensus emerged
in the early 1970s, it revolved initially around the American self, not the
Communist other. The Cold War narrative's rise to dominance and its
subsequent fall were not tightly tied to unexpected shocks. Nor can the
changing realities of global politics explain the pattern: the narrative
was most dominant precisely when the Communist bloc was becoming
more diverse, and a new dominant narrative did not swiftly succeed the
old one.

This theory's expectations and mechanisms – rooted in the conjuncture of the dynamics of public narrative and the domestic politics of the
battlefield – make better sense of both the quantitative content analysis
in Chapter 6 and the qualitative evidence presented in Chapter 7.
I show in the latter chapter that the disheartening Korean War facilitated the Cold War narrative's rise to dominance, that the triumph of
the Cuban Missile Crisis made possible that narrative's breakdown
before the upheaval of Vietnam, that the US military's difficulties in
Vietnam limited how far the responsible opposition would dissent from
Cold War tenets, and, finally, that the domestic upheaval of Vietnam
laid the foundation for a new zone of consensus.

First, the high costs of the Korean War might have undermined the
Cold War globalism in whose name the United States had gone to war.
But leading Republicans, who had resisted the axiom that the world
was so tightly interconnected that global security was indivisible, now
insisted that the war had resulted from the fact that the Truman
administration's battle against Communism had not been global
enough. They thus helped shunt aside the nationalist alternative they
held dear and consolidate the global Cold War that they had long
feared would yield an imperial presidency and an imposing national-
security state.

Second, the Cuban Missile Crisis, seen at the time as a one-sided
triumph for President John F. Kennedy, should have bolstered the
dominant Cold War narrative, according to conventional theory.
Indeed, Republican hawks took the crisis and its resolution as proof
of that narrative's core propositions. Yet, the missile crisis surprisingly

led to greater pluralism in US national security debate. Kennedy had long privately articulated a sophisticated view of Soviet ambitions, Communist diversity, and the superpowers' shared interests, but had hewed in public to the Cold War narrative. Victory in the missile crisis allowed him, and fellow liberal internationalists, to deviate publicly from that narrative and to lay the foundation for détente.

Finally, rather than explode the dominant Cold War narrative, US setbacks in Vietnam had the opposite effect. On the one hand, battlefield disappointments in that protracted war curbed the depth of the liberals' challenge: respectable doves normally criticized the war in Southeast Asia while reaffirming the basic logic of the Cold War. On the other hand, and even more surprising, the war helped to promote a new consensus around America's role in the world – that is, a new dominant narrative of national security. In the wake of Vietnam, elites across the spectrum joined in defense of American exceptionalism and internationalism. The transformation was most striking on the right: radical challenges kindled the fire of a renewed nationalism that seized the Republican Party and sustained the rise of Ronald Reagan.

The rest of Part II proceeds as follows. This introductory chapter continues with a critical overview of the theoretical conventional wisdom on change in dominant ideas and discourses. It then advances an alternative theory of military conflict and the dynamics of narrative. Chapter 6 reconceptualizes the Cold War consensus as a public narrative and proposes a method for measuring its ebbs and flows. The chapter then presents the content analysis findings, explains why they are so puzzling, and shows how they fit better with my theoretical framework. Chapter 7 shows how this theory accounts for the emergence, erosion, and re-emergence of a dominant narrative of national security in the United States in the three decades following the Second World War. Concluding Part II, Chapter 8 explores the theory's generalizability and its implications for key questions of the Cold War. The chapter then returns to the politics of the War on Terror to show that, well beyond the end of the Cold War, even substantial military failures have not prompted a narrative revolution in national security affairs.

National security narratives and theories of change

Fundamental change in national security policy – in its goals and basic orientation, as opposed to the effort expended or the means employed[5] – hinges on change in narrative. Existing literature and folk wisdom rightly suggest that even authoritative speakers' capacity to remake public common sense is limited. A well-known claim, associated with historical institutionalism, attributes change to large-scale policy failure. By this account, powerful psychological, institutional, and social mechanisms mutually reinforce stasis with regard to national security and other policy domains. Only during "critical junctures" can agents make meaningful choices that set a new course.[6] As William Sewell puts it, "lumpiness . . . is the normal texture of historical temporality."[7] To explain how such critical junctures, as moments of structural slack, arise, scholars commonly invoke exogenous shocks that puncture stable equilibria.[8] Thus, David Welch argues that major foreign policy change is undertaken only as a last resort – when the status quo has become too painful and when policy has failed repeatedly or catastrophically.[9] In the national security arena, this normally takes the form of substantial battlefield defeat. Since the latter half of the nineteenth century, when wars became "total" contests between polities, war has been seen as a crucible of the national mettle, in which national identity and the narratives that constitute it are put to the test and are discarded if found wanting.[10]

Scholarship on the life-course of dominant policy ideas and discourses, in national security and other arenas, follows in this vein. A large literature emphasizes the role of the Great Depression in promoting the turn to Keynesianism: a stark failure, the Depression demonstrated that modern national economies were not self-regulating.[11] In Ian Lustick's Gramscian account of imperial collapse, "organic crises" provide the crucial impetus for the collapse of hegemonic conceptions of the nation's boundaries; these crises in turn are the product of policy failures, such as defeat in war, that highlight

---

[5] These distinctions come from Hermann 1990.
[6] Capoccia and Kelemen 2007; Pierson 2004. For an alternative view, see especially Mahoney and Thelen 2010.
[7] Sewell Jr. 1996, 843 and passim.
[8] Regarding economic paradigms, see Hall 1993; industrial policy, Dobbin 1994; postwar associational life, Skocpol *et al.* 2002; organizational practice, Perrow 1984; foreign policy operational code, George 1969; alliance choice, Reiter 1996; and military innovation, Rosen 1991, 8–9.
[9] Welch 2005, esp. 31–51. See also Homolar 2011.
[10] On the nature of "total war," see Imlay 2007.
[11] The classic work is Hall 1989.

"incurable contradictions" between the prevailing discourse and "stubborn realities."[12] In explicating postwar Germany and Japan's "aversion to power politics," Thomas Berger points to the magnitude of the nations' defeats in the Second World War to explain why "new political-military cultures [emerged] that were as profoundly antimilitaristic as the old ones had been militaristic."[13] An especially sophisticated version of this argument is that of Jeffrey Legro: he argues that a necessary condition for the breakdown of dominant conceptions of how states should relate to international society is an unexpected large-scale failure that invalidates old ideas and renders audiences receptive to viable alternatives; success, even when unanticipated, yields no impetus for change.[14]

The conventional wisdom is intuitive. We all know that nothing fails like success and that failure is the lifeblood of change. It stands to reason that defeat in major war should be a shock to settled institutions and ideas. But this historical institutionalist account is insufficiently sensitive to politics. Because institutionalists believe all institutions and discourses are sticky, they differ with realists, who implicitly adopt rationalist models of belief updating, over how much discrepant evidence is required before learning occurs. But both typically treat events, notably military defeat and triumph, as exogenous and as proving policies and ideas right or wrong. While events – from natural disaster to economic recession to war – are unquestionably real, their social import is not determined by their objective features. Whether an event is seen as a shocking crisis or a manageable problem is endogenous to political contestation. As Colin Hay notes, "crises are constituted in and through narrative."[15]

If dominant narratives coalesced and collapsed in response to objective shocks, it would make sense to conceptualize collective learning as an epiphany – per the institutionalist literature. The prevailing image of substantial failure, including battlefield defeat, as a moment of intellectual awakening is apt when defeat is overwhelming and when wars are so short that there is little time for intrawar interpretation. But the collective perception of even major defeats normally comes together only at the end of a protracted process in which actors seek to

---

[12] Lustick 1993, 122–124. [13] Berger 1998, 22.
[14] Legro 2005, esp. 29–35. See relatedly Samuels 2007, ch. 2.
[15] Hay 1996, 254.

make sense of accumulating setbacks. Few military contests have ended as decisively as the Second World War did for Germany and Japan, and even substantial defeats have permitted interpretations, such as the "stab in the back," which legitimate rather than reject the past. While it is true that short wars are common,[16] most wars have provided ample opportunity while combat is raging for debate over their lessons. Very few are as short as Gulf War I, whose ground war went on for just 100 hours, or even the Six Day War of 1967; very few are so fast-paced that the combatants can hardly begin to make sense of events before they end.[17] The average interstate war in the twentieth century lasted nearly one-and-a-half years,[18] and counterinsurgencies, which many forecast as the future of warfare, are especially protracted.[19]

Even when victory and defeat are clear,[20] accounting for these outcomes and assessing their implications are normally a matter of intense public debate – not just in retrospect, but in the moment. Diverse approaches figure crises as times of national unity beyond politics,[21] but protracted conflicts are in fact rife with disputes over the military's stumbles. As battlefield travails come to light, domestic political contestation centers on how these are to be explained. Is the army being outgunned or outsmarted? Does it lack fighting spirit, or did the nation's leaders dispatch it to an unwinnable war? Does the problem lie with tactics or strategy, or with the war's fundamental rationale and thus with its legitimating narrative? An adequate theory must account for this competition over meaning, because, per the logic of path dependence, it conditions the scope and direction of subsequent change. But these public interpretive contests are not a matter of apolitical puzzling. The contestants, stylized here as doves and hawks, as opponents and supporters of military action and hard-line policies, aim to further their political fortunes and strategic agendas, and their public accounts of the conflict should be understood

---

[16] Weisiger 2013, 2.   [17] See Appendix A of Bennett and Stam III 1996.

[18] Levy 1983, 123–124, 133–134, 139, 141.

[19] And they have been getting longer: counterinsurgencies fought between 1800 and 1945 went on for 5.2 years, but post-1945 campaigns have lasted 11.4 years on average. See Johnston and Urlacher 2012.

[20] Though there is evidence that they often lie in the eye of the beholder. See Johnson and Tierney 2006.

[21] Albeit for different reasons – for realists because the stakes are so high, and for securitization theorists because of the discursive power of crisis.

in that light. Both the emergence and breakdown of dominant narratives are deeply political processes.

Battlefield performance and the narrative politics of national security

Political elites are not equally empowered in public contests over the meaning of warfare. Public debates rarely take place on level playing fields, but this is especially true in the national security domain – in which publics are most likely to look to official sources, and especially the executive branch, for the production of meaning.[22] Government spokespeople thus enjoy substantial starting advantages in the exercise of "interpretive leadership."[23] As they are the owners of the military campaign, victory redounds to their benefit. Setbacks, however, erode public trust, diffuse authority, and empower the opposition. Opposition elites' rhetorical choices then have profound narrative implications. Because dominant narratives require continual reproduction, and because they always contain contradictory strands that make possible the remaking of common sense, these elites can, broadly speaking, explain the nation's battlefield travails either by reproducing the security narrative in whose terms the campaign had been legitimated or by charting a new narrative path. Both permit criticism of government policy, but when opposition elites opt for the former, they reinforce the dominant narrative, and when they opt for the latter, they help to undermine it.

All elites operate within a common social environment with shared cultural toolkits, whose contents they draw upon to make public sense of events. But they are also strategic actors seeking to further their political futures via their accounts of the conflict's course.[24] To put strategizing political elites at the center of these dynamics is not to reduce dominant narratives to elite strategizing alone. Whether they can advance specific security narratives depends on more enduring structures of national identity discourse, in which those narratives

---

[22] For related arguments and evidence from rhetoric and communication, see Condit 1985; Perelman and Olbrechts-Tyteca 1969 [1958], 53. From psychology, see Kruglanski 2004, 112–113, 124–126. This is related also to the "two presidencies" thesis: see Canes-Wrone *et al.* 2008; Wildavsky 1966.

[23] Widmaier 2007.

[24] This melding of strategic and cultural action draws on Swidler 1986.

must be grounded. At any given nodal point, the range of legitimate rhetorical moves is limited.[25] While national identity discourse, rhetorical consistency, or strategic incentives do not render political action entirely foreseeable, this theoretical account rests on the wager that, in the context of a failing military venture, both those pressures and the dangers of bucking them are fairly clear and intense. Opposition elites' rhetorical choices are thus irreducibly contingent, but they are also partly the product of a predictable political environment.

Whether opposition elites publicly give voice to other narratives depends in part on whether the alternatives are compatible with their established political identity and in part on whether they see it as politically profitable. I argue that, early in a faltering war whose ultimate outcome is uncertain, all contestants, doves and hawks alike, have incentives to ground their criticisms in the legitimating national security narrative and thereby to preserve or consolidate its dominance. The politics of poor battlefield performance inhibit the opposition from jumping through a more ambitious rhetorical window and pursuing change in the narrative in whose terms the military operation had been publicly justified.

Wartime contestation is complicated by the fact that war's course is fundamentally unpredictable.[26] War is enveloped in fog, as Clausewitz famously put it – not only at the operational level, but when it comes to war's outcome. Great victories are not apparent early on, nor are unsalvageable disasters. Allied missteps on the Pacific front in 1942 so worried Americans that they elected Republicans in droves that fall, and even former non-interventionists escaped punishment for their pre-Pearl Harbor outspoken opposition to war. Initial stumbles, as in Korea, may be followed by breathtaking reversals of fortune (Inchon landing) only to give way to setbacks once more (the Chinese crossing of the Yalu). In retrospect, people commonly identify turning points when an uncertain war became a lost cause, such as the 1968 Tet Offensive in Vietnam.[27] But mass support normally erodes more gradually, as the bloom wears off the rally rose and as battlefield

---

[25] Contrast this to a more purely rationalist account of public rhetoric in Riker 1986, 1996.

[26] Beyerchen 1992.

[27] Although it is now clear that the Tet Offensive was an enormous military setback for North Vietnam.

difficulties mount.[28] And whether an event constitutes a turning point is informed by one's assessment of the war as a whole. Opponents of the Iraq War identified the 2006 bombing of the al-Askari Mosque in Samarra as the moment when the peace was finally lost, when the futility of the war became clear; supporters have argued that the 2007 "surge" of US forces into Iraq subsequently snatched victory from the jaws of defeat.

Consider first political opponents who oppose the war. Doves face a difficult choice: they can seize the opportunity that military struggles provide to assail the underlying narrative, or they can offer a more modest attack on the war that reaffirms that narrative. For instance, the surprising persistence and effectiveness of the Sunni insurgency in Iraq created an opening for Democratic doves to take on the Bush administration after 2003. They could have exploited US struggles in Iraq to confront the Terror narrative, into which administration officials had bound the Iraq invasion. But they also could have criticized the Iraq War from safe narrative terrain – as a distraction from the "real" War on Terror, against Al Qaeda and the Taliban in Afghanistan and Pakistan. When leading Democrats opted for the second course, repudiating the Iraq War by reproducing the Terror narrative, they disappointed many supporters, but their choice was not surprising in light of the fog of war and the politics of military performance.

When evidence of military difficulties has begun to accumulate, but before the perception of irrevocable failure has crystallized, doves are reluctant to launch a thoroughgoing critique that takes on the war's underlying narrative. Criticism in wartime is always dangerous, but the deeper it strikes, the more vulnerable critics are to charges that they are emboldening the enemy, demoralizing the troops, and prolonging the fight. This is especially true early in a war, when its outcome is still seen as uncertain and thus when vocal criticism arguably can affect whether the war ends in victory or defeat, not just the terms and costs of the inevitable conclusion. Should the war's course reverse, critics' judgment will be severely questioned, and should the nation's forces continue to flounder, critics may be held responsible, not lauded for their prescience. Given the stakes, caution reigns, the pressure to conform to the legitimating narrative is intense, and foundational critique is rarely heard. It is safer for doves to criticize the war's

---

[28] For data from the Vietnam War, for instance, see Mueller 1973.

conduct, insist that the strategy's application alone is flawed, or propose withdrawal on grounds of excessive cost or insufficient likelihood of victory. As a result, even as the war's costs mount, doves typically express themselves *within* the terms of the dominant narrative. Politics does not stop at war's edge, at least not for long, but wartime politics is normally waged within narrative bounds.

These political dynamics, narrowing the scope of criticism in a campaign's early stages, have long-term consequences. Once there is widespread agreement of defeat or failure, doves might find it appealing in principle to try to recast the narrative basis of national security, but that option is no longer available. Their past utterances, which reproduced and reinforced the dominant narrative, have established the conventions to which the public expects members of the "responsible opposition" – in both government and civil society – to adhere. Those who move beyond those boundaries of legitimate critique, to embrace an alternative narrative of national security, are predictably assailed as reckless radicals. Had doves known in prospect what they know in retrospect, they might have coupled their wartime criticism to a revision of the nation's security narrative. But the politics of an uncertain and failing war cast narrative alternatives to the margins in war's early stages – and there they remain. This mechanism of lock-in is at work not only when the political opposition's leadership is stable, but even when war shakes up the established order and brings new personalities into politics who are not personally shackled by a wartime rhetorical past. All who wish to avoid the radical label, politicians and pundits alike, are confined to the dominant narrative. Even Barack Obama, who more than any other top Democrat made opposition to the Iraq War the centerpiece of his political persona, remained in thrall to the Terror narrative as a senator and presidential candidate. He joined other leading Democrats in criticizing the Iraq War as having obstructed the War on Terror properly conceived.[29]

Consider now political opponents who support the war. Hawks face a seeming dilemma. On the one hand, they do not wish to undermine public support for the war, which may already be flagging: were they to challenge the war's legitimating logic, the public might lose faith entirely. On the other hand, they wish to exploit battlefield setbacks

---

[29] For details, see Krebs 2013.

for political gain: supporting the policies and echoing the arguments of the wartime leadership will not position them as a credible political alternative. There is at least one way they can sidestep the dilemma: by accusing the government of not having been sufficiently faithful to its own articulated world-view and by suggesting that greater fidelity would have led to better battlefield outcomes, or even have made the war and its attendant sacrifices unnecessary. Criticizing the war's conduct and presenting themselves as the true believers, hawks seek to renew the public's commitment, redouble the military's efforts, and offer the public a distinctive political stance. Opposition hawks thus make political headway, albeit at the cost of principle if their hawkish preferences are rooted in a different narrative of national security from that of the wartime government. In contrast to opposition doves, who seek to evade the perils of criticism, hawks are lured by the prospect of gain. But the effect is the same: to shore up the underlying narrative of national security and stifle change. The politics of military performance can even work to consolidate narrative dominance, when hawks sign on to a narrative they had previously refused to endorse.

In contrast, *success* on the battlefield and in significant episodes of coercive diplomacy opens space for departures from the dominant narrative. This is counterintuitive from the perspective of actors' motives: as Legro argues, when policy produces desirable returns, "societal actors would find little reason to reassess the prevailing orthodoxy."[30] But motive is only half the story, and success alters the opportunity structure facing its owners, in both government and civil society, who wish to narrate the world differently but had previously felt constrained. Success boosts their interpretive authority and thereby loosens those constraints. It creates an opening for them to argue that the rules of the global game have changed *because* the policy they had advocated or implemented was so successful. Diplomatic and military success does not translate smoothly into enduring political power, as leaders from Georges Clemenceau to Winston Churchill to George H. W. Bush have painfully learned.[31] Nor does it, in and of itself, end narrative dominance. But policy success makes the breakdown of narrative dominance possible, depending on whether doves or hawks

[30] Legro 2005, 33.
[31] Thanks to Marc Trachtenberg for reminding me of this.

occupy positions of authority and are success' owners: doves can reveal their true colors, while hawks can continue toeing the narrative line.

Success is not, however, conducive to the consolidation of a new dominant narrative, for two reasons. First, success creates space for alternative futures without delegitimizing the past. It has not only many fathers, but many lessons: it can also be interpreted as proving the wisdom of the status quo from which deviation is dangerous. The erstwhile dominant narrative retains its legitimacy. Even when some seize the opportunity that success provides to advance an alternative narrative, others may remain loyal to what previously had seemed like common sense. The result is at most the erosion of narrative dominance. Second, as suggested in Chapter 2, publics are more tolerant of ontological insecurity and narrative disorder in the wake of victory. Individual human beings, psychologists have learned, are likely to insist on closure as signs mount that deep uncertainty will prove costly.[32] That condition is least likely to hold after victory, when confidence is high. As a result, public demand to return to an ordered state, to restabilize the national narrative, is more muted.

But are not successes like streetcars, to paraphrase McGeorge Bundy's comment on the 1965 attack on the US military base near Pleiku? Cannot adroit leaders always find events they can portray as successes and on which they can hang their claims of a world made new by their skill and determination? Are they not rhetorical alchemists who, with their silvery tongues, transform dross into gold? Success after all is also a narrative, which raises the disturbing possibility that nimble leaders face no real narrative constraints. There are three reasons to be skeptical that such manipulation is widespread. First, were rhetorical alchemy so easy, we would find few leaders tarred with defeat and far more swathed in glory. We would observe leaders regularly declaring victory and withdrawing forces, rather than prolonging wars in the hope of departing under more rosy circumstances. Yet, prolonged exits and charges of failure are common.[33] Second, there is often little dispute about whether a given episode constitutes success or failure, even in its immediate aftermath and even among opponents not inclined to grant credit or among supporters not inclined to blame. This is not because these are objective assessments, nor because of post-facto rhetorical magic, but rather

[32] Kruglanski 2004, 7–13.   [33] Edelstein 2012.

because dominant narratives establish collective benchmarks by which events are judged. Third, if the "fact" of success were the product of rhetorical magic, we would expect the sorcerer's power to extend to the reasons for success as well. But, while there is often much agreement on whether a given war or coercive diplomatic episode went badly, there is often much disagreement on why it went badly and thus on whether it can be salvaged. For instance, no American in the late 1970s looked back on the Vietnam War as a victory, but they embraced divergent interpretations of why the intervention had ended so tragically and whether the war had ever been winnable, and thus whether the United States should have sent forces there in the first place or should even have withdrawn.

Why the Cold War consensus?

The next two chapters assess this theoretical account in light of the experience of the Cold War consensus. Documenting and explaining the rise and fall of the Cold War narrative's dominance is intrinsically important. It speaks to enduring puzzles of the Cold War – from the origins of the US national-security state to the conditions of possibility for détente to the drivers of the intervention in Vietnam. Critics attributed numerous costly, sometimes even disastrous, policies to its stranglehold. The case's prominence also gives it a practical advantage, in that it has been the subject of extensive secondary literature. But, perhaps most importantly, it should be an easy case for two common theories. First, that dominant narratives reflect global realities. Given the high stakes of superpower competition, the high costs of misunderstanding global events, and the nation's intense focus on foreign affairs, one would expect to see an unusually close correspondence between the Cold War narrative and the world it professed to depict, and to observe little dissent among informed observers of the global scene. Second, that stability is undone only by exogenous shocks. Given the long-standing scholarly and popular conventional wisdom that gives the Vietnam War credit (or blame) for the consensus' demise, we would expect the narrative's dynamics to fit the standard theory.

Perhaps, however, there was something distinctive about the Cold War, with its bipolar structure, or about the United States, located far from the bloody battlefield, that altered the political dynamics. Although there is nothing in Part II's theoretical framework that depends on peculiarly American political institutions or culture, it is true that, unlike other nations, the United States, by virtue of its geographical position and the absence of peer competitors in its hemisphere, has normally been located far from the battlefield and somewhat shielded from the costs of war. This might have tempered the intensity with which military failure was felt and its accompanying politics. But the United States has not looked upon its distant wars with equanimity, and its wartime experiences have resonated powerfully in the nation's politics.[34] Since before the Second World War, Michael Sherry famously argues, the United States has lived under, and been deeply shaped by, "the shadow of war."[35] Moreover, when the battle rages nearby, wars can still be protracted, end indecisively, and be subject to multiple interpretations. Even a cursory reading of the history of European politics cannot support the conclusion that war there has been too immediate, too near, and too serious a business for anyone to "play politics" with it. American politicians have not enjoyed a luxury that others have not. Despite America's unusual geopolitical position, there is then little reason to think that its experiences with regard to national security narrative have been unusual.

There was, of course, something distinctive about the Cold War superpower rivalry, conducted under conditions of bipolarity and in the shadow of nuclear Armageddon. But those factors should, if anything, have rendered national security narrative more responsive to presumptive global realities and less subject to the narrative politics of the battlefield. The ways in which the Cold War was an outlier make it an especially hard case, which should give greater credence to the theoretical claims. If conventional theories do not account well for the rise and fall of the Cold War consensus, we need to rethink them. And whatever accounts for its ups and downs deserves consideration as a candidate theory with broader applicability – beyond the United States and beyond the security domain.

---

[34] See, among others, Higgs 1987; Katznelson and Shefter 2002; Mayhew 2005; Saldin 2010; Zelizer 2010.

[35] Sherry 1997.

6 | *Tracking the Cold War consensus*

The conventional view is that a dominant Cold War narrative took shape in the late 1940s. Lasting around two decades, it unraveled during the Vietnam War, and it failed to re-emerge even as détente flickered in the mid 1970s. Although intellectuals and activists began to rebel against Cold War orthodoxy by the end of the 1950s, scholars and contemporary observers alike identified Vietnam as "the acid that dissolved the postwar foreign policy consensus."[1] A minority, however, believes there to have been no substantial change throughout the post-1945 period.[2] Such opposed stances persist because we lack systematic evidence regarding what the consensus was, when it consolidated, and when it collapsed. Yet, a shared public narrative is necessarily observable. The evidence I have gathered suggests that there was an authoritative Cold War narrative that defined the boundaries of legitimate politics in the United States, but that its content and dynamics were quite different from the usual account.

What *was* the Cold War consensus?

The Cold War consensus was a dominant narrative to which American elites – from policymakers to pundits to even professors – felt compelled to adhere in their public pronouncements, regardless of their private qualms. This is what Leslie Gelb meant when he blamed the consensus for driving the United States into the Vietnam fiasco; he knew many Washington insiders had severe misgivings about key

---

[1] Holsti and Rosenau 1986, 376–377. See also Allison 1970–1971; Gelb and Betts 1979, ch. 6; Holsti and Rosenau 1979, 1984. While Russett and Hanson found evidence in public opinion of the Cold War consensus' demise as early as 1960, they still portrayed Vietnam as the turning point; see Russett and Hanson 1975, 134–144. Among contemporary observers, see, for instance, "A New Consensus . . . ," *New York Times*, 18 September 1976.

[2] Bacevich 2007; Craig and Logevall 2009.

pillars of the consensus and its application to Southeast Asia, but he also saw few willing to give public voice to their private dissent.[3] Despite persistent doubts at the highest levels of government that global Communism was "a highly coordinated, conspiratorial, malevolent force" and that local Communists were mere ciphers doing Moscow's bidding[4] – to the point that John Lewis Gaddis has claimed that no US statesman ever really "believed in the existence of an international communist monolith"[5] – rare was the policymaker who openly challenged this representation of global Communism before the early 1960s. They could not say otherwise if they wished to be taken seriously, or so they thought. As a dominant narrative, the Cold War consensus limited the range of policy options that could be legitimately articulated: Riga and Yalta, to employ Daniel Yergin's famous categories, were both approaches *within* the consensus.[6] As Gelb and Richard Betts observe, when it held sway, "debates revolved around how to do things better and whether they could be done, not whether they were worth doing."[7]

. This contrasts with the common view of the Cold War consensus as a broad ideological and policy agreement – a set of beliefs, sincerely held by the vast majority of the nation's elites, and by most common citizens as well, that combined to support a course of action. These beliefs at the heart of Cold War ideology included the centrality of superpower competition, its zero-sum nature, the aggressive disposition of the USSR, the monolithic character of global Communism, the necessity and reliability of US allies, a world so tightly interconnected that even peripheral states "going Communist" posed a danger, and the need for US leadership.[8] These beliefs in turn underpinned a slate of policies, notably substantial defense spending and foreign aid, binding alliances, and military intervention: in short, militarized, unselective, global containment.[9]

---

[3] Gelb 1976.   [4] Selverstone 2009, 4. See also Schrecker 1998, 131–135.
[5] Gaddis 1987, 148; see also Chang 1990, 3.   [6] Wolfe 1979; Yergin 1977.
[7] Gelb and Betts 1979, 190.
[8] The Cold War consensus went beyond merely the bipartisan commitment to liberal internationalism, whose demise has been the subject of much debate. See Busby and Monten 2008; Chaudoin *et al.* 2010; Kupchan and Trubowitz 2007.
[9] The preceding draws on Allison 1970–1971; Gelb and Betts 1979, ch. 6; Hallin 1986; Halperin *et al.* 1974, 11–12; Hoffmann 1978, ch. 1; and esp. Hogan 1998, 10–17.

But the Cold War consensus did not sustain only a single approach. Debate swirled over US national security policy even at the consensus' alleged apex. Deep skepticism of negotiations with the Soviet Union was part of the consensus, we are often told,[10] but in the mid 1950s disagreement was rife over the advisability of negotiating with the Soviet Union, and the Eisenhower administration held high-level summits with Soviet leaders. If there was a consensus in favor of US military intervention to combat Communism's spread, as later critics contended,[11] it was never unselective: the United States passed up many opportunities to send forces abroad in large numbers. Nor in the 1950s did the United States, gripped by Cold War militarism,[12] spend wildly on arms: Eisenhower curtailed defense spending in part by relying heavily on nuclear weapons, members of Congress scrutinized the defense budget for "waste," and conservative intellectuals and politicians warned that military spending was an economic drain and potentially a source of ruinous inflation. Generous foreign aid to the Third World – another alleged pillar of the consensus[13] – was always under intense assault.[14] On policy, there was, before Vietnam and throughout the Cold War, "a workable dissensus ... over how communism could best be combated" – via military measures or via trade, aid, and development.[15]

One cannot, therefore, apprehend this dominant narrative by examining congressional voting patterns on defense expenditures, foreign assistance, treaties of alliance, and authorizations of military intervention.[16] One cannot, therefore, cite debate over policy as evidence of the consensus' passing.[17] Nor can one identify the dominant narrative by analyzing individuals' beliefs, revealed through opinion polls. This was the strategy of survey researchers in the late 1970s, who contrasted the

---

[10] Allison 1970–1971, 150, axioms #1–2; Halperin *et al.* 1974, 11, shared images #1–3; Holsti and Rosenau 1984, 230–232.

[11] Allison 1970–1971, 150–151, axiom #6; Halperin *et al.* 1974, 11–12, shared images #6–8; Holsti and Rosenau 1984, 218–223; Katzenbach 1973, 6.

[12] Allison 1970–1971, 151, axiom #9; Fordham 1998; Halperin *et al.* 1974, 12, shared images #13–14.

[13] Allison 1970–1971, 151, axiom #7; Halperin *et al.* 1974, 12, shared image #11; Holsti and Rosenau 1984, 218–223.

[14] Pach Jr. 1987, esp. 140–144.

[15] Hughes 1980, esp. 49–53. Similarly, though less explicitly, see van Oudenaren 1982.

[16] As in, among others, Fordham 1998, 2002, 2008a.

[17] As in Holsti and Rosenau 1984, 2.

deep divides they discovered with the putative consensus of the past.[18]
They admitted that, because sampling procedures were flawed in the
1950s, they could not properly document that public opinion had
become more fractured. But even if such data existed,[19] the method
would miss the mark. First, polls are not neutral instruments for
gauging the public's views. Pollsters operate within the bounds of
the respectable, and they embed narrative presuppositions in their
questions. They are better at detecting cleavages than establishing
zones of consensus and identifying the limits of the legitimate.[20] One
would never know, from Ole Holsti and James Rosenau's seminal
work, that internationalists dominated in the 1980s or that the elite
spectrum shifted rightward at the end of the 1970s.[21] Second, and even
more important, the Cold War narrative's dominance was rooted less
in what individuals believed than in the stances they thought they could
legitimately defend in public.[22]

To identify the consensus with a dominant narrative is not to deny
that there was a material reality to the Cold War. In the wake of the
Second World War, there were two acknowledged great powers whose
material resources exceeded those of all others.[23] The United States and
the Soviet Union were "enemies by position," in Raymond Aron's
famous phrase, consigned to rivalry and competition. But there were
nevertheless multiple ways in which Americans might have narrated
the global drama, and those different narratives implied very different
policies. Was superpower competition the central axis of world affairs,
or did local forces drive events without Washington's and Moscow's
input? Were the superpowers' interests purely competing, or did they
overlap? Were the leading Communist powers extreme revisionists,
moderate revisionists, or semi-satisfied? Was the world so tightly
interconnected that one state embracing Communism would set off a
cascade of falling dominoes? Was global Communism diverse, or did
local Communists slavishly do Moscow's bidding? The observed facts

[18] In addition to those cited in n. 1 above, see also Wittkopf 1986, 1987, 1990;
Wittkopf and Maggiotto 1983. For a partial reconsideration, see Wittkopf and
McCormick 1990.
[19] Sophisticated techniques could compensate for the flawed sampling, as Berinsky
has done for opinion data from the 1930s and 1940s. See Berinsky 2009.
[20] Kegley Jr. 1986, 450–455.   [21] For this critique, see Ferguson 1986.
[22] See, relatedly, Noelle-Neumann 1993.
[23] Although the material foundation of bipolarity was less than clear. See especially
Wagner 1993.

did not alone provide clear answers to these questions. When elites suggested answers, they generated narratives of national security, which in turn sustained policy menus and thereby had material consequences. Partly a reflection of the material world, the Cold War narrative also brought a world into being. It shaped global flows of goods, services, and people, and physically divided regions and even countries into two. Those material realities in turn made this particular national security narrative seem not only plausible, but natural.

Measuring the Cold War consensus

Dominant narratives constitute the boundaries of legitimate politics. As a result, one cannot ascertain whether a public narrative is dominant by looking to only a single source, such as official government pronouncements, since that narrative may not be shared and since other narratives may retain legitimate standing. Nor can one look to politicians or media that address only narrow constituencies, since it is possible that their views would be ignored or dismissed by broader audiences.[24] One should, therefore, be able to observe the presence or absence of a dominant narrative of national security in a relatively consistent corpus of elite discourse, drawn from multiple sources that are within the pale, but that occupy distant points on an ideological scale. That body of elite discourse should be present over the entire period, to make possible comparisons over time.

Given these considerations, to track the Cold War narrative, I undertook a longitudinal content analysis of editorials on foreign affairs between the end of the Second World War (1945) and the dissolution of the USSR (1991). They were drawn from two leading newspapers that inhabited opposed poles on the ideological spectrum, especially with regard to foreign affairs: the consistently internationalist and liberal *New York Times* and the reliably nationalist and conservative *Chicago Tribune*. Although the length, style, and daily number of editorials varied between the two newspapers and over time, as did the degree to which each editorialized on foreign affairs, both ran

---

[24] This is one reason that speeches in the *Congressional Record*, often directed at audiences in a congressperson's district, are not an ideal source. Moreover, marginal and extreme figures are sometimes over-represented in the proceedings, perhaps because congressional leaders hope that allowing them to spout will disarm them.

editorials throughout the span on what they saw as the major issues of the day. The database contains nearly 9,100 editorials on foreign affairs, an annual average of 87.4 from the *Tribune* (with a range of 42 to 142) and of 101.8 from the *Times* (with a range of 33 to 188). Overall, 46.2 percent of the editorials in the database come from the *Tribune* and 53.8 percent from the *Times*.[25] I look to these editorials as reflections of a potentially dominant narrative and the changes it underwent, not as influential sources of narrative change.

Based on existing catalogs of Cold War axioms, I constructed a fourteen-point questionnaire (reproduced in Appendix D) on the editorial's central concern, its representations of Communist powers and superpower competition, its portrait of US allies, its stance on the domino theory, and its position on US leadership.[26] Human coders completed the questionnaire for each editorial in the database,[27] with additional double-blind coding to establish intercoder reliability.[28] Due to the interpretive demands of the coding, intercoder reliability rates are lower than ideal, but nevertheless strong.[29] When the scores of

[25] Undergraduate research assistants collected editorials from every fifth day over the time span. If that method failed to generate sufficient editorials in a given year, editorials were collected from every third day.

[26] In decomposing the Cold War narrative into its various elements and in abstracting from specific incidents and episodes, the questionnaire necessarily de-emphasizes plot in favor of protagonist. It does, however, capture certain general plot lines in its examination of editorials for representations of, among others, Communist aggression, superpower competition, the domino theory, and the impact of US intervention.

[27] Coders, mostly Ph.D. candidates in political science, were provided with written guidelines for the coding, and all coders went through two rounds of training to harmonize their codings.

[28] Due to the extensiveness of the project, double-blind coding was not conducted for the full run of both newspapers. The first twenty editorials per year from each paper – at least 10 percent and sometimes nearly 50 percent of a given year's editorials – were analyzed by an additional coder. This practice is standard with large data sets. Thanks to Tim Johnson for guidance on intercoder reliability procedures.

[29] Intercoder reliability tests indicate average agreement of 78.04 percent across all questionnaire items. Cohen's kappa scores on individual items ranged from a low of 0.2337 to a high of 0.6656, with an average of 0.49. Landis and Koch would classify this as a "moderate" level of agreement, although they admit that such a classification is "arbitrary" (Landis and Koch 1977, 165). While these rates of agreement exceed some commonly cited rules of thumb (Stemler and Tsai 2008, 48), many statisticians are skeptical of efforts to interpret the magnitude of kappa statistics and to establish such fixed conventions (Krippendorff 2004; Uebersax 2013). I also calculated other, more complex

an element across the two newspapers are statistically indistinguishable (p > 0.05), or when statistically significant differences are substantively negligible (< 5 percent), I identify it as a zone of narrative agreement and thus as part of the dominant narrative. To my knowledge, this is the first time anyone has disaggregated the Cold War narrative into its possible components and traced their prominence in public elite discourse on foreign affairs. This method makes it possible to establish whether there was a dominant Cold War narrative in the United States, of what it consisted, when it consolidated, and when it collapsed. The findings cannot tell us why the narrative arena narrowed or broadened, why a narrative acquired or lost dominance, but it establishes the trends that require explanation.

The validity of this study depends on three assumptions. First, the questionnaire represents the Cold War narrative's farthest reach. To design the questionnaire, I drew from a wide range of secondary sources, and the resulting list of questionnaire items is inclusive and extensive. I am not familiar with any elements that are commonly viewed as part of the Cold War consensus but do not appear on the questionnaire.

Second, we cannot reasonably speak of a *dominant* national security narrative if either of these two newspapers regularly departed from it. The *New York Times* and the *Chicago Tribune* are two of only three newspapers nationwide that ranked in the top ten in circulation in every decade over the span.[30] Both were widely seen as opinion leaders, and both regularly made lists of the nation's best newspapers.[31]

---

measures of intercoder reliability, such as Scott's pi and Krippendorff's alpha. These were in the same range as Cohen's kappa; see the online appendix, located at https://sites.google.com/a/umn.edu/rkrebs/home/publications/data, for details. For comprehensive critical discussions of various methods of intercoder reliability, see the sources cited above.

[30] Based on decennial data compiled from: *Editor & Publisher International Year Book*; *The World Almanac & Book of Facts*; and the *Information Please Almanac, Atlas, and Yearbook*.

[31] See John Tebbel, "Rating the American Newspaper – Part I," *Saturday Review*, 13 May 1961, 60–62, and "Rating the American Newspaper—Part II," *Saturday Review*, 10 June 1961, 54–56; "The Ten Best American Dailies," *Time*, 21 January 1974, 66–72; "The Ten Best U.S. Dailies," *Time*, 30 April 1984, 64–72. *Time* excluded the *Tribune* from its 1964 rankings, although it acknowledged the paper's worthiness in the years before the passing of its long-time publisher, Col. Robert McCormick ("The Top U.S. Dailies," *Time*, 10 January 1964, 60–67).

The *Times* in particular was, for much of the period under study, tightly tied to the national establishment,[32] had reporting resources that dwarfed its competitors,[33] and was the only newspaper that elites truly felt compelled to read.[34] While the *Tribune* was not in the *Times'* league, it was a mighty regional newspaper with a national profile: on its 100th anniversary in 1946, *Time* declared it "the loudest and perhaps the most widely feared and hated" of the nation's dailies;[35] in 1961, a survey of journalism school faculty ranked it fourth among 119 major dailies in respondents' familiarity with the paper (and first among newspapers beyond the east coast);[36] and *Time* included it on its lists of the nation's top dailies in 1974 and 1984. In short, both operated within the bounds of legitimate discourse. Moreover, the two papers were also unusually ideologically consistent, especially on foreign affairs.[37] The *Tribune* endorsed a Republican for president in every election between 1932 and 1996 and was generally seen as a leading conservative voice. The *Times* usually endorsed Democrats[38] and was generally seen as the paragon of liberal internationalism. One cannot classify a narrative as dominant if either the nation's paper of record or the heartland's spokesman deviated from it.[39]

---

[32] See esp. Talese 1970, 121–124.

[33] As *Time* put it in 1974, "There is no other U.S. daily quite like the Times. Its total news staff is by far the largest (about 650), its scope and coverage the most exhaustive, its influence on national and world leaders daunting" ("The Ten Best American Dailies," *Time*, 21 January 1974). See also generally Talese 1970; Tifft and Jones 1999.

[34] See the findings in Rosenau 1963, 186–202.

[35] Quoted in Wendt 1979, 674.

[36] John Tebbel, "Rating the American Newspaper – Part II," *Saturday Review*, 10 June 1961, 55.

[37] The *Times* was, in a comprehensive study of nominations, one of two consistently center-left newspapers, along with the less prominent *St. Louis Post-Dispatch*, and the *Tribune* was one of four consistently center-right papers, alongside the *Detroit News* and two less prominent regional outlets. See Ansolabehere *et al.* 2006.

[38] Although it did endorse four Republicans between 1940 and 1956 while noting their internationalist commitments.

[39] Other primary sources, including certain magazines, might have done equally well in mapping the boundaries of mainstream discourse on foreign affairs, as might other newspapers occupying similar points along the ideological spectrum. I hope others will replicate this study's methods and apply the questionnaire in Appendix D to a different corpus of elite discourse on foreign affairs.

Third, these two newspapers represent the boundaries of legitimate American views of the global scene.[40] On the one hand, it is
conceivable that there were respectable papers, "within" the pale,
substantially to the right of the *Tribune* and to the left of the *Times*,
whose foreign affairs editorials either endorsed key propositions
later or diverged from them earlier or never joined the consensus
at all. I cannot discount this possibility fully, without surveying a
broader range of news outlets and undertaking a similar content
analysis of those sources. This would be easy if computerized content analysis tools could be adapted to this purpose, but the sensitivity of this analysis requires human coding, and extending it to
other newspapers would be prohibitively expensive and time-
consuming. Moreover, it is not obvious what other newspapers
besides the *New York Times* and the *Chicago Tribune* one should
consult, for alternatives lacked similar long-standing national status
and/or ideological consistency.[41] On the other hand, it is possible
that newspapers' editorial boards, in contrast to politicians who
worry about re-election, are insensitive to the confines of legitimacy.
However, newspapers are at their core businesses, and their editorial
pages cannot go too far out on a limb, or it may affect advertising
and sales – which, as I discuss below, led the publisher of the
New York Times to rein in the editorial board in the 1970s.
Moreover, there is evidence that major newspapers' editorial stances
follow national politicians, at least those in their ideological and
partisan camp.[42]

Content analysis, especially when conducted with computerized
tools, has well-known limitations: it is well suited to counting words
with stable meanings, but misses the flux of meaning; it has difficulty
with units of analysis beyond the word or short-word complex; and,
treating what is rarely uttered as less important, it overlooks the
significance of silence.[43] This study is less afflicted by these problems.

---

[40] Thanks to Jeremi Suri for pressing me on this point.
[41] Thanks to James Baughman for consultation on these issues.
[42] Habel 2012.
[43] For a good overview, see the various short essays in Herrera and Braumoeller
2004. On the possibilities and limits of computerized content analysis, see
Morris 1994; and West 2001, esp. the essays by Stevenson, Hart, and
Linderman.

First, human coders can be trained to identify larger linguistic constructs. There is, however, a trade-off: given the inferential challenges of coding more complex linguistic structures, intercoder reliability rates are necessarily lower than on simpler tasks. Second, human coders can be trained to code for meaning, not just to record the presence of absence of a given word or phrase, and they need not presume that words or phrases have stable meanings. Third, content analysis is a useful tool for recording the absence of articulations as well as their presence. It does not, though, resolve the interpretive problem: textual silence may reflect an unspoken foundation for argument, or it may mean that the item was not in fact part of the dominant narrative. Content analysis thus provides evidence of certain linguistic elements' presence or absence, but it does not tell us what they mean. Nor does it explain the patterns it records: why particular narrative constructs become dominant or are later contested. Complementary methods, such as discourse analysis and historical process-tracing, are necessary to make sense of the patterns that content analysis reveals.

Narrating the Cold War anew

The content analysis yields four novel empirical claims regarding what the dominant Cold War narrative was, when it rose to dominance, and when it eroded. First, the dominant narrative, or consensus, of the 1950s was not nearly as broad as conventional accounts suggest. Second, this narrow narrative achieved dominance later – not in the late 1940s, but into the 1950s. Third, its dominance began to erode in the early 1960s – before the United States committed substantial forces to the defense of South Vietnam and long before mass opinion turned against the war. Fourth, while the original consensus revolving around the Communist Other failed to re-form in the wake of the Vietnam War, establishment elites from both the right and left joined forces in the 1970s to beat back the assault from the margins; for the first time, they clearly affirmed America's peculiar amalgam of exceptionalism and internationalism.

First, there was a dominant Cold War narrative in the 1950s, but it was narrow. Traditional accounts of the consensus claim that it revolved around three clusters of items: the centrality of the Cold War, representations of the Communist adversary and superpower

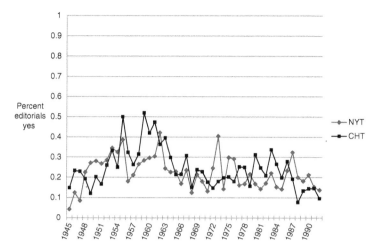

Figure 6.1 Superpower competition: central concern?

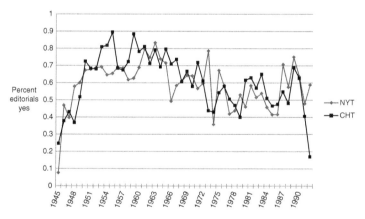

Figure 6.2 Central concern linked to Cold War?

conflict, and representations of the United States, its role in global politics, and its allies. The content analysis suggests that there is some truth to this. As Figures 6.1 and 6.2 show, the two newspapers' editorials largely moved in lock-step regarding the centrality of superpower competition, and more broadly the Cold War, in global affairs. On this issue, the gap between the two papers was small and stable, per

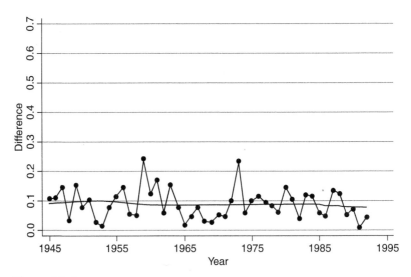

Figure 6.3 Superpower concern.

Figures 6.3 and 6.4.[44] Over the full span, superpower competition was
the central concern of 25 percent of the *Tribune*'s editorials on foreign
affairs and 23 percent of those in the *Times* (Figure 6.1); if one includes
also those foreign-affairs editorials that, although primarily concerned
with other matters, depict those issues as linked to superpower competition, those figures rise to 61 percent for the *Tribune* and 59 percent for
the *Times* (Figure 6.2). These substantively small differences were also
not statistically significant (Table 6.1, top row). Over time, both papers
devoted editorial attention to other issues[45] and reduced the Cold
War's place: whereas both narrated 75 percent or more of global
politics through the prism of the Cold War before the mid 1960s,
that figure fell to between 40 and 60 percent afterwards.

---

[44] Figures 6.3 and 6.4 show on the y-axis the differences between the two
      newspapers' scores. The curves in these figures are relatively flat, indicating that
      the differences between the two newspapers on the centrality of the Cold War
      were stable; they also reveal that these differences were generally small. The
      statistical method used in these figures, locally weighted scatterplot smoothing
      (LOWESS), plots a smooth curve through data without requiring the analyst to
      specify a global function, i.e. one that fits all the data.
[45] Space constraints prevent presentation of this data. For this data, see the online
      appendix on the author's website.

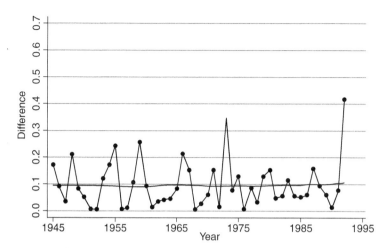

Figure 6.4 Cold War.

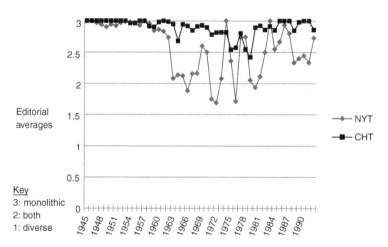

Figure 6.5 Unity of global Communism.

Furthermore, the two newspapers agreed that: the Communist world was monolithic (Figure 6.5); leading Communist powers were expansionist and aggressive (Figure 6.6); the threat was real; relations between the two blocs were generally conflictual (Figure 6.7); and the domino theory held (Figure 6.8). As indicated in Table 6.1 (bottom five rows), between 1945 and the early 1960s, the differences between the two papers' editorial stances on these matters were either statistically insignificant ($p > 0.05$)

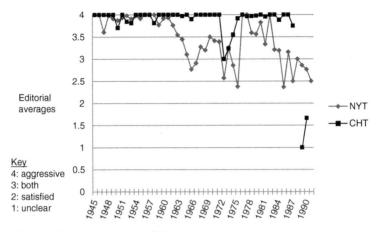

Figure 6.6 Aggressiveness of Communist powers.

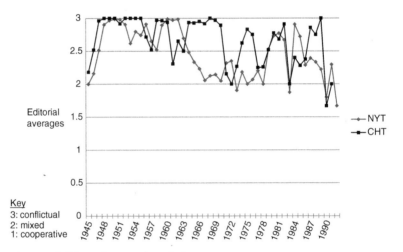

Figure 6.7 West–Communist relations.

or, when they were statistically significant, substantively negligible (3 percent or less, per the "ratio" column).

However, that is as far as the consensus went. Throughout the 1950s, until the early 1960s, the two papers' editorials diverged greatly over the reliability of allies, over whether the United States had special responsibilities in global politics, over the value of foreign assistance, and even over whether the United States had in the past acted, or would in the future act,

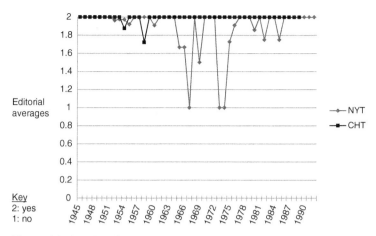

Figure 6.8 Domino theory.

as a force for good in world affairs.[46] The *Times* had greater faith than the *Tribune* in US allies, the utility of foreign aid, and the need for and virtues of US leadership. Per Table 6.2, the differences were statistically significant ($p < 0.05$) and substantively large (on average, 68 percent).[47]

Second, the usual periodization of even the narrow Cold War consensus is problematic: it did not consolidate until well into the Korean War.[48] This is not readily apparent from Figures 6.5 to 6.8: *when* the conservative nationalist *Tribune* editorialized about the Communist powers or free world–Soviet bloc relations or global interconnectedness, it lagged only slightly behind the liberal internationalist, Cold Warrior *Times*. It is, rather, strikingly reflected in the paltry *amount* of editorial coverage the *Tribune* devoted, relative to the *Times*, to narrating the Cold War – that is, to representing the free world's adversaries and the nature of the global conflict. Between 1948 and 1955, 48.3 percent of foreign affairs editorials in the *Times* identified the character of the leading Communist powers, compared to just 28.7 percent in the *Tribune*; over that span, 25.1 percent of foreign affairs editorials in the *Times* made reference to the perils of states going Communist, compared to just 13.6 percent in the

---

[46] For graphical representations of the two papers' scores, see the online appendix.

[47] One exception: the necessity of allies. This is not surprising, given the *Tribune*'s small-government commitments: allies were necessary to keep the government's budget limited. The gap between the two papers was statistically and substantively significant, but it was *much* smaller than the gaps associated with issues clearly outside the consensus.

[48] Important exceptions include Fordham 1998; Snyder 1991.

Table 6.1 *Cold War consensus I: representations of the Communist Other*

Questionnaire item	Substantive interpretation of editorial score	Year range	Chicago Tribune: no. editorials	NY Times: no. editorials	Chicago Tribune: average editorial score	NY Times: average editorial score	p-value	ratio (of higher to lower average editorial score)
Cold War centrality	1: central 0: not central	1945–1992	4192	4884	0.61	0.59	0.576	1.03
Communist aggressiveness	3: aggressive 2: both 1: peaceful	1945–1962	477	1170	2.97	2.92	0.035*	1.02
Communist threat	2: real 1: inflated	1945–1964	533	956	1.98	1.98	0.63	1
West–Comm. relations	3: conflictual 2: mixed 1: cooperative	1945–1962	493	1050	2.77	2.84	0*	1.03
Communist unity	3: monolithic 2: both 1: diverse	1945–1960	613	1281	2.98	2.95	0.007*	1.01
Domino theory	1: yes 0: no	1945–1964	304	638	0.98	0.98	0.67	1

Key:
* Statistically significant (p < 0.05).
† Substantively significant (> 10 percent).

Table 6.2 *Limits of Cold War consensus I*

Questionnaire item	Substantive interpretation of editorial score	Year range	Chicago Tribune: no. editorials	NY Times: no. editorials	Chicago Tribune: average editorial score	NY Times: average editorial score	p-value	ratio (of higher to lower average editorial score)
Allies necessary?	2: necessary 1: not necessary	1945–1970	217	920	1.8	2	0*	1.11[†]
Allies reliable?	3: reliable 2: contingent 1: not reliable	1945–1970	486	907	1.66	2.64	0*	1.59[†]
Special US leadership role?	1: yes 0: no	1945–1975	43	304	0.4	0.96	0*	2.40[†]
Foreign aid valuable?	2: valuable 1: not valuable	1945–1975	178	425	1.08	1.96	0*	1.81[†]
US past constructive?	2: yes 1: no	1945–1964	304	471	1.09	1.82	0*	1.67[†]
US future constructive?	3: yes 2: contingent 1: no	1945–1971	439	795	1.67	2.54	0*	1.52[†]

* Statistically significant (p < 0.05).
† Substantively significant (> 10 percent).

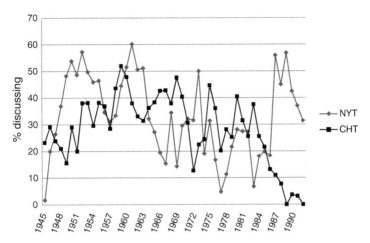

Figure 6.9 Character of Communist powers: editorial coverage.

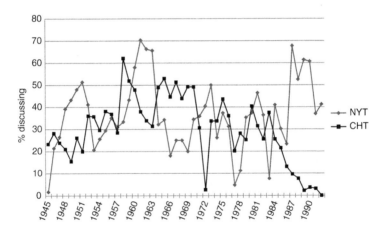

Figure 6.10 West–Communist relations: editorial coverage.

Tribune. Between 1948 and 1952, 44.6 percent of foreign affairs editorials in the *Times* presented a view of Western–Soviet bloc relations, while only 23.7 percent in the *Tribune* did. As Figures 6.9 and 6.10 show, by the mid 1950s, the editorial coverage gap had narrowed: the *Tribune* had joined the consensus.

Third, the two papers' articulated views did eventually diverge, marking a significant erosion of the Cold War narrative's dominance, and they diverged earlier than conventional accounts recognize. As Table 6.3 indicates, from the early to mid 1960s through the end of the Cold War,

Table 6.3 *Erosion of Cold War consensus I*

Questionnaire item	Substantive interpretation of editorial score	Year range	Chicago Tribune: no. editorials	NY Times: no. editorials	Chicago Tribune: average editorial score	NY Times: average editorial score	p-value	ratio (of higher to lower average editorial score)
Communist aggressiveness	3: aggressive 2: both 1: peaceful	1963–1989	710	491	2.9	2.25	0*	1.29[†]
Communist threat	2: real 1: inflated	1965–1989	544	234	1.98	1.78	0*	1.11[†]
West–Comm. relations	3: conflictual 2: mixed 1: cooperative	1963–1989	777	633	2.66	2.42	0*	1.10[†]
Communist unity	3: monolithic 2: both 1: diverse	1961–1989	1110	654	2.85	2.39	0*	1.19[†]
Domino theory	1: yes 0: no	1965–1989	426	147	1	0.85	0*	1.18[†]

* Statistically significant ($p < 0.05$).
† Substantively significant (> 10 percent).

statistically significant gaps (p < 0.01) arose between the two newspapers on *every* question that had previously constituted the dominant narrative. The *Tribune* hewed to the traditional Cold War narrative, hardly departing from the stance it had endorsed in the 1950s, whereas the *Times* deviated substantially. Those differences were also substantively significant, averaging over 17 percent (per the "ratio" column). It is not the fact of the Cold War consensus' ultimate collapse that is surprising, but its timing – *before* leading figures in Congress, and certainly before the American people, turned against the Vietnam War, and even before the Americanization of the war in 1965. The gaps in the papers' stances generally emerged around 1962 with regard to Communist powers' aggressiveness and unity, West–Communist relations, and the domino theory (see Figures 6.5 to 6.8). As the Vietnam War dragged on, there was even less agreement on representations of the Communist Other, but the trend pre-dates the war.

The differences between the liberal internationalists at the *Times* and their conservative counterparts at the *Tribune* were real and growing by the early 1960s, but the former did not adopt editorial stances *diametrically* opposed to the erstwhile consensus. The *Times* did not represent the Soviet Union as a status quo power: between 1962 and 1975, its editorials averaged 3.21 on the scale – somewhat closer to expansionist/aggressive (4) than to satisfied/peaceful (2).[49] It did not cast West–Communist relations as generally cooperative, but as a mix of cooperation and conflict: even in 1966 to 1970, a period of sustained optimism, its editorials averaged 2.12 on this question – close to a mixed-motive game (2), but slightly inclined toward zero-sum competition (3), rather than a positive-sum game (1). It did not even decisively rebuff the domino theory, the pre-eminent legitimating logic of the Vietnam War: between 1965 and 1975, its editorials more often endorsed than rejected the claim that the United States should be concerned with other states "going Communist," averaging 1.60 (with 1.50 representing substantive indifference).[50] These gaps were

---

[49] However, in 1976, its editorials did, on this measure, average 2.38—the lowest score across the entire span, including the late Gorbachev period.

[50] This is consistent with Daniel Hallin's finding regarding the limits of the mainstream media's coverage and criticism of the Vietnam War. See Hallin 1986, esp. 48–58 and passim.

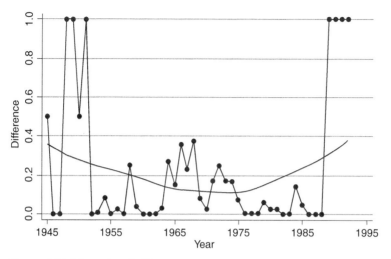

Figure 6.11 Necessity of allies.

not trivial, but the differences in the 1950s (Table 6.2) were four times larger than in this new zone of dissensus (Table 6.3).

Fourth, a new zone of consensus emerged in the last days of the Vietnam War. By the early to mid 1970s, on a range of previously divisive issues – the necessity and reliability of allies, America's status as a leader, the capacity of the United States to play a constructive role in world affairs, and even the value of foreign aid – the two papers' editorial stances for the first time converged (Figures 6.11 to 6.14). On these issues, as Table 6.4 indicates, the differences between the two newspapers' editorials were either statistically insignificant or, when they were statistically significant, substantively small (generally under 5 percent). The distance between liberal Cold Warriors and conservative nationalists had shrunk dramatically – on precisely those putative elements of the Cold War consensus that had not actually been part of the consensus in the 1950s. This was partly because liberals had lost their faith during and after Vietnam, but the most striking movement took place on the right: on these dimensions, the *Times*' scores fell, on average, just 9.7 percent from the first to the second half of the Cold War, while the *Tribune*'s rose 55.8 percent.[51]

---

[51] See the online appendix for these calculations.

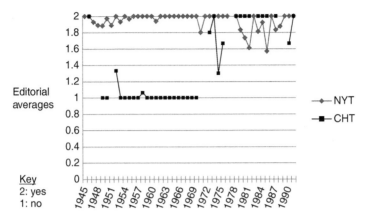

Figure 6.12 Foreign aid valuable?

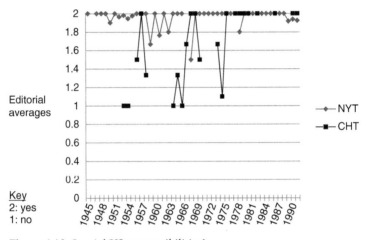

Figure 6.13 Special US responsibilities?

Evaluating contending explanations

The content analysis challenges the conventional historical narrative and periodization of the Cold War consensus. It is also theoretically puzzling: standard models of change in the basic ideas and discourses informing national security do not explain its findings. First, as the previous chapter elucidated, the most common and intuitive explanation attributes change to unexpected, large-scale failure. Defeat in major war is a classic exogenous shock that invalidates old ideas and

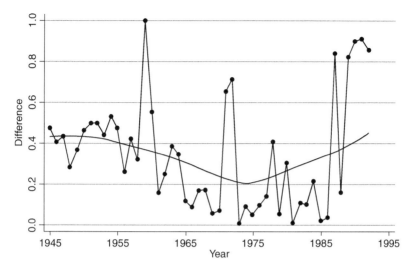

Figure 6.14 US future actions.

renders audiences receptive to alternatives.[52] While this explanation accords with histories that credit the Vietnam War with the dominant Cold War narrative's demise, it cannot make sense of a Cold War narrative that coalesced in the first half of the 1950s, amidst a frustrating war in Korea, and that collapsed in the early 1960s, when there was no unsettling shock.

Second, national security narratives might straightforwardly reflect global realities, as structural realists would argue.[53] Perhaps the Cold War narrative became dominant because it mirrored the bipolar structure of international politics, aggressive Soviet behavior, and a tightly controlled Soviet orbit, and perhaps it lost its grip on US national security debate because it was out of step with developments like the Sino–Soviet split and Soviet moderation. But the dominant Cold War narrative came together only around Stalin's death, and it was

---

[52] Legro 2005; Welch 2005. For other relevant citations, see Chapter 5, nos. 8–9, 11–14.

[53] While structural realists, as confirmed materialists, would not put much stock in narratives, this is a fair extrapolation from the logic of the theory. Neoclassical realists agree that the international system yields clear imperatives that states should obey, but they would acknowledge the possibility that sometimes, and even often, dominant narratives of national security deviate from the system's objective lessons.

Table 6.4 *Cold War consensus II: representations of the American Self and its allies*

Questionnaire item	Substantive interpretation of editorial score	Year range	Chicago Tribune: no. editorials	NY Times: no. editorials	Chicago Tribune: average editorial score	NY Times: average editorial score	p-value	ratio (of higher to lower average editorial score)
Allies necessary?	2: necessary 1: not necessary	1971–1989	175	234	1.97	1.96	0.67	1.01
Allies reliable?	3: reliable 2: contingent 1: not reliable	1971–1989	266	246	2.41	2.18	0.001*	1.11[†]
Special US leadership role?	1: yes 0: no	1976–1989	10	65	1	0.98	0.32	1.02
Foreign aid valuable?	2: valuable 1: not valuable	1976–1989	29	134	1.97	1.88	0.24	1.05
US past constructive?	2: yes 1: no	1965–1989	330	478	1.3	1.42	0*	1.09
US future constructive?	3: yes 2: contingent 1: no	1972–1989	152	486	2.15	2.16	0.82	1

* Statistically significant ($p < 0.05$).
† Substantively significant (> 10 percent).

strongest afterwards – that is, when, under Khrushchev, the Soviet bloc was becoming more diverse and Soviet policy growing more tolerant of difference, and thus when the Cold War narrative was less apposite. Moreover, those presumably most attuned to international realities, realists like George Kennan and Walter Lippmann, took issue early on with the Cold War narrative's view of global Communism as monolithic and of superpower competition as zero-sum.[54] Indeed, realist scholars later often treated militarized global containment as irrational and puzzling.[55] Finally, according to this realist theory, a new narrative should have become dominant in the 1960s that reflected crucial changes in global politics, notably a divided Communist world following the eruption of Sino–Soviet conflict and shared superpower interests following the resolution of the Cuban Missile Crisis – but none did.

Third, perhaps national security narratives shift course along with presidential administration. When new presidents come into office, they often bring a different vision of global politics, conception of the national interest, and foreign policy priorities, a different group of advisers upon whom they are reliant, and a different set of major contributors to whom they are beholden – especially when the new president comes from another political party.[56] Leaving aside the partisan presidential account's overall merits, it does not fit the Cold War narrative's dynamics. The key periods of change do not correspond to changes of presidential administration or party control of the White House. Those have been too frequent, and some key changes have occurred during times of partisan presidential stability. This stands to reason from a narrative perspective. Policy debate typically occurs within the bounds imposed by dominant narratives, and changes in presidential administration and party control might explain policy change *within* those constraints – for instance, the relative weight given to military force in Cold War strategy. It would in fact be surprising if new administrations regularly challenged narrative structures: after all, policy advisers of both parties are typically creatures of the establishment, and elected politicians of both parties are normally highly sensitive to the limits of sustainable argument.

---

[54] Gaddis 1982, 25–53, 89–109; Steel 1980, 466–476.
[55] See, for instance, Dueck 2006; Snyder 1991.
[56] See, for instance, Spiegel 1985, and to some extent Gaddis 1982.

Fourth, one might argue that intense threat, and the need for national unity of purpose, crush dissent, whereas diminished threat opens space for long-suppressed challenge. Certainly, the pressures and politics of threat and wartime stifle debate.[57] That is why wartime criticism often remains shallow even when the military effort has run into trouble and when many are skeptical of the possibility of victory – as Chapter 5 argued. Yet, it would hardly be surprising that threat perceptions correlated with the rise and fall of the Cold War narrative, for that narrative depicted the drama of world politics, including the threat environment. An explanation of a national security narrative's dynamics that relied on threat perceptions would be a tautology.

Fifth, perhaps the data are not capturing shifts in the nation's security narrative, but changes in the two newspapers' leadership teams. Some evidence appears, on the surface, consistent with this possibility: Clayton Kirkpatrick became editor of the *Chicago Tribune* in 1969,[58] just as the paper became less ambivalent about US leadership; the *New York Times* saw the appointment of new publishers in 1961 (Orvil Dryfoos) and 1963 (Arthur Ochs "Punch" Sulzberger) and of a new editorial page editor, John Oakes, in 1961,[59] who, with the support of the publishers, imparted both new verve and a more left-leaning edge to the *Times'* editorials.[60]

Yet, it would be a mistake to attribute too much to personnel changes. The *Tribune* had joined the Cold War consensus while still under the tight control of its long-time hard-core conservative publisher, Colonel Robert McCormick.[61] While Kirkpatrick did transform the paper beginning in the late 1960s, his innovations focused on eliminating the partisan tone of news coverage, introducing greater diversity into the opinion pages, and giving the paper a more modern look. The editorials, contemporaries noted, were a bit less strident, but

[57] Krebs 2009.
[58] Although Kirkpatrick was hardly new to the paper. He had spent his entire career since 1938 at the *Tribune* and had served throughout the 1960s in various editorial positions.
[59] Oakes, too, was hardly new to the paper or the editorial page. A cousin of the publishers (Oakes' father had Anglicized the spelling of the family name), he had been a member of the editorial board since 1949 and had even been considered a candidate for publisher in 1961.
[60] Talese 1970, 79–81, 95–105; Tifft and Jones 1999, 324–325.
[61] On McCormick's dictatorial ways, especially in the final years, see Wendt 1979, 689–691.

the basic outlook remained, as Kirkpatrick had promised at the start of his tenure, "basically conservative ... generally Republican in politics."[62]

The *Times* unquestionably tilted left after Oakes assumed the reins, and neither Dryfoos nor (to an extent) Sulzberger much intervened, except on rare occasions.[63] Yet, the key question is not why the *Times* adopted more liberal editorial positions, but how the reading public reacted to those positions. When the *Times* departed from the putative mainstream in the early 1960s, inhabitants of the Oval Office and Foggy Bottom were less than pleased: John F. Kennedy reportedly declared that "if I tried to run the country the way Oakes writes editorials, we'd all be in a ditch."[64] But neither circulation nor advertising were much affected. After the *Times* in 1961 called for recognition of the People's Republic of China, Oakes recalled: "I really was prepared for an avalanche of abuse. We did not get ... the vituperation that I would have expected ... [I]t does suggest to me that the feeling in this country is much less violent on this subject than the particularly interested parties would want us all to believe. Because instead of getting absolutely crucified, which I thought we were going to be, we got good intelligent letters, which is all anyone can ask."[65] When Oakes began to go too far, to the point that the paper's marketing and sales department became exercised,[66] Punch Sulzberger stepped in, appointing former Nixon speech-writer William Safire to the op-ed page in 1972 over Oakes' opposition and eventually forcing Oakes out in 1976 in "Punch's putsch." This was no mere personality clash, according to the *Times* columnist Tom Wicker, but a reflection of

[62] Wendt 1979, esp. 750–757, quote at 756. On the *Tribune*'s transformation, see also "The Press: The Ten Best American Dailies," *Time*, 21 January 1974; Seth S. King, "Chicago Tribune Shows New Face," *New York Times*, 10 October 1971; Bruckner 1972; Squires 1993, esp. 27–45.

[63] On Dryfoos' hands-off management style, in contrast to his predecessor Arthur Hays Sulzberger, see Tifft and Jones 1999, 323–324; and John B. Oakes Oral History, Columbia University Libraries, 121, available at www.columbia.edu/ cu/lweb/digital/collections/nny/oakesjb/. Punch Sulzberger occasionally objected to particular editorial positions or language, but, in general, he thought it best to leave the editorial page alone and supported its more controversial stances, such as on the Vietnam War. See Talese 1970, 441–443; Tifft and Jones 1999, 385–387, 502–504, 520–527; and also Oakes Oral History, 123–130, 152–162, 170–171, 188–221.

[64] Quoted in Tifft and Jones 1999, 388.   [65] Oakes Oral History, 50–51.

[66] Tifft and Jones 1999, 502.

the country's "rightward shift ... My mail told me where the country was going, and I'm sure Punch's did too."[67]

The puzzle of the Cold War narrative's rise and fall is all the greater when one considers the events surrounding the key nodal points. They coincide with the signal events of the first half of the Cold War: the Korean War, which was the first large-scale US military engagement of the bipolar era, which settled into a bloody stalemate, and which Americans experienced as deeply disappointing and chastening; and the Cuban Missile Crisis, which was the closest the two superpowers came to direct military confrontation and whose resolution Americans across the political spectrum initially saw as an unvarnished triumph. The consensus consolidated amidst (perceived) military failure, and it began to erode after (perceived) victory in a major episode of coercive diplomacy. Equally surprising is that the Cold War narrative's erosion was limited despite an unremitting torrent of bad news from Vietnam and that a new zone of consensus emerged as that traumatic war sputtered to a close. These outcomes, I argue, are not mere coincidence. The Cold War narrative rose to dominance not despite, but because of, the poor US performance in Korea; its dominance slipped not despite, but because of, the seemingly one-sided US victory in Cuba; that erosion remained limited and a new consensus took shape not despite, but because of, the politics of the Vietnam War. The next chapter delves more deeply into the history, politics, and rhetoric of Cold War America to show why the Cold War narrative rose and fell as it did. War and crisis in Korea, Cuba, and Vietnam – key episodes in any history of the Cold War – remain crucial, but in unexpected ways.

[67] Quoted in Diamond 1993, 139.

7 | *Tracing the Cold War consensus*

Viewed through the prism of public narrative, the Cold War consensus takes on a surprising shape. A narrow shared narrative of national security regarding the Communist adversary and the interconnected nature of global politics rose to dominance in the first half of the 1950s, amidst a frustrating war in Korea. It fell apart in the early 1960s, even before the Johnson administration ramped up the US commitment to South Vietnam. A new consensus regarding the protagonists in global politics and their relationship failed to coalesce through the mid 1970s. However, a common elite narrative on America's role in the world emerged from the domestic turmoil unleashed by the Vietnam War. These were not the faithful and straightforward reflections of global realities, nor were they the usual expected responses to policy failure and success.

Rather, as this chapter shows in detail, they were the result of the narrative politics of the military and diplomatic battlefield, per the theoretical logic of Chapter 5. As expected, opposition hawks and doves alike responded to battlefield setbacks by reproducing the narrative in whose terms the war had been legitimated. Thus, during the Korean War, conservative hawks in the Republican opposition blamed the Truman administration not for wasting blood and treasure in a peripheral conflict, but for having left East Asia vulnerable to Communist predation through its inconsistent pursuit of containment – that is, for a policy that was not global enough. They thereby deprived a non-globalist alternative narrative of its leading voices and helped to consolidate the Cold War consensus. During the Vietnam War, "responsible" critics in both parties – all but the most extreme doves – did not take advantage of the faltering and increasingly unpopular intervention to break with the logic of the Cold War. Rather, they maintained that the war was not worth the candle or that it was a misapplication of containment. Both lines of argument re-inscribed the Cold War, rather than upend it. Meanwhile, hawks in the

Republican Party did not seize upon the US military's setbacks in that faraway land to revive the nationalist narrative, but rather embraced their new role as standard-bearers of Cold War globalism and aggressive internationalism. In so doing, they joined liberals to beat back the "radical" challengers to American exceptionalism. Triumph, however, made possible narrative change: the Cuban Missile Crisis permitted John F. Kennedy and other liberal internationalists to deviate from the dominant Cold War narrative and to offer publicly a vision of the adversary and the global environment that sustained détente. This chapter examines these key turning points in America's postwar national security narrative: the Cold War narrative's rise to dominance amidst the Korean War, its erosion in response to the Cuban Missile Crisis, and the limits to that erosion and the rise of a new dominant narrative in response to the Vietnam War.

Consolidation: the Korean War and the end of the nationalist alternative

The dominant Cold War narrative took shape through the marginalization of two alternatives. Accommodationists, like former Vice President Henry Wallace, shared the Cold War's internationalist premises – the indivisible nature of global security, the need for allies, the imperative of US leadership, the potential for constructive US engagement – but they differed in their representation of the adversary, their understanding of local conflicts, and the nature of superpower relations. Conservative nationalists, like Republican party leader Senator Robert Taft, could not be outdone when it came to anti-Communism, but they accepted neither global interconnectedness nor a special US role in global affairs. For the Cold War narrative to become dominant, both these alternative narratives could no longer enjoy legitimacy.

Conventional theory would not expect the Korean War to have led to the Cold War narrative's consolidation. That accommodationists, in response, swiftly transformed themselves into ardent Cold Warriors is not a surprise: the outbreak of war in Korea seemed to confirm a Moscow-driven agenda of Communist aggression.[1] But it was not

---

[1] On Wallace and other accommodationists, see Meyers 2007, 291–298; Paterson 1971.

obvious that the war should have proved fatal to the conservative nationalist narrative. The North Korean invasion was in line with their anti-Communism, and it did not inherently undercut their skepticism of a *global* Cold War – that is, their representation of the setting of global politics. In fact, the public's frustration with the costly stalemate might have been expected to bolster their challenge to globalist premises, as Secretary of State Dean Acheson feared.[2] In human terms, the war was overall nearly as costly for the United States as the subsequent war in Vietnam, and, on an annualized basis, it was much more so, and the Republicans made political hay of the high casualties.[3] And the Korean War was equally unpopular: after Chinese forces crossed the Yalu River in November 1950 and a bloody deadlock set in, the home front's patience grew as thin as it would two decades later.[4] So desperate were Americans to bring the boys home that the war hero Dwight Eisenhower's vague promise, "I shall go to Korea," won them over in 1952.[5] Even as the Korean War's memory faded, Americans continued to see it as a waste: the most popular reason to support Republican candidates in 1956 was that the party had extricated the country from Korea.[6] In short, the Cold War narrative did not become dominant because the Korean War had demonstrated its key pillars' undeniable truth. Across the political spectrum, among civilians and military officers, a main

---

[2] Acheson 1969, 494.

[3] A slightly higher percentage of serving US soldiers was killed and wounded in the course of the Korean War (2.4 percent) than the Vietnam War (2.3 percent). As a percentage of total population (at the start of the war), however, the cost in battle deaths and wounded was slightly higher in Vietnam (0.103%), versus Korea (0.090%). But because the Korean War (1950–1953) was much shorter than the Vietnam War (1965–1973), its annualized human cost was far greater. Calculated from figures in Chambers II 1999, 849; and US Census Bureau, Historical National Population Estimates, 1 July 1900 to 1 July 1999, www.census.gov/popest/data/national/totals/pre-1980/tables/po pclockest.txt. On the politics of casualties in Korea, see Casey 2010.

[4] On public opinion in the two wars, see Mueller 1971, 42–65.

[5] That declaration's decisive impact was widely noted at the time and afterwards. For contemporaries' assessments, see Divine 1974, 74–76, 82–84; Hughes 1957. Among scholars, see Bernstein 1971, 349–350; Caridi 1968, 234; Donovan 1982, 401; Greene 1985, 219–220; Pach Jr. and Richardson 1991, 26; Perret 1999, 418. For analysis of the speech itself, see Medhurst 2000.

[6] Gallup Poll #568, Questions 15–16, 1 August 1956, available at http://brain. gallup.com/documents/questionnaire.aspx?STUDY=AIPO0568&p=2.

lesson of the war – ignored but a decade later – was that the United States should not again become embroiled in a limited conflict, and possibly any land war, in Asia.[7] There is good reason to think that the war's course could, if not should, have led to the rejection of its legitimating Cold War logic and bolstered the nationalist alternative.

Yet, the opposite occurred. By war's end, globalist premises ruled US foreign affairs debate: the Cold War consensus had been consolidated, the nationalist narrative cast to the periphery. For the institutionalist conventional wisdom, this outcome is confounding, but it makes perfect sense from the perspective of the theoretical account in Chapter 5. As military setbacks in Korea accumulated, nationalists, who then dominated the congressional Republican leadership, did not invoke them as evidence of the folly of a militarized global crusade against Communism – which would have accorded with both their narrative and their domestic priorities. Rather, these opposition hawks exploited the US military's misfortune for political gain by trying to out-Cold War the Cold Warriors. Taking the Truman administration to task for waging that militarized global crusade inconsistently and ineptly – on purpose, the more conspiratorially minded suggested – they thrust aside the nationalist alternative to which they had long given voice. By the mid 1950s, responsible Republicans no longer challenged the global Cold War.[8]

The global Cold War, resting on a portrait of the international scene as tightly interconnected, had not yet achieved axiomatic status in the late 1940s – even though many scholars believe that earlier the domestic bases of internationalism had become dominant, Axis aggression had discredited isolationism, and the Allies' triumph had consolidated internationalism.[9] Nationalism was hardly beyond the pale after the Second World War.[10] Thus,

---

[7] See Gacek 1994, 87–90. On the public's fading view over time of the Korean War's futility and error, see Mueller 1973, 170–172.

[8] For supporting data from roll-call votes, see Fordham 2007; Reichard 1975. Some credit Eisenhower's leadership (Dueck 2010, 85–116; Reichard 1975), but the evidence is meager.

[9] For the best accounts, see, from different perspectives, Legro 2005; Trubowitz 1998.

[10] Brian Rathbun (2011, 2012) agrees that there continued to be a vigorous debate after the Second World War over how security should be provided – via unilateral or multilateral means. But even he argues that the war marked a decisive turn to internationalism.

the *New York Times* endorsed Thomas Dewey for president in 1948 even though "isolationism still dominates the Republican leadership of the House of Representatives," and in 1952 it hoped that Eisenhower would silence the party's powerful "semi-isolationists."[11] Traveling in the nation's heartland in spring 1945, Senator J. William Fulbright warned Archibald MacLeish, then Assistant Secretary of State for Cultural Affairs, that Anglophobia and isolationism continued to thrive in the Midwest.[12] Nationalist non-interventionists remained prominent in Republican circles and especially among the party's congressional leaders until the mid 1950s. The transformed Senator Arthur Vandenberg aside, few radically changed their tune after Pearl Harbor or even after the war.[13] This was especially true after 1948: Truman's surprise victory that year ended a short-lived bipartisan moment and reinvigorated a stridently partisan politics.[14] The prospects for GOP moderation declined further when John Foster Dulles failed to win election to the Senate from New York in 1949 and when illness sidelined Vandenberg in 1950. The hegemonic standing of the global Cold War was not a sure thing at the start of the Korean War – or, as Richard Barnet pithily puts it, "the American people were not ready for the American Century."[15]

Important elite-bargaining accounts, notably those of Benjamin Fordham and Jack Snyder, agree that nationalist Republicans remained central and legitimate figures in postwar politics and that the Korean War was crucial to the consolidation of the Cold War consensus. But they differ on the causal logic: they argue that the consensus was the product of a tacit logroll between Europe-first internationalists of both parties and conservative Republicans. As all legitimated their pet projects in the name of an indiscriminate anti-Communism, the latter joined the Cold War abroad in exchange for a shrunken welfare state and Cold War at

[11] "The Choice of a Candidate," *New York Times*, 3 October 1948; "Eisenhower," *New York Times*, 7 January 1952.
[12] Woods 1995, 104.
[13] Gould 2003, 291–292; Westerfield 1955. On the prominent party leader, Sen. Robert Taft, see Dueck 2010, 63–76; Hamby 1985, 102; Patterson 1972, 247–248, 285–298.
[14] Caridi 1968, esp. ch. 1; Kepley 1988; Reinhard 1983, 18–20, 54–67.
[15] Barnet 1990, 249–254, quote at 253.

home.[16] These accounts, however, are unsatisfying. First, they slide too quickly from anti-Communism to globalism:[17] passionate anti-Communism had long been compatible with selective engagement.[18] Second, the Truman administration was no latecomer to the domestic Cold War. By February 1950, when Senator Joseph McCarthy first publicly charged the State Department with employing known Communists, the administration was already deeply enmeshed via the federal employee loyalty program, its harassment of Communist Party leaders, and its ramped-up rhetoric. As David Caute observes: "It was the Truman administration that manured the soil from which the prickly cactus called McCarthy suddenly and awkwardly shot up" – well before prominent conservative nationalists had taken substantial steps toward the global Cold War.[19] Third, evidence of a logroll is meager. The Truman administration did not give much ground on executive power, and it was the controlling political alliance between conservative Republicans and southern Democrats, not the administration, that killed the Fair Deal.[20] Fourth, these accounts fail to explain why the logroll endured. Nationalists could presumably have scored political gains, and come closer to achieving their domestic ends, by pulling out of the bargain and by offering an alternative to the global Cold War that had trapped US forces in a bloody, unpopular, stalemated war.

---

[16] Fordham 1998; Snyder 1991. However, Fordham elsewhere suggests that the consensus did not coalesce until the second half of the 1950s: see Cronin and Fordham 1999; Fordham 2007.

[17] For the view that embracing intense anti-Communism required embracing the global Cold War, see Green 1987, 171, 185–189; Hamby 1985, 103–115; Miles 1980, 119; Snyder 1991, 264. This problem is noted also by Fordham 1998, 103.

[18] Jonas 1966, 54, 64, 87; Powers 1995, 162–170, 183–184, 192.

[19] Caute 1978, 28, and generally 25–40. On Truman's contributions to the domestic Cold War, see also Hogan 1998; Theoharis 1971, esp. 98–122. For a more sympathetic portrait, see Powers 1995, 191–233.

[20] Fordham (1998, 103–130) asserts that Truman's commitment to the Fair Deal was "largely rhetorical," but neither he nor the historians on whom he relies present evidence that a more committed Truman could have brought about its enactment. In fact, Zelizer (2010, 67–68) argues that Truman's move to the right on Communism, at home and abroad, had the opposite intent: to generate political space to move left in domestic affairs. That Truman was ultimately unsuccessful was a sign not of his lack of commitment, but of the political constraints he confronted.

Conservative nationalists were not outside the mainstream when the Korean War erupted. Avid anti-Communists, they welcomed and echoed Truman's increasingly Manichean rhetoric, which painted a stark portrait of a world divided between free and slave. Quantitative measures confirm that Truman's rhetoric on foreign affairs became markedly more storied after March 1947 and then again after the start of the Korean War.[21] Yet, while Truman boldly narrated the protagonists in the emerging global drama, his articulation of the global scene was muddy. With good reason: this was a matter of dispute within the administration through early 1950. When it came to how tightly the fabric of international security was woven, the administration's influential realists, who advocated a more selective slate of US commitments abroad, differed from the nationalists in degree and tone alone. Only with Truman's final endorsement of NSC-68 in December 1950 was the administration finally ready to embrace a truly global Cold War.[22] By that time, however, its credibility had already begun to wane thanks to battlefield struggles in Korea. The Truman administration's hesitancy, and then the Korean War, gave conservative nationalists an opening. It was up to them to seize it or spurn it.

Korea and the politics of failure

At first, conservatives, like the nation as a whole, rallied around the flag: every Republican senator, even as orthodox a nationalist and as harsh a critic of Truman as Senate Minority Leader Kenneth Wherry of Nebraska, supported the administration's forceful response to the North Korean invasion.[23] But they held true to their vision even as they rallied. Senator Robert Taft of Ohio – the nation's most prominent conservative,[24] "Mr. Republican," so unquestionably the party's

---

[21] See Appendix C, Table C.6.

[22] The NSC had issued its first draft in April 1950, but Truman had sent it back for cost estimates. Soon after those were submitted in September, Truman approved the document's basic approach, but asked for further revisions. Only in December did he finally endorse NSC-68 as the basis for a multi-year build-up.

[23] Caridi 1968, 35–38. On Wherry, see Stromer 1969.

[24] Taft was widely seen as the leader of the GOP's "Old Guard," but he was not dogmatically conservative. His inclination to compromise sometimes rendered him suspect to those farther to his right. However, given Taft's national and organizational prominence, and the decline of the traditional Republican Right

leader that *The New Republic* quipped that "Congress now consists of the House, the Senate, and Bob Taft"[25] – backed the administration's policy, but challenged the legitimating globalist logic: the independence of Korea, he declared on the Senate floor, was "not vitally important to the United States," and the choice to draw the line there against Communist aggression was arbitrary.[26] The White House was surprised to hear of Taft's support; Press Secretary Charles Ross noted, only half in jest: "My God, Bob Taft has joined the UN and the US."[27] But it overlooked how little Taft had actually conceded. The *Chicago Tribune* was unusual in declaring openly, the day after North Korea invaded, that "not one American in a thousand believes that the defense of Korea is worth the life of a husband, son, or brother" and in objecting to the president's apparent belief that "it is the duty of the United States to oppose the spread of Russian communism anywhere, at anytime."[28] But, even as most newspapers united behind the administration in the war's early days, notes of cautious dissent could be heard. The concerned editor of the conservative *Richmond News Leader* reasonably asked: "Over how many Koreas have we spread our wings?"[29]

Wild reversals characterized the war's first six months. The steady North Korean advance through September 1950 was succeeded by a dramatic momentum swing to the US-led UN forces following the Inchon landing and Pusan breakout. The pendulum then swung back after Chinese forces crossed the Yalu River in mid October. Prominent conservatives agreed with Acheson that the war's ups and downs had rendered Cold War globalism vulnerable. Noting that "it is clear that the United Nations are defeated in Korea," sensing the administration's weakness, and seizing on its announcement that it planned to station

upon his death, I treat him as a key figure in understanding the dynamics of the hawkish opposition during wartime. On conservatives' suspicion of Taft, see Reinhard 1983, 27–30 and passim.

[25] *Time* similarly referred to the period of the 80th Congress as "the Age of Taft." *New Republic* quoted in Patterson 1972, 337; *Time* quoted in Reinhard 1983, 39.

[26] Excerpts from Senate Speech on Korean War, 28 June 1950, in Wunderlin 2006, quote at 168.

[27] Quoted in Patterson 1972, 453.

[28] "Korea," 26 June 1950; "A Popular War So Far," 30 June 1950 – both in *Chicago Tribune*. See also Caridi 1968, 116–120.

[29] Quoted in "Report from the Nation: All Eyes on Korea," *New York Times*, 2 July 1950.

several divisions permanently in Europe, GOP elder statesman and former President Herbert Hoover initiated the so-called "Great Debate" in late December 1950.[30] It dominated debate over national security affairs in both Congress and the nation's leading publications until late into spring 1951.[31] Well into the Korean War, there was clearly no consensus on the nature of the postwar world.

Hoover's public addresses that winter challenged not only the administration's military policy, but the deeper narrative of national security in which it was grounded. He did not question the emerging narrative on the motives or unity of the Soviet Union or global Communism or on the conflictual nature of Communist-free world relations; "there is today only one center of aggression on the earth," he declared, and "that is the Communist-controlled Asian-European land mass." But, calling upon his fellow Americans "to preserve for the world this Western hemisphere Gibraltar of Western Civilization," Hoover did question the liberal internationalist claim that the fabric of global politics was so tightly interwoven that security was indivisible. National security, he averred, was not dependent on global order. Drawing a defensive perimeter that stretched from Britain across the Western hemisphere to Japan, Formosa (Taiwan), and the Philippines, he pointedly excluded continental Europe, where "minds are confused with fears and disunities" and which appeared to lack "the spiritual force" to defend itself against "the red flood." Despite the Communist advantage in land forces, the military threat was limited: "they can no more reach Washington in force than we can reach Moscow," he concluded. As a result, even in a world in which Soviet-led Communism was on the march, the United States could thrive "indefinitely." What was tightly interwoven, Hoover contended, were the national defense effort and US prosperity: current rates of spending were, he maintained, "beyond the long endurance of any nation and fatal to the preservation of a system of free men." He lobbied for specific policies – more selective engagement, a smaller standing army, greater reliance on naval and air power – and he justified those policies with a very different portrait of the global scene.[32]

---

[30] "Our National Policies in this Crisis," 20 December 1950, reprinted in Hoover 1955, 3–10.

[31] Carpenter 1986; Casey 2008, 181–198.

[32] "Our National Policies in this Crisis," 20 December 1950, and "We Should Revise Our Foreign Policies," 9 February 1951, reprinted in Hoover 1955, 3–10, 11–22.

The press covered the Great Debate at length. Citing the "Korean defeat" and the prospect of its "repetition ... on a grander scale," the *Chicago Tribune*, true to form, endorsed Hoover's stance. Anti-Communist "hysteria" and administration propaganda, which the *Tribune* labeled "the enemy within," had blinded Americans to the true implications of the Korean intervention.[33] But, beyond the predictably supportive *Tribune*, the media and public response to Hoover was, in the words of one historian, "overwhelmingly favorable" – so much so that the *Nation* bemoaned this sign of the "widespread revival of blind isolationism."[34] Committed liberal internationalists in the media found Hoover's positions passé and even laughable, but they could not ignore the clarion call of one of America's elder statesmen. A *New York Times* review of regional reaction to the Great Debate revealed that many newspapers, even those that did not endorse Hoover's proposals, "applauded" him for calling the administration to account; some quarters of the country were "fertile ground" for Hoover's message, in others the debate "rage[d] hotly," but everywhere there was confusion and dissatisfaction.[35] The military's travails in Korea set off, in *Life*'s words, "a great debate on foreign policy that tugged at the nation's mind and soul."[36] In short, there was no dominant narrative as of the winter of 1950 to 1951. Americans had just then reached the critical juncture – not before.

Yet, conservative nationalism would soon be strangled by the politics of Korea. In contrast to Hoover, whose political time had passed, younger conservatives readily sacrificed their nationalism on the altar of political expediency and pressed themselves into the global Cold War's service. Eager to score gains against an administration on the ropes, they abandoned their nationalism in favor of Cold War globalism in winter-spring of 1951. As hawks, they had to back the war as a matter of both principle and articulated identity: "there is no alternative except to support the war," Taft admitted. But patriotism alone would not allow them to make political headway. The solution,

[33] "Feeble Reply," 26 December 1950; "The Enemy Within Our Gates," 10 January 1951. See also "Mr. Hoover Speaks for the Nation," 22 December 1950. All in *Chicago Tribune*.
[34] Kaufman 1986, 123; *Nation* quoted in Carpenter 1986, 404. Carpenter (1986, 405) agrees that the response was "generally favourable."
[35] "Report from the Nation on Foreign Policy Issue," *New York Times*, 14 January 1951.
[36] *Life*, 8 January 1951, quoted in Kaufman 1986, 124.

Taft privately strategized just a month into the war, was to "point out that [the war] has resulted from a bungling of the Democratic administration."[37] Conservative Republicans, hawks in the political opposition, followed Taft's playbook for more than two years. They cast Korea as but the latest debacle, and they invoked the domino theory to explain it: by selling out the nationalists in Formosa (Taiwan), Truman had invited aggression in Korea and soon in Indochina. Even Harold Stassen, the moderate former governor of Minnesota and a serious presidential contender (before he became a perennial punch-line), could not restrain himself: the war, he contended in November 1950, resulted from "five years of coddling Chinese Communists, five years of undermining General MacArthur, five years of snubbing friendly freedom-loving Asiatics, and five years of appeasing the arch-Communist, Mao-Tse-Tung."[38]

Conservative hawks could have charged the Truman administration with dragging the nation into a pointless, costly war in a location of little strategic import. This line of attack would have been consistent with their nationalism, and it might have been good politics too as casualties mounted, battlefield progress proved fleeting, and stalemate set in. But they did not. Rather, they charged Truman with not having been sufficiently faithful to the global Cold War. The basic logic was hardly new to Republicans, who spat out Yalta as if the word itself were evidence of Democratic perfidy,[39] but the Korean War gave it renewed impetus and, crucially, a new Asian twist. Unlike the party's "China bloc" – notably Senator William Knowland of California, whose moniker "the Senator from Formosa" did him little injustice – the orthodox Republican Right of Taft, Wherry, Speaker of the House Joseph Martin, and many lesser lights had, before the Korean War, shown as little interest in committing substantial US resources to East Asia as to Europe.[40] After North Korea's invasion, however, they discovered a love of Asia, endorsing policies toward that region that

[37] Quoted in Patterson 1972, 455.
[38] Caridi 1968, 95. For other examples, see Caridi 1968, 39–49, 54–56, 84–85, and passim; Casey 2008, 82–84, 109–111, and passim; Kepley 1988, 85, 88–89, 93–96; Patterson 1972, 453–454, 475; Radosh 1975, 173.
[39] Republicans accused Democrats of having sold out Eastern Europe at the February 1945 Yalta Conference, and they claimed that postwar Soviet aggression was the direct result of Democratic cowardice, if not treason. On the Yalta Myth and its political uses, see Theoharis 1970.
[40] Kepley 1988, 49–50, 61, 131. See also Zelizer 2010, 99.

they found anathema elsewhere. So avidly did the party's conservative wing embrace the global Cold War when it came to Asia that it was commonly noted that "a neo-isolationist was one who wanted to fight in China."[41]

A further sign of how far conservative hawks, under the pressure of the Korean War, had moved from their nationalist commitments was their enthusiastic backing of General Douglas MacArthur. MacArthur called for escalating the war to China, and Truman cashiered the imperious general in April 1951 when he publicized his objections to the Commander-in-Chief's strategy. Republicans welcomed MacArthur back home as a crucified hero. Hoover hailed him as "the reincarnation of St. Paul into a great general of the Army who has come out of the East," while Wherry declared him a "tower of strength and deserving idol of the American people," a "giant" beset by "pygmies." Sacking MacArthur, the House Republican Policy Committee alleged, was prelude to a "Super-Munich" in Asia.[42] This was good politics, for MacArthur was extraordinarily popular with Republicans' constituents. But nationalists thereby entangled themselves in the global Cold War. MacArthur's zealous commitment to Asia followed from Cold War logic pursued to its extreme: if containment was necessary in Europe to prevent Soviet aggression and bolster sagging European resolve, it was even more warranted in Asia, where Communists had actually engaged in aggression and where capable Nationalist Chinese were chomping at the bit to help. The deep interconnectedness of global politics, MacArthur warned House Speaker Martin in a letter that became public, required the United States to beat back Communism in Asia: "If we lose the war to Communism in Asia, the fall of Europe is inevitable. Win it, and Europe most probably will avoid war and yet preserve freedom." MacArthur's view of the Cold War was so global and so unselective – "I believe we should defend every place from Communism. I believe we can. I believe we are able to," he testified to Congress[43] – that other Cold Warriors found it puzzling. MacArthur "has a strange idea that we should back anybody who

---

[41] Graebner 1956, 27.
[42] Quoted in Caridi 1968, 150, 149; quoted in Zelizer 2010, 110.
[43] Quoted in Kepley 1988, 126.

will fight communism," Averell Harriman reported to Truman after meeting the general.[44]

MacArthur's stance was attractive to opposition hawks for obvious reasons: it scored political points while shoring up the war effort.[45] But conservative Republicans could not follow MacArthur and preserve their opposition to the global Cold War. After all, for MacArthur, the chief problem with the administration's policy was that it was not global *enough*. Moreover, only by reproducing the logic of the global Cold War could hawks make their criticisms stick; if global security were divisible and if the battle against Communism were selective, the administration's lack of resolve in East Asia may not have been very consequential. Thus, in May 1951, Taft echoed MacArthur in declaring that his quarrel was "with those who wished to go all out in Europe, even beyond our capacity, and at the same time refuse to apply our general program and strategy to the Far East." The administration's half-hearted commitment to the Cold War, Senator William Jenner of Indiana charged in fall 1951, had produced a "treadmill war."[46] Had they been true to their principles, members of the Republican Right should have pressed to scale back US efforts in Asia, but instead they sanctioned the expansion of what they had previously condemned as illogical and unaffordable. As the long-time pacifist A. J. Muste observed ironically: "For isolationists, these Americans do certainly get around."[47] In a July 1951 private letter, Taft admitted that his endorsement of an aggressive global Cold War was political in design: MacArthur may not be completely right when it comes to foreign policy, he wrote, but "we cannot possibly win the next election unless we point out the utter failure and incapacity of the present Administration to conduct foreign policy and cite the loss of China and the Korean war as typical examples of their very dangerous control."[48]

[44] Caridi 1968, chs. 5–6, quote at 145, 61. See also Doenecke 1979, chs. 8–9; Kepley 1988, ch. 7; Radosh 1975, 184–189; Snyder 1991, 266–268, 288–289. On the Republicans' embrace of MacArthur, see also Stueck 1995, 182–184.
[45] For similar interpretations, see Caridi 1968; Kepley 1988. See also Foot 1985, 69–70.
[46] Caridi 1968, quotes at 163, 183, and, for other examples, see 112–113, 116–120, 153–159. On similar rhetoric during the highly partisan 1952 campaign, see Kaufman 1986, 261.
[47] Quoted in Patterson 1972, 482. See also Radosh 1975, 156.
[48] Quoted in Patterson 1972, 491.

As battlefield setbacks and the war's uncertain course cowed administration officials, who feared being overtaken by events or overheating the mass public,[49] opposition hawks seized the national rostrum – but not to advance an alternative narrative of national security. They lobbed their grenades from the safe terrain of the Cold War narrative in whose terms the war had been legitimated. Taft's contribution to the Great Debate was typical. He was superficially in line with his mentor Hoover, whom he affectionately called "Chief":[50] he warned against stationing US forces in Europe, and he urged deeper investment in naval and air forces.[51] But he did not launch "a smashing attack against the whole internationalist position," contrary to Acheson's later claim.[52] In fact, Taft narrated a world that looked very much like that of Cold War globalism.[53] He conceded that the spread of Communism, *anywhere*, was necessarily inimical to American interests: because global interconnectedness was great, the US national interest knew no bounds. Hoover depicted the Soviet threat as primarily military, but Taft, like the Truman Doctrine, cast the Communist menace as largely ideological and global liberty as indivisible.[54] Unlike Hoover, Taft's objection to the global Cold War was entirely instrumental, and he called for protecting far-flung regions from Communist advance where this could be achieved at low cost.[55] Hoover had thrown down the gauntlet to the Cold Warriors, but Taft reworked his elder's proposals into merely an alternate *means* of waging the Cold War. It was, as one historian has written, "an alternative strategy *of* containment" – not an alternative *to* containment.[56]

In the end, the Great Debate was not very great, as the distance between nationalists and internationalists shrank considerably during its course. Republican Henry Cabot Lodge, Jr., announced on the Senate floor: "There are no fundamental principles which divide us. There are questions of degree and questions of method – but nothing

---

[49] Casey 2008, 82–84, 207–210, 226–228, and passim.

[50] Patterson 1972, 243.

[51] Republicans' preference for strategic nuclear weapons and airpower persisted throughout the Cold War. See Fordham 2002.

[52] Acheson 1969, 491. See also Dueck 2010, 80.

[53] See, for a similar interpretation, Berger 1971, 168–169 and passim; Kepley 1988, 101–102 and generally ch. 7; Radosh 1975; Wunderlin 2005, 158–170.

[54] Wunderlin 2005, 170–172.

[55] "'Great Debate' Speech in the U.S. Senate," 5 January 1951, in Wunderlin 2006, 230–252.

[56] MacDonald 1986, 79 [emphasis added].

which really goes to the heart of the matter"; Taft wrote Lodge that he agreed.[57] Eisenhower was, in his diary, blistering in his criticism of the Great Debate as "nothing more than a heterogeneous collection of personal, partisan, and private quarrels"; the NATO Supreme Commander saw it as a dispute over "the various means and methods open to us for waging effective war against communism" – not over the more fundamental questions raised by Hoover at the start.[58] Muste saw even less daylight between Truman and Taft: their joint objective remained "war to the finish against Russia and Communism."[59] It is revealing that Taft's greatest critics were not liberal Cold Warriors, but more consistent nationalists like Wherry or libertarians like Murray Rothbard.[60]

Globalism ascendant

Once the GOP Old Guard had publicly endorsed the global Cold War, the nationalist narrative not only lost its most prominent spokesmen, but descended into the realm of the irrelevant and irresponsible. Downplaying the threat posed by global Communism and portraying global security as divisible – pillars of the nationalist alternative narrative – were clear signs that one was not serious and respectable. Thus, by 1953, few conservatives elected to national office still publicly voiced reservations to Cold War globalism. Although Eisenhower may have decided to run for president in 1952 because he did not trust Taft's commitment to internationalism,[61] he noted in his diary with pleasant surprise, shortly after entering office, that, when it came to foreign policy, he and Taft never disagreed "academically or theoretically" – that is, on principles – only on questions of application to and implementation in specific cases.[62] Even Hoover had by the middle of 1954 given up the fight against the global Cold War: "our dangers from the Communist source of gigantic evil are unending," he insisted.[63]

---

[57] Quoted in Bell 2004, 240–241.
[58] Eisenhower diary, 27 April 1951, in Ferrell 1981, 192–193.
[59] Muste to Taft, 1 March 1951, enclosed "Taft and Truman: Memo on Crisis in Foreign Policy," in Wunderlin 2006, 267, n. 1.
[60] Patterson 1972, 482; Rothbard 2007, 85–86.
[61] Eisenhower 1967, 371–372.
[62] Eisenhower diary, 1 June 1953, in Ferrell 1981, 242.
[63] "The Protection of Freedom," 10 August 1954, reprinted in Hoover 1955, quote at 79.

If conservatives needed any reminder of the boundaries of legitimation in the early 1950s, they just had to look at the remaining old progressives, who railed against the global Cold War and found themselves ignored, dismissed as "hick provincials" and renegade isolationists.[64] Conservative intellectuals were also coming to terms with the new reality. In the mid 1950s, the *National Review* led the intellectual effort to fuse Burkean conservatism and anti-statist individualism under the banner of anti-Communism.[65] The prominent libertarian Murray Rothbard ruefully recalled that, by the mid 1950s, "old libertarian and isolationist compatriots who should have known better ... [and] who used to scoff at the 'Russian threat' and had declared The Enemy to be Washington, D.C.[,] now began to mutter about the 'international Communist conspiracy.'"[66]

The 1953 confirmation fight over Eisenhower's nominee for ambassador to the USSR, Charles Bohlen, is instructive. Right-wing Republican senators took issue not with Bohlen's internationalism, but with his spine. Because he had been FDR's interpreter at Yalta, and had subsequently defended the agreement, the Right viewed him as of too weak a mettle to wage the Cold War. Everett Dirksen of Illinois asked: "If we are going to disavow Yalta, how can we accept the architect?" Styles Bridges of New Hampshire spoke for many: "When Bohlen, the exponent of appeasement and containment[, rather than rollback,] is elevated to the vital role of Ambassador to Moscow, the cause of freedom suffers the world over." Taft, ever "Mr. Republican," pushed the nomination through, but privately he conceded that his colleagues' opposition was "perfectly reasonable." The fight was so bruising that Taft reportedly told the White House, "No more Bohlens," and the administration listened.[67] By 1953, hawkishness alone had overtaken whatever objections the Old Guard had once had to Cold War globalism.

Once conservative nationalists took up the Cold War narrative, the scope of contestation narrowed in ways they did not anticipate or desire: they found themselves in a rhetorical vise of their own making. Most immediately, they limited their capacity to oppose deepening the US military commitment to Europe. The logic of the global Cold War

---

[64] Griffith 1979, 346–347.
[65] On this transformation, see Himmelstein 1990; Hodgson 1996, 69–90.
[66] Rothbard 2007, 127.
[67] Hulsey 2000, 55; Reinhard 1983, 105–106; Theoharis 1970, 165–175.

required conservative hawks to concede that a European bulwark against Communism was crucial. When Eisenhower testified before Congress in 1951 that, based on his recent tour of NATO capitals, the allies evinced great determination and will to resist the Soviets, but lacked the requisite human and material resources,[68] nationalists found themselves in an untenable position. Taft wavered: he "would not object to a few more divisions," if only to shore up the Europeans' confidence. When Secretary of Defense George Marshall subsequently presented the administration's plan in detail, the substantive difference had come down to a single division.[69] Great Debate indeed!

More generally, the globalism embraced by nationalist hawks in the political opposition in the midst of the Korean War proved "a devil's bargain."[70] They would help to craft compromises that stopped short of the dreaded garrison state, but, as Donald Critchlow concludes, even though "they continued to inveigh against New Deal collectivism, the welfare state, and government regulation of business, . . . the leviathan state continued its advancement in the United States."[71] Voices within the consensus, they could not justify denying the government the resources it needed to wage the global struggle, and they quietly gave their blessing to the national-security state. With the Cold War narrative firmly in place, advocates of limited government were left only with points of constitutional principle, embodied in Senator John Bricker's repeated efforts to confine the president's capacity to make foreign policy via executive agreement. But this debate over the separation of powers and the status of international law took place within the bounds of the Cold War national-security state: at one time, the Bricker Amendment had sixty-four co-sponsors in the Senate.[72] The Old Right's maneuvering in the shadow of the Korean War paved the way for the rise of the globalist, interventionist New Right of Barry Goldwater and later Ronald Reagan.

The Right never did shake the isolationist label, however. So pilloried, they were a useful foil to Cold Warriors in both parties. Eisenhower, who would as president build a strong relationship with Majority Leader

---

[68] Eisenhower was, in private communications with Truman, more skeptical of Europeans' commitment, to the point that he sounded more like Hoover. See Carpenter 1986, 410–411.

[69] Acheson 1969, 495; Patterson 1972, 480–481.   [70] Zelizer 2010, 6.

[71] Critchlow 2007, 26. See also Hogan 1998.

[72] Tananbaum 1988, 69–71. For a similar interpretation, see also Zelizer 2010, 124.

Taft,[73] denounced the senator as an isolationist during the brutal race for the nomination in 1952. Just three years after Taft's death, the journalist Samuel Lubell wrote of that contest: "If a playwright had tried to contrive a pair of characters to dramatize the isolationist-internationalist cleavage in the Republican party he could not have found two better prototypes."[74] Taft's ill-deserved reputation as a doctrinaire conservative and isolationist would serve him well in the wake of the Vietnam War. Critics of that intervention would proclaim the much-maligned Taft a "sober, wise, and realistic voice" who had counseled "restraint and liberty at a moment when these themes appeared as anachronistic cries from a past age."[75]

It is thus more than a little ironic that the consolidation of the Cold War narrative is perhaps Taft's most significant historical legacy. Amidst the frustrating, bloody, and deeply unpopular Korean stale-mate, Taft and other leading conservatives abandoned the nationalist narrative of national security – even though the faltering war might plausibly have bolstered its skepticism of global interconnectedness. As Chapter 5 expects of opposition hawks, they supported the war effort vigorously and signed on to the globalist narrative in whose terms the war had been legitimated. They left their nationalism behind and joined the Cold War consensus.

Collapse: Cuba and the end of the Cold War consensus

This narrow Cold War narrative's dominance lasted around a decade. Beginning in 1963, while the *Chicago Tribune* remained faithful to that narrative, and even hardened its stance, the *New York Times'* assessment of Communist aggressiveness declined substantially (over 21 percent); its judgment of Western–Communist relations moved much closer to a mixed-motive game;[76] it more often thought the Communist threat exaggerated; and its portrait of the Communist world became more nuanced.[77] Neither exogenous shock nor alleged

[73] See various diary entries: Ferrell 1981, 226–227, 240–242, 269.
[74] Lubell 1956, 16.   [75] Radosh 1975, 195.
[76] The *Times'* score on this question fell from 2.84 to 2.37, with 3 representing a "generally conflictual" relationship and 2 a "cooperative and conflictual" one.
[77] On the question of Communism's unity or diversity, the *Times'* editorials remained circumspect, however. In no year did the *Times'* editorials average less than 1.69, which is still closer to "both" (2) than to "diverse" (1). Even between 1962 and 1967 – the *Times'* longest sustained period of relatively low scores – it

global realities can account for liberal internationalists' drift from the Cold War narrative. It was surprisingly, and consistent with the logic of Chapter 5, triumph in the Cuban Missile Crisis that made possible the demise of the Cold War consensus. However, as expected, no new consensus portrait of the Communist Other took its place: conservative Cold Warriors continued to toe the old Cold War line, charging liberals with naïvely confusing a tactical flash in the pan with enduring strategic change.

Liberal activists and intellectuals had for years been poking holes in the Cold War narrative.[78] Behind closed doors, some officials, including John F. Kennedy himself, questioned key elements, especially the zero-sum nature of superpower competition. In a 1959 background interview, Kennedy noted that what impeded the two powers from achieving a stable *modus vivendi* was less Soviet ideology or ambition than preconceptions and miscommunication: "You have two people ... who are both of goodwill, but neither of whom can communicate because of a language difference."[79] In his March 1962 draft Basic National Security Policy, Walt Rostow, the head of policy planning at the State Department, observed that "it may become increasingly possible to make [the Soviets] feel that we share a common interest in the exercise of restraint"; their Communist system did not preclude "constructive participation."[80] This view at times influenced Kennedy's decision-making: during the Bay of Pigs operation, he refused to authorize air cover for the Cuban exiles because he feared provoking Soviet action against Berlin, which struck Eisenhower and his former Vice President Richard Nixon as a misguided reading of the sources of Soviet aggression.[81] By mid 1961, US officials were working assiduously toward a "basic settlement" with the Soviet Union premised on the division of Germany and a permanent US troop presence on the continent.[82]

But these stirrings on the margins and in private rarely penetrated mainstream public discourse before the Cuban Missile Crisis. The

hovered somewhat above "both," and thus closer to "monolithic" (3), with an average score of 2.18.

[78] Kadushin 1974, ch. 4; Matusow 1984; Suri 2003, ch. 3.
[79] Quoted in Beschloss 1991, 20. See also Gaddis 1982, 198–236; Halberstam 1969, 14–24, 60.
[80] Quoted in Gaddis 1982, 228.   [81] Beschloss 1991, 133, 144–146.
[82] Trachtenberg 1999, 321–328, 343–351.

major exception was the Sino–Soviet split, whose importance experts and policymakers publicly recognized by the early 1960s,[83] and they perceived centrifugal forces – "polycentrism" was the inelegant term – elsewhere in the Communist world.[84] In general, however, the *Times'* editorials on foreign affairs remained faithful to Cold War axioms, and the Kennedy administration's public rhetoric hewed to Cold War orthodoxy. The gap between the president's private musings, which displayed a "mentality extraordinarily free from preconceived prejudices," and his public rhetoric startled former Ambassador to the USSR Chip Bohlen.[85] Pressure from the Right, reinforced by the administration's own rhetoric, kept Kennedy from closing that gap: Khrushchev "would like to prevent a nuclear war but is under severe pressure from his hard-line crowd ... I've got similar problems," he told Norman Cousins, editor of the *Saturday Review*.[86] Britain's Prime Minister Harold Macmillan later recalled that, when Kennedy entered office, he "wanted to do something big" in US-Soviet relations, but did not "know how to do it" and remained "constricted by the political situation internally."[87] Not until the mid 1960s did US officials lay the Communist leviathan to rest, with Secretary of State Dean Rusk stating at the 1966 Senate Vietnam Hearings that "Communism today is no longer monolithic; it no longer wears one face but many."[88]

Real events underlay the erosion of the Cold War narrative's dominance. Khrushchev's "secret speech" at the 1956 Communist Party Congress, in which he lashed out at Stalin, had given license to Communists in other nations to grope toward a more independent stance. By 1960, the Sino–Soviet split was out in the open, and it soon seemed that these tensions had advanced beyond a familial spat. These events meant that an alternative portrait of the agents and action of global politics was plausible. But they were clearly not sufficient for liberal Cold Warriors at the *New York Times* or in the halls of power to change their tune. They preceded by several years the willingness of most liberal internationalists, whether editorialists at the *Times*, government officials, or elected representatives, to acknowledge them

---

[83] Lüthi 2008; Zagoria 1962.   [84] Chang 1990; Laqueur and Labedz 1962.
[85] Beschloss 1991, 62–65, 70; Gaddis 1982, 210–212, 232–235; Giglio 1991, 45;
    Halberstam 1969, 13. On Kennedy's sensitivity to the domestic political
    implications of his foreign policy, see, generally, Freedman 2000.
[86] Cousins 1972, 114.   [87] Quoted in See 2002, 163.
[88] US Senate 1966, 239.

publicly. Nor did the changed reality of global politics necessitate a new narrative. Liberal Cold Warriors might have continued plausibly to interpret welcome Soviet behavior as a tactical adjustment to circumstance, rather than as a sign of a more fundamental shift. Kennedy himself pooh-poohed Sino–Soviet differences as late as January 1963, portraying them as "a strain, not a fracture," as a dispute over means, "over how best to bury the free world."[89] Barry Goldwater, during his 1964 presidential run, agreed that Sino–Soviet disagreements were much less meaningful than what united them: "I don't care how you spell it, it's still Communism."[90]

What permitted liberal internationalists to begin deviating from the dominant Cold War narrative? Not large-scale failure, but success – specifically what seemed to be an unambiguous US victory in the episode that was the closest that the two superpowers had come to blows: the Cuban Missile Crisis. Although we now know that the crisis' resolution was a negotiated outcome, in which the United States accommodated Soviet and Cuban concerns, neither Left nor Right in the United States understood it that way at the time, because the administration went to great lengths to keep secret its agreement to remove the Jupiter missiles from Turkey.[91] Afraid that, under pressure, the Soviets might reveal the Jupiter deal, Kennedy and other officials refrained from publicly gloating, and they asked for the press' cooperation.[92] But the prevailing view across the political spectrum was that Kennedy had scored a great triumph, and journalists had trouble exercising restraint. As Richard Rovere wrote in *The New Yorker*, it was "perhaps the greatest personal diplomatic victory of any President in our history."[93]

---

[89] Kennedy, Annual Message to the Congress on the State of the Union, 14 January 1963, available at *The Public Papers of the President*, American Presidency Project, www.presidency.ucsb.edu/ws/; unless otherwise indicated, all further references to presidential speeches come from this source. This was at odds, however, with a CIA report published that same month concluding that "the USSR and China are now two separate powers whose interests conflict on almost every major issue" (quoted in Chang 1990, 235).

[90] Charles Mohr, "Goldwater Says He'd Curb Court," *New York Times*, 16 September 1964.

[91] Hershberg 2010, 85; Nash 1997, 141–160, 166–167.

[92] Which the Soviets, via Czech intelligence, knew and for which they gave the Americans credit. See Fursenko and Naftali 1997, 305.

[93] Beschloss 1991, 542, 547–549, quote at 568. For review of reaction to the crisis' resolution, see also Dobbs 2008, 337; George 2003, 103–105; Weisbrot 2001, 188–191, 193.

Yet, this great success did not produce narrative continuity – just the opposite. According to the *Times*, "reason prevailed" in October 1962. The Soviet Union had finally come around to the long-standing US view of the nuclear balance of terror. Kennedy had "made clear time and again his understanding of [the] basic fact" that violence was not a rational tool of policy in a nuclear-armed world, and it was "encouraging" that Khrushchev finally agreed. The two sides had not stepped back equally from the brink: Khrushchev had suffered a "humiliating defeat" in Cuba that he would never live down, while Kennedy deserved "the chief credit … [for] the fateful decision to confront Soviet Russia head-on" and for his prudent display of "American military might and firmness of purpose."[94] His resolve had brought about not merely tactical adjustment on the Soviets' part, but "a turning point in the Cold War" heralding an era of "great détente." Under the shadow of mutual assured destruction whose implications, thanks to liberal Cold Warriors, both superpowers now grasped, liberal internationalists at the *Times* looked forward to the possibility of ending the Cold War. A year later, they affirmed that strategic change was a fact, not "mere wishful thinking."[95] Thus, when negotiations stalled in 1963 to 1964 and the Soviets adopted a hard line, the *Times* interpreted this not as evidence of Soviet duplicity (as they had in the past), but as "ritualistic" posturing to appease Peking. Once a skeptic of negotiations, the *Times* had become an unequivocal advocate: "as long as the Russians are willing to talk, the possibilities of agreement exist, and we must continue to explore them."[96]

Afterwards, Kennedy felt free to articulate more consistently a vision for transcending the Cold War, which he linked expressly to the crisis.[97] In mid December, in a nationally televised interview, the president told

---

[94] "A Triumph of Reason," 29 October 1962; "Khrushchev's Sober Speech," 20 July 1963; "Khruschevism sans Khruschev," 17 October 1964; "The Days that Shook the World," 4 November 1962; "The Side of the Hill," 16 January 1963; "The Changing Atmosphere," 3 October 1963 – all in *New York Times*.

[95] "A Triumph of Reason," 29 October 1962; "As We Step Back from Danger," 30 October 1962. See similarly "Beyond Cuba," 31 October 1962 – all in *New York Times*.

[96] "The Changing Atmosphere," 3 October 1963; "Focus on Germany," 14 June 1964; "Test Talks with Moscow," 26 April 1963 – all in *New York Times*.

[97] Gaddis 1982, 234–235. Carefully tracking the shift in numerous public policy documents, as well as presidential speeches, is Beukel 1989, 37–48. For an alternative view, see Giglio 1991, 219.

the public that Khrushchev had finally "showed his awareness of the nuclear age[,] . . . of the dangers of the United States and the Soviet Union clashing over an area of vital importance."[98] At American University's commencement in June 1963, he forthrightly challenged the Cold War narrative, calling on his fellow Americans to re-examine their most basic attitudes – "toward the possibilities of peace, toward the Soviet Union, toward the course of the Cold War and toward freedom and peace here at home." Kennedy shared his fear of nuclear holocaust arising less from Soviet aspirations to world domination than from a security dilemma: "a vicious and dangerous cycle in which suspicion on one side breeds suspicion on the other." The danger of nuclear war derived from "a distorted and desperate view of the other side," from the "trap . . . [of] see[ing] conflict as inevitable, accommodation as impossible, and communication as nothing more than an exchange of threats." Only after the Cuban Missile Crisis could Kennedy preach publicly what he had long preached privately – that the superpowers shared "a mutually deep interest in a just and genuine peace and in halting the arms race" and that this trumped both ideological commitments and legitimate conflicts of interest.[99]

Victory in the Cuban Missile Crisis freed liberals from the strictures of the Cold War narrative. It opened political space for them to narrate the world in public the way in which many long had behind closed doors.[100] Written entirely in the White House and hidden until the last moment from the administration's hard-liners, the American University speech was "probably the most authentic statement of Kennedy's views on the nuclear arms race."[101] Informed by Kennedy that the address would not need the customary Cold War bombast – "the usual threats of destruction, boasts of nuclear stockpiles and lectures on Soviet treachery" – his chief speech-writer, Theodore Sorensen, drew in part on draft language that had been deleted from earlier major addresses for being in those days too great a departure.[102] As Michael Beschloss notes, "there was not a sentence in this speech with which he would have privately disagreed in 1960. The change was

---

[98] Television and Radio Interview: "After Two Years – A Conversation with the President," 17 December 1962.

[99] Commencement Address at American University in Washington, 10 June 1963.

[100] Similarly, see Freedman 2000, 267 and passim; Fursenko and Naftali 1997, 320, 336–337; Gaddis 1982, 234–235; See 2002.

[101] Freedman 2000, 267.   [102] Sorensen 1965, 730–731.

not in Kennedy but in what he perceived to be his political environment."[103]

Other liberals followed the trail Kennedy had blazed. From 1957, Fulbright had been a vocal critic of US foreign policy, but always from within the consensus: he had offered a different vision of *how* to wage the Cold War, but he did not deny that it needed waging. He called for more development aid, and later supported the formation of the OECD, as more effective tools than military force in the battle for hearts and minds. He warned against blind US support for the status quo in the Third World, fearing that it would drive ideologically flexible revolutionary nationalist regimes into Soviet arms. He cautioned against far-flung US military commitments in "peripheral struggles" because they would hamper America's ability to respond effectively to challenges from "the principal communist powers." As early as 1959, Fulbright believed that the Soviet Union had become a status quo power and that it recognized the superpowers' shared interests in avoiding nuclear war.[104] But it was not until after the missile crisis that Fulbright broke publicly with the Cold War narrative. Openly embracing realist principles, he called on Americans in March 1964 to abandon "old myths" in favor of "new realities" – specifically, that zero-sum superpower competition was a thing of the past, replaced by the prospect of "peaceful coexistence." How a state organized its domestic economy and politics was of little concern to the United States: "Insofar as a nation is content to practice its doctrines within its own frontiers, that nation, however repugnant its ideology, is one with which we have no proper quarrel." What mattered, declared Fulbright, were its intentions: "Insofar as a great nation mobilizes its power and resources for aggressive purposes, that nation, regardless of ideology, makes itself our enemy."[105] This was radical stuff by the standards of the Cold War. It drew predictable howls from the Right, but it was welcomed and praised by such mainstream journalists as Drew Pearson and Arthur Krock.[106]

Campbell Craig and Frederik Logevall claim that, although after the missile crisis "American political discourse had begun to change in subtle ways," nevertheless "the underlying dynamic had not

[103] Beschloss 1991, 600 and generally 597–601. See also Gaddis 1990, 254–255.
[104] Woods 1995, 225, 237–239, 249–250, 262–263, 313–314, 317–318.
[105] Fulbright 1964.   [106] Woods 1995, 336–338.

changed": "If in doubt, spout the eternal verities: the Soviet menace is as great as ever, the Kremlin as untrustworthy."[107] But this was no longer true for a substantial portion of the political spectrum. Regardless of liberals' reasons for straying from Cold War orthodoxy – changing economic interests,[108] new values derived from unprecedented prosperity, or puzzling about the world – it was the Cuban Missile Crisis that freed them to give voice to that vision. That vision did not become more sustainable simply because the crisis woke Americans up to the dangers of a nuclear-armed world. Although the crisis amplified fears of nuclear holocaust, Cold Warriors had previously grasped the superpowers' common interest in avoiding direct confrontation. That premise underlay the Eisenhower administration's strategy of "massive retaliation," which presumed that the Soviets would heed American threats, if only in extremis. That the Soviets backed away from the brink in Cuba was consistent with Cold War expectations and did not necessarily mean that they were open to genuine dialogue and a permanent settlement. That inference would have been reasonable if the Soviet Union had substantially changed its behavior after the crisis. But the USSR took few concrete steps in the months after October 1962 to alter that view, aside from not precipitating a new crisis.[109] Neither the CIA nor the State Department substantially altered its assessment of Soviet motives or superpower relations, and Kennedy himself concluded from the crisis that his early policy of "consideration and courtesy" may have been mistaken.[110] The Cuban Missile Crisis made possible, but did not require, abandoning the Cold War narrative.

Indeed, many did not, because the missile crisis equally lent itself to another interpretation: that it revealed the wisdom of staying the course. For conservative Cold Warriors at the *Tribune*, the *outcome* of the missile crisis was a great success, a "Red backdown," and they even had complimentary things to say about the president's "unexpected show of ... firmness."[111] But the *fact* of the missile crisis

---

[107] Craig and Logevall 2009, 214.
[108] Cutrone and Fordham 2010; Fordham 2008a, 2008b.
[109] Garthoff 1989, esp. 133.   [110] See 2002, 165; Trachtenberg 1999, 355.
[111] "Russia Now Favors Inspection," 29 October 1962. See also "Getting Back on Our Own Feet," 25 October 1962; "Invitation to a Ride on the Merry-Go-Round," 26 October 1962; "The New Adlai," 27 October 1962 – all in *Chicago Tribune*.

reinforced the dominant Cold War narrative. It seemed to confirm how implacable the Soviet Union was and how pointless, even dangerous, it would be to negotiate with such a deceitful foe. The crisis, conservatives argued, demonstrated the imprudence of deviating from the path of strength.[112] House Minority Leader Charles Halleck's view before the Cuban Missile Crisis applied in spades afterwards: even if the Soviets were "mellowing, why change a policy that brought it about? It doesn't make sense. Improvements? Certainly. Basic change? No. Let's keep that policy tough. We must maintain a course of action that is determined and firm."[113] Before long, many, including Nixon and then Republican Party Chairman George H. W. Bush, were taking the administration to task for allowing the Soviets to maintain a troop presence on the island.[114] Whereas liberal internationalists around the globe greeted the crisis' end with hope, the retired Eisenhower, hardly a rabid Cold Warrior, warned against such optimism, citing a history of Communist trickery and insisting that "the conflict of ideas, ideologies which defines what we have called the cold war, will continue." Months later, the *Tribune* labeled the Nuclear Test Ban Treaty a "delusion" and perhaps a "snare."[115] Senate minority leader Everett Dirksen, who often backed Kennedy in foreign affairs, averred that the president's aspirations for a test ban treaty constituted a "renunciation of the policy of strength" that had proved its worth in Cuba.[116]

The theoretical conventional wisdom would suggest that triumph in the Cuban Missile Crisis should have bolstered the dominant Cold War narrative. But, in fact, the crisis fostered challenges to the Cold War consensus from prominent erstwhile loyalists. As the theoretical framework of Chapter 5 would expect, Kennedy, his aides, and liberal internationalists in civil society emerged with renewed narrative authority. Free to articulate long-suppressed views of the Soviet

---

[112] "Our Course is Set," *Chicago Tribune*, 23 October 1962. Nor was this the interpretation only of Republican partisans: in 1964, the realist scholar Hans Morgenthau, a leading critic of the US intervention in Vietnam, thought Fulbright dangerously naïve when it came to the Soviet Union. See "J. William Fulbright," in Morgenthau 1970, 174–181.

[113] Quoted in Dietz 1986, 45.

[114] Beschloss 1991, 564–568, 581–583; Dietz 1986, 49–51; Fursenko and Naftali 1997, 327–329; Weisbrot 2001, 189–191.

[115] "Ike Counsels No Relaxing in Wake of Crisis," 30 October 1962; "The Test Ban Treaty," 27 July 1963 – both in *Chicago Tribune*.

[116] Hulsey 2000, 176–180, quote at 177.

Union and global Communism at odds with the dominant narrative, they laid the foundation for détente. Although victory in Cuba made possible the dissolution of the Cold War consensus, it did not yield a new dominant narrative – again consistent with Chapter 5. Conflicting interpretations of US adversaries, superpower relations, and the magnitude of the threat were sustainable in its wake. Social unrest would soon grip America's campuses and cities, with the Vietnam War both the focus and trigger of mass protest. But the battles over Vietnam at home took place on a narrative terrain that had already begun to fracture.

The limits of erosion: the Vietnam War and responsible dissent

If events spoke for themselves – if the implications of the Cuban Missile Crisis and the Sino–Soviet split, and the origins of the conflict in Vietnam, had been obvious to all – then a new dominant national security narrative, revolving around new portraits of the agents, action, and scene of global politics, should have replaced the old Cold War consensus in the early 1960s. None did. Liberal and conservative elites did not share a common narrative foundation. Yet, even as liberals departed from the Cold War narrative, they did not swing to the opposite extreme. They did not become accommodationists. They continued to express skepticism of Soviet motives, to think the USSR ambitious, and to acknowledge the abiding reality of superpower rivalry. Even in the darkest days of Vietnam and even at the giddiest heights of détente, liberal and conservative narratives were not diametrically opposed. Both conventional theoretical wisdom and our general sense of the period support the expectation that leading liberal internationalists would react to the strategic failure and domestic turmoil of Vietnam by careening in the opposite direction. Surprisingly, they did not.

Histories of the era tend to focus on the dramatic challengers to the Cold War at the edges of civil society. They were an obsession of both the Johnson and Nixon administrations, and they articulated a narrative opposed on nearly every dimension to Cold War dogma. But such dissent proved beyond the bounds of legitimacy: not only did it fail to resonate with Americans, but, together with anarchist violence, it tarred all anti-war protesters with the radical brush and turned

Americans off, despite their displeasure with the war.[117] War critics
who remained respectable curbed the depth of their dissent from the
Cold War narrative. In their public speeches and writings, these responsible critics assailed the administration's claims regarding the war's
prospects and purposes, while reaffirming the larger logic of superpower rivalry and the wisdom of global containment. In setting the
boundaries of legitimate dissent early on, they confined their capacity
later to articulate a thoroughgoing alternative to the global Cold War.
Their caution was warranted: critics who took on the Cold War found
themselves marginalized and often out of office. Consistent with
Chapter 5, these limits had their roots in the politics of the Vietnam
War: this protracted, uncertain, and foundering military campaign
reined in the impulse to narrative revolution. The US military's travails
in Vietnam did not accelerate leading liberal internationalists' escape
from the global Cold War's narrative chains. Just the opposite.

Doves in Cold War cages

From late 1962, liberal internationalists increasingly gave voice to a
narrative that might sustain superpower détente, but these doves did
not fully liberate themselves from the Cold War.[118] The Johnson
administration insisted that the common threat of nuclear holocaust
bequeathed to the two superpowers common interests and common
responsibilities – as Dean Rusk put it, "for the first time in history, two
nations live each with its hands on the jugular of the other – and of
every other nation" – but it was careful always to affirm that the
fundamental ideological differences that had led to the Cold War
were enduring.[119] Whereas Stalin had been represented as always
"probing" US resolve, the Soviet Union during and after Vietnam
was cast as a more cautious power. But it was hardly a satisfied one.
It would wait patiently for windows of vulnerability to open, but it was
not content for them to remain permanently shut, and it would take
American power and will to keep them closed. William Welch's 1970
study of scholars' images of the Soviet Union ran from ultra-hard to
hard to mixed – that is, from extremely to moderately expansionist.[120]

---

[117]   See Jeffreys-Jones 1999; Matusow 1984, ch. 11.
[118]   Which was reflected in the mainstream media as well. See Hallin 1986, 48–58
        and passim.
[119]   Beukel 1989, 48–60, quote at 49.   [120]   Welch 1970.

At the height of détente in 1973, the dovish Sovietologist Marshall Shulman acknowledged that the Soviet Union was "not a status quo power" and that its long-term ambition remained to supplant the United States.[121]

Although occasional flights of rhetorical fancy during détente represented the superpowers as partners in the construction of a harmonious global order, for the most part they remained, in administration rhetoric and more generally in US political debate, rivals for global influence.[122] In their reports on progress in arms control, officials insisted that they were under no illusions about the Soviet Union and its ultimate vision.[123] In Stanley Hoffmann's felicitous formulation, détente meant that "containment through negotiation" had replaced "containment by confrontation," but containment it remained.[124] Détente did not supplant the Cold War, but was merely another way of prosecuting it. Robert Legvold mourned the passing of détente in 1980, but he admitted: "None of this implies that the Soviet Union is less ambitious, less a country on the make, or less antipathetic to much that the West values in the world."[125] The mass of Americans agreed. Amidst ongoing détente, 83 percent presumed that the USSR was "generally expansionist"; this was among the most commonly cited lessons of the Vietnam War.[126] While the portion of the public "concerned" about "the threat of Communism" and "Soviet Russia" declined substantially between 1964 and 1972, a clear majority – 69 and 61 percent respectively – remained concerned.[127] Even the domino

---

[121] Shulman 1973, 37.

[122] Garthoff (1994, 1145–1146) blames Kissinger and Nixon for overselling détente and for cultivating unrealistic expectations at odds with their own beliefs about enduring competition. While one can point to examples, one would be hard-pressed to see that as a consistent theme in administration rhetoric. Moreover, if Garthoff were right that Kissinger and Nixon had rendered Americans temporarily naïve, one would expect to see it reflected in the public opinion data. As I explain later, the opinion data do not bear Garthoff out.

[123] Beukel 1989, 60–73; Garthoff 1994, 28–39. This became an increasingly significant theme as domestic criticism of détente intensified in the Ford administration: see Beukel 1989, 74–84. For similar retrospective statements, see Kissinger 1979, 114–125, 128; Nixon 1978, 941.

[124] Hoffmann 1978, 43. For more recent retrospective assessments along similar lines, see Hanhimäki 2008; Schulzinger 2010; Suri 2003.

[125] Legvold 1980, 79.

[126] Barton 1974–1975, 518. See also Russett and Hanson 1975, 70–75.

[127] Wattenberg 1974, 204.

theory, the chief legitimating logic of the Vietnam War, survived intact:
over two-thirds of Americans surveyed in 1976 forecast that the US
withdrawal from Vietnam the year before would provoke Communist
aggression.[128] According to Raymond Garthoff, among the reasons
détente ultimately failed was each side's stable view of the other as
ultimately seeking world domination.[129]

Although the Vietnam War was, from the US perspective, a strategic
failure that unleashed unprecedented domestic turmoil, it "produced ...
no confrontation with the language that had been used to justify the war
in the first place"[130] – at least among dissenters who could not easily be
dismissed by the White House. Doves' early criticisms of the war fell
along two lines, both of which were consistent with the heart of the
Cold War narrative. First, they offered an instrumental argument,
alleging that victory would come, if at all, at too great a cost.[131] For
some, the cost was the risk of escalation to war with one of the two
leading Communist powers. Senator Albert Gore challenged Dean
Rusk at the 1966 Foreign Relations Committee hearings: "many
members of Congress do not believe, that the costs, the risk of nuclear
war, the dangers of a war with China or perhaps both China and
Russia, are worth the endeavor."[132] For others, the excessive cost
would come with the larger interventionist agenda implied by the
Vietnam War. The United States would find itself seeking, in Senator
Frank Church's words, "to damp down the fires of smoldering revolution throughout the whole of the awakening world." That was more
than the United States could afford: "no nation – not even our own –
possesses an arsenal so large, or a treasury so rich" as to achieve that
end.[133] Others focused on opportunity costs: by siphoning so much
of America's military might, the Vietnam War would degrade the

[128] Holsti and Rosenau 1980, 270–271. Not surprisingly, the response was even
stronger in 1980: Holsti and Rosenau 1984, 62.
[129] Garthoff 1994, 1128.   [130] Green 1987, 255.
[131] Averch 2002, 97–98, 108–111. See also Clifford 1969.
[132] US Senate 1966, 14–15 and also, from other senators, 80–83, 92–93. See also
Longley 2003; 2004, 205–206. On similar themes from Sen. Mike Mansfield,
see Ritchie 2003, 202; from Sen. John Sherman Cooper, see Logevall 2003,
249; from Prof. Hans Morgenthau, "War with China?", in Morgenthau 1965,
50–60.
[133] Church, "How Many Dominican Republics and Vietnams Can We Take On?"
New York Times Magazine, 28 November 1965. See also Ashby and Gramer
1994, 192 and passim; Schmitz and Fousekis 1994. See similarly Fulbright
1966, 4.

country's general deterrent posture. This theme emerged as early as the debate over the Gulf of Tonkin Resolution, where an early Republican critic, Senator John Sherman Cooper, worried, "I do not know how widely we can spread our resources and our men in the military forces."[134] Realists, like George Kennan, warned that the protracted war would make it harder to advance core strategic interests, like the negotiation of a stable *modus vivendi* with the USSR.[135]

These instrumental critiques left the Cold War narrative essentially intact. Kennan spoke plainly: "If we had been able – without exorbitant cost in American manpower, American resources, in the attention of our government, in the emphasis of our foreign policy – if we had been able to do better in Vietnam, I would have been delighted and I would have thought that the effort was warranted."[136] Others were rarely so explicit, but they typically conceded the Johnson administration's portrait of the protagonists and stakes in Vietnam. That shared foundation helped sustain their instrumental arguments; Cold War considerations figured centrally in their calculations that deemed victory in Vietnam not worth the cost. The doves' star witness in the 1966 Senate hearings was retired General James Gavin, but his testimony revealed that he too was "still a prisoner of the Cold War mind-set and the devotion to containment."[137] Such "responsible" dissent had much in common with bureaucratic "back-door" criticism that questioned merely the feasibility of the US mission, not its value: "tactical arguments, not fundamental ones, were the order of the day," Leslie Gelb and Richard Betts later observed.[138]

A second line of argument, associated with the scholar Hans Morgenthau and with Church and Fulbright, held that the war improperly applied containment.[139] They argued vociferously in public, as in private did Senate majority leader Mike Mansfield, formerly a scholar and teacher of Asian history, that the origins of the Vietnam conflict did not lie in global Communist aggression and thus that it was not another front in the Cold War. Ho Chi Minh, despite his Communist trappings, was primarily a nationalist, not a loyal servant of either the PRC or the

---

[134] Quoted in Logevall 2003, 245–246.   [135] US Senate 1966, 124–127.
[136] US Senate 1966, 131.   [137] Fry 2006, 38–39.
[138] Gelb and Betts 1979, 236 and passim.
[139] Church, "How Many Dominican Republics"; Fulbright 1966, 106–119 and passim; on Morgenthau, See 2001. See also US Senate 1966; Woods 1995, 392–394, 401–402.

USSR. The Vietnam conflict was a civil war and an anti-colonial struggle. As Fulbright colorfully put it, "loving corn [nationalism] and hating lima beans [communism], we simply cannot make up our minds about succotash."[140]

However, this critique also owed much to Cold War premises. To say that containment was not germane to Vietnam was to suggest that it was often relevant elsewhere, that the strategy itself, and the narrative that underpinned it, were basically sound. In 1965 to 1966, Fulbright and Church agreed that Communism's spread was inherently contrary to US interests. Revolutionary insurgencies were, Church wrote, "often infected by the Communist virus," and the United States should strive for the neutralization of Southeast Asia "providing it is not a camouflage for a Communist takeover."[141] Fulbright said he would tolerate a revolution with "Communist-associated" elements, implying that a Communist-*dominated* revolution was unacceptable. He even wrapped himself in the mantle of Cold War righteousness, insisting that he – more than the hawks – was the true upholder of the faith.[142] In other words, even the most trenchant mainstream critics of the Vietnam War were not yet prepared in the early years to break from the Cold War.[143] They did not offer audiences a very different view of lima beans. Their point – controversial enough in those days – was that succotash had more in common with tasty corn. This argument lay more within, than in opposition to, the Cold War consensus.[144] The one important seeming exception was that these critics insisted that Communism was diverse, not monolithic. But the Johnson administration had already acknowledged that the Sino–Soviet divide was real. It was not a great leap to seeing other Communist regimes as independent of the Red giants. Under questioning from senators in 1966, Rusk conceded that Hanoi did not take strict orders from Peking, that Ho Chi Minh was not Mao's puppet.[145]

---

[140] Fulbright 1966, 77.
[141] Church, "How Many Dominican Republics"; Jack Raymond, "Senator Church Sees Need for a Major Shift on Asia," *New York Times*, 27 December 1964. See also Schmitz and Fousekis 1994, 566.
[142] Fulbright 1966, 90–91, 30–31.
[143] Sitting in the ivory tower, Morgenthau was an important, if lonely, exception. See his "Globalism: The Moral Crusade," in Morgenthau 1965, 81–91. On Morgenthau's exceptional status, see See 2001.
[144] For a reading of Fulbright that reaches similar conclusions, see Berman 1988, 42, 66, 75, 77–78.
[145] US Senate 1966, 269.

Critics did often challenge the Cold War narrative's portrait of global politics as tightly interconnected. The US national interest, they argued, did not demand a pro-Western or even independent government in South Vietnam: if it fell, America's reputation for resolve and general deterrent capacity would be unaffected. But they were still careful not directly to take on the domino theory.[146] Misguided though they believed the initial intervention to be, they normally opposed withdrawal precisely because of the presumed costs to the nation's reputation for resolve. During the 1966 Vietnam hearings, speaker after speaker took the administration to task for getting the country into a mess, but speaker after speaker acknowledged that, as Kennan put it, "a sudden precipitate withdrawal of our activities in South Vietnam ... would be exploited mercilessly by the Chinese and the North Vietnamese ... [I]f we simply turned tail and fled the scene, obviously we would do great damage around." Even Fulbright endorsed the point. Shying away from fully following through their narrative challenge, early doves came off as ambivalent and confused.[147]

Flight paths and fortunes

These doves, in other words, remained within Cold War cages: they criticized the Vietnam War while reaffirming much of its legitimating logic. Their caution was not incidental to the war, but rather followed directly from its politics – per the logic of Chapter 5. In the war's early years, it was not yet obvious that the US intervention was futile. It was one thing for doves to challenge an ongoing war as misguided or overly expensive. It was entirely another for them to launch a direct assault on the war's central legitimation, on the narrative that underpinned it. Fulbright and his fellow doves were careful not to bite off more than the American people could chew. Joseph Fry similarly concludes: "Making the antiwar case with the Congress and the American public was a formidable undertaking. Challenging Cold War America's ardent anticommunism and reflexive inclination to combat the enemy on all

---

[146] Logevall 2003, 247–248.
[147] Fulbright 1966, 196–197; US Senate 1966, 121–122 and passim. Morgenthau was more consistent and advocated withdrawal. See his "Shadow and Substance of Power," and "Another Korea?," in Morgenthau 1965, 9–14, 33.

fronts was a Herculean task" – one they were too politically astute to take on.[148] These cautious doves took notice of the fate of the rarer birds that flew completely free, perpendicular to the Cold War flight path. Those birds paid the price: they became known as radicals and lost their respectability.

Fear and ambition were a potent combination in moderating the rhetoric of establishment doves. If they were as "strident" as Senator Wayne Morse of Oregon, they might be tossed from office; at the very least, they would be unwelcome in the Johnson White House and would lose all hope of shaping policy. "Up until now, I have been trying to work within the context of the existing situation, hoping in this way, to exercise some influence upon events," Church wrote a friend in July 1965, because "only those who stay have any chance to reach the President's ear." Eventually, declared Church, "I may wash my hands of the whole affair, as Wayne Morse has done, and enter the 'Never-Never-Land' of radically ineffectual dissent" – but not yet.[149] According to his administrative assistant, Fulbright did not break with the deeper logic of the Cold War or with the administration because he feared "turning off the public."[150] In May 1967, Church and other prominent doves issued a letter publicly opposing unilateral withdrawal and calling on North Vietnam to show greater flexibility. Their "cheap hawk position," as even one Church aide called it, pinned the blame on Hanoi. It was designed, thought the more impatient Senator Ernest Gruening of Alaska, "to get Frank [Church] off the hook at home." Senator George McGovern of South Dakota conceded that Gruening was right in principle, but he excused his decision to co-sign "because of the extremely conservative nature of my state and my forthcoming campaign." But, McGovern went on apologetically, "my heart is always with you even when I have not been able to vote with you."[151]

Who could blame them? Lyndon Johnson was famously temperamental, and he froze out those who ran afoul of him – as Gore and

[148] Fry 2006, 46.
[149] Quoted in Ashby and Gramer 1994, 213; Schmitz and Fousekis 1994, 571, 577. On Church's ambition and caution, see Ashby and Gramer 1994, 143–145, 213–215, 222–223, 318–323, and passim.
[150] Quoted in Berman 1988, 69.   [151] Quoted in Johnson 1998, 290–291.

Fulbright had discovered long before.[152] And those who struck the Cold War narrative head-on were politically cast aside. Consider Gruening. The only two senators to vote against the Gulf of Tonkin Resolution, he and Morse directly challenged the Cold War narrative, and, as Church confided to McGovern, they "may be right, but they have been 'written off'" as a result.[153] Like others, Gruening pointed out the war's futility and its costs: in blood and treasure, in domestic upheaval and public distrust, in sacrifice of America's good name, in hearts and minds.[154] But his progressive anti-imperialism had deep roots, and he refused to view US policy through Cold War lenses.[155] As early as December 1965, he assailed the US role "of self-appointed 'citizen fixit,' of world policeman." There was no need for the United States to throw its "young men into every cockpit in the world where Communist totalitarianism rears its ugly head." By mid 1966, Gruening publicly named the United States the aggressor; he thereby distanced himself from American exceptionalism, from the dominant identity narrative that portrayed the United States as inherently virtuous and its misdeeds as honest mistakes.[156] The Alaskan, unlike his colleagues, refused to accept the narrative limits of the responsible opposition. He embraced radical protesters, voted against all defense appropriations, and declared NATO an impediment to peace.[157] His fate? Gruening was kicked out of office at the first opportunity, defeated in the 1968 primaries by a candidate, Mike Gravel, whose greatest asset was his boring moderation.[158] Gruening was not alone: of seven anti-war senators up for re-election in 1968, three lost, thanks in large part to their positions on the war. As Gruening's biographer concludes: "The political climate was still not ready to tolerate a

---

[152] On Gore's troubled relationship with Johnson, see Longley 2004, 118–119. On Fulbright and Johnson, Woods 1995, 384–389. On Church and Johnson, Ashby and Gramer 1994, 194–196, 206–207, 220–221.
[153] Quoted in Schmitz and Fousekis 1994, 577.
[154] Gruening 1973, 476–478; Johnson 1998, 241–242.
[155] Johnson 1998, 192–193, 205–206, 219–221, 234–235, and passim.
[156] Quoted in Johnson 1998, 274, 277.
[157] Contrast Gruening to McGovern. The South Dakotan adopted some similar positions, but he normally paid homage to the Cold War. He kept his distance from what he saw as the "undisciplined radicalism" of the campuses. He was, like Fulbright, among "the foremost critics *within* the Liberal Establishment which had itself conceived the war." Knock 2003, quote at 113 (emphasis added).
[158] Johnson 1998, 294–314.

full-blown congressional assault on the basic assumptions of Cold War foreign policy."[159]

By setting the limits of "responsible" dissent early in the Vietnam War, establishment doves restricted the possibility of escaping the Cold War in the 1970s. Even as the war exhausted the patience of the US public, as anti-war members of Congress entered the House, and as the Senate voted to cut military aid and to restrict military operations,[160] instrumental argument was still the order of the day. Opponents of the Vietnam War's expansion to Cambodia asserted that the benefits were nil, due to the war's futility, and the costs, notably domestic havoc, were high. Thus, Gore continued in 1970 to argue that the war in Southeast Asia was not worth the candle: "for the stated high purpose of restoring stability and unity to a war-wracked and divided little country ... [,] we have lost friends around the world, have sent more than two million young Americans to participate [in that war] ... and, in the end, have influenced the Vietnamese only to fight each other and *us* all the more fanatically."[161] Fulbright similarly explained on television to a national audience in August 1970: "A war is fought for political objectives, and when it is recognized that those objectives are unattainable at a reasonable cost, the appropriate course of action is to end that war in an orderly and expeditious way."[162] Vietnam may have been hopeless, but the Cold War lived on. For Gore, helping nations "withstand the onslaught of Communism" had been "to our great honor"; the United States could scale back only because the Soviet Union had declined and because technocrats had come to dominate the Soviet bureaucracy. Even so, Gore insisted, "fundamental and dangerous problems" would rightly continue to mark superpower relations because of the two nations' "basic ideological antagonism."[163]

Gore was typical of the rhetorical constraints binding mainstream doves, even when they were not elected politicians. Charles Kadushin's 1970 survey of "leading intellectuals," a disproportionately liberal group, found that war critics did not take issue with the larger narrative in which the war had been embedded. Eighty percent of his subjects

[159] Johnson 2006, 149.   [160] Fordham 2007, 2008a.
[161] Gore 1970, 2; see also Longley 2004, 214, 220. See, similarly, on Church, Schmitz 2003, 138.
[162] Quoted in Woods 1995, 580.   [163] Gore 1970, 54–55, 60.

raised instrumental objections – the limits of US power, domestic and reputational costs, futility – and 50 percent did so exclusively. As Kadushin concluded, this "allowed old Cold Warriors to have opposed the war in Southeast Asia with considerable vigor and even occasional militancy and yet continue to hold views of the world that are not appreciably different from those they held in 1960."[164] What Gelb observed later of the mass public was equally true of elites in Vietnam's waning days: they "did not reject the consensus behind the war in any intellectual or conceptual sense ... [T]heir message was simply 'we've had enough.'"[165] The consistency of elites' views may have been the product of psychological mechanisms: the priority to maintain stable belief systems and the capacity of especially the well-informed and educated to reconcile their beliefs with discrepant data. But the logic of public narrative suggests a more political mechanism. Opinion leaders remained trapped within the strictures of the responsible opposition, and they could advance any comprehensive alternative only at the risk of being branded reckless and radical.

As a result, the intense foreign policy debates of the 1970s took place on familiar narrative terrain. The "new internationalists" did not argue that the Communist threat was minimal or that superpower relations could and should be harmonious. What they opposed was a *militarized* Cold War.[166] Their purpose in opposing assistance to repressive regimes and in attaching human-rights riders to foreign economic legislation was to bolster the US position in the Cold War, not transcend the Cold War. They argued that a consistently pro-democratic and pro-rights stance would bequeath substantial advantages in the battle for hearts and minds in the Third World. Jimmy Carter was an ardent Cold Warrior first and a human-rights advocate second, and he saw no contradiction: containment, he averred, was most effective when guided by a moral compass.[167] In Carter's words, "respect for human rights is one of the most significant advantages of a free and democratic nation in the peaceful struggle for influence."[168] The new internationalists, despite their maverick image, challenged the means

[164] Kadushin 1974, quote at 195. See also Matusow 1984, ch. 13.
[165] Gelb 1976, 112.
[166] On the rise and fall of the "new internationalists," see Johnson 2006, ch. 6.
[167] On Carter as Cold Warrior, see Smith 1986; and, more recently, along similar lines, Mitchell 2010; Schmitz 2006, ch. 5; Zelizer 2010, 274–275.
[168] Quoted in Schmitz 2006, 144.

by which the Cold War would be prosecuted, not the need for its prosecution.[169] And they opposed further US military intervention due to its likely costs, especially domestic divisiveness, not the objectives those proposed deployments were intended to further.[170]

Fulbright's political demise illustrates the consequences of ignoring the limits of responsible dissent. By the early 1970s, he had left behind his earlier, relatively cautious rhetoric to tackle the Cold War itself. The Truman Doctrine's ideological blinders had long since outlived their usefulness, he asserted. How Vietnam or any other nation organized its economics and politics should be utterly irrelevant to the United States. Even Communist-dominated regimes no longer troubled the long-serving chairman of the Senate Foreign Relations Committee: "As with Mao Tse-Tung in China, we might have gotten along tolerably well – maybe even quite well – with a unified, independent Vietnam under Ho Chi Minh, if our leaders' minds had not been hopelessly locked in by the imprisoning theory of the international Communist conspiracy." The later Fulbright blamed the United States for the Cold War's origins and missed opportunities and for human suffering around the globe. Postwar crises "could and should have been avoided with comparative ease," and it was "only partly true ... that our global role was thrust upon us." That the United States should be the world's policeman was "dubious and dangerous," he declared.[171] The Soviet Union was "a traditional, cautious, and rather unimaginative great power" that posed little threat to the United States – certainly less than the United States posed to itself.[172] Fulbright's *The Crippled Giant*, published in summer 1972, was the sequel to his 1966 blockbuster, *The Arrogance of Empire*. Whereas the earlier book's blistering critique had been framed in familiar terms, its successor systematically rejected the most bare Cold War essentials. And it was a flop.[173] Fulbright's rhetoric on Vietnam became intensely moralizing, damning US policy

---

[169] See, similarly, Buckaloo 2008.
[170] See also Russett and Hanson 1975, 87–94.
[171] "Reflections: In Thrall to Fear," *New Yorker*, 8 January 1972, 41–62; Fulbright 1972, quotes at 68, 157–158, 170.
[172] "Old Myths and New Realities," address to US Senate, 2 April 1970; "What Students can do for Peace," *Progressive*, June 1970 – both quoted in Woods 1995, 559–560, 567.
[173] For other reasons it may have failed to attract much attention, see Berman 1988, 162.

as "barbarous, inhumane, and obscene."[174] He had become a radical. The Fulbright of the early 1970s would not be bound by prevailing rhetorical conventions. He did not seem much to care whether he remained within the pale. Although he ran for re-election in 1974, he was a reluctant and indifferent campaigner.[175] He was the exception that proves the rule.

In standard histories, the domestic reverberations of the Vietnam War tore America, and the Cold War consensus, apart. I showed earlier that this was not true: the consensus was already fraying well before Americans assumed substantial combat responsibility and before the body-bags began streaming home. One might nevertheless have argued that, although the Vietnam War did not initiate the consensus' collapse, it exacerbated existing trends. But I maintain the opposite: even as this failing war inspired some Americans to radical critique, it also curbed the scope of dissent among those who wished to remain legitimate and respectable.. Senators, scholars, journalists, and other elite critics opposed the war while reaffirming much of the deeper Cold War logic that had legitimated the intervention. They thus, early in the war, established the boundaries that responsible opponents of the war – that is, non-radicals – dared not cross, even once the bulk of the US public had given up on the war and had become desperate to bring the boys home. Contrary to the usual theory, the politics of a faltering war, even as traumatic a war as Vietnam, served to bolster its legitimating narrative.

Consensus reborn: Vietnam and the rise of the Right

The 1970s is usually remembered as a decade when the nation came unraveled, when a vast gulf opened up between Left and Right. The Left began to question the nation's foundational myths, while the Right clung to them as tightly as ever.[176] It is certainly true that dissenters were more vocal and numerous than in the past, but the content analysis findings, reported in Chapter 6, suggest that the 1970s was a time of surprising elite unity: elites on the Right and Left responded to challenge from the margins by circling the wagons and publicly

---

[174] Quoted in Berman 1988, 153, 159. See also Fulbright 1972, 80, 83.
[175] For a full analysis of his 1974 defeat, see Woods 1995, 654–659, 670–671.
[176] See, for instance, Quester 1980.

defending a common portrait of America and its unique mission in sustaining global order. While liberals and conservatives remained divided over the Communist Other, the distance between them shrank dramatically on many other narrative pillars: the necessity and reliability of allies, America's status as a leader, the capacity of the United States to play a constructive role in world affairs, and even the value of foreign aid. In other words, a new consensus was forged, revolving not around representations of the Soviet Union and superpower relations, but around a crusading American exceptionalism. My confidence in these findings is a little weaker than in the previous sections, because the number of annual editorials touching on these themes is sometimes small and the annual standard deviation is correspondingly high.[177] But observers at the time thought they detected much the same. As the 1976 presidential campaign got under way, the *New York Times* noted that the current debate on foreign policy was largely about tactics, obscuring "an underlying agreement on many fundamental principles."[178] Ironically, the failed intervention in Vietnam and the accompanying domestic tumult, normally seen as responsible for shattering the Cold War consensus, helped crystallize the new dominant narrative.

In the 1970s, the chattering classes were obsessed with America's crisis of confidence.[179] The New Left challenge was real – real enough that the keepers of the narrative defended with gusto America's right and duty to exercise moral leadership in global affairs. Both Gerald Ford and Jimmy Carter felt compelled on multiple occasions to address what they perceived as Americans' lagging enthusiasm for the nation's global calling. Carter's (in)famous "malaise" address was intended to overcome that crisis of confidence, by hectoring Americans to belief and action. He had no doubt that the United States had "a unique role" to play as "a pioneer in shaping more decent and just relations among people and among societies."[180] In an age of slow growth and resource shocks, retrenchment was the watchword of the day, but it was not

---

[177] For supporting data, see the online appendix, located at https://sites.google.com/a/umn.edu/rkrebs/home/publications/data. Thanks to Ben Fordham for pressing me on this.

[178] "A New Consensus . . . ," *New York Times*, 18 September 1976.

[179] Although some at the time chalked up the crisis to the momentary pain of gas lines and high inflation. Historians have reached no consensus on the depth or roots of the crisis. See Kalman 2010, 325–327.

[180] Quoted in Schmitz 2006, 148.

incompatible with steadfast adherence to American exceptionalism.[181] Retrenchment appealed both to radicals, who questioned what business a deeply flawed America had telling others how to arrange their affairs, and to stalwarts, who sometimes thought the United States had long neglected its own needs or believed its allies had long taken advantage of its munificence. Even hawks presumed that after Vietnam local allies would bear the greatest burden in combating Communist threats – as the Nixon Doctrine stated and as the Reagan Doctrine implied. Elites across the spectrum joined forces to combat the heretics who questioned the national faith. And it worked. The average American did not doubt the nation's worthiness as leader of the free world. Overwhelming majorities continued to affirm the value of US engagement. Frustrated by the war in Vietnam, many were reluctant to dispatch troops around the globe, but they did not see the United States as just one state among many. They did not doubt that world order rested on US leadership.[182] American exceptionalism remained intact.

That the "Gray Lady," the *New York Times*, spokesman of the mainstream liberal-left and critic of the Vietnam War, did not much stray from the exceptionalist creed is somewhat surprising, given the usual account of how the Left lost faith in the wake of Vietnam and how the war chased liberal hawks out of the Democratic Party. But the greatest movement, according to the content analysis, took place on the Right. On the *Chicago Tribune*'s editorial pages, the Old Guard of the GOP finally gave way to the New Right of Reagan. Conservative Cold Warriors shed the last vestiges of nationalism as they came fully into the internationalist fold and became the keepers of the interventionist flame. Some of this may have been particular to the *Tribune*, which had into the 1960s clung tightly to the hard-core nationalism of its deceased long-time publisher, Colonel Robert McCormick, and which was thus starting from an unusual baseline. But the changes on the *Tribune*'s editorial page – whose stances on global affairs were by the 1970s almost indistinguishable from the *Times* of the 1950s – were part and parcel of a narrative shift taking place in the conservative movement and the Republican Party as a whole.

---

[181] On exceptionalism and US foreign policy, see McDougall 1997.
[182] Holsti and Rosenau 1984, 66–68, 72–74, 94–97; Wittkopf 1986, 434.

That transformation was a direct, though not exclusive, result of the Vietnam War. Chapter 5 argued that the politics of poor military performance give hawks in the opposition incentives to redouble their commitment to the narrative in whose terms the war had been legitimated and to accuse the government and governing party of insufficient fidelity to that narrative. That basic incentive structure was borne out during the Vietnam War. It was also buttressed by the war's peculiar politics, in which most congressional critics were members of the Democratic Party, on whose watch the war had intensified and which bore responsibility for the disappointment on the battlefield. It was further reinforced by a popular conservative backlash among white, working-class Americans against the rise of the counterculture, the shrillness of left-wing protest, and the assertiveness of ethnic and racial minorities. The hawkishness of the populist New Right and elitist neoconservatism was principled, but those principles also made for good politics. The Vietnam War not only laid the mass underpinnings of the rise of Reagan,[183] but galvanized the philanthropists who would bankroll conservatism's ideological infrastructure: a network of think tanks to sustain conservative intellectuals and policy wonks. Much of this energy was focused on domestic affairs, but homes, at such places as the Foreign Policy Research Institute and the Hoover Institution, arose for a new generation of conservative foreign policy experts to battle the erosion of Cold War orthodoxy.[184]

The Vietnam War had a profound impact on right-wing discourse on global affairs via two intertwined paths: neoconservatism and the new nationalism. Liberals had begun to break with the Cold War narrative before the war, but radicals' wartime assaults on America's exceptionalist traditions awakened the Democratic hawks who would later become known as neoconservatives.[185] In the early 1960s, they too had expressed doubts about Cold War axioms, notably at Norman Podhoretz's *Commentary* magazine. But such questioning came to seem a foolish youthful dalliance. Nathan Glazer attributed his own return to the fold to the "increasing radicalization, increasing

---

[183] Berman 1998; Wilentz 2008.
[184] Critchlow 2007, 104–122; O'Connor 2008; Schneider 2009, 112.
[185] I focus here on those Vaïsse labels "second-age neoconservatives"; first-age neocons concentrated on domestic matters. See Vaïsse 2010, chs. 3–4. See also Ehrman 1995, 33–57.

vituperation, [and] increasing disaffection with the country and its institutions" that had come to suffuse anti-war protest.[186] Jeanne Kirkpatrick, who would serve as a key bridge between Reagan and estranged liberal anti-Communists, became a neoconservative because: "'We' affirmed the validity of the American dream and the morality of the American society. 'They' adopted the characterizations of intellectuals ... who described the U.S. as a sick society drunk on technology and materialism. 'We' rejected the effort to revise American history, making it a dismal tale of dead Indians and double-dealing white settlers, imperialism, and war."[187] The Vietnam War, in the neoconservatives' view, had revealed not that the Cold War consensus was blinkered or passé, but that liberal anti-Communism was fragile. They sought to re-infuse superpower relations with the high moral tones of the 1950s. Theirs was the counterattack of the "vital center" against the New Left.[188] It is not too great a stretch to conclude: no Vietnam, no neoconservatism.[189]

Neoconservatives fought a losing battle in the first half of the 1970s to take back the Democratic Party. They might have languished in obscurity had they not hitched their star to the rising Right, to whose nationalist message they lent their intellectual heft and wonkish expertise. The New Right traced its roots to the ideological revolution spurred at the *National Review* in the mid 1950s.[190] But Goldwater's trouncing in 1964 had returned it to the party's margins. Conservatives remained divided until Vietnam over how tightly global politics was interconnected, how selective the United States could be in its battle against Communism, and how constructively the United States could engineer both global affairs and other societies. Before 1965, many conservatives were skeptical of the wisdom of deepening the US military presence in South Vietnam. With the Americanization of the war, however, the fractured conservative movement unified around this cause as the central front in the Cold War and around a crusading

---

[186] Quoted in Hodgson 1996, 128–129.   [187] Quoted in Vaïsse 2010, 98.
[188] Himmelstein 1990, 14; Peele 1984, 46–48.
[189] Some also attribute the Democratic hawks' transformation to the effects of the 1967 War on Jewish intellectuals, who allegedly recommitted to Cold War globalism to ensure US support for an Israel of whose vulnerability they had become increasingly aware. See Klinghoffer 1999; Vaïsse 2010, 58–62.
[190] On this transformation, see Himmelstein 1990; Hodgson 1996, 69–90; Judis 1988; Miles 1980, 80–93; Rothbard 2007, 147–172. On the various conservatisms, see Nash 1976.

internationalism.[191] That message resonated. As Kevin Phillips, strategist of the permanent Republican majority, later observed, the trauma of Vietnam and the vehemence of the New Left stirred up popular nationalism among the mass of Americans whose "superabundance of frustration and anomie" needed an outlet.[192] The New Right gave voice to and capitalized on "a pervasive, deeply felt sense [after Vietnam] that the country was in trouble; that it was in danger of losing its reputation as well as its power in the world; and that the rot could be stopped not by government, but only by a robust reassertion" of American exceptionalism and by new victories against the Communist menace.[193]

Gerald Ford believed most Americans just wanted to forget all about Vietnam, but the New Right refused to abide such collective amnesia. For the New Right, Vietnam had not been a lost cause or an unwinnable war. It had been lost at home, when liberals capitulated to Leftists who exhibited greater affection for Hanoi than Peoria and when self-declared realists' promise of détente sapped the nation's anti-Communist fighting spirit. Vietnam was both the impetus for and a signal moment in the New Right narrative of national betrayal – of an America betrayed by leaders of both parties who had sold out anti-Communist allies the world over.[194] If only the nation's elites had maintained their faith in America and the good Cold War fight, the Vietnam War could have been won. Whatever doubts conservatives had once harbored about the national-security state, whatever tortured logic Robert Taft had once employed to reconcile the global Cold War with his domestic priorities, the politics of the Vietnam War put them to rest. From the mid 1960s, Congressional conservatives' voting patterns shifted markedly toward an aggressive internationalism.[195]

The New Right's nationalist message came into its own just two years after the fall of Saigon, during the brouhaha over revision of the

---

[191] Offenbach 2012. Actually, as Offenbach records with greater nuance
       elsewhere, the war transformed the conservative movement by exacerbating
       the divide between mainstream and libertarian conservatives and by casting the
       latter out. See Offenbach 2010.
[192] Phillips 1982, 26–28, quote at 5.
[193] Hodgson 1996, quote at 219, also 306–307.
[194] On the complex conservative response to Vietnam, see Offenbach 2010;
       Scanlon 2009. On conservatives and détente, see Kalman 2010, 117–131;
       Schulzinger 1997, 305–327; Suri 2008; Wilentz 2008, 51–67.
[195] Cronin and Fordham 1999, 978.

Panama Canal treaties. Relinquishing US control over the canal had been a bipartisan executive initiative since the mid 1960s, but presidents had long delayed finalizing treaties. The issue had revitalized Ronald Reagan's flagging campaign against Ford in the 1976 Republican primaries – although not quite enough to put the Californian over the top. After entering office, Jimmy Carter bit the bullet and concluded a treaty in less than a year. He and his advisers anticipated a fight over ratification, but they got more than they bargained for. New Right activists mobilized the nascent conservative movement in opposition to the treaty, putting in the crosshairs not just the administration, but also moderate Republicans. Although the treaty passed narrowly, energized conservative organizations did not let the issue die, and indeed used it effectively to bludgeon and even defeat some senators who had ratified it.[196] That the New Nationalism erupted over the canal was not accidental, noted the historian David McCullough, whose award-winning and best-selling book on its digging would be published later that year. "There is a grandeur about the Panama Canal ... of a kind we like to think of as peculiarly American," he wrote to Carter. "The Canal is a triumph of an era we remember fondly for its confidence and energy, youth and sense of purpose."[197] He left unsaid what he and Carter both knew: that the nation's confidence and sense of purpose had come crashing down during Vietnam. The New Nationalism offered self-assurance and optimism, the promise of a new beginning – which Reagan's rhetoric captured with perfect pitch. The *Tribune*'s conversion in the final years of the Vietnam War reflected the New Right's growing influence within American conservatism and the Republican Party.

During and after the Vietnam War, American identity narratives came under assault. But this questioning from the margins, prompted by the war's setbacks and the counterinsurgency's brutality, served to consolidate a new consensus. Elites on the Right and Left reaffirmed American exceptionalism, proclaimed that the United States still had special responsibilities in a world buffeted by challenges, and pledged the nation's commitment to meeting its responsibilities. The politics of military failure in the Vietnam War thus gave rise to a new dominant public narrative, no longer regarding representations of the adversary,

---

[196] Clymer 2008; Zaretsky 2011. See also Moffett 1985.
[197] Quoted in Hodgson 1996, 227.

but of the American Self and its role in the world. The political con-
frontations of the late 1970s took place on that common narrative
terrain.

Victory and defeat do not speak for themselves. Elites interpret events
for mass audiences. But they do not offer their interpretations unen-
cumbered: they operate within a narrative and political context, and
their interpretive moves – to reproduce a dominant narrative, or to
break with it – reflect that context. This chapter has shown how major
episodes of victory and defeat on the military and diplomatic battlefield
of the Cold War – the Korean War, the Cuban Missile Crisis, the
Vietnam War – intertwined with the political calculations of US elites
to produce the Cold War narrative's consolidation, collapse, and subsequent transformation. What difference this made to US policy is the
subject, in part, of the next chapter, which concludes Part II.

8 | *Puzzles of the Cold War, lessons for the War on Terror*

After the Vietnam War, there was much disagreement in the United States about the merits of consensus in the making of foreign policy. Some bemoaned the unraveling of the Cold War consensus and called for a new bipartisan accord to guide US foreign policy. Others saw in the Vietnam intervention the danger of consensus and warned against forging new rigid doctrines about the world. Still others concluded that consensus has been the exception, rather than the rule, in US foreign policy and thought the effort to forge it anew quixotic.[1] It was a strange debate, in presuming that consensus was something nations self-consciously chose or rejected, that they could refashion their public narratives at will. But it was also strange in imagining that one can operate in a world without structures of meaning. Even those who yearned for consensus believed it possible, albeit regrettable, to conduct a policy debate that, in Ernest May's terms, involved only "calculated" choices and did not rest on any "axiomatic" principles.[2]

Part II has explored what leads dominant public narratives of national security to endure and to erode. It should now be clear that the dynamics of national security narrative in the United States since the Second World War cannot be explained by reference either to the simple, unmediated realities of global politics or to an accumulation of costly and otherwise inexplicable failures. I start instead with the politics of uncertain and protracted military campaigns, in combination with the public nature of narrative competition. Per the theoretical framework of Chapter 5, and supported by the quantitative and qualitative evidence of Chapters 6 and 7, I argue that dominant narratives normally endure despite substantial battlefield setbacks, and that major

---

[1] See, for the first view, Katzenbach 1973; for the second, Gelb and Betts 1979, 362–369; for the third, Chace 1978; Kristol 1976.
[2] May 1962.

battlefield successes, or the equivalent in crisis diplomacy, make possible their erosion.

This is a provocative claim. The literature on institutions, ideas, and discourses identifies a large and unanticipated policy failure – a shock – as the motor of change. Histories of the Cold War consensus support this intuitive argument, for they typically credit the Vietnam War with its collapse. But this reconsideration of the content and timing of the dominant Cold War narrative suggests otherwise. When challenging so well-established a conventional wisdom, caution is warranted. The limitations of this study are clear, with its focus on the politics of the Cold War and on the United States. Given the resource- and time-intensive nature of this research, especially the content analysis, those trade-offs were not only acceptable, but necessary.

In Chapter 5, I explained why there is good reason to think that the argument travels beyond the Cold War and beyond the United States. Although space constraints preclude much consideration of the argument's cross-national applicability, it is unquestionably common for political oppositions to criticize military operations from the safe terrain of the dominant narrative. Everywhere the natives proved ungrateful for the graces of liberal empire. But their continual resistance, and the imperial forces' regular setbacks, typically led to questions about methods and means, rarely to fundamental challenges to the imperial enterprise and its civilizing mission. The initial stages of the Yom Kippur War of October 1973 were so disastrous that it came in Israel to be known as the *mehdal* – the failure – despite the subsequent operational triumphs. But the oft-heard charges of complacency, arrogance, and poor judgment directed at the political and military leadership and the intense demand for political accountability resulted in no fundamental rethinking of Israel's strategic environment, strengthened the right and the rhetoric of siege, and left the dominant narrative largely intact. France's floundering in Indochina and Algeria in the 1950s led to constitutional change, but opposition leader and then President Charles de Gaulle's calls for the restoration of French grandeur were rhetorically conservative, framed as an adjustment of means, not ends. Even Mikhail Gorbachev, who as a junior Politburo member in 1979 bore little responsibility for the invasion of Afghanistan and who as premier shared his Politburo colleagues' pessimism that the Soviet Union could stabilize that country, was reluctant to break with his nation's dominant Cold War narrative: he long hesitated to withdraw Soviet forces from Afghanistan because he expressly feared it would harm the Soviet Union in the continuing superpower competition for Third World allegiances. And, as we will see below, the same dynamics were at work in American politics in the decade after 9/11. These examples are merely suggestive. I leave it to future scholars to explore these and other cases, to identify scope conditions beyond the extent and rapidity of military struggles, and to investigate whether the argument, in some form, extends to other policy domains beyond national security.

Skeptical readers will fairly ask what light this revised version of the Cold War narrative sheds on the policies actually pursued by the United States. Consider three enduring puzzles. First, US state development. One of these chapters' findings is that the dominant Cold War narrative of the 1950s was narrow and that it emerged thanks to nationalists' self-marginalization during the Korean War. From one vantage point, it is puzzling that the Cold War did not produce a garrison state.[3] But, from another, the puzzle is why the Cold War brought about a national-security state *despite* America's anti-statist traditions.[4] This would not be terribly puzzling if US policy had been an unavoidable response to the pressures of the international system, and specifically to the Soviet/global Communist threat. But many realists at the time – supposedly clear-eyed observers of the global scene, like George Kennan – thought the unselective and militarized vision of NSC-68, which underpinned the growth of unaccountable executive power and a huge defense bureaucracy, dangerous and overly static.[5] Even if NSC-68's interpretation of global Communism's intentions, capabilities, and unity was plausible, so too were other interpretations that might have avoided the perils of the military-industrial complex and the imperial presidency. If the emergence of the Cold War national-security state remains a puzzle, the Old Right's machinations during the Korean War provide part of the answer.

Second, the changed character of superpower conflict after the early 1960s. A more rule-governed and stable superpower relationship emerged after the Cuban Missile Crisis. The traditional view is that the crisis' close call illuminated for both superpowers the irresponsibility of nuclear brinkmanship. What had seemed like clever *realpolitik* in the 1950s came, after October 1962, to seem reckless and anything

[3] Friedberg 2000.   [4] Hogan 1998.   [5] Gaddis 2011, 391–392.

but clever.[6] It is true that the missile crisis heightened the mass public's awareness of the danger of nuclear Armageddon. But key decision-makers were already deeply aware of those dangers and of the super-powers' common interests in avoiding nuclear war. Soviet leaders were, by the mid 1950s, openly acknowledging as much, despite the ideological challenges this posed.[7] Well before the missile crisis, Marc Trachtenberg has shown, the Kennedy administration was keen on pursuing a *modus vivendi* with the Soviet Union, based on reassurance of both America's European allies (that the United States truly was committed to their security) and the Soviet Union (that Germany would not acquire nuclear weapons).[8] As John Lewis Gaddis observes: "The Cuban Missile Crisis did not ... frighten Soviet and American leaders into embracing a policy of détente. Whatever their motives, both sides had for some time sought a relaxation of Cold War tensions, although by different means."[9] Prior to the missile crisis, however, US leaders could not openly move toward that vision and the less confrontational policy it implied. They did not believe they could legitimately advance in public the requisite nuanced understanding of the Communist Other. Détente, including the taming of the arms race, hinged, in the United States, on the demise of the Cold War narrative's dominance. That in turn required political space for liberal internationalists to break with the prevailing narrative. The Kennedy administration's triumph in the Cuban Missile Crisis, acknowledged across the political spectrum, created that space. It opened a window of change through which liberal internationalists jumped.

Third, the Vietnam War. Large-scale US military intervention in Southeast Asia was not a direct result of Cold War groupthink. We now know that Lyndon Johnson thought victory unlikely and that he only reluctantly escalated the US presence, in part because he feared the impact of "losing Vietnam" on his treasured Great Society programs.[10] Had a new consensus taken shape after the Cuban Missile Crisis, along the lines Kennedy had proposed at American University and arguably as realists might expect, the charge of having "lost" Vietnam would have had little bite and the war's Americanization might have been avoided. But that indictment continued to resonate in the mid 1960s,

---

[6] For a classic statement, see Halle 1967, 408–411. See also Hershberg 2010.
[7] Garthoff 1990, 33–37.   [8] Trachtenberg 1999.   [9] Gaddis 1990, 254.
[10] Bator 2008; Johns 2010; Logevall 1999.

with tragic consequences. The theoretical argument sheds light on why no new consensus consolidated after the Cuban Missile Crisis around the act, agent, and scene of the global drama, yet also why US elites came together in the 1970s to defend American exceptionalism and a national sense of mission.

The world and the United States are, in this second decade of the twenty-first century, very different from those of the Cold War. Its end did not usher in a new world order of peace and prosperity, and the US military has, in the two decades since, operated at a much higher tempo. Does the military crucible remain relevant? The events of the last decade seem to suggest that the answer is yes. This chapter concludes by returning to the puzzle with which Part II opened: the Terror narrative, which long outlived the Iraq War that had been so tightly bound into it.

Coda: Iraq and the persistent War on Terror[11]

The political dynamics of the Cold War consensus and the War on Terror run parallel. Setbacks on the Iraqi battlefield undercut the Bush administration's, and more generally Republicans', authority with regard to national security.[12] One might have thought that the dominance of the Terror narrative would have shattered amidst the dunes of Iraq – just like, according to the conventional wisdom, the Cold War consensus shattered amidst the paddies and jungles of Vietnam. One might have thought that the Bush administration's Democratic opponents, eager to distance themselves from an increasingly unpopular war, would jump at the chance to articulate a different narrative of national security. They did stridently criticize a war they had once supported in droves. But they did not launch a frontal assault on the War on Terror. Even as US forces in Iraq faced an increasingly sophisticated and effective insurgency and even as the insurgency morphed into a sectarian civil war, leading Democrats left the underlying Terror narrative untouched. They cast the Iraq War as a betrayal of the War on Terror properly conceived. Many, including Senator and then presidential candidate Barack Obama, turned their backs on the former by rushing headlong into a renewed embrace of the latter.

---

[11] This section draws on a lengthier essay: Krebs 2013.
[12] Goble and Holm 2009.

They more deeply entrenched the Terror narrative, and they ultimately led the United States into a greater military commitment in
Afghanistan and the frontier regions of Pakistan.[13] As in Vietnam,
the politics of poor military performance curbed the degree to which
Democrats confronted the Terror narrative early on, and that bound
their tongues, and their hands, later. Their rhetorical choices amidst a
failing and uncertain war were understandable – from the perspective
of the theoretical framework – but they were also fateful: Democrats
missed an opportunity to alter the narrative terrain of US national
security.[14] If Democrats complain that the War on Terror lasted too
long, and in ways is still with us, they partly have themselves to
blame.

The Terror narrative maintained its dominant position for much of
the decade after 9/11 – even though another mass-casualty attack on US
soil had not taken place, even though there was little evidence that
infringements on Americans' liberty and investments in homeland
security could take much credit,[15] even though both America's overseas adventures and its domestic War on Terror had proved extremely
costly,[16] and even though the public had soured on the wars in Iraq and
Afghanistan. International terrorism and Islamist extremism topped
the list of Americans' fears throughout the decade. Although the
proportion of Americans who identified international terrorism as a
"critical threat" to vital US interests fell substantially after 2002, it still
ranked first in 2008, and it had declined less than China's rise, which
also ranked much lower.[17] There were, from the start, those who
charged that a "war" on terror would legitimize Al Qaeda, predispose
the United States to militarized counterterrorism, alienate Muslim
populations sympathetic to Al Qaeda's grievances, and hand Al

---

[13] Thus, five years after 9/11, there began to emerge only occasional cracks in the
      imposing edifice of the Terror narrative. See, among others, Cole 2006, 26;
      Dobson 2006; Lustick 2006; Mueller 2006; Frank Rich, "Whatever Happened
      to the America of 9/12?," *New York Times*, 10 September 2006. For a partial
      break, see Gordon 2007.
[14] For a different – and, to my mind, too static – account of continuity, see Jackson
      2011, as well as various essays in Bentley and Holland 2014.
[15] Mueller and Stewart 2012.
[16] Stiglitz and Bilmes 2008, and for an update Bilmes 2013. See also
      http://costsofwar.org/.
[17] For relevant data from the Pew Research Center, Gallup, and the Chicago
      Council of Foreign Relations, see Holsti 2011, 112–114.

Qaeda a psychological victory, but, as Chapter 3 argued, their preference for a law-enforcement paradigm (terrorism as crime) did not
depart nearly as far from the dominant Terror narrative as was often
thought. That criticism remained so thin throughout the decade is also
surprising because substantial segments of the public had lost trust in
the administration, in the official narrators of the War on Terror.

I have argued that, early in a struggling war, opposition doves have
little incentive to take on the war's underlying rationale. Even as war's
costs mount, critics typically frame their arguments *within* the terms of
the dominant narrative. This fits to a tee leading Democrats' rhetoric in
the decade after 9/11: even when they condemned the Iraq War, they
left the Terror narrative intact.[18] Echoing the Vietnam debates of 1965
to 1966, narrow criticisms of the Iraq War's strategy, operational
doctrine, and tactics were succeeded by a buyer's remorse: the Iraq
War had been an error, but the United States could not withdraw.
During the 2004 Democratic primaries, every candidate, even the
hawkish Senator Joseph Lieberman, criticized how the war was
conducted – without the imprimatur of the United Nations, with
too few allies, based on false pretenses. But they did not differ with
the administration over whether to prosecute the War on Terror,
just how. Andrew Bacevich's rueful observation of the Democratic
nominee, Senator John Kerry – that his "differences with George
W. Bush's national security policies" lay in "tactics rather than first
principles"[19] – applied to nearly all of his rivals in the primaries.

In 2004, all of the Democratic candidates for president, save
Lieberman, converged around the representation of Iraq as a distraction from the real War on Terror. As early as December 2003,
Governor Howard Dean charged that "the Iraq war diverted critical
intelligence and military resources, undermined diplomatic support for
our fight against terror, and created a new rallying cry for terrorist
recruits."[20] Kerry took the same line of attack. Awkwardly echoing
Bush, he declared in a debate, "I can do a better job of waging a
smarter, more effective war on terror and guarantee that we go after

[18] See similarly King and Wells 2009.
[19] Bacevich 2005, 15. See also Croft 2006, 44, 219–220.
[20] Howard Dean, "Fulfilling the Promise of America: Meeting the Security
Challenges of the New Century," remarks to the Pacific Council on
International Policy, Los Angeles, CA, 15 December 2003, available at
www.crocuta.net/Dean/Dean_Speeches.htm (hereinafter, Dean Speeches).

the terrorists. I will hunt them down and will kill them, will capture them, will do whatever's necessary to be safe."[21] When it came to the stakes of the War on Terror, Kerry again could have been confused with Bush: "The war on terror is as monumental a struggle as the Cold War. Its outcome will determine whether we and our children live in freedom or in fear ... This is a clash between civilization and the enemies of civilization; between humanity's best hopes and most primitive fears."[22] The Democratic candidates even tried to outdo the administration in fear-mongering, regularly invoking the specter of mushroom clouds on US soil.[23] The perennial maverick candidate Congressman Dennis Kucinich was the only one to hazard breaking with the War on Terror's first principles, with the Terror narrative.

Little changed in 2008. True, foreign policy was no longer the over-riding issue, given the financial meltdown and economic slowdown. True, the War on Terror, once established as an unquestioned common sense, had begun to lose that status: during the first debate among Democratic hopefuls, they were asked whether they thought the United States was, or should be, engaged in a global War on Terror.[24] Nevertheless, of the eight candidates who appeared at that first debate, nearly all made clear, then and afterwards, that they accepted the Terror narrative's premises and that their differences with the Bush administration lay in the realm of means, not ends.[25] Even those who sought to avoid the slogan, War on Terror, often substituted combative synonyms like fight, battle, or struggle, and they did not normally insist that its targets be more concrete: terrorism, as an abstraction, was still the adversary. The candidates almost

[21] "Transcript of Debate between Bush and Kerry," *New York Times*, 14 October 2004.
[22] Kerry, Speech at Temple University, 24 September 2004, available at www.presidentialrhetoric.com/campaign/index.html.
[23] Dean, "Restoring American Leadership: A New Direction for American Foreign Policy," speech to the Council on Foreign Relations, 25 June 2003 (Dean Speeches). See also John Edwards in Vice-Presidential Debate at Case Western Reserve University, Cleveland, Ohio, 5 October 2004, available at www.presidency.ucsb.edu/debates.php (hereinafter, Debates).
[24] Democratic Presidential Candidate Debate, Orangeburg, South Carolina, 26 April 2007 (Debates).
[25] While Joseph Biden, John Edwards, Mike Gravel, and Dennis Kucinich all distanced themselves from the *War* on Terror as a slogan, only Gravel and Kucinich broke with the Terror narrative.

universally agreed that the administration's misguided war in Iraq had undermined the more important battle being waged on what Senator Hillary Clinton called "the forgotten frontlines in the war against terror," in Afghanistan and Pakistan.[26] By going to war in Iraq, the United States, Obama alleged, had "taken [its] eye off the ball" – the War on Terror – and the result was that al Qaeda was "stronger now than [at] any time since 2001."[27] Most importantly, they did not offer an alternative narrative, with a different set of protagonists, paramount issues, historical moments, and causal story. What motivated terrorists to target the United States? A "toxic, distorted, and hate-filled ideology" that made them "intent upon foisting their way of life" on others – hardly a far cry from Islamofascism.[28] Criticizing the Bush administration and specifically the Iraq War from the terrain of the Terror narrative was a tried-and-true technique that thrived through 2008.

More than any other major Democratic candidate in 2008, Barack Obama made opposition to the Iraq War the centerpiece of his campaign. It is telling that even he reproduced the Terror narrative. The chief problem confronting the United States in the global arena remained for Obama that vague abstraction, terrorism.[29] And that was the problem with the Iraq War: "the military defeat of the Iraqi insurgency," he said in 2005, will not bring about "the defeat of international terrorism." Just the opposite, as that misbegotten war, in Obama's view, hampered the War on Terror, properly conceived – via a "deteriorating" situation in Afghanistan, "lagg[ing]" improvement in intelligence collection and analysis, unimplemented "critical homeland security measures," and "improved coordination with our

---

[26] Democratic Presidential Candidate Debate, Los Angeles, California, 31 January 2008 (Debates).
[27] Barack Obama in Democratic Candidates Forum, Chicago, Illinois, 7 August 2007 (Debates).
[28] See Dodd, "Understanding the Stakes"; Hillary Clinton in Democratic Presidential Candidate Debate, Manchester, New Hampshire, 3 June 2007 (Debates).
[29] See, among many others, Obama, "A Way Forward in Iraq," speech to the Chicago Council on Global Affairs, 20 November 2006, available at http://obamaspeeches.com/ (hereinafter, Obama Speeches); and Remarks at the VFW National Convention, Orlando, Florida, 19 August 2008, available at http://2008election.procon.org/view.resource.php?resourceID=001568 (hereinafter, Campaign Speeches).

global allies and partners."[30] Many saw in Obama a radical critic of
the War on Terror, but he was no such thing. He regularly employed
the phrase, or various closely related variants, although he assailed its
use as a "political football."[31] He too portrayed terrorists not as
rational actors with a political agenda, but as "fanatical" ideologues.[32]
He too represented the events of 9/11 as a historical rupture. "The
attacks of September 11 brought this new reality into a terrible and
ominous focus," he asserted during his presidential campaign. "On
that bright and beautiful day, the world of peace and prosperity that
was the legacy of our Cold War victory seemed to suddenly vanish
under rubble, and twisted steel, and clouds of smoke." That new
reality, Obama claimed, was that "the American people cannot be
protected by oceans or the sheer might of our military alone." He
agreed that the stakes were high, implicitly the nation's very survival:
the danger of terrorism was "no less grave" than the threat posed by the
Soviet Union during the Cold War.[33]

The Bush administration was primarily responsible for the "war on
terror" that stoked Americans' nightmares after September 11, 2001.
But Democrats were hardly innocent. Taking the politically safe rhetorical route, they blunted their own spears and gave the Terror narrative
life. It took a (hopefully) once-in-a-generation economic recession, and
a further two-and-a-half years, for the Obama administration to shake
the Terror narrative's firm grip – so that terrorism was a concern, but
no longer pre-eminent; so that counterterrorism no longer took pride of
place above all other foreign policy initiatives; so that a war against
terror or violent extremism was narrowed to a war against a specific
organization, Al Qaeda, and its affiliates.[34] This transpired with hardly
a word of criticism from the Right: partisans were busy fighting their
battles on economic terrain, and Republicans were divided over the
definition of vital interests in times of austerity.[35] All this was in place
by the time US forces finally found and killed Osama bin Laden in

[30] Obama, "Moving Forward in Iraq," speech to the Chicago Council on Foreign Relations, 22 November 2005 (Obama Speeches).
[31] Obama, "A Way Forward in Iraq."
[32] Obama, "Moving Forward in Iraq."
[33] Obama, "A New Strategy for a New World," remarks delivered in Washington, DC, 15 July 2008 (Campaign Speeches).
[34] For evidence, see Krebs 2013, 71–76.
[35] See Alex Roarty, "Foreign Policy Opens Fissures in GOP," *National Journal*, 29 June 2011; Eli Lake, "All Over the Map," *New Republic*, 28 July 2011.

May 2011. Had he been killed earlier, perhaps the Terror narrative's dominance might have been challenged earlier too – although that seems unlikely if the Bush administration had owned that triumph. But, in May 2011, the greater danger, the Obama administration believed, was that Americans would conclude that terrorism was a thing of the past, that they would, with relief, look inward. Thus, though proud of the accomplishment and eager to capitalize on it politically to guard the president's flank, the administration insisted that the threat posed by Al Qaeda and its affiliates endured unabated. And so, somewhat altered, did the Terror narrative itself.

9 | *Narrative in an age of fracture*

Running for re-election in the summer of 2012, Barack Obama offered a public confession – albeit a safe one. His biggest mistake of the past four years, he told Charlie Rose, was not the substance of his policy, but the style of his leadership: "the nature of this office is also to tell a story to the American people that gives them a sense of unity and purpose and optimism, especially during tough times."[1] Self-proclaimed "serious" people prefer to debate the intricacies of policy and tend to dismiss style as superficial. But, Obama hinted, he had learned that, in the real world of presidential politics, style and substance are linked. The policy wonks who hold forth in Washington's seminar rooms gravitate toward the instrumental mode of argumentation, toward the assessment of costs and benefits. Sometimes, they embrace the normative mode, a rhetorical world of rights and wrongs. But they generally frame their arguments within an existing conversation. However, a president who refuses to play his part as narrator-in-chief, and who thus allows others to seize the rostrum and set the terms of debate, will find himself stymied. Obama's confession granted some credence to critics on the Left who charged that he had failed to use his bully pulpit – although, had the moderate Obama followed his own advice, he would not have set forth a narrative to their liking.

In that interview, Obama emphasized the importance of narrative leadership in domestic affairs, but both the demand for and limits of such storytelling apply equally to the realm of foreign affairs, specifically national security. Policy arguments in this arena too always rest on implicit, often truncated, narratives depicting the protagonists, the setting, and the action of a global drama. Such narratives define the national interest and identify the global challenges and opportunities

---

[1] Lindsey Boerma, "Obama Reflects on His Biggest Mistake as President," 12 July 2012, www.cbsnews.com.

facing the polity. In their absence, leaders could not set priorities or fashion a menu of appropriate responses. Such narratives, in other words, constitute the basis for grand strategy – the state's plan for how it can achieve its ends abroad, given limited resources. Were such narratives countless, or were they readily adopted and abandoned as events demand, a narrative perspective would add little to more traditional accounts of national security policy. This book takes issue with, and provides evidence against, both of these propositions.

First, debates over national security are typically not unstructured. Sometimes, the terrain and texture of global politics seem deeply and persistently uncertain, and legitimate debate is free-ranging. But, eventually, a narrative rises to dominance. This dominant narrative permits only a range of policy options to be articulated, placing others beyond the limits of legitimacy. It does not quash all contestation and render the outcome of deliberation a foregone conclusion. But, by fixing the boundaries of legitimation, it tilts the tables. We have seen how the dominant narratives of the interwar period, of the Cold War, and after 9/11 structured debates over US national security, sustaining some policy options and setting conceivable – and arguably preferable – alternatives beyond the pale. When policies lack a basis for legitimation, they have few vocal advocates, and those few advocates are either ignored or castigated.

Second, events require interpretation, and narratives thus do not reflect some unmediated reality. Yet, narratives also do not rise and fall thanks simply to motivated and rhetorically talented actors imposing their vision and shaking up the established order of things. There is at work a delicate interplay between structure and agency. This book argues for an explanatory framework rooted in speech acts, broadly conceived: who is speaking and what relations of authority they bring to bear; when they speak, which affects whether audiences demand storytelling and who can claim authority; whether they reproduce or break with dominant narratives (i.e. what they say); and how they express themselves (i.e. rhetorical mode). Both Part I, on the emergence of dominant narratives of national security, and Part II, on their persistence and demise, draw on these elements, in different configurations and combinations.

Narratives of national security are ubiquitous – as most would readily acknowledge. But, contrary to the putative mainstream of international relations, they often leave a distinctive mark on debates over foreign affairs and thus on the policies that states pursue. We cannot understand how leading politicians publicly talk about security, nor can we explain the resulting policies, and crucially why some alternatives received little consideration, without an eye to the dominant narratives that constitute the terrain for legitimation. For those already convinced that narratives matter to politics, these claims will be welcome, but hardly novel. For them, this book's contribution is to shed light on how particular narratives of national security become relatively dominant and how and when those dominant narratives come undone.

This concluding chapter continues by summarizing what I hope readers have learned about when dominant national security narratives have come together in the United States and when they have collapsed. To that end, it presents briefly the theoretical configurations and empirical evidence at the heart of the preceding chapters. It elaborates on the implications for scholarship and sketches out a research agenda. Second, the chapter examines whether this study's core claims are resilient to changes in technologies of communication, in the ideological and discursive fabric, and in the constitution of audiences and authority. The Right, bemoaning nations' unraveling, and the Left, welcoming the prospect of a less confined politics, agree that dominant structuring narratives are a thing of the past. I argue otherwise: alongside the many pressures toward fragmentation in a world of rapid change, there is great public demand for meaning-making and interpretive order. Third, the chapter explores the normative stakes: should we lament or celebrate the endurance of dominant narratives of national security? A world without narrative order is impossible – and also, I believe, deceptive in its appeal.

The chapter closes by reflecting on the future of US national security. Dominant narratives continue to shape debate in the United States over strategy and policy, and not surprisingly so does the quest for narrative dominance. Strategy that cannot be effectively legitimated is brittle, and obstacles to legitimation entice leaders down the sometimes dangerous path of covert action. Persistent narrative competition makes policy seem incoherent and inconsistent, and it entices leaders down the sometimes dangerous path of a rhetoric clearer than truth. The politics of narrative will shape how America's leaders make sense of developments at home and abroad in the years to come, whether they cast these developments as threats or opportunities, as urgent crises or manageable problems, and thus whether the United States greets change by opening its arms or manning the barricades. We ignore the politics of narrative at our peril.

Arguments, evidence, and implications

Narratives of national security do not rise to dominance simply because they reflect reality, mirroring the plain meaning of events, for events have little meaning except insofar as they are woven into coherent stories. Such narratives do not emerge from nowhere, out of the cultural ether, for political agents self-consciously and strategically seek to make sense of the world and to shape how others make sense of the world. Such narratives do not vanquish their competitors just because their advocates are more rhetorically skilled or hold a larger megaphone, for even charismatic speakers backed by resources may lack the requisite authority, and even they cannot fling open the windows of transformation at their insistence.

The key to narrative dominance in the United States in the domain of national security, I argue in Part I, is for the president – in this arena an authoritative speaker – to embrace a rhetoric of storytelling – as opposed to argument – during a time of narrative crisis, when multiple narratives command legitimacy and when public demand for narrative order is elevated. When, during such critical junctures, presidents express themselves in a mode marked by storytelling, other political elites find it difficult to advance alternatives, allowing the president's preferred narrative to rise unopposed. The elements in this conjuncture – moment, authority, and rhetorical mode – are jointly necessary and sufficient for narrative projects to achieve dominance.

Franklin Delano Roosevelt's and George W. Bush's rhetorical performances after Pearl Harbor and 9/11 respectively epitomized the conjuncture and met with the expected success – even though, I argue in Chapter 4, there were other plausible ways of narrating those events, of representing the drama's setting, its actors, and their purposes. The attack on Pearl Harbor did not itself decisively settle the public dispute over the interconnectedness of global politics and the divisibility of security (scene), the ends of US military intervention and the unity of the battlefield (purpose, scene), or the sources of aggression (agent). Al Qaeda's bold assault on the pre-eminent symbols of US economic and military might did not itself establish that the United

States had been targeted for its values rather than its actions (purpose), that terrorism and ideological extremism were the adversary rather than the specific organization Al Qaeda (agent), that transnational terrorism was the pre-eminent threat rather than one among many (scene), or that 9/11 marked a turning point in global history (scene). Each of these pillars of the dramatic pentad was contestable, yet Roosevelt's and Bush's narratives came to seem like common sense. They marginalized alternatives that could have legitimated strikingly different policies: in Roosevelt's case, a more limited response to Japan's provocation rather than total war and unconditional surrender, a more intensive effort in the Asian theater at the expense of the European campaign, a harsh postwar peace rather than Germany's reconstruction and reintegration; in Bush's case, terminating US support for authoritarian Arab leaders rather than leaning on them heavily to root out extremism, focusing on managing China's rise rather than waging campaigns to spread democracy, degrading Al Qaeda rather than spreading counterterrorist resources thin.

When the conjuncture is not properly aligned – because the speaker adopts a rhetorical mode inappropriate to the moment, by embracing storytelling under conditions of narrative stability or by employing predominantly argument in an unsettled narrative situation – even considerable presidential rhetorical efforts fall short. The reasons for misalignment range from individual rhetorical predilections to misperception and miscalculation. Regardless, national leaders are then unable to silence their opponents. When they turn to storytelling when public demand for such stabilizing rhetoric is low, they invite counter-stories. When they turn to argument when public demand for storytelling is high, they permit political opponents to advance alternative arguments in a rhetorical space that is comparatively unstructured and thus that is not conducive to rhetorical coercion. When they are silent, they allow others to supply the meaning and order for which the attentive public is so keen.

The two cases in Chapter 3 illustrate the dynamics of rhetorical and political contestation under these misaligned conditions. Non-interventionists retained legitimacy through the end of 1941, even as public support for their positions eroded, because Roosevelt's argument-heavy rhetoric, and his more occasional weakly drawn narrative, did not match the increasingly unsettled narrative situation. Ronald Reagan's concerted storytelling about Nicaragua, after the fall of détente when the Cold War again held sway, ran into an opposed narrative of that conflict. The consequences of these talented communicators' failures were substantial: tentative intervention in a war in which FDR saw vital national interests at stake, paltry overt assistance and illegal covert action in civil wars in which Reagan saw vital national interests at stake.

For theorists of international relations and foreign policy, Part I reveals how deeply political and power-laden are the processes that give rise to social meaning. Contra realism, both structural and neoclassical, the international system does not yield clear imperatives: the system requires interpretation, and what appears to be common sense is in fact the result of contingent political contest. Contra liberalism, there are not as many publicly sustainable narratives as there are domestic interests: political contest normally takes place on a shared narrative terrain. Contra liberal constructivism, the sedimentation of meaning is shot through with power: it cannot be persuasion all the way down, as persuasion rests on common metrics and standards and a shared agenda. This is hardly news to critical theorists, who have long advanced these arguments, but have refrained from offering a generalizable account of dominant narratives' rise and fall – and would think my effort to do so misguided. Inspired by critical theory, but parting ways with its epistemological commitments, I bring together in Part I the realist's grasp of coercion, the liberal's focus on contestation, and the constructivist's sensitivity to structures of meaning, with an appreciation of agency. Starting with broadly constructivist premises, but emphasizing conflictual and coercive processes of meaning-making, Part I's synthetic theoretical framework embodies a politics that has much in common with the spirit of realism, albeit not with strict materialism. It seeks to promote dialogue between an enriched realism and a redirected constructivism.[2] Finally, it introduces, and demonstrates the analytical purchase of, a novel concept: rhetorical mode. If Part I is persuasive, that is partly because it focuses on presidential rhetoric alone and holds constant the institutional embeddedness of authority. Yet, the authority to "speak security" varies. This is a key point of departure for Part II – on the consolidation, endurance, and breakdown of dominant narratives of national security.

[2] On potential areas of compatibility between realism and constructivism, see also Barkin 2010; Jackson 2004.

Part II begins from the insight that US presidents' narrative authority with regard to national security erodes when their signature security initiatives falter, when the forces they have dispatched into battle experience setbacks. As narrative authority diffuses, political opponents can advance alternative security stories and shift the bases of debate. Whether a dominant narrative endures depends on whether opponents seize that opportunity. Theorists commonly attribute large-scale ideational and discursive change to substantial policy failure, but they reach that conclusion by overlooking the politics of failure. Chapter 5 argues that, in the context of a troubled and protracted military mission, the political disincentives to launching a wholesale assault are substantial. Far more likely are narrower attacks that serve to reproduce, consolidate, and buttress the narrative that sustained the mission's legitimation. In the wake of a substantial triumph on the battlefield or in an episode of coercive diplomacy, however, those who can take credit for that victory emerge with their authority bolstered and can leverage that redoubled authority to challenge the dominant narrative – if that accords with their preferences.

Part II's contribution is empirical as well as theoretical. Chapters 6 and 7 offer a reinterpretation of what the Cold War consensus held, when it consolidated, and when it collapsed. The consensus is normally understood as a set of widely held beliefs and policies associated with militarized global containment. It has been blamed, perhaps unfairly, for a host of American blunders. Yet, despite its importance to both policy and history, the consensus has never been rigorously studied. It is on its face a hard case for my theory: the usual account, according to which it collapsed amidst the trauma of the Vietnam War, seems to fit the long-standing theoretical conventional wisdom. Chapter 6 re-conceptualizes the Cold War consensus as a dominant public narrative and tracks it via a content analysis of foreign affairs editorials. The result is a dramatically different history: the zone of narrative agreement was fairly narrow; this narrow narrative did not achieve dominance until well into the 1950s; its dominance began to erode even before the Johnson administration dispatched hundreds of thousands of Americans to Vietnam; no new dominant narrative emerged regarding the Communist Other in the 1960s; and, when a new consensus finally took shape in the early 1970s, it revolved around a peculiarly American blend of exceptionalism and internationalism. The unique data I have collected revises our understanding of an intrinsically important period in global, and American, history.

Exogenous shocks, alleged global realities, and change in administration cannot account for the ups and downs of national security narrative in the United States between 1945 and 1991. Yet, the pattern is consistent with the provocative theory of Chapter 5, revolving around the narrative politics of the battlefield. From that perspective, it makes perfect sense that the frustrations of the Korean War facilitated the Cold War narrative's consolidation, that the triumph of the Cuban Missile Crisis made possible the consensus' breakdown, and that US setbacks in Vietnam generated blistering criticism that nevertheless in crucial ways reproduced Cold War axioms. Chapter 7 delves into the history, politics, and rhetoric of Cold War America to show why the narrative rose and fell as it did over four decades.

There are at least three ways in which it would be productive to extend this line of inquiry into the narrative life-cycle and its consequences. First, narrative and the making of national security beyond the United States. There were good methodological and substantive reasons for tailoring this book's theoretical framework and empirical research to the United States, as Chapter 1 explains. But this choice unfortunately reproduced the discipline's traditional biases and raised questions about whether these arguments and findings travel beyond America's borders. The earlier chapters could speak only briefly to the question of the theoretical accounts' cross-national and cross-temporal generalizability. Follow-on work might consider whether and how these dynamics are different in parliamentary regimes and non-totalitarian non-democracies, in countries that have felt the pressures of global politics more intensely than the United States, and in countries that have waged costly wars on their own territory. While both the desire for ontological security and the impulse to storytelling seem universal, the attribution of authority varies across time and space. How and why it varies is less clear. It may vary by regime type: perhaps leaders in parliamentary regimes who are not directly elected are also not their nations' narrators-in-chief, or perhaps semi-presidential regimes, on the French model, more closely approximate pure presidential systems.[3] It may vary by form of civil-military interaction: in

---

[3] Although there is evidence that politics everywhere is becoming presidentialized and personalized: see Poguntke and Webb 2005; Karvonen 2010.

some countries, militarism rules, and civilians show great deference to how current and ex-officers narrate global affairs, while, in other countries, those wearing the uniform are not uniquely authorized to shape debates over national security. Or perhaps authority varies independently of institutional design and is more the product of nations' unique histories.

Second, the politics of narrative in other policy domains. The security arena is different from others: its stakes are generally represented as being much greater. At the extreme, poorly designed security policies threaten state survival and the lives of citizens and residents. True, public health, fiscal, or educational policy can also have implications for the fate of collectives and individuals, and even their mortality, but the links are generally less direct. While one might rightly question whether security is truly unique, the fact remains that it is commonly considered and treated as a realm apart. We expect politics to inform the appropriation of public funds, appointments to bureaucratic offices, and the design of regulations, and we accept the resulting inefficiency. We reject, and are offended by, political interference in national security. Arnold Wolfers long ago pointed out that no polity actually seeks to maximize security, that in practice all balance security against other priorities, and that politics necessarily drives the precise mix.[4] But, Wolfers notwithstanding, we still treat security as distinctive, and we still invoke security to signal the exclusion of politics.[5] The upshot is that authority may be more fragmented, and narratives may less commonly or easily emerge as dominant, in other domains. Moreover, national security narratives may be especially enduring: while security's high stakes might in principle call forth more attentive publics and more rational learning,[6] the potentially high costs of being wrong would seem likely to inhibit possible challengers.

Finally, the politics of narrative in what Daniel Rodgers has aptly called "an age of fracture." In Rodgers' intellectual and political history of the last decades in the United States, the central theme is the prevalence of fissures and fluidity, especially among institutions and

[4] Wolfers 1962, 147–165.
[5] The literature on "securitization" claims that the invocation of security "takes politics beyond the established rules of the game and frames the issue either as a special kind of politics or as above politics": Buzan *et al.* 1998, 23.
[6] Extending the logic of Posen 1984.

ideas. Cultural production has diversified, community has eroded, constraints on individual choice have worn away, authority has fragmented.[7] The new media environment has reinforced these trends by providing an ever-expanding array of entertainment. As the attentive public shrinks and occupies the more extreme ends of the political spectrum, politics becomes polarized.[8]

Meanwhile, the power of traditional authorities to enforce discipline in the public sphere has diminished. In Bruce Lincoln's reading of the *Iliad*, Odysseus could drive the lesser-born Thersites from the rostrum with the golden scepter that is the symbol of legitimate authority and with a public tongue-lashing. That is not possible today.[9] In the internet age, the public sphere is not a well-ordered agora, but a chaotic marketplace – akin to how Lewis Morris, New York's representative to the Continental Congress, describes his state's legislature in the musical *1776*: "They speak very fast and very loud, and nobody listens to anybody else."[10] When Thersites spoke without authorization, Odysseus could put him in his place. But there are today few costs to speaking out of turn. Shame is less easily produced in a society in which there is less consensus regarding social norms, in which audiences are varied and dispersed, and in which communications are distantiated. Alternative narratives seem to be everywhere, but also nowhere – advanced, yet ignored. Once upon a time, dissenters had trouble finding a forum. A latter-day Thersites has access to unlimited forums, but discovers that acquiring anything beyond a niche audience has become harder. The challenge for Thersites was to speak. The challenge for his successors is to be heard. Perhaps narrative projects – of presidents or anyone else – are today doomed to failure, as countless narratives vie for the public's attention, approbation, and assent. Perhaps no narrative can dominate national debate as the Cold War consensus once did.[11] The next section takes up this challenge.

---

[7] Rodgers 2011.   [8] Prior 2007.
[9] Lincoln 1994, 34–36, 128–130, 138–143.
[10] Stone and Edwards 1976 [1970], 160.
[11] Drawing on Fiske's concept of "multiaxiality" (Fiske 1996), this is the position of Williams and Delli Carpini 2011, esp. 116–121, although their discussion of the post-9/11 period substantially undercuts the claim.

Narrative projects and leadership in the internet age

The internet is still in its toddlerhood. Its penetration is uneven, across
the globe and within nations, but ever deepening. Its effects on human
habits, behaviors, and attitudes vary by socioeconomic class, genera-
tional cohort, and personal preferences – and it is not obvious that these
gaps will close over time.[12] The technology is still evolving, seemingly
always in the direction of more information, more transparency, and
more tightly interconnected systems, toward a world in which we can
never turn off the constant stream nor tune it out. Scholars are just
beginning to come to terms with the "new media environment" for
political behavior, structures, and identity. However, what we do
know about the impact of the internet suggests that we should not be
too quick either to declare dominant narratives of national security a
thing of the past or to consign presidential rhetorical leadership to the
trash.

Amidst the churn of technological change, there is a palpable anxiety
that new media are abetting pre-existing tendencies toward the
breakdown of community and nation.[13] If the nineteenth and much
of the twentieth centuries were, in Europe and North America, marked
by aggregation – the emergence of transnational mega-companies, the
growth of national civil society, the explosion of national government,
the consolidation of nation-states – the last decades have seen at least a
partial reversal – celebrating the virtues of local communities, embracing the creativity of small start-ups, assailing the waste and rigidity of
large bureaucracies, diffusing power, and eroding authority.[14] Many
fear that the internet, like cable television before it, exacerbates
these trends by tempting audiences into ideological and partisan echo
chambers, and that the consequences will be the corrosion of citizens'
sense of commonality and the attenuation of democracy.[15] They can
cite evidence in support of their brief. The wealth of media options has
diminished the audience for hard news: those who care little about
politics can find ever more ways to avoid learning about it.[16] At the
same time, because information is now plentiful and low-cost, news

[12] On these gaps, see DiMaggio *et al.* 2004; Hargittai and Hsieh 2013, esp.
134–137.
[13] For such concerns before the internet age, see Huntington 1981; Schlesinger Jr.
1992.
[14] Naím 2013; Rodgers 2011.   [15] See, among others, Sunstein 2001.
[16] For a review, see Just 2011.

junkies can feed their addiction more richly and cheaply than ever.[17] When it comes to those most passionate about politics, the fear of echo chambers, or "selective exposure," has some purchase. Bloggers overwhelmingly provide links to the sites of like-minded bloggers, and their readers are more ideologically committed and partisan than typical citizens and more likely to gravitate toward online sources whose views they share.[18] There is some evidence that this extends to mass audiences: conservatives turn to more conservative news outlets, liberals do the same.[19]

But, on the whole, overwrought pundits need not wring their hands so vigorously. First, relatively few news consumers visit the political blogs where ideologues congregate. Far more popular are the general news sites, whose presentation tends to be more balanced.[20] In fact, most of the top news websites are old media companies, and the others are news aggregators who link mostly to traditional sources, such as wire services.[21] When blogs – whose emergence was the preeminent symbol of how the internet would change the news industry and which began as private and small-scale enterprises – prove popular, they join commercial media outlets, where they are subject to corporate pressures and where readers are exposed to a range of views. And blogs do not seem to be the agenda-setters: political issues and news overwhelmingly appear first in traditional media before blogs pick them up.[22]

Second, studies comparing Americans' news consumption online and offline have found little evidence of deepening echo chambers. Consumers of online news tend to be fairly omnivorous. A visitor to a left-wing website is more likely than the typical online news reader to have visited foxnews.com, and the same is true of those who visit right-wing websites, that they are more likely to have visited nytimes. com. While audiences' selective news exposure on the internet – the

---

[17] See especially Prior 2007. See, relatedly, Bimber 2003; Hindman 2010. Also Boulianne 2009; Brundidge and Rice 2009.

[18] Bennett and Iyengar 2008; Hargittai *et al.* 2008; Lawrence *et al.* 2010.

[19] Iyengar and Hahn 2009; Stroud 2011.

[20] Gentzkow and Shapiro 2011.

[21] For 2013 data, see http://stateofthemedia.org/2013/digital-as-mobile-grows-ra pidly-the-pressures-on-news-intensify/digital-by-the-numbers/. See also Chadwick 2013.

[22] Leskovec *et al.* 2009, as cited in Neuman *et al.* 2011. See also http://snap. stanford.edu/infopath/papers.html.

medium's "isolation index" – is somewhat higher than for some offline news sources, such as television, it is lower than for national news-papers, and it is much, much lower than the self-segregation in which people routinely engage via civil society, work, home, friends, and family. Equally important, there is no evidence that ideological segre-gation is increasing over time.[23] Other studies have confirmed that, while Americans are seeking out the like-minded online, they are not avoiding those with whom they disagree. In fact, they also seem to be searching for divergent views.[24] Only the most politically attentive and engaged may be entering echo chambers,[25] but the evidence is mixed at best even for that population.

If the internet is not bringing about a political dystopia, it is also not the democratic Eden that some once forecast.[26] Optimists hoped the internet would break down existing barriers to deliberation and promote more active political conversations among the masses of citizens.[27] But online patterns mirror those offline: the internet largely reproduces existing inequalities with regard to political knowledge and participation.[28] Taking part in political discussion online has, if any-thing, only a "slight" positive impact on willingness to engage those whose views strongly differ from one's own.[29] Moreover, the top news sites are becoming increasingly homogeneous, due to the costs of providing news and to marketplace pressures,[30] which is presumably detrimental to deliberation. Finally, if news consumers are exploring divergent views online, they are likely not doing so in a spirit of open-minded deliberation, but to know the enemy.[31]

All of this may be bad news for theorists of deliberative democracy, but it suggests that we have not escaped, and are unlikely to escape, foundational narratives. A common political culture is not about

[23] The preceding draws on the impressive, large-scale study of Gentzkow and Shapiro 2011.
[24] Garrett 2009; Garrett *et al.* 2013. For similar findings, using different popula-tions and methodologies, see Kahne *et al.* 2012.
[25] Farrell 2012, 42; Prior 2013, 123.   [26] See, generally, Hindman 2010.
[27] Recent research, however, suggests that there is a trade-off between people's exposure to diverse views and their engagement in political activity. See Mutz 2006.
[28] Bimber 2003; Brundidge and Rice 2009, 146–149; Schlozman *et al.* 2010. For evidence from outside the United States, see Larsson 2013.
[29] Brundidge and Rice 2009, 149–154.
[30] Boczkowski 2010; Prior 2007, 261–262.   [31] Nahon and Hemsley 2014.

shared attitudes – although the substantive divisions among Americans have long been narrowing, not widening, despite the culture wars and rampant partisanship[32] – but about shared points of reference. Political community rests on agreement not on the substance of policy, but on what it is worth disagreeing about and on the range of legitimate policy stances.[33] Ideological warriors' exposure to what the other side has to say, even if only to discredit it, reinforces those boundaries. Relatively uniform news sources reproduce the limits of the legitimate for their readers. Stylized debates among extreme partisans, in which each side rehearses its own stale lines to pre-empt the other side's, both reflect and bolster the underlying structure of political discourse. In the absence of dominant narratives, there cannot be a politics of legitimacy, charging others with violating sacred boundaries. Ugly though such politics are, contending claims of il/legitimacy cannot resonate unless there are boundaries to cross.

Despite the pressures toward fragmentation, the human need for ontological security, and thus the public demand for narrative order, remain intact. This is the subterranean secondary theme pulsing through Rodgers' wide-ranging history. "Amid the exaggerations, the false nostalgia, the racial and ethnic mythmaking," Rodgers observes of the debates over multiculturalism, "the concern for a common culture was genuine and palpable" and not restricted to one side of the political spectrum. Dueling visions of educational curricula all "drew from the same well of desire for common, national ideals and knowledge."[34] With regard to global affairs, the demand for narrative stabilization will only mount – thanks to the "rise of the rest" and shifting power dynamics, the crumbling of global authority, and broadly the acceleration of space and time. If the shape of global order is uncertain, it follows that mass publics will look to the nation's leaders more, not less, to make sense of the world around them.

The dissatisfaction that so many expressed with Barack Obama's rhetorical leadership bears this out. The summer after Obama's re-election in 2012, Thomas Friedman of the *New York Times* reviewed the challenges that had confronted the United States in the last decade

---

[32] DiMaggio *et al.* 1996; Fiorina *et al.* 2011; Fischer and Mattson 2009; Page and Jacobs 2009.

[33] This builds on, and modifies, Laitin 1988. For a contrary view, see Wildavsky 1987.

[34] Rodgers 2011, 211–212.

and especially the limits of America's power and desire to shape domestic politics elsewhere. He concluded: "Obama knows all of this. He just can't say it. But it does explain why his foreign policy is mostly 'nudging' and whispering."[35] In response, the realist commentator Stephen Walt protested: "Why in heaven's name can't he? What's the big secret that Obama or his administration dare not speak of?" By "fall[ing] back on ... familiar rhetorical bromides," rather than "educating the American people about how global interests are changing and how our policies must adapt to reflect new realities," Obama had failed to rally the public behind his policies toward the Middle East's upheaval, had half-heartedly pursued interventions that ran counter to his realist inclinations, and had contributed to the perception, and reality, of American inconsistency.[36] Walt was not alone in taking Obama to task. Daniel Drezner insisted that Obama's strategy was coherent, but scolded the president for leaving that strategy "poorly articulated" and letting others fill the "vacuum of interpretation."[37] Michael O'Hanlon concluded that "Obama will have to find a more coherent way to explain his foreign policy vision – and more generally, his presidency – to the American people."[38]

It is true that the pragmatic Obama was hesitant to articulate a grand strategy and a narrative of national security – even telling *The New Yorker*'s David Remnick that "'I don't really even need George Kennan right now,' ... just the right strategic partners." Part of the reason may have been the president's inborn caution, what Remnick calls "the archetypal Obama habit of mind and politics, the calm, professorial immersion in complexity"[39] that prevented him from issuing sweeping statements. Part of the reason, his admirers suggest, may have been the fact that global politics is increasingly complex and rapidly changing and that it defies simple narratives. As Fareed Zakaria puts it: "In today's multipolar, multilayered world, there is no central hinge upon which all American foreign policy rests. Policymaking looks more

---

[35] Friedman, "Foreign Policy by Whisper and Nudge," *New York Times*, 24 August 2013.

[36] Walt, "'Obama Just Can't Say It,'" 26 August 2013, walt.foreignpolicy.com/posts/2013/08/26/he_just_cant_say_it.

[37] Drezner 2011.

[38] Michael E. O'Hanlon, "Is Libya Policy Cornerstone of an Obama Doctrine?" *USA Today*, 29 August 2011.

[39] David Remnick, "Going the Distance: On and Off the Road with Barack Obama," *The New Yorker*, 27 January 2014.

varied, and inconsistent, as regions require approaches that don't necessarily apply elsewhere."[40] Yet, the president's reluctance, however justified, failed to satisfy the public need for narrative order.

This is one lesson Obama, whose soaring campaign oratory brought him renown, never really grasped. Consider a flare-up in spring 2014. During a trip to Asia, frustrated with his critics, and in a fit of pique during a press conference with the Philippine president, Obama defended his prudence in deploying military force:

But we can continue to speak out clearly about what we believe. Where we can make a difference using all the tools we've got in the toolkit, well, we should do so. And if there are occasions where targeted, clear actions can be taken that would make a difference, then we should take them . . . [T]hat may not always be sexy. That may not always attract a lot of attention, and it doesn't make for good argument on Sunday morning shows. But it avoids errors. You hit singles, you hit doubles; every once in a while we may be able to hit a home run. But we steadily advance the interests of the American people and our partnership with folks around the world.[41]

The response was, from many quarters, swift and harsh. It was a gift-horse to Republican presidential aspirants, seeming to bolster the very charge of weakness that Obama had sought to counter. The governor of New Jersey, Chris Christie, eager to put his own far worse missteps behind him, seized the opportunity to charge "the lack of American leadership" with creating a "vacuum that [is] being filled . . . by evil." He called for a return to traditional principles: "We need to stand once again loudly for these values, and sometimes that is going to mean standing in some very messy, difficult places and standing strong and hard for those things that we believe in."[42] So much was predictable. But even those normally in the president's corner were quick to distance themselves. The columnist Maureen Dowd ridiculed Obama's modesty: "A singles hitter doesn't scare anybody. It doesn't feel like

[40] Fareed Zakaria, "Stop Searching for an Obama Doctrine," *Washington Post*, 6 July 2011. See also Michael Hirsh, "Obama Has No Doctrine," 29 March 2011, www.theatlantic.com/politics/archive/2011/03/obama-has-no-doctrine/73171/. Although see also, ironically, Zakaria, "Wanted – A New Global Strategy," *Newsweek*, 28 November 2008.

[41] Remarks by President Obama and President Benigno Aquino III of the Philippines in Joint Press Conference, Malacañang Palace, Manila, Philippines, 28 April 2014, available at www.whitehouse.gov/the-press-office/2014/04/28/remarks-president-obama-and-president-benigno-aquino-iii-philippines-joi.

[42] Justin Sink, "Christie Blasts Obama's Foreign Policy," *The Hill*, 19 May 2014.

leadership. It doesn't feel like you're in command of your world. What happened to crushing it and swinging for the fences? Where have you gone, Babe Ruth?"[43] Without citing Obama's press conference, Zakaria observed that Obama "has put forward an agenda that is ambitious and important, but he approaches it cautiously, as if his heart is not in it, seemingly pulled along by events rather than shaping them. Once more, with feeling, Mr. President!"[44] While the *New York Times* defended the administration's foreign policy, it acknowledged that there was something "to [the] criticism that [Obama] is not articulating a strong, overarching blueprint for the exercise of American power." It ruefully observed that Obama has "a sadly pinched view of the powers of his office." In contrast, it wrote, "American presidents who stood as strong global leaders did so by setting high expectations in clear, if sometimes overly simplistic, ways."[45] A few months later, Hillary Clinton signaled that she had gotten the message. Seeking to distinguish herself from Obama, she implicitly criticized her former boss: "Great nations need organizing principles, and 'Don't do stupid stuff' is not an organizing principle." The problem, Clinton declared, was that "we don't even tell our own story very well these days." If Americans were fretting over an absence of leadership and vision coming from the Obama White House, she implied, a Clinton White House would have it in spades – and wouldn't be shy about telling the world.[46]

This incident, little more than a contretemps, is nevertheless revealing of the abiding expectation that presidents will exercise rhetorical leadership, that they are needed to make public sense of things, and that they occupy a singular position, despite the cacophony of today's public square. The fragmentation of authority, which has provoked so much disquiet, is real. But authority is contextual, and the demand for narrative order has always been episodic. The White House may no longer regularly dominate the nation's news, but there are nevertheless times and domains in which Americans, even those not inclined to

---

[43] Maureen Dowd, "Is Barry Whiffing?", *New York Times*, 29 April 2014.

[44] Fareed Zakaria, "Obama Needs to Lead with Feeling," *Washington Post*, 8 May 2014.

[45] "President Obama and the World," *New York Times*, 3 May 2014.

[46] Jeffrey Goldberg, "Hillary Clinton: 'Failure' to Help Syrian Rebels Led to the Rise of ISIS," 10 August 2014, available at www.theatlantic.com/international/archive/2014/08/hillary-clinton-failure-to-help-syrian-rebels-led-to-the-rise-of-isis/375832/.

follow the news, still look to the president.[47] In responding, national leaders face a Goldilocks problem. They must be careful not to raise expectations so high that they cannot possibly meet them. As the former president of Brazil Fernando Henrique Cardoso put it: "The gap between our real power and what people expect from us is the source of the most difficult pressure any head of state has to manage."[48] But they still must lay out an aspirational vision, a sense of where we've been and, as important, where we are headed – a narrative. Modesty born of slump-shouldered realism does not inspire. Barack Obama's problems are thus partly structural and partly of his own making.

Yet, the obstacles to leaders negotiating this Goldilocks problem are only likely to get worse. On the one hand, public demand for a simplifying narrative to cut through the complexity of global politics is as intense as ever. Perhaps more so, since enduring uncertainty has real consequences in a tightly interconnected global economy that offers both opportunities and vulnerabilities. On the other hand, if swiftly moving events continually dislocate efforts to make public sense of them, dominant narratives will be more short-lived, and the public demand for the restoration of order will be not only more intense, but more regular. To alleviate the perpetual anxiety, national leaders will be tempted to point toward the fences, promising more certainty than they can assuredly deliver. Or, like Obama, they may play small ball and leave the crowd booing. Even were the public not being continually distracted by voices shouting on all sides, leaders in the twenty-first century would face a devilish problem.

A world without narrative?

Periodically, Americans debate the vices and virtues of doctrine in foreign policy. Rigidity and ignorance of local nuance, detractors warn. Rational decision-making under conditions of uncertainty and scarcity, defenders shoot back. These have, in effect, been disputations over the vices and virtues of dominant public narratives of national security, over what Ernest May called the "axiomatic" dimension of foreign policy.[49] Not that we can really *choose* whether we share a set

---

[47] See, relatedly, Althaus 2002; Prior 2007, 260.
[48] Quoted in Naím 2013, xii.   [49] May 1962.

of underlying stories about global politics. But these periodic debates are nevertheless useful – first, because they help clarify the stakes and alternatives, and, second, because we can design institutions that impede, or conversely facilitate, the consolidation of dominant narratives and the ease of challenging them.

For two reasons, we might prefer an imagined social world in which no unquestioned common sense reigned. First, dominant narratives can lead to poor policies because of the way in which they structure choice. The course of action that might, to an outsider, seem best might also be incapable of legitimation, and the resulting policy would then be suboptimal or even potentially damaging. Dominant narratives also impede smooth adjustment to changing realities. This is akin to realist charges levied against the pernicious impact of, variously, bureaucracy, human psychology, and domestic politics. How problematic dominant narratives are depends on how often they pervert decision-making and how severely they harm the national interest. Second, dominant narratives undermine liberal government by hampering open debate. They do not directly restrict freedom of speech, throwing dissenters behind bars or banning them from the airwaves. But they have the same effect indirectly, when they dissuade prospective dissenters from coming forward and when they prime audiences to ignore or dismiss arguments. If one values liberal politics on instrumental grounds, because they produce the best outcomes or at least help polities to avoid disaster, this second concern melds with the first. But if one values liberal politics for its own sake, then dominant narratives are inherently troubling, because they curtail the free exchange of ideas and prevent the expression of people's true preferences.

These are legitimate concerns, but they are outweighed by three considerations. First, they misrepresent the alternative. Realist broadsides against bureaucracy, for instance, measure its negative impact by comparing the real world, in which bureaucracy is ubiquitous and necessary, to an imagined world in which states are rational unitary actors.[50] Yet, states without bureaucracy would lack not only the pathologies that bureaucracy can introduce, but also the capabilities that bureaucracy generates. Organizations without bureaucratic standard operating procedures would render government less predictable and more subject to the foibles of individual office-holders.[51] By that

---

[50] This is the strategy in the classic account of Allison and Zelikow 1999 [1971].
[51] Bendor and Hammond 1992.

standard, bureaucracy looks more appealing, despite its flaws. The same is true of the decision-making errors that result from human beings' cognitive limitations. The alternative is not a computer with infinite processing speed and capacity, but a human being who, without mental short-cuts, would fall prey to information overload and paralysis. Similarly, the imagined alternative to narrative domination – limitless, free-wheeling debate – would also entail endemic ontological insecurity. Without stable identity structures, human beings cannot formulate their own interests or assess those of others, and thus they cannot calculate alternatives or engage in rational action. A world without narrative order would be a world without meaning, without political vision, and without sacrifice for the common good.

Second, dominant narratives sustain ex-ante and ex-post mechanisms for constraining leaders. In an imaginary world without dominant narratives, leaders could offer legitimate public justifications for any policy they like. Since everyone would know that where there is a will, there is a rhetorical way, attentive publics would have no reason to demand of their nations' leaders publicly acceptable rationales for their policy stances and actions. Leaders would then be able to mobilize public resources for whatever agenda they desired. Dominant narratives thus underpin the imperative to legitimation and whatever ex-ante rhetorical and policy constraints it imposes. Legitimation is also important to accountability ex post: previously articulated goals provide a common focal point and set of standards according to which attentive audiences can deem policy a failure or success. Without such shared metrics, publics can still punish leaders, but it will be harder to pull together a unified coalition of the sufficiently discontented. While legitimation is most regular in democracies, and is essential to their healthy operation, it is not dependent on a broad public. It has even been a central feature of authoritarian governance: recall, for instance, Soviet leaders' adherence to Communist ideology and their intense debates over its precepts. In fact, because mass publics are often distracted and ignorant, they are not the key to legitimation. What legitimation requires is a shared narrative foundation and a narrower audience, or selectorate, sufficiently attentive to enforce it.

Third, dominant narratives make possible leadership in the service of the common good. One can certainly have policy without a consensus narrative of national security. Often, one must. But one cannot have grand strategy. Grand strategy, I argued earlier, rests on a narrative of national security, on a portrait of the nation's security environment. Due to bureaucratic pulling and hauling, pressure from other branches of government, the limits of human cognition, and the inherent complexity and unpredictability of global politics, many are duly skeptical that states can pursue anything like a coherent and consistent strategy. Given strategy's well-known dangers, some question whether it is worth the candle and advocate pragmatism instead.[52] Yet, pragmatic foreign policy is always in danger of seeming aimless, creating the impression that government is simply lurching from crisis to crisis. A pragmatic foreign policy, therefore, does not provide a sound basis for mobilizing public resources. Leaders who wish to call on domestic resources must project coherence. Strategy may be an illusion,[53] but it is a necessary illusion. And so too, in turn, is a dominant narrative of national security. To integrate their various missions and ventures into a cogent strategy, leaders must advance a compelling narrative.

As long as there are political communities, there will be dominant narratives. It would be foolish to lament their persistence, and there are good reasons to celebrate them. Yet, we need not passively accept the dangers posed by dominant narratives. We must protect outlets for the free expression of alternative storylines; they can then circulate, even if only on the margins, ready to be picked up when circumstances are ripe. We must protect a vibrant press and a culture of investigative journalism. It will not generally operate outside the mainstream, and the discrepant information it turns up will rarely be enough to overturn orthodoxy. But dominant narratives will endure too long if they are not compelled to confront and make sense of evidence, which investigative journalists expose. We must, as much as possible, ensure that alternatives receive a hearing in the halls of power, preferably not purely ritualized in the form of an in-house devil's advocate.[54] But, most of all, we need to be aware that we are ourselves actors, tinkering with scripts that we are rarely conscious of having been handed. Perhaps then we can write a new and better play.

---

[52] Edelstein 2013.   [53] I am taking liberties here with Betts 2000.
[54] This is what Alexander George called "multiple advocacy." See George 1972, 1980.

Whither US national security policy?

Politicians worry a great deal about narratives. With good reason, for unspoken narratives often govern their professional lives and shape the contours of legitimate debate. They can acquire an aura of invincibility even when persuasion is not possible or is not in play. This, I have contended, is as true when it comes to national security as in other arenas. The politics of narrative are central to US national security – to ongoing debates over that policy's broad outlines, to whether security policy succeeds and endures, and to the driving forces that will shape it in the future.

Debates over the present and future of US national security policy not only overlook the politics of narrative, but they are blind to the narrative of their own politics. Proponents of US restraint (or, as critics would have it, retrenchment), selective engagement, and deep or global engagement (or, as critics would have it, liberal hegemony) offer very different concrete recommendations for when the United States should use its military might, how it should configure its armed forces, and what security commitments it should extend. These debates do not turn on facts alone, however, for the contending stances rest on different narratives of national security. These underlying narratives determine what facts are relevant and thus how proponents tally the costs and benefits of their preferred approach and the alternatives. As a result, the proponents of competing strategies talk past each other.

Calls for restraint in US grand strategy rest on an expressly narrow definition of national security, limited to the preservation of sovereignty, safety, territorial integrity, and power position. To this portrait of the actors, they add a depiction of the global scene as constituted by discrete events, rather than as an interconnected web. Hence, they focus only on "direct, imminent, and plausible military threats."[55] Defenders of deep engagement charge restraint's advocates with overestimating the costs of current grand strategy and underestimating its benefits, but their calculations derive from divergent portraits of the actors of global politics, and especially its scene. Their conception of the national interest is broader, including domestic prosperity and the preservation of liberty. They adopt a richer typology of actor motives. Most importantly, whereas restraint's advocates see global events as

---

[55] The most sophisticated account is Posen 2014, quote at 3.

either fairly disconnected or as enmeshed in causal chains so complex and unpredictable that teasing them out is impossible, the case for deep engagement seeks to tease out the complex causal chains linking the global economy and international institutions to US national security.[56] As a result, the threats, costs, and benefits they examine and invoke are quite different, as are their conclusions. Key issues remain unresolved – and they must remain so, because such fundamental claims about the nature of states and the global scene resist disproof. When policy stances reside in different narrative worlds, ascertaining who is right becomes a narrative proposition, not a purely factual one.

The politics of narrative go far in explaining why US national security policy succeeds or falls short. The usual answer focuses on the mismatch between strategy and reality: on strategy's failure to adapt sufficiently quickly to changing realities or, conversely, strategy's too rapid adjustment to momentary, rather than enduring, trends. Yet, valuable as this realist-style analysis is, it overlooks the politics of legitimation. This is, in a way, surprising, since the ideal realist state is one whose leaders are so expert at legitimation that they mobilize the entire polity to the service of national ends.[57] Yet, legitimation is never automatic, which causes realists to gnash their teeth at parochial interests' interference with the pursuit of the national interest. Strategy cannot succeed unless it can endure, and that is a matter of getting right not just the policy, but the narrative that defines the debate and fixes the range of legitimate alternatives.

On the one hand, strategy that cannot be defended to the American people is not sustainable in the long run. It cannot lay claim to substantial national resources. It lacks the resilience to weather setbacks. When leaders, rightly or wrongly, anticipate the difficulty they may face in legitimating policy, they don't even try. This is Barack Obama's foreign policy of whispers and nudges, as Tom Friedman aptly put it. Leaders are then especially tempted to embrace covert action, which is hidden from public view and does not require legitimation. The challenges of legitimation lay behind Richard Nixon's secret bombing of Cambodia, Ronald Reagan's reliance on

[56] For an exemplary defense, see Brooks *et al.* 2012/13.
[57] Thus, Randall Schweller (2006, 117–125) concludes that the ideal realist state is the fascist state.

the Iranian backchannel to provide funding to the Nicaraguan rebels, and George W. Bush's handover, via "extraordinary rendition," of suspected terrorists to sometimes unsavory allies who were less squeamish about torture. Incapable of legitimation, these policies exploded into controversy once they came into the open. The resulting tumult spoke volumes about the dangers of pursuing illegitimate policies by stealth.

On the other hand, even when policy can be legitimated effectively, it cannot prove enduring in the face of persistent and wide-ranging narrative competition. When the narrative space is so unstructured, policy seems disjointed, as if it were merely lurching from crisis to crisis. Although the government's policy seems coherent from one standpoint, it seems incoherent from another, equally legitimate standpoint – from which its critics launch their attacks. This was the knock on US foreign policy in the 1990s: despite Bill Clinton's obsession with authoring a new doctrine for the post-Cold War period, none of his many stabs took hold. Frustrated policymakers are then especially tempted to oversimplify threats, so as to quash wide-ranging debate and dissent. The subtle realist thinking of George Kennan thus gave way to the global Cold War of NSC-68, written to bludgeon the mind of government. And if such simplified narratives successfully clear away the competition and secure a dominant position, as did the Cold War consensus, beware when they confront a complex world. Although Lyndon Johnson did not unthinkingly foray into Vietnam, under the Cold War consensus' spell, that powerful narrative played its part. He swallowed hard and reluctantly ramped up the US commitment to South Vietnam, despite the evident risks and despite his gloomy projections, because that narrative, though no longer dominant, still had many adherents. Johnson feared that the charge that he had lost Vietnam to Communism would resonate so powerfully that his beloved Great Society would never be born.

Finally, if this book's analysis has merit, the politics of narrative will prove central in shaping the future of US national security policy. Ideally, realists say, strategy adjusts appropriately to shifting realities – as experience reveals that our prior beliefs regarding the state of the world were incorrect. Yet, strategy rarely adjusts so smoothly. This is not just because concrete interests resist policy changes that threaten to gore their oxen. It is also because reasonable people can disagree about the meaning of global developments.

Recognizing these narrative divides, politicians are eager for advice on how to overcome them. No surprise, then, that there are plenty of how-to guides in the marketplace, providing advice on how politicians can rhetorically seize their destinies. This book is not one of them. It does not contain an instruction manual for the enterprising political rhetorician. It offers no ready-made solutions to politicians' narrative problems. It is too sensitive to the limits of agency: even charismatic speakers cannot open windows at will through which they might jump. At the same time, one lesson of this book is that these narrative divides are not inherently fixed. Whether a dominant narrative emerges, erodes, or endures depends on what leading political figures say, when they say it, and how they say it. Whether narrative divides persist or whether they are transcended depends on how real events bolster or undercut the authority to speak security and on the rhetorical choices of leading politicians – whether they grasp the rhetorical confines and expectations of the moment, and whether and how they seize the very real possibilities. The fate of narrative rests on leadership, right-sized.

The future of US national security policy will be shaped by numerous unknowns. Will the rest, especially China, continue to rise? Will new nuclear powers emerge? Will extremist Islamist groups gain new adherents and keep the United States and its allies in their sights? Will the US economy collapse under the weight of Washington's dysfunction? Will the dollar remain the world's reserve currency? But equally unknown, and equally important, is how America's leaders will make public sense of the challenges that lie ahead. The nation's security, and the strategy adopted by the US Government, depend on it.

Appendix A Content analysis: method

Content analysis in general, and computerized content analysis in particular, have often been criticized for making heroic assumptions. First, whether one measures the frequency with which particular words or phrases appear in a given text or set of texts (as in the Yoshikoder tool described below), or whether one measures the centrality of words or phrases in a rhetorical network (as in the Crawdad tool described below), one presumes that their meaning is stable over time – or at least sufficiently stable to permit analysis[1] – and can be grasped without sensitivity to context. Second, because all content analysis tools necessarily analyze what has been said or printed, they assume that what is articulated is of greater substantive import than what is not articulated, and they do not help the analyst probe the meaning of silence.[2]

These critiques are fair, but content analysis still has utility, and it can be productively joined to methods like discourse analysis. Concerns about the instability of meaning can be alleviated by analyzing a narrower range of texts – from a single or relatively homogeneous set of speakers, from a relatively short time span, from a single country – and by generating search-terms and coding rules based on context-sensitive reading of select texts and secondary literature. Analysts sensitive to the silences within texts might employ content-analytic methods to explore explicit articulations and then turn to more critical methods to identify and probe crucial silences. Content analysis is a blunt but suggestive method, and it necessarily

[1] Content analysis need not presume, contra Hardy *et al.* 2004, that language exists as some reality independent of processes of social construction. The key rather is the relative stability of those social constructions – whether they are stable enough to be treated, for the purposes of analysis, as social facts.

[2] On content and discourse analysis, see Herrera and Braumoeller 2004, and, for exceptionally insightful discussions, especially the essays by Fierke, Hopf, and Laffey and Weldes. See also Fierke 2007, 81–85.

leaves it to the analyst to interpret the findings. But content analysis can reinforce, or potentially challenge, the qualitative analyst's impressionistic observations about what linguistic patterns are more or less common. It can thereby strengthen discourse analyses, which normally rest on assertions that a particular discourse, or set of elements, is commonplace or even dominant ("the main signifying elements of the discourse ... must be identified"), as are certain "chains of connotations among these signifying elements."[3] Content analysis, whether conducted by computers or human beings, is never sufficient on its own, but it has an important role to play in the study of language – as long as analysts do not rest conclusions exclusively on it, as long as analysts combine it with other methods and approaches, and as long as analysts are aware of its limits. I disagree that discourse and content analysis are "fundamentally incompatible."[4]

This book follows those guidelines. Like discourse analysis, it is centrally concerned with how relations of power structure and produce the systems of meaning embodied in linguistic practices.[5] But to sustain its claims regarding the processes that give rise to dominant narratives, it sees a place both for quantitative (sometimes computerized) content analysis, as well as for critical discourse analysis. It employs content analysis, especially in Chapters 3 and 4, to corroborate empirical claims regarding the substance and style of presidents' speech. But content analysis cannot explicate what presidents' public rhetoric *does* – how it produces particular social relations, what strategies of legitimation and what policy stances it makes possible and which it forecloses, how it silences some alternatives and facilitates others, how it structures political contest. This is where other methods of analyzing structures and processes of communication, notably discourse analysis, enter. The study of social reality is inherently an interpretive exercise, and content analysis can take us only so far.

---

[3] Laffey and Weldes 2004, 29.
[4] Contra Hopf 2004. On the compatibility of content and discourse analysis, see Neuendorf 2004. Given Hopf's conception of discourse analysis, however, I wonder if he might view this book as discourse analytic in its aims, notwithstanding some of its methodological choices.
[5] For this characterization of the goals of discourse analysis, see Laffey and Weldes 2004.

There is still debate about the relative merits of computerized content analytic tools versus human coders.[6] But there is less to this debate than meets the eye, for content analyses of all sorts share the presuppositions discussed above and thus the same constraints. For some tasks, as in Part I, computers are superior due to their ability to process large quantities of text quickly and reliably. For other tasks, however, as in Part II, they are less appropriate – when seeking to analyze linguistic structures beyond the simple word or bundled phrase, when coding requires substantial interpretation, and when coders must display great sensitivity to irony, silences, sarcasm, and other aspects of tone and style to grasp the speaker's or writer's meaning.

Tools

This book employs three kinds of content-analytic tools to analyze presidential rhetoric. The first simply measures word frequency in a given text – the number of times a given word/term and its "children" (that is, plurals, possessives, etc.) appear. There are several such tools available, and I have chosen a flexible, multilingual, and free content analysis platform known as Yoshikoder (version 0.6.3-preview.3), available at www.yoshikoder.org/ (downloaded 2 March 2010). Yoshikoder can list all words, with their frequency and proportion, in a given text. It can also search for bundles of words – what it calls "categories." It also allows for easy comparison of categorical frequencies across a pair of texts. To generate relevant categories, as discussed in more detail in Appendix B, I first reviewed the overall word list for a given text. In Chapters 3 and 4, I use Yoshikoder to support or challenge some of my more impressionistic observations regarding presidents' rhetoric.

Second, scholars of communication have long recognized that these simple tools, while powerful, can be misleading in that they presume that words that appear more frequently in a given text are also more important. CRA – "centering resonance analysis," employed in a computer program called Crawdad[7] – seeks to measure instead a particular noun phrase's centrality in a rhetorical network. More specifically, it focuses on "betweenness centrality" – that is, "the

---

[6] See Morris 1994; West 2001.   [7] Corman and Dooley 2006.

extent to which a particular centering word (represented by a network node) mediates chains of association in the CRA network," as a way of capturing the "rush" of meaning through a network. How this is computed mathematically is complicated, but it revolves around examining how two noun phrases (x and y) are most directly connected and how often a third noun phrase (z) is included in the most direct (shortest) connecting path between x and y. The more z appears in the x–y path, the more central, or influential, z is said to be. Large rhetorical networks have many such combinations of noun phrases, and the more combinations in which z appears to play an intervening role, the more central z is in that network. Crawdad uses this method to generate quantitative influence scores for individual words or phrases. Most revealing though, I have found, are its graphical representations of the relationships between influential noun phrases in a rhetorical network, including the strength of the connections between those influential words. These appear throughout Chapters 3 and 4 to represent shifts in presidents' foreign affairs rhetoric over time. Crawdad can also compute the "resonance" of two texts – that is, how similar two texts are in terms of their influence networks.[8]

Third, one of the key concepts in this book is rhetorical mode, and perhaps most novel for political scientists in general, and scholars of international relations in particular, is the storytelling mode. Because a narrative is a linguistic structure, content analysis, which focuses on individual words and their combinations, would seem poorly suited to measuring storytelling rhetoric. However, the theoretical discussion suggests that certain kinds of words should appear disproportionately in texts in which the storytelling mode is dominant. Roderick Hart has developed a content-analysis tool, called Diction, with a set of thirty-three separate dictionaries that can be flexibly combined. Diction searches texts of any length for the words in designated dictionaries and then normalizes its findings by

[8] For an introduction to CRA, placing it in the context of other text-analytic tools and explaining how Crawdad computes its influence scores, see Corman *et al.* 2002, quote at 177. This method has not been widely used by political scientists, but see Wedeking 2010. For other scholarly work employing CRA, see www.crawdadtech.com/html/03_customers.html (accessed 19 March 2010).

calculating a separate dictionary score for an average 500-word sample.[9] In published work, Hart has used Diction to calculate the "narrative style" in presidential candidates' speeches – an additive measure of Diction's dictionaries for spatial awareness, temporal awareness, motion, and human interest.[10] This has face validity: narratives contain protagonists (human interest), involve action (motion), and take place in particular locations in space and time (spatial and temporal awareness). I have considered other measures of storytelling that were specifically tailored to the politics of national security and to the *content* of such narratives – including Diction's dictionaries for collectives, praise, blame, inspiration, hardship, and cooperation – but in practice these more complex categories proved less discriminating than I would have liked.[11] The data presented in Chapters 3 and 4 thus generally employ Hart's simpler measure of narrative style, which I refer to as the storytelling mode. However, in Appendix C, I report both measures – of storytelling mode and content.

Document selection

These content-analytic tools are applied to presidential speech. While it would have been relatively simple to collect all documents in the *Public Papers of the President* series, that would not have produced useful findings for this study. First, the series includes many documents that lack large-scale public audiences and that were never delivered in public. There is no reason to expect such documents to be influential in shaping dominant narratives. Nor are they necessarily useful in reflecting such narratives, since all actors have more freedom to speak in ways contrary to dominant narratives when key audiences are not in the room, so to speak. Second, the balance of documents across categories is not equal over time. Since the 1970s, the statutory (congressionally imposed) reporting requirements for the executive

---

[9] See www.dictionsoftware.com. The analyses here were generated using a beta version of Diction 6, which employs a different (and more justifiable) method of normalizing the output than earlier versions of the program. Diction 5.0 has been used to good effect by many social scientists: for a select list of publications, see www.dictionsoftware.com/published-studies/.

[10] See Hart and Childers 2005. On the Diction dictionaries, see Hart 2000.

[11] For similar efforts, see research on "charismatic leadership" – notably Bligh *et al.* 2004a, 2004b; Seyranian and Bligh 2008; Shamir *et al.* 1994.

branch have grown dramatically. As presidents have had difficulty in recent decades reaching the mass public, they have also spent more time cultivating narrower audiences. To include all documents in the series would overweight precisely those categories of speech that matter less to this book's central focus: dominant national-security narratives.

Students of presidential speech are of course sensitive to these problems, but they often take the easy route – by analyzing all documents in the *Public Papers* series, which is problematic for the reasons just discussed, or by applying excessively restrictive rules and limiting the analysis to, for instance, only State of the Union addresses or, slightly more broadly, speeches before nationally televised audiences. But State of the Union addresses are a rhetorical genre all on their own, with their own conventions, and nationally televised addresses are rare, and those focused on foreign affairs even more so. Presidents often deliver major addresses on both domestic and foreign affairs that receive substantial media attention, but are not televised.

Because the official *Public Papers of the President* series begins with President Harry S. Truman, I have collected documents from the easy-to-search online database maintained by the American Presidency Project at the University of California at Santa Barbara (www.presidency.ucsb.edu/ws/). This study's set of presidents' major domestic and foreign affairs addresses includes documents that meet the following guidelines.

- Prepared speeches to domestic audiences. This was signaled early in the series as an "Address" or "Special Message"; for later presidents, I relaxed this criterion to include "Remarks," as their documents label few as "Addresses," and rigorously applying this rule would have excluded important speeches with substantial public profiles. Excluded documents from the *Public Papers* include: informal remarks at press conferences; speeches by other administration figures; White House statements; reports submitted to Congress; toasts to visiting dignitaries; addresses in foreign locales; messages "transmitting" and vetoing legislation; remarks on signing legislation or executive orders; election speeches.

- Documents longer than 500 words. This rule was applied to exclude very short messages that are purely formulaic or that would not be expected to have much impact. It does generally include presidents' relatively short national radio addresses, delivered every Saturday since 1982.

- Documents were separated into those primarily involved with domestic affairs and those primarily involved with foreign affairs. Certain addresses – notably the State of the Union address and the Annual Budget Message – normally speak at some length to both policy arenas, and in those cases, I divided the document to include relevant portions in both databases.

A list of all the speeches included in the analysis, along with the text files for replication, appears in the online appendix located on my website: https://sites.google.com/a/umn.edu/rkrebs/home/publications/data.

Appendix B Content analysis: FDR's major foreign affairs addresses, 1935 to 1945

Data on President Franklin Delano Roosevelt's major foreign affairs addresses was generated using two content-analysis platforms, Yoshikoder and Crawdad, whose approaches to text are summarized in Appendix A. Yoshikoder permits the analyst to identify "categories" based on a set of specific single words. The categorical terms below were developed after examination of the full range of words in the data.

- *Category*: Hitler
  Included terms: Hitler, Hitler's, Hitler-dominated, Hitlerism, Hitlerisms, Hitlerite, Hitlerites
- *Category*: Nazi and variants
  Included terms: Nazi, Nazi-dominated, Nazi-fascists, Nazis, Nazism, Goering
- *Category*: German nation
  Included terms: German, German-occupied, Germany, Germany's, Prussia, Junker, Junkers, Kaiser, Kaiserism
- *Category*: Japanese leadership
  Included terms: Tojo, Tojo's, emperor, emperor's, Hirohito, Hirohito's
- *Category*: Japanese nation
  Included terms: Japan, Japan's, Japanese, Japanese-dominated, Japs
- *Category*: ideological war terms
  Included terms: free, freedom, freedom-loving, freedoms, freely, freemen, democracies, democracy, democracy's, democratic, democrats, civilization, civilized, fascism, fascist, fascists, totalitarian, dictator, dictators, dictatorship, dictatorships, slave, slavery, enslave, enslave, enslavement, barbaric, barbarism, barbarous
- *Category*: legal terms
  Included terms: crime, crimes, criminal, gangster, gangsters, gangsterism, law, lawless, lawlessness
- *Category*: civilizational terms
  Included terms: barbaric, barbarism, barbarous, civilization, civilized

Table B.1 *FDR major addresses on foreign affairs, 1935–1945**

	No. of words	Axis	Hitler	Nazi	German nation	Japanese leadership	Japanese nation	Italian leadership	Italian nation	Ideological terms	Legal terms	Civilizational terms
1/1/35 – 8/31/39	9,051	0	0	0	0	0	1	0	0	21	17	11
9/1/39 – 5/16/40	6,993	0	0	0	1	0	0	0	0	10	16	3
5/26/40 – 12/7/41	26,485	21	44	55	51	0	1	0	2	164	13	7
12/8/41 – 12/23/43	42,196	41	48	43	86	9	274	12	66	145	17	16
12/24/43 – 4/45	35,164	4	18	45	133	1	54	3	46	98	16	9

Note:
* Data run through Yoshikoder, 16–17 March 2010 and 17 July 2012.

The analysis in Chapters 3 and 4 relies in part on Yoshikoder's computations of the frequency with which these categories appear in FDR's major public addresses. The complete processed data is reproduced here in Table B.1.

These categories were used also as the bases for the "bundled terms" in the Centering Resonance Analysis performed using Crawdad. All CRA data presented in Chapters 3 and 4 involves some "pre-processing" of the data, in which certain proper nouns are instructed to be treated as equivalent (for example, United States, US, USA). The data was then run a second time with more extensive pre-processing that involved bundling key terms.

- *Bundled term*: hitlernazienemy
  Included: Hitler category + Nazi category
- *Bundled term*: germanenemy
  Included: German nation category
- *Bundled term*: japanenemy
  Included: Japanese nation category
- *Bundled term*: tojoemperorenemy
  Included: Japanese leadership category
- *Bundled term*: ideologicalterms
  Included: ideological war terms category

The CRA results are represented graphically in the figures in Chapters 3 and 4. As the numerical results are harder to interpret, I do not include them in the chapters or here in the appendix, but the data files are posted to the online appendix, located on the author's website: https://sites.google.com/a/umn.edu/rkrebs/home/publications/data.

Appendix C Presidential speech and storytelling: descriptive data

As Appendix A relates, the analysis of the storytelling mode in Chapters 3 and 4 is based on an additive measure of Diction 6.0's dictionaries for spatial awareness, temporal awareness, motion, and human interest. Because national-security narratives entail a specific set of substantive questions about global politics, I also considered measures of story "content," based on Diction's dictionaries for collectives, praise, blame, inspiration, hardship, and cooperation (in addition to those associated with the storytelling mode). Data from the tables that follow, which include measures for presidents' major addresses only, are interspersed throughout Chapters 3 and 4.

Table C.1 *Presidential rhetoric devoted to foreign affairs, 1935–2009*

	Words	Words per year	Foreign vs. domestic*
Roosevelt, 1935–1945	119,308	11,931	0.51
1935–Sept. 1939	9,062	2,266	
Sept. 1939–Dec. 1941	33,334	14,306	
Sept. 1939–Apr. 1945	110,334	19,459	
Dec. 1941–Apr. 1945	77,000	23,123	
Truman, 1945–1953	236,578	29,572	0.55
Eisenhower, 1953–1961	245,687	30,711	0.79
Kennedy, 1961–1963	106,565	35,522	0.56
Johnson, 1963–1969	119,805	23,961	0.32
Nixon, 1969–1974	123,333	22,424	0.23
Ford, 1974–1977	35,118	14,047	0.46
Carter, 1977–1981	83,208	20,802	0.41
Reagan, 1981–1989	248,428	31,054	1.36
Central America	50,540	6,318	
Bush, G. H. W., 1989–1993	48,432	12,108	1.17

Table C.1 (*cont.*)

	Words	Words per year	Foreign vs. domestic*
Clinton, 1993–2001	284,974	35,622	0.39
Bush, G. W., 2001–2009	386,440	48,305	1.02

Note:

* Ratio of the number of words in major presidential speeches devoted to foreign affairs to the number of words in major presidential speeches devoted to domestic affairs.

Table C.2 *Comparisons across presidents – storytelling*

President	Domestic		Foreign		All*	
	Mode	Content	Mode	Content	Mode	Content
Roosevelt	40.94	58.99	64.41	69.30	48.92	62.50
Truman	39.85	63.11	60.61	75.73	47.12	67.53
Eisenhower	37.65	64.58	54.28	75.42	44.97	69.35
Kennedy	42.06	64.00	58.12	72.43	47.84	67.04
Johnson	49.82	70.67	67.22	80.27	53.99	72.97
Nixon	48.07	68.05	67.54	80.42	51.77	70.40
Ford	46.24	67.75	64.91	83.16	52.21	72.68
Carter	41.53	63.41	66.05	82.07	48.64	68.82
Reagan	50.67	65.72	63.07	74.31	57.86	70.70
Bush, G. H. W.	59.56	70.11	64.44	77.52	62.20	74.11
Clinton	71.98	68.33	75.52	77.10	72.97	70.79
Bush, G. W.	63.11	66.53	70.72	78.34	66.92	72.44

Note:

* Weighted, based on the proportion of rhetoric devoted to foreign and domestic affairs.

Table C.3 *President as narrator: storytelling averages, 1935–2009**

	Cold War**		All	
	Mode	Content	Mode	Content
Domestic	46.16	66.38	49.29	65.94
Foreign	62.92	77.93	64.74	77.17
All	51.85	70.40	54.62	69.94

Notes:

* Averages across presidents, not taking into account volubility or length of term.
** Cold War presidents: Truman – G. H. W. Bush.

Table C.4 *Presidents vs. the storytelling average, 1935–2009**

| President | Foreign affairs major speeches | | | | All major speeches | | | |
| | vs. Cold War** | | vs. all | | vs. Cold War** | | vs. all | |
	Absolute	%	Absolute	%	Absolute	%	Absolute	%
Roosevelt	1.50	2.38	-0.33	-0.51	-2.92	-5.64	-5.70	-10.43
Truman	-2.31	-3.67	-4.13	-6.38	-4.73	-9.12	-7.50	-13.74
Eisenhower	-8.64	-13.73	-10.46	-16.16	-6.88	-13.27	-9.65	-17.67
Kennedy	-4.80	-7.62	-6.62	-10.23	-4.00	-7.72	-6.77	-12.40
Johnson	4.30	6.84	2.48	3.83	2.15	4.15	-0.62	-1.14
Nixon	4.62	7.35	2.80	4.32	-0.08	-0.14	-2.85	-5.21
Ford	1.99	3.17	0.17	0.26	0.37	0.71	-2.40	-4.40
Carter	3.14	4.99	1.31	2.03	-3.20	-6.18	-5.98	-10.94
Reagan	0.16	0.25	-1.67	-2.58	6.02	11.61	3.25	5.94
Bush, G. H. W.	1.52	2.42	-0.30	-0.47	10.35	19.96	7.58	13.87
Clinton	12.60	20.03	10.78	16.65	21.13	40.75	18.35	33.60
Bush, G. W.	7.80	12.40	5.98	9.23	15.07	29.07	12.30	22.52

Notes:

* Averages across presidents, not taking into account volubility or length of term.

** Cold War presidents: Truman – G. H. W. Bush.

Table C.5 *FDR and storytelling in foreign affairs*

	Mode	Content
Quarantine Address	51.73	79.90
Jan. 1935–Oct. 1937	27.23	46.65
Oct. 1937–Sept. 1939	43.91	69.18
Jan. 1935–Sept. 1939	41.49	65.57
Sept. 1939–Dec. 1941	62.73	68.44
Dec. 1941–April 1945	67.88	70.16

Table C.6 *Truman and storytelling in foreign affairs*

	Mode	Content
January 1946 – Truman Doctrine	53.45	74.56
Truman Doctrine – Start of Korean War	58.36	76.85
Truman Doctrine – 1953	62.06	76.71
Start of Korean War – 1953	64.80	76.60

Table C.7 *Ronald Reagan – telling the story of Central America*

	Mode	Content
1983–1988	59.43	73.00
1983	66.12	76.17
1984	59.22	75.71
1985	62.43	70.97
1986	58.38	73.02
1987	52.90	69.87
1988	64.04	72.65
1983–1984	62.02	75.89
1985–1986	58.97	72.72
1987–1988	58.50	71.43

Appendix D Coding the Cold War consensus

The data presented in Part II, and in the online appendix, derives from a large-scale coding project of foreign affairs editorials in two major national newspapers, the *New York Times* and the *Chicago Tribune*. The coding procedures and the content analysis results are summarized in Chapter 6. The questionnaire applied by the coders to each editorial is reproduced below.

Date:
Newspaper:
Title (if applicable):

1. **What is the editorial's central concern in international affairs?**
   - superpower/bipolar competition: _____
   - something else: _____
       – if so, what else?
       ____ Western alliance politics/relations
       ____ Soviet/Communist bloc politics/relations
       ____ local/regional instability/conflict
       ____ human rights
       ____ global economy
       ____ energy scarcity/dependence
       ____ global inequality/underdevelopment
       ____ domestic politics of foreign nation (if does not fit into above categories)
       ____ other – specify: _____

       – is the problem(s) listed above explicitly or implicitly linked to competition with the USSR or global Communism? if so, how?
       ____ yes – how: _____
       ____ no

2. Representations of Communist powers/Communism:
   (a) *Leading* Communist powers/global Communism are portrayed as having the following character:
      - expansionist/aggressive: ____
      - both: ____
      - satisfied/peaceful: ____
      - unclear/uncertain: ____
      - not discussed: ____

   (b) The threat (to the United States or its allies) from *leading* Communist powers/global Communism is portrayed as:
      - real: ____
      - exaggerated/inflated: ____
      - not discussed: ____

   (c) Relations between the United States/the West/etc. and the USSR, the People's Republic of China, or global Communism are portrayed as:
      - generally conflictual: ____
      - cooperative and conflictual: ____
      - generally cooperative: ____
      - not discussed: ____

   (d) The Communist world is represented as:
      - monolithic: ____
      - both: ____
      - diverse: ____
      - not discussed: ____

3. Representations of US allies:
   (a) US allies are portrayed as:
      - necessary: ____
      - unnecessary: ____
      - not discussed: ____

   (b) US allies are portrayed as:
      - reliable or unified: ____
      - potentially either: ____
      - unreliable or divided: ____
      - not discussed: ____

4. Global politics and interconnectedness:
   Should the United States be concerned with other states "going Communist" or joining the Soviet bloc?
   - yes: _____
   - no: _____
   - not discussed: _____

5. US role in the world:
   (a) Does the United States have, or should it embrace, special responsibilities/leadership?
      - yes: _____
      - no: _____
      - not discussed: _____

   (b) With regard to its financial or military commitments abroad, the United States should:
      - expand: _____
      - maintain: _____
      - reduce: _____
      - not discussed: _____

   (c) With regard to its diplomatic engagements and commitments abroad, the United States should:
      - expand: _____
      - maintain: _____
      - reduce: _____
      - not discussed: _____

   (d) Foreign aid is portrayed as:
      - valuable: _____
      - not valuable: _____
      - not discussed: _____

   (e) US leadership, and its interventions, in world affairs *in the past* are portrayed as:
      - constructive: _____
      - destructive: _____
      - not discussed: _____

(f) **Future US leadership and US interventions in world affairs are portrayed as:**
  - constructive: _____
  - potentially either: _____
  - destructive: _____
  - not discussed: _____

References

Acheson, Dean. 1969. *Present at the Creation: My Years in the State Department*. New York: W. W. Norton.

Ackerman, Bruce. 2006. *Before the Next Attack: Preserving Civil Liberties in an Age of Terrorism*. New Haven, CT: Yale University Press.

Adamthwaite, Anthony. 1977. *France and the Coming of the Second World War, 1936–1939*. London: Frank Cass.

  1995. *Grandeur and Misery: France's Bid for Power in Europe, 1914–1940*. London: Arnold.

Alexander, Jeffrey C. 2004. Cultural Pragmatics: Social Performance between Ritual and Strategy. *Sociological Theory* 22(4): 527–573.

  2010. *The Performance of Politics: Obama's Victory and the Democratic Struggle for Power*. New York: Oxford University Press.

Alker Jr., Hayward R., James P. Bennett, and Dwain Mefford. 1980. Generalized Precedent Logics for Resolving Insecurity Dilemmas. *International Interactions* 7(2): 165–206.

Allison, Graham T. 1970–1971. Cool It: The Foreign Policy of Young America. *Foreign Policy* 1: 144–160.

Allison, Graham and Philip Zelikow. 1999 [1971]. *Essence of Decision: Explaining the Cuban Missile Crisis*, 2nd edn. New York: Longman.

Alpers, Benjamin L. 2003. *Dictators, Democracy, and American Public Culture: Envisioning the Totalitarian Enemy, 1920s–1950s*. Chapel Hill, NC: University of North Carolina Press.

Althaus, Scott L. 2002. American News Consumption During Times of National Crisis. *PS: Political Science & Politics* 35(3): 517–521.

Angstrom, Jan. 2011. Mapping the Competing Historical Analogies of the War on Terrorism: The Bush Presidency. *International Relations* 25(2): 224–242.

Ansolabehere, Stephen, Rebecca Lessem, and James M. Snyder, Jr. 2006. The Orientation of Newspaper Endorsements in U.S. Elections, 1940–2002. *Quarterly Journal of Political Science* 1(4): 393–404.

Appleby, R. Scott. 2002. History in the Fundamentalist Imagination. *Journal of American History* 89(2): 498–511.

Aristotle. 1991. *The Art of Rhetoric*. Translated by H. C. Lawson-Tancred. London: Penguin.

Arnson, Cynthia and Philip Brenner. 1993. The Limits of Lobbying: Interest Groups, Congress, and Aid to the Contras, in *Public Opinion in U.S. Foreign Policy: The Controvery over Contra Aid*, edited by Richard Sobel. Lanham, MD: Rowman & Littlefield, pp. 191–219.

Arnson, Cynthia J. 1993. *Crossroads: Congress, the President, and Central America, 1976–1993*, 2nd edn. University Park, PA: The Pennsylvania State University Press.

Ashby, LeRoy and Rod Gramer. 1994. *Fighting the Odds: The Life of Senator Frank Church*. Pullman, WA: Washington State University Press.

Aune, James Arnt. 2001. *Selling the Free Market: The Rhetoric of Economic Correctness*. New York: Guilford Press.

    2009. Coping with Modernity: Strategies of 20th-Century Rhetorical Theory, in *The Sage Handbook of Rhetorical Studies*, edited by Andrea A. Lunsford. Los Angeles, CA: Sage, pp. 85–108.

Austin, John L. 1975. *How To Do Things With Words*, 2nd edn. Cambridge, MA: Harvard University Press.

Averch, Harvey. 2002. *The Rhetoric of War: Language, Argument, and Policy During the Vietnam War*. Lanham, MD: University Press of America.

Azar, Edward E. and Chung-in Moon. 1988. Legitimacy, Integration, and Policy Capacity: The "Software" Side of Third World National Security, in *National Security in the Third World: The Management of Internal and External Threats*, edited by Edward E. Azar and Chung-in Moon. College Park, MD: Center for International Development and Conflict Management, University of Maryland, pp. 77–101.

Bacevich, Andrew J. 2005. *The New American Militarism: How Americans are Seduced by War*. New York: Oxford University Press.

    2007. Introduction, in *The Long War: A New History of U.S. National Security Policy Since World War II*, edited by Andrew J. Bacevich. New York: Columbia University Press, pp. vii–xiv.

    2008. *The Limits of Power: The End of American Exceptionalism*. New York: Metropolitan Books.

Balzacq, Thierry. 2005. The Three Faces of Securitization: Political Agency, Audience and Context. *European Journal of International Relations* 11(2): 171–201.

    (ed.). 2011. *Securitization Theory: How Security Problems Emerge and Dissolve*. Abingdon, UK: Routledge.

Banerjee, Sanjoy. 1998. Narratives and Interaction: A Constitutive Theory of Interaction and the Case of the All-India Muslim League. *European Journal of International Relations* 4(2): 178–203.

Banta, Benjamin. 2013. Analyzing Discourse as a Causal Mechanism. *European Journal of International Relations* 19(2): 379–402.

Barkin, J. Samuel. 2010. *Realist Constructivism: Rethinking International Relations Theory.* Cambridge, UK: Cambridge University Press.

Barnet, Richard J. 1990. *The Rockets' Red Glare: When America Goes to War – The Presidents and the People.* New York: Simon & Schuster.

Barnett, Michael N. 1998. *Dialogues in Arab Politics: Negotiations in Regional Order.* New York: Columbia University Press.

1999. Culture, Strategy and Foreign Policy Change: Israel's Road to Oslo. *European Journal of International Relations* 5(1): 5–36.

Barnett, Michael N. and Raymond Duvall. 2005. Power in International Politics. *International Organization* 59(1): 39–76.

Barsamian, David. 2001. The United States is a Leading Terrorist State: An Interview with Noam Chomsky. *Monthly Review* 53(6): 10–19.

Barthes, Roland. 1972. *Mythologies.* Translated by Annette Lavers. New York: Hill and Wang.

1975. An Introduction to the Structural Analysis of Narrative. *New Literary History* 6(2): 237–272.

Barton, Allen H. 1974–1975. Consensus and Conflict among American Leaders. *Public Opinion Quarterly* 38(4): 507–530.

Bates, Robert H., Avner Greif, Margaret Levi *et al.* 1998. *Analytic Narratives.* Princeton, NJ: Princeton University Press.

Bates, Toby Glenn. 2011. *The Reagan Rhetoric: History and Memory in 1980s America.* DeKalb, IL: Northern Illinois University Press.

Bator, Francis M. 2008. No Good Choices: LBJ and the Vietnam/Great Society Connection. *Diplomatic History* 32(3): 309–340.

Baum, Matthew A. and Tim Groeling. 2010a. Reality Asserts Itself: Public Opinion on Iraq and the Elasticity of Reality. *International Organization* 64(3): 443–479.

2010b. *War Stories: The Causes and Consequences of Public Views of War.* Princeton, NJ: Princeton University Press.

Baum, Matthew A. and Samuel Kernell. 1999. Has Cable Ended the Golden Age of Presidential Television? *American Political Science Review* 93(1): 99–114.

Baumgartner, Frank R., Jeffrey M. Berry, Marie Hojnacki *et al.* 2009. *Lobbying and Policy Change: Who Wins, Who Loses, and Why.* Chicago, IL: University of Chicago Press.

Beasley, Vanessa B. 2009. Between Touchstone and Touch Screens: What Counts as Contemporary Political Rhetoric? in *The Sage Handbook of Rhetorical Studies*, edited by Andrea A. Lunsford. Los Angeles, CA: Sage, pp. 587–603.

Beasley, Vanessa B. and Deborah Smith-Howell. 2006. No Ordinary Rhetorical President? FDR's Speechmaking and Leadership, 1933–1945, in *American Rhetoric in the New Deal Era, 1932–1945*, edited by Thomas W. Benson. Lansing, MI: Michigan State University Press, pp. 1–32.

Beinart, Peter. 2006. *The Good Fight: Why Liberals – and Only Liberals – Can Win the War on Terror and Make America Great Again*. New York: HarperCollins.

Bell, Jonathan. 2004. *The Liberal State on Trial: The Cold War and American Politics in the Truman Years*. New York: Columbia University Press.

Bendor, Jonathan and Thomas H. Hammond. 1992. Rethinking Allison's Models. *American Political Science Review* 86(2): 301–322.

Benford, Robert D. and David A. Snow. 2000. Framing Processes and Social Movements: An Overview and Assessment. *Annual Review of Sociology* 26: 611–639.

Bennett, D. Scott and Allan C. Stam III. 1996. The Duration of Interstate Wars, 1816–1985. *American Political Science Review* 90(2): 239–257.

Bennett, W. Lance. 1989. Marginalizing the Majority: Conditioning Public Opinion to Accept Managerial Democracy, in *Manipulating Public Opinion: Essays on Public Opinion as a Dependent Variable*, edited by Michael Margolis and Gary A. Mauser. Pacific Grove, CA: Brooks/Cole, pp. 321–361.

1990. Toward a Theory of Press-State Relations in the United States. *Journal of Communication* 40(2): 103–125.

Bennett, W. Lance and Shanto Iyengar. 2008. A New Era of Minimal Effects? The Changing Foundations of Political Communication. *Journal of Communication* 58(4): 707–731.

Bennett, W. Lance, Regina G. Lawrence, and Steven Livingston. 2007. *When the Press Fails: Political Power and the News Media from Iraq to Katrina*. Chicago, IL: University of Chicago Press.

Benoit, William J. 2000. Beyond Genre Theory: The Genesis of Rhetorical Action. *Communication Monographs* 67(2): 178–192.

Bentley, Michelle and Jack Holland (eds.). 2014. *Obama's Foreign Policy: Ending the War on Terror*. London: Routledge.

Bercovitch, Sacvan. 1978. *The American Jeremiad*. Madison, WI: University of Wisconsin Press.

Berenskoetter, Felix. 2014. Parameters of a National Biography. *European Journal of International Relations* 20(1): 262–288.

Berger, Henry W. 1971. Senator Robert A. Taft Dissents from Military Escalation, in *Cold War Critics: Alternatives to American Foreign Policy in the Truman Years*, edited by Thomas G. Paterson. Chicago, IL: Quadrangle Books, pp. 167–204.

Berger, Thomas U. 1998. *Cultures of Antimilitarism: National Security in Germany and Japan*. Baltimore, MD: The Johns Hopkins University Press.

Berinsky, Adam J. 2009. *In Time of War: Understanding American Public Opinion from World War II to Iraq*. Chicago, IL: University of Chicago Press.

Berinsky, Adam J. and Donald R. Kinder. 2006. Making Sense of Issues through Media Frames: Understanding the Kosovo Crisis. *Journal of Politics* 68(3): 640–656.

Berman, William C. 1988. *William Fulbright and the Vietnam War: The Dissent of a Political Realist*. Kent, OH: Kent State University Press.

   1998. *America's Right Turn: From Nixon to Clinton*, 2nd edn. Baltimore, MD: The Johns Hopkins University Press.

Bernstein, Barton J. 1971. Election of 1952, in *History of American Presidential Elections, 1789–1968*, vol. 4, edited by Arthur M. Schlesinger, Jr. New York: Chelsea House, pp. 385–436.

Beschloss, Michael R. 1991. *The Crisis Years: Kennedy and Khrushchev, 1960–1963*. New York: HarperCollins.

   2002. *The Conquerors: Roosevelt, Truman and the Destruction of Hitler's Germany, 1941–1945*. New York: Simon & Schuster.

Betts, Richard K. 2000. Is Strategy an Illusion? *International Security* 25(2): 5–50.

Beukel, Erik. 1989. *American Perceptions of the Soviet Union as a Nuclear Adversary*. London: Pinter.

Beyerchen, Alan. 1992. Clausewitz, Nonlinearity and the Unpredictability of War. *International Security* 17(3): 59–90.

Bially Mattern, Janice. 2005. *Ordering International Politics: Identity, Crisis, and Representational Force*. New York: Routledge.

   2009. The Concept of Power and the (Un)Discipline of International Relations, in *The Oxford Handbook of International Relations*, edited by Christian Reus-Smit and Duncan Snidal. Oxford, UK: Oxford University Press, pp. 691–698.

Bilmes, Linda J. 2013. The Financial Legacy of Iraq and Afghanistan: How Wartime Spending Decisions Will Constrain Future National Security Budgets. Unpublished manuscript, Harvard University, Kennedy School of Government, Faculty Research Working Paper Series RWP13-006.

Bimber, Bruce. 2003. *Information and American Democracy: Technology in the Evolution of Political Power*. Cambridge, UK: Cambridge University Press.

Birdwell, Michael E. 1999. *Celluloid Soldiers: The Warner Bros. Campaign against Nazism*. New York: New York University Press.

Blachman, Morris J. and Kenneth E. Sharpe. 1987. Central American Traps: Challenging the Reagan Agenda. *World Policy Journal* 5(1): 1–28.

Black, Edwin. 1992. *Rhetorical Questions: Studies of Public Discourse.* Chicago, IL: University of Chicago Press.

1994. Gettysburg and Silence. *Quarterly Journal of Speech* 80(1): 21–36.

Bleiker, Roland (ed.). 2001. Images and Narratives in World Politics. *Millennium: Journal of International Studies* (special issue) 30(3): 509–894.

Bligh, Michelle C., Jeffrey C. Kohles, and James R. Meindl. 2004a. Charisma under Crisis: Presidential Leadership, Rhetoric, and Media Responses Before and After the September 11th Terrorist Attacks. *Leadership Quarterly* 15(2): 211–239.

2004b. Charting the Language of Leadership: A Methodological Investigation of President Bush and the Crisis of 9/11. *Journal of Applied Psychology* 89(3): 562–574.

Blum, John Morton. 1967. *From the Morgenthau Diaries: Years of War, 1941–1945.* Boston, MA: Houghton Mifflin.

1976. *V was for Victory: Politics and American Culture During World War II.* New York: Harcourt Brace Jovanovich.

Boczkowski, Pablo J. 2010. *News at Work: Imitation in an Age of Information Abundance.* Chicago, IL: University of Chicago Press.

Boje, David M. 1991. The Storytelling Organization: A Study of Story Performance in an Office Supply Firm. *Administrative Science Quarterly* 36(1): 106–126.

Borg, Dorothy. 1957. Notes on Roosevelt's "Quarantine" Speech. *Political Science Quarterly* 72(3): 405–433.

Bostdorff, Denise M. 2003. George W. Bush's Post-September 11 Rhetoric of Covenant Renewal: Upholding the Faith of the Greatest Generation. *Quarterly Journal of Speech* 89(4): 293–319.

2008. *Proclaiming the Truman Doctrine: The Cold War Call to Arms.* College Station, TX: Texas A&M University Press.

Boulianne, Shelley. 2009. Does Internet Use Affect Engagement? A Meta-Analysis of Research. *Political Communication* 26(2): 193–211.

Brace, Paul and Barbara Hinckley. 1992. *Follow the Leader.* New York: Basic Books.

Brands, H. W. 1999. The Idea of the National Interest. *Diplomatic History* 23(2): 239–261.

Braumoeller, Bear F. 2010. The Myth of American Isolationism. *Foreign Policy Analysis* 6(4): 349–371.

Brenner, Philip and William M. LeoGrande. 1991. Congress and Nicaragua: The Limits of Alternative Policy Making, in *Divided Democracy: Cooperation and Conflict Between the President and Congress,* edited by James A. Thurber. Washington, DC: CQ Press, pp. 219–253.

Brewer, Susan A. 2009. *Why America Fights: Patriotism and War Propaganda from the Philippines to Iraq*. Oxford, UK: Oxford University Press.

Brooks, Stephen G., G. John Ikenberry, and William C. Wohlforth. 2012/13. Don't Come Home, America: The Case Against Retrenchment. *International Security* 37(3): 7–51.

Bruckner, D. J. R. 1972. 'High Noon' in Chicago. *Columbia Journalism Review* 10(5): 23–33.

Brundidge, Jennifer and Ronald E. Rice. 2009. Political Engagement Online: Do the Information Rich Get Richer and the Like-Minded More Similar? in *Routledge Handbook of Internet Politics*, edited by Andrew Chadwick and Philip N. Howard. London: Routledge, pp. 144–156.

Bruner, Jerome. 1986. *Actual Minds, Possible Worlds*. Cambridge, MA: Harvard University Press.

1990. *Acts of Meaning*. Cambridge, MA: Harvard University Press.

2002. *Making Stories: Law, Literature, Life*. New York: Farrar, Straus and Giroux.

Bruner, Jerome S. 1944. *Mandate from the People*. New York: Duell, Sloan, and Pearce.

Buckaloo, Dereck N. 2008. Carter's Nicaragua and Other Democratic Quagmires, in *Rightward Bound: Making America Conservative in the 1970s*, edited by Bruce J. Schulman and Julian E. Zelizer. Cambridge, MA: Harvard University Press, pp. 246–264.

Buhite, Russell D. and David W. Levy (eds.). 2010. *FDR's Fireside Chats*. Norman, OK: University of Oklahoma Press.

Bukovansky, Mlada. 2002. *Legitimacy and Power Politics: The American and French Revolutions in International Political Culture*. Princeton, NJ: Princeton University Press.

Burgos, Russell A. 2008. Origins of Regime Change: "Ideapolitik" on the Long Road to Baghdad, 1993–2000. *Security Studies* 17(2): 221–256.

Burke, Kenneth. 1969 [1945]. *A Grammar of Motives*. Berkeley, CA: University of California Press.

1969 [1950]. *A Rhetoric of Motives*. Berkeley, CA: University of California Press.

Burke, Peter J. 1991. Identity Processes and Social Stress. *American Sociological Review* 56(6): 836–849.

Burns, E. Bradford. 1987. *At War in Nicaragua: The Reagan Doctrine and the Politics of Nostalgia*. New York: Harper & Row.

Burns, James MacGregor. 1956. *Roosevelt: The Lion and the Fox*. New York: Harcourt, Brace.

Busby, Joshua and Jonathan Monten. 2008. Without Heirs? Assessing the Decline of Liberal Internationalism in U.S. Foreign Policy. *Perspectives on Politics* 6(3): 451–472.

Bush, George W. 2002. *The National Security Strategy of the United States of America*. Washington, DC: The White House.

  2006. *National Strategy for Combating Terrorism*. Washington, DC: The White House.

Buzan, Barry, Ole Wæver, and Jaap de Wilde. 1998. *Security: A New Framework for Analysis*. Boulder, CO: Lynne Rienner.

Callahan, William A. 2006. War, Shame, and Time: Pastoral Governance and National Identity in England and America. *International Studies Quarterly* 50(2): 395–419.

Campbell, David. 1998. *Writing Security: United States Foreign Policy and the Politics of Identity*, revised edn. Minneapolis, MN: University of Minnesota Press.

Campbell, Karlyn Kohrs and Kathleen Hall Jamieson. 1990. *Deeds Done in Words: Presidential Rhetoric and the Genres of Governance*. Chicago, IL: University of Chicago Press.

  2008. *Presidents Creating the Presidency: Deeds Done in Words*. Chicago, IL: University of Chicago Press.

Canes-Wrone, Brandice. 2005. *Who Leads Whom? Presidents, Policy, and the Public*. Chicago, IL: University of Chicago Press.

Canes-Wrone, Brandice, William G. Howell, and David E. Lewis. 2008. Toward a Broader Understanding of Presidential Power: A Re-evaluation of the Two Presidencies Thesis. *Journal of Politics* 70(1): 1–16.

Cantril, Hadley (ed.). 1951. *Public Opinion, 1935–1946*. Princeton, NJ: Princeton University Press.

Capoccia, Giovanni and R. Daniel Kelemen. 2007. The Study of Critical Junctures: Theory, Narrative, and Counterfactuals in Historical Institutionalism. *World Politics* 59(3): 341–369.

Caridi, Ronald J. 1968. *The Korean War and American Politics: The Republican Party as a Case Study*. Philadelphia, PA: University of Pennsylvania Press.

Carothers, Thomas. 1991. *In the Name of Democracy: U.S. Policy toward Latin America in the Reagan Years*. Berkeley, CA: University of California Press.

Carpenter, Ronald H. 1978. The Historical Jeremiad as Rhetorical Genre, in *Form and Genre: Shaping Rhetorical Action*, edited by Karlyn Kohrs Campbell and Kathleen Hall Jamieson. Falls Church, VA: Speech Communication Association, pp. 103–118.

  1987. Ronald Reagan, in *American Orators of the Twentieth Century: Critical Studies and Sources*, edited by Bernard K. Duffy and Halford R. Ryan. New York: Greenwood Press, pp. 331–336.

Carpenter, Ted Galen. 1986. United States' NATO Policy at the Crossroads: The "Great Debate" of 1950–1951. *International History Review* 8(3): 389–415.

2008. *Smart Power: Toward a Prudent Foreign Policy for America.* Washington, DC: Cato Institute.

Carroll, Lewis. 1954 [1865]. *Alice's Adventures in Wonderland and Through the Looking-Glass.* London: J. M. Dent & Sons.

Casey, Steven. 2001. *Cautious Crusade: Franklin D. Roosevelt, American Public Opinion, and the War Against Nazi Germany.* New York: Oxford University Press.

2008. *Selling the Korean War: Propaganda, Politics, and Public Opinion in the United States, 1950–1953.* Oxford, UK: Oxford University Press.

2010. Casualty Reporting and Domestic Support for War: The US Experience during the Korean War. *Journal of Strategic Studies* 33(2): 291–316.

Caute, David. 1978. *The Great Fear: The Anti-Communist Purge under Truman and Eisenhower.* New York: Simon & Schuster.

Chace, James. 1978. Is a Foreign Policy Consensus Possible? *Foreign Affairs* 57(1): 1–16.

Chadwick, Andrew. 2013. *The Hybrid Media System: Politics and Power.* Oxford, UK: Oxford University Press.

Chadwin, Mark Lincoln. 1968. *The Hawks of World War II.* Chapel Hill, NC: University of North Carolina Press.

Chambers II, John Whiteclay (ed.). 1999. *The Oxford Companion to American Military History.* Oxford, UK: Oxford University Press.

Chang, Gordon C. and Hugh B. Mehan. 2006. Discourse in a Religious Mode: The Bush Administration's Discourse in the War on Terrorism and its Challenges. *Pragmatics* 16(1): 1–23.

Chang, Gordon H. 1990. *Friends and Enemies: The United States, China, and the Soviet Union.* Palo Alto, CA: Stanford University Press.

Charland, Maurice. 1987. Constitutive Rhetoric: The Case of the Peuple Québécois. *Quarterly Journal of Speech* 73(2): 133–150.

Chatman, Seymour. 1975. Towards a Theory of Narrative. *New Literary History* 6(2): 295–318.

Chaudoin, Stephen, Helen V. Milner, and Dustin H. Tingley. 2010. The Center Still Holds: Liberal Internationalism Survives. *International Security* 35(1): 75–94.

Chilton, Paul. 2004. *Analysing Political Discourse: Theory and Practice.* London: Routledge.

Chollet, Derek and James Goldgeier. 2008. *America between the Wars: From 11/9 to 9/11.* New York: PublicAffairs.

Clancy, Susan. 2005. *Abducted: How People Come to Believe They Were Kidnapped by Aliens.* Cambridge, MA: Harvard University Press.

Clifford, Clark M. 1969. A Viet Nam Reappraisal: The Personal History of One Man's View and How It Evolved. *Foreign Affairs* 47(4): 601–622.

Clifford, J. Garry. 1989. Both Ends of the Telescope: New Perspectives on FDR and American Entry into World War II. *Diplomatic History* 13(2): 213–230.

Clymer, Adam. 2008. *Drawing the Line at the Big Ditch: The Panama Canal Treaties and the Rise of the Right.* Lawrence, KS: University Press of Kansas.

Coe, Kevin, David Domke, Erica S. Graham *et al.* 2004. No Shades of Gray: The Binary Discourse of George W. Bush and an Echoing Press. *Journal of Communication* 54(2): 234–252.

Cohen, Jeffrey E. 2008. *The Presidency in the Era of 24-Hour News.* Princeton, NJ: Princeton University Press.

2010. *Going Local: Presidential Leadership in the Post-Broadcast Age.* Cambridge, UK: Cambridge University Press.

Cohen, Jeffrey E. and John A. Hamman. 2005. Presidential Ideology and the Public Mood: 1956–1994, in *In the Public Domain: Presidents and the Challenges of Public Leadership*, edited by Lori Cox Han and Diane J. Heith. Albany, NY: State University of New York Press, pp. 141–162.

Cole, Juan. 2006. Think Again: 9/11. *Foreign Policy* 156: 26–32.

Cole, Wayne S. 1983. *Roosevelt & the Isolationists, 1932–1945.* Lincoln, NE: University of Nebraska Press.

Condit, Celeste M. 1985. The Functions of Epideictic: The Boston Massacre Orations as Exemplar. *Communication Quarterly* 33(4): 284–299.

Corman, Steven R. and Kevin J. Dooley. 2006. *Crawdad Text Analysis System 2.0.* Chandler, AZ: Crawdad Technologies, LLC.

Corman, Steven R., Timothy Kuhn, Robert D. McPhee *et al.* 2002. Studying Complex Discursive Systems: Centering Resonance Analysis of Communication. *Human Communication Research* 28(2): 157–206.

Cornog, Evan. 2004. *The Power and the Story: How the Crafted Presidential Narrative Has Determined Political Success from George Washington to George W. Bush.* New York: Penguin Press.

Costigliola, Frank. 2012. *Roosevelt's Lost Alliances: How Personal Politics Helped Start the Cold War.* Princeton, NJ: Princeton University Press.

Cousins, Norman. 1972. *The Improbable Triumvirate: John F. Kennedy, Pope John, Nikita Khrushchev.* New York: W. W. Norton.

Crable, Richard E. and Steven L. Vibbert. 1983. Argumentative Stance and Political Faith Healing: "The Dream Will Come True." *Quarterly Journal of Speech* 69(3): 290–301.

Craig, Campbell and Fredrik Logevall. 2009. *America's Cold War: The Politics of Insecurity*. Cambridge, MA: Harvard University Press.

Crawford, Neta C. 2002. *Argument and Change in World Politics: Ethics, Decolonization, and Humanitarian Intervention*. Cambridge University Press.

2009. Homo Politicus and Argument (Nearly) All the Way Down. *Perspectives on Politics* 7(1): 103–124.

Crile, George. 2003. *Charlie Wilson's War: The Extraordinary Story of the Largest Covert Operation in History*. New York: Atlantic Monthly Press.

Critchlow, Donald T. 2007. *The Conservative Ascendancy: How the GOP Right Made Political History*. Cambridge, MA: Harvard University Press.

Croft, Stuart. 2006. *Culture, Crisis, and America's War on Terror*. Cambridge University Press.

Cronin, Patrick and Benjamin O. Fordham. 1999. Timeless Principles or Today's Fashion? Testing the Stability of the Linkage Between Ideology and Foreign Policy in the Senate. *Journal of Politics* 61(4): 967–998.

Cutrone, Ellen A. and Benjamin O. Fordham. 2010. Commerce and Imagination: The Sources of Concern about International Human Rights in the US Congress. *International Studies Quarterly* 54(3): 633–655.

Dallek, Robert. 1979. *Franklin D. Roosevelt and American Foreign Policy, 1932–1945*. New York: Oxford University Press.

Darilek, Richard E. 1976. *A Loyal Opposition in Time of War: The Republican Party and the Politics of Foreign Policy from Pearl Harbor to Yalta*. Westport, CT: Greenwood Press.

Depoe, Stephen P. 1988. Arthur Schlesinger, Jr.'s "Middle Way Out of Vietnam": The Limits of "Technocratic Realism" as the Basis for Foreign Policy Dissent. *Western Journal of Speech Communication* 52(2): 147–166.

Der Derian, James and Michael J. Shapiro (eds.). 1989. *International/Intertextual Relations: Postmodern Readings of World Politics*. Lexington, KY: Lexington Books.

Derrida, Jacques. 1981. The Law of Genre, in *On Narrative*, edited by W. J. T. Mitchell. Chicago, IL: University of Chicago Press, pp. 51–77.

Devetak, Richard. 2009. After the Event: Don DeLillo's *White Noise* and September 11 Narratives. *Review of International Studies* 35(4): 795–815.

Diamond, Edwin. 1993. *Behind the Times: Inside the New New York Times*. New York: Villard Books.

Dietz, Terry. 1986. *Republicans and Vietnam, 1961–1968*. Westport, CT: Greenwood Press.

DiMaggio, Paul, John Evans, and Bethany Bryson. 1996. Have Americans' Social Attitudes Become More Polarized? *American Journal of Sociology* 102(3): 690–755.

DiMaggio, Paul, Eszter Hargittai, Coral Celeste, and Steven Shafer 2004. Digital Inequality: From Unequal Access to Differentiated Use, in *Social Inequality*, edited by Kathryn Neckerman. New York: Russell Sage, pp. 355–400.

Dirks, Nicholas B., Geoff Eley, and Sherry B. Ortner (eds.). 1994. *Culture/Power/History: A Reader in Contemporary Social Theory*. Princeton, NJ: Princeton University Press.

Divine, Robert A. 1965. *The Reluctant Belligerent: American Entry into World War II*. New York: John Wiley & Sons.

    1974. *Foreign Policy and U.S. Presidential Elections: 1952–1960*. New York: New Viewpoints.

Dobbin, Frank. 1994. *Forging Industrial Policy: The United States, Britain, and France in the Railway Age*. Cambridge, UK: Cambridge University Press.

Dobbs, Michael. 2008. *One Minute to Midnight: Kennedy, Khrushchev, and Castro on the Brink of Nuclear War*. New York: Alfred A. Knopf.

Dobson, William J. 2006. The Day Nothing Much Changed. *Foreign Policy* 156: 22–25.

Doenecke, Justus D. 1979. *Not to the Swift: The Old Isolationists in the Cold War Era*. Lewisburg, PA: Bucknell University Press.

    2000. *Storm on the Horizon: The Challenge to American Intervention, 1939–1941*. Lanham, MD: Rowman & Littlefield.

Doherty, Thomas. 1993. *Projections of War: Hollywood, American Culture, and World War II*. New York: Columbia University Press.

Domke, David. 2004. *God Willing? Political Fundamentalism in the White House, the "War on Terror," and the Echoing Press*. London: Pluto Press.

Donovan, John C. 1951. Congressional Isolationists and the Roosevelt Foreign Policy. *World Politics* 3(3): 299–316.

Donovan, Robert J. 1982. *Tumultuous Years: The Presidency of Harry S. Truman, 1950–1953*. New York: W. W. Norton.

Dorn, Walter L. 1957. The Debate over American Occupation Policy in Germany in 1944–1945. *Political Science Quarterly* 72(4): 481–501.

Doty, Roxanne Lynn. 1996. *Imperial Encounters: The Politics of Representation in North-South Relations*. Minneapolis, MN: University of Minnesota Press.

Dower, John. 1986. *War without Mercy: Race and Power in the Pacific War*. New York: Pantheon.

Doyle, Michael W. 1997. *Ways of War and Peace: Realism, Liberalism, Socialism*. New York: W. W. Norton.

Drezner, Daniel W. 2011. Does Obama Have a Grand Strategy? Why We Need Doctrines in Uncertain Times. *Foreign Affairs* 90(4): 57–68.

Dueck, Colin. 2006. *Reluctant Crusaders: Power, Culture, and Change in American Grand Strategy*. Princeton, NJ: Princeton University Press.

2010. *Hard Line: The Republican Party and U.S. Foreign Policy Since World War II*. Princeton, NJ: Princeton University Press.

Edelman, Murray. 1971. *Politics as Symbolic Action: Mass Arousal and Quiescence*. Chicago, IL: Markham.

1988. *Constructing the Political Spectacle*. Chicago, IL: University of Chicago Press.

Edelstein, David M. 2008. *Occupational Hazards: Success and Failure in Military Occupations*. Ithaca, NY: Cornell University Press.

2012. Withdrawal Symptoms: The Politics of Exit Strategies. Unpublished manuscript, Georgetown University, Washington, DC.

2013. Why Grand Strategy Isn't So Grand: The Case for Strategic Pragmatism. Unpublished manuscript, Georgetown University, Washington, DC.

Edkins, Jenny. 1999. *Poststructuralism and International Relations: Bringing the Political Back In*. Boulder, CO: Lynne Rienner.

2003. *Trauma and the Memory of Politics*. Cambridge University Press.

Edwards III, George C. 2003. *On Deaf Ears: The Limits of the Bully Pulpit*. New Haven, CT: Yale University Press.

2009. *The Strategic President: Persuasion and Opportunity in Presidential Leadership*. Princeton, NJ: Princeton University Press.

Ehrman, John. 1995. *The Rise of Neoconservatism: Intellectuals and Foreign Affairs, 1945–1994*. New Haven, CT: Yale University Press.

Eisenhower, Dwight D. 1967. *At Ease: Stories I Tell to Friends*. Garden City, NY: Doubleday.

Elshtain, Jean Bethke. 1987. *Women and War*. Chicago, IL: University of Chicago Press.

Elster, Jon. 1995. Strategic Uses of Argument, in *Barriers to Conflict Resolution*, edited by Kenneth Arrow, Robert H. Mnookin, and Amos Tversky. New York: W. W. Norton, pp. 236–257.

Entman, Robert M. 2004. *Projections of Power: Framing News, Public Opinion, and U.S. Foreign Policy*. Chicago, IL: University of Chicago Press.

Erickson, Paul D. 1985. *Reagan Speaks: The Making of an American Myth*. New York: New York University Press.

Eshbaugh-Soha, Matthew and Jeffrey S. Peake. 2011. *Breaking through the Noise: Presidential Leadership, Public Opinion, and the News Media*. Palo Alto, CA: Stanford University Press.

Esposito, John L. and Dalia Mogahed. 2010. *Measuring the State of Muslim–West Relations: Assessing the "New Beginning."* Washington, DC: Gallup, Inc.

Etzold, Thomas and John Lewis Gaddis (eds.). 1978. *Containment: Documents on American Policy and Strategy.* New York: Columbia University Press.

Fairclough, Norman. 2003. *Analysing Discourse: Textual Analysis for Social Research.* London: Routledge.

Fallows, James. 2006. Declaring Victory. *Atlantic Monthly* 298(2): 60–73.

Farrell, Henry. 2012. The Consequences of the Internet for Politics. *Annual Review of Political Science* 15: 35–52.

Fearon, James D. 1991. Counterfactuals and Hypothesis Testing in Political Science. *World Politics* 43(2): 169–195.

Ferguson, Thomas. 1986. The Right Consensus? Holsti and Rosenau's New Foreign Policy Belief Surveys. *International Studies Quarterly* 30(4): 411–423.

Ferrell, Robert H. 1981. *The Eisenhower Diaries.* New York: W. W. Norton.

Fiaz, Nazya. 2014. Constructivism Meets Critical Realism: Explaining Pakistan's State Practice in the Aftermath of 9/11. *European Journal of International Relations* 20(2): 491–515.

Fierke, K. M. 1998. *Changing Games, Changing Strategies: Critical Investigations in Security.* Manchester, UK: Manchester University Press.
    2007. *Critical Approaches to International Security.* Cambridge, UK: Polity Press.

Finnemore, Martha. 1996. *National Interests in International Society.* Ithaca, NY: Cornell University Press.
    2003. *The Purpose of Intervention: Changing Beliefs about the Use of Force.* Ithaca, NY: Cornell University Press.

Finnemore, Martha and Kathryn Sikkink. 1998. International Norm Dynamics and Political Change. *International Organization* 52(4): 887–917.

Fiorina, Morris P., Samuel J. Abrams, and Jeremy C. Pope. 2011. *Culture Wars? The Myth of Polarized America*, 3rd edn. New York: Pearson Longman.

Fischer, Claude S. and Greggor Mattson. 2009. Is America Fragmenting? *Annual Review of Sociology* 35: 435–455.

Fisher, Walter R. 1984. Narration as a Human Communication Paradigm: The Case of Public Moral Argument. *Communication Monographs* 51(1): 1–22.

Fiske, John. 1996. *Media Matters: Race and Gender in U.S. Politics.* Minneapolis, MN: University of Minnesota Press.

Foot, Rosemary. 1985. *The Wrong War: American Policy and the Dimensions of the Korean Conflict, 1950–1953*. Ithaca, NY: Cornell University Press.

Fordham, Benjamin O. 1998. *Building the Cold War Consensus: The Political Economy of U.S. National Security, 1949–51*. Ann Arbor, MI: University of Michigan Press.

　2002. Domestic Politics, International Pressure, and the Allocation of American Cold War Military Spending. *Journal of Politics* 64(1): 63–88.

　2007. The Evolution of Republican and Democratic Positions on Cold War Military Spending: A Historical Puzzle. *Social Science History* 31(4): 603–636.

　2008a. Economic Interests and Congressional Voting on Security Issues. *Journal of Conflict Resolution* 52(5): 623–640.

　2008b. Economic Interests and Public Support for American Global Activism. *International Organization* 62(1): 163–182.

Foucault, Michel. 1984. The Order of Discourse, in *Language and Politics*, edited by Michael J. Shapiro. New York: New York University Press, pp. 108–138.

Franzosi, Robert. 1998. Narrative Analysis – or Why (and How) Sociologists Should be Interested in Narrative. *Annual Review of Sociology* 24: 517–554.

Freedman, Lawrence. 2000. *Kennedy's Wars: Berlin, Cuba, Laos, and Vietnam*. New York: Oxford University Press.

　2004. War in Iraq: Selling the Threat. *Survival* 46(2): 7–50.

Friedberg, Aaron L. 2000. *In the Shadow of the Garrison State: America's Anti-Statism and Its Cold War Grand Strategy*. Princeton, NJ: Princeton University Press.

Frieden, Jeffry A. 1999. Actors and Preferences in International Relations, in *Strategic Choice and International Relations*, edited by David A. Lake and Robert Powell. Princeton, NJ: Princeton University Press, pp. 39–76.

Fry, Joseph A. 2006. *Debating Vietnam: Fulbright, Stennis, and their Senate Hearings*. Lanham, MD: Rowman & Littlefield.

Frye, Northrop. 1957. *Anatomy of Criticism: Four Essays*. Princeton, NJ: Princeton University Press.

Fulbright, J. William. 1964. *Old Myths and New Realities, and Other Commentaries*. New York: Random House.

　1966. *The Arrogance of Power*. New York: Random House.

　1972. *The Crippled Giant: American Foreign Policy and its Domestic Consequences*. New York: Random House.

Fuller, Robert C. 1995. *Naming the Antichrist: The History of an American Obsession*. Oxford, UK: Oxford University Press.

Fursenko, Aleksandr and Timothy Naftali. 1997. *"One Hell of a Gamble": Khrushchev, Castro, and Kennedy, 1958–1964*. New York: W. W. Norton.

Gabriel, Yiannis. 2000. *Storytelling in Organizations: Facts, Fictions, and Fantasies.* Oxford, UK: Oxford University Press.

Gacek, Christopher M. 1994. *The Logic of Force: The Dilemma of Limited War in American Foreign Policy.* New York: Columbia University Press.

Gaddis, John Lewis. 1982. *Strategies of Containment: A Critical Appraisal of Postwar American National Security Policy.* New York: Oxford University Press.

1987. *The Long Peace: Inquiries into the History of the Cold War.* New York: Oxford University Press.

1990. *Russia, the Soviet Union, and the United States: An Interpretive History,* 2nd edn. New York: McGraw-Hill.

2004. *Surprise, Security, and the American Experience.* Cambridge, MA: Harvard University Press.

2011. *George F. Kennan: An American Life.* New York: Penguin.

Gaines, Robert N. 2000. Aristotle's *Rhetoric* and the Contemporary Arts of Practical Discourse, in *Rereading Aristotle's Rhetoric,* edited by Alan G. Gross and Arthur E. Walzer. Carbondale, IL: Southern Illinois University Press, pp. 3–24.

Garrett, R. Kelly. 2009. Politically Motivated Reinforcement Seeking: Reframing the Selective Exposure Debate. *Journal of Communication* 59(4): 676–699.

Garrett, R. Kelly, Dustin Carnahan, and Emily K. Lynch. 2013. A Turn toward Avoidance? Selective Exposure to Online Political Information, 2004–2008. *Political Behavior* 35(1): 113–134.

Garsten, Bryan. 2006. *Saving Persuasion: A Defense of Rhetoric and Judgment.* Cambridge, MA: Harvard University Press.

Garthoff, Raymond L. 1989. *Reflections on the Cuban Missile Crisis.* Washington, DC: The Brookings Institution Press.

1990. *Deterrence and the Revolution in Soviet Military Doctrine.* Washington, DC: The Brookings Institution Press.

1994. *Détente and Confrontation: American-Soviet Relations from Nixon to Reagan,* revised edn. Washington, DC: The Brookings Institution Press.

Garver, Eugene. 1996. The Political Irrelevance of Aristotle's *Rhetoric. Philosophy and Rhetoric* 29(2): 179–199.

Gates, Robert M. 1996. *From the Shadows: The Ultimate Insider's Story of Five Presidents and How They Won the Cold War.* New York: Simon & Schuster.

2014. *Duty: Memoirs of a Secretary at War.* New York: Alfred A. Knopf.

Gelb, Leslie H. 1976. Dissenting on Consensus, in *The Vietnam Legacy: The War, American Society, and the Future of American Foreign Policy,* edited by Anthony Lake. New York: New York University Press, pp. 102–119.

Gelb, Leslie H. and Richard K. Betts. 1979. *The Irony of Vietnam: The System Worked*. Washington, DC: The Brookings Institution Press.

Gentzkow, Matthew and Jesse M. Shapiro. 2011. Ideological Segregation Online and Offline. *Quarterly Journal of Economics* 126(4): 1799–1839.

George, Alexander L. 1969. The "Operational Code": A Neglected Approach to the Study of Political Leaders and Decision Making. *International Studies Quarterly* 13(2): 190–222.

1972. The Case for Multiple Advocacy in Making Foreign Policy. *American Political Science Review* 66(3): 751–785.

1980. *Presidential Decisionmaking in Foreign Policy: The Effective Use of Information and Advice*. Boulder, CO: Westview.

George, Alexander L. and Andrew Bennett. 2005. *Case Studies and Theory Development in the Social Sciences*. Cambridge, MA: MIT Press.

George, Alice L. 2003. *Awaiting Armageddon: How Americans Faced the Cuban Missile Crisis*. Chapel Hill, NC: University of North Carolina Press.

Gerrig, Richard J. and Giovanna Egidi. 2003. Cognitive Psychological Foundations of Narrative Experiences, in *Narrative Theory and the Cognitive Sciences*, edited by David Herman. Stanford, CA: CSLI Publications, pp. 33–55.

Giddens, Anthony. 1979. *Central Problems in Social Theory: Action, Structure and Contradiction in Social Analysis*. Berkeley, CA: University of California Press.

1991. *Modernity and Self-Identity*. Palo Alto, CA: Stanford University Press.

Giglio, James N. 1991. *The Presidency of John F. Kennedy*. Lawrence, KS: University Press of Kansas.

Gilbert, Martin. 1966. *The Roots of Appeasement*. London: Weidenfeld and Nicolson.

Gilovich, Thomas. 1991. *How We Know What Isn't So: The Fallibility of Human Reason in Everyday Life*. New York: Free Press.

Gimbel, John. 1968. *The American Occupation of Germany: Politics and the Military, 1945–1949*. Palo Alto, CA: Stanford University Press.

Goble, Hannah and Peter M. Holm. 2009. Breaking Bonds?: The Iraq War and the Loss of Republican Dominance in National Security. *Political Research Quarterly* 62(2): 215–229.

Goddard, Stacie E. 2009. *Indivisible Territory and the Politics of Legitimacy: Jerusalem and Northern Ireland*. New York: Cambridge University Press.

2015. The Rhetoric of Appeasement: Hitler's Legitimation and British Foreign Policy, 1938–1939. *Security Studies* 24(1): 95–130.

Goddard, Stacie E. and Ronald R. Krebs. 2015. Rhetoric, Legitimation, and Grand Strategy. *Security Studies* 24(1): 5–36.

Goffman, Erving. 1974. *Frame Analysis: An Essay on the Organization of Experience*. Cambridge, MA: Harvard University Press.

Goldman, Aaron. 1979. Germans and Nazis: The Controversy over "Vansittartism" in Britain during the Second World War. *Journal of Contemporary History* 14(1): 155–191.

Goldstein, Joshua S. 2001. *War and Gender: How Gender Shapes the War System and Vice Versa*. Cambridge, UK: Cambridge University Press.

Goodman, Nelson. 1978. *Ways of Worldmaking*. Indianapolis, IN: Hackett.

Goodnight, G. Thomas. 1986. Ronald Reagan's Re-formulation of the Rhetoric of War: Analysis of the "Zero Option," "Evil Empire," and "Star Wars" Addresses. *Quarterly Journal of Speech* 72(4): 390–414.

　2002. Ronald Reagan and the American Dream: A Study in Rhetoric Out of Time, in *The Presidency and Rhetorical Leadership*, edited by Leroy G. Dorsey. College Station, TX: Texas A&M University Press, 200–231.

Gordon, Michael R. and General Bernard E. Trainor. 2012. *The Endgame: The Inside Story of the Struggle for Iraq, from George W. Bush to Barack Obama*. New York: Pantheon.

Gordon, Philip. 2007. *Winning the Right War: The Path to Security for America and the World*. New York: Times Books.

Gore, Albert. 1970. *The Eye of the Storm: A People's Politics for the Seventies*. New York: Herder and Herder.

Gould, Lewis L. 2003. *Grand Old Party: A History of the Republicans*. New York: Random House.

Graber, Doris A. 2005. Introduction: The President and the Public Revisited, in *In the Public Domain: Presidents and the Challenges of Public Leadership*, edited by Lori Cox Han and Diane J. Heith. Albany, NY: State University of New York Press, pp. 1–13.

Graebner, Norman A. 1956. *The New Isolationism: A Study in Politics and Foreign Policy Since 1950*. New York: Ronald Press.

Gramsci, Antonio. 1992. *Prison Notebooks*. Translated by Joseph A. Buttigieg and Antonio Callari. New York: Columbia University Press.

Green, David. 1987. *The Language of Politics in America: Shaping Political Consciousness from McKinley to Reagan*. Ithaca, NY: Cornell University Press.

Greenberg, Stanley B. 2009. *Dispatches from the War Room: In the Trenches with Five Extraordinary Leaders*. New York: Thomas Dunne.

Greene, John Robert. 1985. *The Crusade: The Presidential Election of 1952*. Lanham, MD: University Press of America.

Griffin, Larry J. 1993. Narrative, Event-Structure Analysis, and Causal Interpretation in Historical Sociology. *American Journal of Sociology* 98(5): 1094–1133.

Griffith, Robert. 1979. Old Progressives and the Cold War. *Journal of American History* 66(2): 334–347.

Gruening, Ernest. 1973. *Many Battles: The Autobiograpy of Ernest Gruening*. New York: Liveright.

Gutman, Roy. 1988. *Banana Diplomacy: The Making of American Policy in Nicaragua, 1981–1987*. New York: Simon & Schuster.

Habel, Philip D. 2012. Following the Opinion Leaders? The Dynamics of Influence among Media Opinion, the Public, and Politicians. *Political Communication* 29(3): 257–277.

Habermas, Jürgen. 1984. *The Theory of Communicative Action*. Translated by Thomas McCarthy. Boston, MA: Beacon.

Hajer, Maarten A. 1989. *City Politics: Hegemonic Projects and Discourse*. Aldershot: Avebury.

  1997. *The Politics of Environmental Discourse: Ecological Modernization and the Policy Process*. New York: Oxford University Press.

Halberstam, David. 1969. *The Best and the Brightest*. New York: Random House.

  2001. *War in a Time of Peace: Bush, Clinton, and the Generals*. New York: Simon & Schuster.

Hall, Peter. 1989. *The Political Power of Economic Ideas*. Princeton, NJ: Princeton University Press.

  1993. Policy Paradigms, Social Learning, and the State: The Case of Economic Policymaking in Britain. *Comparative Politics* 25(3): 275–296.

Hall, Stuart. 1988. *The Hard Road to Renewal: Thatcherism and the Crisis of the Left*. London: Verso.

Halle, Louis J. 1967. *The Cold War as History*. New York: Harper & Row.

Hallin, Daniel C. 1986. *The "Uncensored War": The Media and Vietnam*. New York: Oxford University Press.

Halper, Stefan and Jonathan Clarke. 2007. *The Silence of the Rational Center: Why American Foreign Policy is Failing*. New York: Basic Books.

Halperin, Morton and Priscilla Klapp, with Arnold Kanter. 1974. *Bureaucratic Politics and Foreign Policy*. Washington, DC: The Brookings Institution Press.

Hamby, Alonzo. 1985. *Liberalism and its Challengers: FDR to Reagan*. New York: Oxford University Press.

Hammack, Phillip L. and Andrew Pilecki. 2012. Narrative as a Root Metaphor for Political Psychology. *Political Psychology* 33(1): 75–103.

Hancock, Jan. 2011. Human Rights Narrative in the George W. Bush Administrations. *Review of International Studies* 37(2): 805–823.

Hanhimäki, Jussi M. 2008. Conservative Goals, Revolutionary Outcomes: The Paradox of Détente. *Cold War History* 8(4): 503–512.

Hansen, Lene. 2006. *Security as Practice: Discourse Analysis and the Bosnian War*. London: Routledge.

Hardy, Cynthia, Bill Harley, and Nelson Phillips. 2004. Discourse Analysis and Content Analysis: Two Solitudes? *Qualitative Methods* 2(1): 19–22.

Hargittai, Eszter, Jason Gallo, and Matthew Kane. 2008. Cross-Ideological Discussions among Conservative and Liberal Bloggers. *Public Choice* 134(1–2): 67–86.

Hargittai, Eszter and Yuli Patrick Hsieh. 2013. Digital Inequality, in *The Oxford Handbook of Internet Studies*, edited by William H. Dutton. Oxford, UK: Oxford University Press, pp. 129–151.

Hart, Roderick P. 2000. *Diction 5.0: The Text-Analysis Program*. Thousand Oaks, CA: Sage.

    2008. Thinking Harder About Presidential Discourse, in *The Prospect of Presidential Rhetoric*, edited by James Arnt Aune and Martin J. Medhurst. College Station, TX: Texas A&M University Press, pp. 238–250.

Hart, Roderick P. and Jay P. Childers. 2005. The Evolution of Candidate Bush: A Rhetorical Analysis. *American Behavioral Scientist* 49(2): 180–197.

Hart, Roderick P., Jay P. Childers, and Colene J. Lind. 2013. *Political Tone: How Leaders Talk and Why*. University of Chicago Press.

Harvey, Frank P. 2012. *Explaining the Iraq War: Counterfactual Theory, Logic, and Evidence*. Cambridge, UK: Cambridge University Press.

Hauser, Gerard A. 1999. Aristotle on Epideictic: The Formation of Public Morality. *Rhetoric Society Quarterly* 29(1): 5–23.

Hay, Colin. 1996. Narrating Crisis: The Discursive Construction of the "Winter of Discontent." *Sociology* 30(2): 253–277.

Hayes, Danny and Matt Guardino. 2010. Whose Views Made the News? Media Coverage and the March to War in Iraq. *Political Communication* 27(1): 59–87.

Hazony, Yoram. 2000. *The Jewish State: The Struggle for Israel's Soul*. New York: Basic Books.

Hearden, Patrick J. 2002. *Architects of Globalism: Building a New World Order During World War II*. Fayetteville, NC: University of Arkansas Press.

Heinrichs, Waldo. 1988. *Threshold of War: Franklin D. Roosevelt and American Entry into World War II*. New York: Oxford University Press.

Hermann, Charles F. 1990. Changing Course: When Governments Choose to Redirect Foreign Policy. *International Studies Quarterly* 34(1): 3–21.

Herrera, Yoshiko M. and Bear F. Braumoeller (eds.). 2004. Symposium: Discourse and Content Analysis. *Qualitative Methods* 2(1): 15–39.

Herring, George C. 1985. Vietnam, El Salvador, and the Uses of History, in *The Central American Crisis: Sources of Conflict and the Failure of U.S. Policy*, edited by Kenneth M. Coleman and George C. Herring. Wilmington, DE: Scholarly Resources, pp. 97–110.

Hershberg, James G. 2010. The Cuban Missile Crisis, in *The Cambridge History of the Cold War*, vol. II: *Crises and Deténte*, edited by Melvyn P. Leffler and Odd Arne Westad. Cambridge University Press, pp. 65–87.

Herz, John H. 1948. The Fiasco of Denazification in Germany. *Political Science Quarterly* 63(4): 569–594.

Hess, Gary R. 2006. Presidents and the Congressional War Resolutions of 1991 and 2002. *Political Science Quarterly* 121(1): 93–118.

Hess, Stephen and Marvin Kalb (eds.). 2003. *The Media and the War on Terrorism*. Washington, DC: The Brookings Institution Press.

Heymann, Philip B. 2003. *Terrorism, Freedom, and Security: Winning Without War*. Cambridge, MA: MIT Press.

Higgs, Robert. 1987. *Crisis and Leviathan: Critical Episodes in the Growth of American Government*. New York: Oxford University Press.

Hill, Richard F. 2003. *Hitler Attacks Pearl Harbor: Why the United States Declared War on Germany*. Boulder, CO: Lynne Rienner.

Himmelstein, Jerome L. 1990. *To the Right: The Transformation of American Conservatism*. Berkeley, CA: University of California Press.

Hinckley, Barbara. 1990. *The Symbolic Presidency: How Presidents Portray Themselves*. New York: Routledge.

Hindman, Matthew. 2010. *The Myth of Digital Democracy*. Princeton, NJ: Princeton University Press.

Hodges, Adam. 2011. *The "War on Terror" Narrative: Discourse and Intertextuality in the Construction and Contestation of Sociopolitical Reality*. Oxford, UK: Oxford University Press.

Hodgson, Godfrey. 1990. *The Colonel: The Life and Wars of Henry Stimson, 1867–1950*. New York: Knopf.

1996. *The World Turned Right Side Up: A History of Conservative Ascendancy in America*. Boston, MA: Houghton Mifflin.

Hoenicke-Moore, David W. 2001. *Americans See Terrorist Attacks as "Act of War" – But Want Culprits Clearly Identified Before United States Retaliates*. Washington, DC: Gallup, Inc.

Hoenicke-Moore, Michaela. 2010. *Know Your Enemy: The American Debate on Nazism, 1933–1945*. Cambridge, UK: Cambridge University Press.

Hoff, Joan. 2007. *A Faustian Foreign Policy from Woodrow Wilson to George W. Bush: Dreams of Perfectibility*. Cambridge, UK: Cambridge University Press.

Hoffmann, Stanley. 1978. *Primacy or World Order: American Foreign Policy since the Cold War*. New York: McGraw-Hill.

Hofstadter, Richard 1973. *The American Political Tradition and the Men Who Made It*. New York: Knopf.

Hogan, Michael J. 1998. *A Cross of Iron: Harry S. Truman and the Origins of the National Security State, 1945–1954*. Cambridge, UK: Cambridge University Press.

Holland, Jack. 2009. From September 11th, 2001 to 9–11: From Void to Crisis. *International Political Sociology* 3(3): 275–292.

    2012. *Selling the War on Terror: Foreign Policy Discourses After 9/11*. London: Routledge.

Holsti, Ole R. 2011. *American Public Opinion on the Iraq War*. Ann Arbor, MI: University of Michigan Press.

Holsti, Ole R. and James N. Rosenau. 1979. Vietnam, Consensus, and the Belief Systems of American Leaders. *World Politics* 32(1): 1–56.

    1980. Cold War Axioms in the Post-Vietnam Era, in *Change in the International System*, edited by Ole R. Holsti, Randolph M. Siverson, and Alexander L. George. Boulder, CO: Westview, pp. 263–301.

    1984. *American Leadership in World Affairs: Vietnam and the Breakdown of Consensus*. Boston, MA: Allen & Unwin.

    1986.Consensus Lost. Consensus Regained? Foreign Policy Beliefs of American Leaders, 1976–1980. *International Studies Quarterly* 30(4): 374–409.

Homolar, Alexander. 2011. Rebels without a Conscience: The Evolution of the Rogue States Narrative in US Security Policy. *European Journal of International Relations* 17(4): 705–727.

Hoover, Herbert. 1955. *Addresses Upon the American Road, 1950–1955*. Palo Alto, CA: Stanford University Press.

Hopf, Ted. 2004. Discourse and Content Analysis: Some Fundamental Incompatibilities. *Qualitative Methods* 2(1): 31–33.

    2010. The Logic of Habit in International Relations. *European Journal of International Relations* 16(4): 539–561.

    2012. *Reconstructing the Cold War: The Early Years, 1945–1958*. New York: Oxford University Press.

Horten, Gerd. 2002. *Radio Goes to War: The Cultural Politics of Propaganda During World War II*. Berkeley, CA: University of California Press.

Howard, Michael. 2002. What's in a Name? *Foreign Affairs* 81(1): 8–13.

    2006–2007. A Long War? *Survival* 48(4): 7–14.

Howard-Pitney, David. 2005. *The African American Jeremiad: Appeals for Justice in America*. Philadelphia, PA: Temple University Press.

Huddy, Leonie, Stanley Feldman, and Erin Cassese. 2005. Threat, Anxiety, and Support of Antiterrorism Policies. *American Journal of Political Science* 49(3): 593–608.

Hughes, Emmet John. 1957. The Critical Last Ten Days. Unpublished manuscript, Seeley Mudd Manuscript Library, Princeton University.

Hughes, Thomas L. 1980. The Crack-Up: The Price of Collective Irresponsibility. *Foreign Policy* 40: 33–60.

Hull, Cordell. 1948. *The Memoirs of Cordell Hull*. New York: Macmillan.

Hulsey, Byron C. 2000. *Everett Dirksen and his Presidents: How a Senate Giant Shaped American Politics*. Lawrence, KS: University Press of Kansas.

Huntington, Samuel P. 1981. *American Politics: The Promise of Disharmony*. Cambridge, MA: Harvard University Press.

Hutcheson, John, David Domke, Andre Billeaudeaux, *et al*. 2004. U.S. National Identity, Political Elites, and a Patriotic Press Following September 11. *Political Communication* 21(1): 27–50.

Hutto, Daniel D. 2007. The Narrative Practice Hypothesis: Origins and Applications of Folk Psychology, in *Narrative and Understanding Persons*, edited by Daniel D. Hutto. Cambridge University Press, pp. 43–68.

Ickes, Harold L. 1954a. *The Secret Diary of Harold L. Ickes*, vol. II: *The Inside Struggle, 1936–1939*. New York: Simon & Schuster.

1954b. *The Secret Diary of Harold L. Ickes*, Vol. III: *The Lowering Clouds, 1939–1941*. New York: Simon & Schuster.

Imlay, Talbot. 2007. Total War. *Journal of Strategic Studies* 30(3): 547–570.

Ish-Shalom, Piki. 2011. Defining by Naming: Israeli Civic Warring over the Second Lebanon War. *European Journal of International Relations* 17(3): 475–493.

Isikoff, Michael and David Corn. 2006. *Hubris: The Inside Story of Spin, Scandal, and the Selling of the Iraq War*. New York: Crown.

Ivie, Robert L. 1984. Speaking "Common Sense" About the Soviet Threat: Reagan's Rhetorical Stance. *Western Journal of Speech Communication* 48(1): 39–50.

Iyengar, Shanto and Kyu S. Hahn. 2009. Red Media, Blue Media: Evidence of Ideological Selectivity in Media Use. *Journal of Communication* 59(1): 19–39.

Jackson, Patrick T. (ed.). 2004. *Bridging the Gap: Toward a Realist-Constructivist Dialogue*. *International Studies Review* (Special issue) 6(2): 337–352.

Jackson, Patrick Thaddeus. 2006. *Civilizing the Enemy: German Reconstruction and the Invention of the West*. Ann Arbor, MI: University of Michigan Press.

Jackson, Richard. 2005. *Writing the War on Terrorism: Language, Politics, and Counter-Terrorism*. Manchester, UK: Manchester University Press.

2011. Culture, Identity and Hegemony: Continuity and (the Lack of) Change in US Counterterrorism Policy from Bush to Obama. *International Relations* 48(2/3): 390–411.

Jacobs, Lawrence R. and Robert Y. Shapiro. 2000. *Politicians Don't Pander: Political Manipulation and the Loss of Democratic Responsiveness.* Chicago, IL: University of Chicago Press.

Jacobson, Jon. 1972. *Locarno Diplomacy: Germany and the West, 1925–1929.* Princeton, NJ: Princeton University Press.

James, Scott C. 2009. Historical Institutionalism, Political Development, and the Presidency, in *The Oxford Handbook of the American Presidency*, edited by George C. Edwards III and William G. Howell. Oxford, UK: Oxford University Press, pp. 51–81.

Jamieson, Kathleen Hall. 1973. Generic Constraints and the Rhetorical Situation. *Philosophy and Rhetoric* 6(3): 162–170.

Jarvis, Lee and Jack Holland. 2014. "We [For]got Him": Remembering and Forgetting in the Narration of bin Laden's Death. *Millennium – Journal of International Studies* 42(2): 425–447.

Jeffreys-Jones, Rhodri. 1999. *Peace Now! American Society and the Ending of the Vietnam War.* New Haven, CT: Yale University Press.

Jervis, Robert. 2005. *American Foreign Policy in a New Era.* New York: Routledge.

Jessop, Bob. 1982. *The Capitalist State: Marxist Theories and Methods.* New York University Press.

Johns, Andrew L. 2010. *Vietnam's Second Front: Domestic Politics, the Republican Party, and the War.* Lexington, KY: University Press of Kentucky.

Johnson, Dominic D. P. and Dominic Tierney. 2006. *Failing to Win: Perceptions of Victory and Defeat in International Politics.* Cambridge, MA: Harvard University Press.

Johnson, Robert David. 1998. *Ernest Gruening and the American Dissenting Tradition.* Cambridge, MA: Harvard University Press.

2006. *Congress and the Cold War.* Cambridge, UK: Cambridge University Press.

Johnson, Robert H. 1994. *Improbable Dangers: U.S. Conceptions of Threat in the Cold War and After.* New York: St. Martin's Press.

Johnson, Walter. 1944. *The Battle against Isolation.* Chicago, IL: University of Chicago Press.

Johnston, Patrick B. and Brian R. Urlacher. 2012. Explaining the Duration of Counterinsurgency Campaigns. Unpublished manuscript, RAND Corp. and University of North Dakota.

Jonas, Manfred. 1966. *Isolationism in America, 1935–1941.* Ithaca, NY: Cornell University Press.

Jones, Howard. 1989. *"A New Kind of War": America's Global Strategy and the Truman Doctrine in Greece.* New York: Oxford University Press.

Jones, Joseph M. 1955. *The Fifteen Weeks.* New York: Viking Press.

Jones, Michael D. and Mark K. McBeth. 2010. A Narrative Policy Framework: Clear Enough to Be Wrong? *Policy Studies Journal* 38(2): 329–353.

Jones, Michael D. and Geoboo Song. 2013. Making Sense of Climate Change: How Story Frames Shape Cognition. *Political Psychology* 35(4): 447–476.

Judis, John B. 1988. *William F. Buckley, Jr.: Patron Saint of the Conservatives.* New York: Simon & Schuster.

Just, Marion R. 2011. What's News: A View from the Twenty-First Century, in *Oxford Handbook of American Public Opinion and the Media*, edited by George C. Edwards, Lawrence R. Jacobs, and Robert Y. Shapiro. Oxford, UK: Oxford University Press, pp. 105–121.

Kadushin, Charles. 1974. *The American Intellectual Elite.* Boston, MA: Little, Brown.

Kahne, Joseph, Ellen Middaugh, Nam-Jin Lee, and Jessica T. Feezell. 2012. Youth Online Activity and Exposure to Diverse Perspectives. *New Media & Society* 14(3): 492–512.

Kahneman, Daniel and Jonathan Renshon. 2007. Why Hawks Win. *Foreign Policy* 158: 34–38.

Kalman, Laura. 2010. *Right Star Rising: A New Politics, 1974–1980.* New York: W. W. Norton.

Karvonen, Lauri. 2010. *The Personalisation of Politics: A Study of Parliamentary Democracies.* Colchester: ECPR Press.

Katzenbach, Nicholas de B. 1973. Foreign Policy, Public Opinion, and Secrecy. *Foreign Affairs* 52(1): 1–19.

Katznelson, Ira and Martin Shefter (eds.). 2002. *Shaped by War and Trade: International Influences on American Political Development.* Princeton, NJ: Princeton University Press.

Kaufman, Burton I. 1986. *The Korean War: Challenges in Crisis, Credibility, and Command.* New York: Temple University Press.

Kaufman, Stuart J. 2009. Narratives and Symbols in Violent Mobilization: The Palestinian-Israeli Case. *Security Studies* 18(3): 400–434.

  2012. "Constructivism, Social Psychology, and Interlocking Theory (I)." Available at www.whiteoliphaunt.com/duckofminerva/2012/06/con structivism-social-psychology-and.html.

Kaufmann, Chaim. 2004. Threat Inflation and the Failure of the Marketplace of Ideas: The Selling of the Iraq War. *International Security* 29(1): 5–48.

Keck, Margaret and Kathryn Sikkink. 1998. *Activist beyond Borders: Activist Networks in International Politics.* Ithaca, NY: Cornell University Press.

Kegley Jr., Charles W. 1986. Assumptions and Dilemmas in the Study of Americans' Foreign Policy Beliefs: A Caveat. *International Studies Quarterly* 30(4): 447–471.

Kennedy, David M. 1999. *Freedom From Fear: The American People in Depression and War.* New York: Oxford University Press.

Kennedy, Paul (ed.). 1991. *Grand Strategies in War and Peace.* New Haven, CT: Yale University Press.

Kenworthy, Eldon. 1987a. Selling the Policy, in *Reagan Versus the Sandinistas: The Undeclared War on Nicaragua,* edited by Thomas W. Walker. Boulder, CO: Westview, pp. 159–181.

1987b. Where Pennsylvania Avenue Meets Madison Avenue: The Selling of Foreign Policy. *World Policy Journal* 5(1): 107–127.

1995. *America/Américas: Myth in the Making of U.S. Policy toward Latin America.* University Park, PA: Pennsylvania State University Press.

Kepley, David R. 1988. *The Collapse of the Middle Way: Senate Republicans and the Bipartisan Foreign Policy, 1948–1952.* Westport, CT: Greenwood.

Kermode, Frank. 1981. Secrets and Narrative Sequence, in *On Narrative,* edited by W. J. T. Mitchell. Chicago, IL: University of Chicago Press, pp. 79–97.

Kernell, Samuel. 2007. *Going Public: New Strategies of Presidential Leadership,* 4th edn. Washington, DC: CQ Press.

Kimball, Warren F. 1976. *Swords or Ploughshares? The Morgenthau Plan for Defeated Nazi Germany, 1943–1946.* Philadelphia, PA: J. B. Lippincott.

1991. *The Juggler: Franklin Roosevelt as Wartime Statesman.* Princeton, NJ: Princeton University Press.

1997. *Forged in War: Roosevelt, Churchill, and the Second World War.* New York: William Morrow.

Kimmens, Andrew C. (ed.). 1987. *Nicaragua and the United States.* New York: H. W. Wilson.

King, Erika G. and Robert A. Wells. 2009. *Framing the Iraq War Endgame: War's Denouement in an Age of Terror.* New York: Palgrave Macmillan.

King, Ronald F. and Thomas S. Langston. 2008. Narratives of American Politics. *Perspectives on Politics* 6(2): 235–252.

Kissinger, Henry. 1979. *White House Years.* Boston, MA: Little, Brown.

Klinghoffer, Judith A. 1999. *Vietnam, Jews, and the Middle East: Unintended Consequences.* New York: St. Martin's Press.

Klotz, Audie and Cecelia Lynch. 2007. *Strategies for Research in Constructivist International Relations.* Armonk, NY: M. E. Sharpe.

Knock, Thomas. 2003. "Come Home America": The Story of George McGovern, in *Vietnam and the American Political Tradition: The Politics of Dissent*, edited by Randall B. Woods. Cambridge, UK: Cambridge University Press, pp. 82–120.

Kohut, Andrew, Carroll Doherty, Scott Keeter *et al.* 2004. *News Audiences Increasingly Politicized.* Washington, DC: Pew Research Center for the People and the Press.

Koppes, Clayton R. and Gregory D. Black. 1987. *Hollywood Goes to War: How Politics, Profit, and Propaganda Shaped World War II Movies.* New York: Free Press.

Kornbluh, Peter. 1987. *Nicaragua: The Price of Intervention – Reagan's Wars Against the Sandinistas.* Washington, DC: Institute for Policy Studies.

Kornprobst, Markus. 2008. *Irredentism in European Politics: Argumentation, Compromise, and Norms.* Cambridge University Press.

Krasner, Stephen. 1984. Approaches to the State: Alternative Conceptions and Historical Dynamics. *Comparative Politics* 16(2): 223–246.

Krebs, Ronald R. 2006. *Fighting for Rights: Military Service and the Politics of Citizenship.* Ithaca, NY: Cornell University Press.

2009. In the Shadow of War: The Effects of Conflict on Liberal Democracy. *International Organization* 63(1): 177–210.

2013. The Rise, Persistence, and Fall of the War on Terror, in *How 9/11 Changed Our Ways of War*, edited by James Burk. Stanford, CA: Stanford University Press, pp. 56–85.

Krebs, Ronald R. and Patrick T. Jackson. 2007. Twisting Tongues and Twisting Arms: The Power of Political Rhetoric. *European Journal of International Relations* 13(1): 35–66.

Krebs, Ronald R. and Jennifer K. Lobasz. 2007. Fixing the Meaning of 9/11: Hegemony, Coercion, and the Road to War in Iraq. *Security Studies* 16(3): 409–451.

Krippendorff, Klaus. 2004. Reliability in Content Analysis: Some Common Misconceptions and Recommendations. *Human Communication Research* 30(3): 411–433.

Kristol, Irving. 1976. Consensus and Dissent in U.S. Foreign Policy, in *The Vietnam Legacy: The War, American Society, and the Future of American Foreign Policy*, edited by Anthony Lake. New York University Press, pp. 80–101.

Kristol, William and Robert Kagan. 1996. Toward a Neo-Reaganite Foreign Policy. *Foreign Affairs* 75(4): 18–32.

Kruglanski, Arie W. 2004. *The Psychology of Closed Mindedness.* New York: Psychology Press.

Kull, Steven. 2007. *Muslim Public Opinion on US Policy, Attacks on Civilians, and al Qaeda*. College Park, MD: Program on International Policy Attitudes, University of Maryland.

Kull, Steven, Clay Ramsay, and Evan Lewis. 2003–04. Misperceptions, the Media and the Iraq War. *Political Science Quarterly* 118(4): 569–598.

Kupchan, Charles A. and Peter L. Trubowitz. 2007. Dead Center: The Demise of Liberal Internationalism in the United States. *International Security* 32(2): 7–44.

Laclau, Ernesto. 1977. *Politics and Ideology in Marxist Theory*. London: New Left Books.

Laclau, Ernesto and Chantal Mouffe. 2001. *Hegemony and Socialist Strategy: Toward a Radical Democratic Politics*, 2nd edn. London: Verso.

Laffey, Mark and Jutta Weldes. 2004. Methodological Reflections on Discourse Analysis. *Qualitative Methods* 2(1): 28–30.

Laitin, David D. 1988. Political Culture and Political Preferences. *American Political Science Review* 82(2): 589–593.

Lakoff, George. 2004. *Don't Think of an Elephant! Know Your Values and Frame the Debate: The Essential Guide for Progressives*. New York: Chelsea Green.

2008. *The Political Mind*. New York: Viking.

Lakoff, George and Mark Johnson. 1980. *Metaphors We Live By*. Chicago, IL: University of Chicago Press.

Landis, J. Richard and Gary G. Koch. 1977. The Measurement of Observer Agreement for Categorical Data. *Biometrics* 33(1): 159–174.

Landy, Marc and Sidney M. Milkis. 2000. *Presidential Greatness*. Lawrence, KS: University Press of Kansas.

Laqueur, Walter and Leopold Labedz (eds.). 1962. *Polycentrism: The New Factor in International Communism*. New York: Praeger.

Larsson, Anders Olof. 2013. "Rejected Bits of Program Code": Why Notions of "Politics 2.0" Remain (Mostly) Unfulfilled. *Journal of Information Technology & Politics* 10(1): 72–85.

László, János. 2008. *The Science of Stories: An Introduction to Narrative Psychology*. London: Routledge.

Lawrence, Eric, John Sides, and Henry Farrell. 2010. Self-Segregation or Deliberation? Blog Readership, Participation, and Polarization in American Politics. *Perspectives on Politics* 8(1): 141–157.

Lebow, Richard Ned. 1984. *Between Peace and War: The Nature of International Crisis*. Baltimore, MD: Johns Hopkins University Press.

2000. What's So Different about a Counterfactual? *World Politics* 52(4): 550–585.

Leff, Michael C. 1993. The Uses of Aristotle's *Rhetoric* in Contemporary American Scholarship. *Argumentation* 7(3): 313–327.

Leffler, Melvyn P. 2004. Think Again: Bush's Foreign Policy. *Foreign Policy* 144: 22–28.

Legro, Jeffrey W. 2005. *Rethinking the World: Great Power Strategies and International Order*. Ithaca, NY: Cornell University Press.

Legvold, Robert. 1980. Containment without Confrontation. *Foreign Policy* 40: 74–98.

LeoGrande, William M. 1998. *Our Own Backyard: The United States in Central America, 1977–1992*. Chapel Hill, NC: University of North Carolina Press.

LeoGrande, William M. and Philip Brenner. 1993. The House Divided: Ideological Polarization Over Aid to the Nicaraguan "Contras." *Legislative Studies Quarterly* 18(1): 105–136.

Leskovec, Jure, Lars Backstrom, Jon Kleinberg *et al.* 2009. Meme-tracking and the Dynamics of the News Cycle, in *Proceedings of the 15th ACM SIGKDD International Conference on Knowledge Discovery and Data Mining*. Paris, France.

Levy, Jack S. 1983. *War in the Modern Great Power System, 1495–1975*. Lexington, KY: University Press of Kentucky.

2008. Counterfactuals and Case Studies, in *Oxford Handbook of Political Methodology*, edited by Janet Box-Steffensmeier, Henry Brady, and David Collier. New York: Oxford University Press, pp. 627–644.

Lim, Elvin T. 2003. The Lion and the Lamb: De-Mythologizing Franklin Roosevelt's Fireside Chats. *Rhetoric & Public Affairs* 6(3): 437–464.

Lincoln, Bruce. 1994. *Authority: Construction and Corrosion*. Chicago, IL: University of Chicago Press.

2003. *Holy Terrors: Thinking About Religion after September 11*. Chicago, IL: University of Chicago Press.

Lindsay, James M. 1994. *Congress and the Politics of U.S. Foreign Policy*. Baltimore, MD: Johns Hopkins University Press.

Lippmann, Walter. 1943. *U.S. Foreign Policy: Shield of the Republic*. Boston, MA: Little, Brown.

Lobell, Steven E., Norrin Ripsman, and Jeffrey Taliaferro (eds.). 2009. *Neoclassical Realism, the State, and Foreign Policy*. Cambridge University Press.

Lockerbie, Brad and Stephen A. Borrelli. 1990. Question Wording and Public Support for Contra Aid, 1983–1986. *Public Opinion Quarterly* 54(2): 195–208.

Logevall, Fredrik. 1999. *Choosing War: The Lost Chance for Peace and the Escalation of War in Vietnam*. Berkeley, CA: University of California Press.

2003. A Delicate Balance: John Sherman Cooper and the Republican Opposition to the Vietnam War, in *Vietnam and the American Political Tradition: The Politics of Dissent*, edited by Randall B. Woods. Cambridge, UK: Cambridge University Press, pp. 237–258.

Longley, Kyle. 2003. The Reluctant "Volunteer": The Origins of Senator Albert A. Gore's Opposition to the Vietnam War, in *Vietnam and the American Political Tradition: The Politics of Dissent*, edited by Randall B. Woods. Cambridge, UK: Cambridge University Press, pp. 204–236.

2004. *Senator Albert Gore, Sr.: Tennessee Maverick*. Baton Rouge, LA: Louisiana State University Press.

Lowenthal, Abraham F. 1985. The United States and Central America: Reflections on the Kissinger Commission Report, in *The Central American Crisis: Sources of Conflict and the Failure of U.S. Policy*, edited by Kenneth M. Coleman and George C. Herring. Wilmington, DE: Scholarly Resources, pp. 205–215.

Lubell, Samuel. 1956. *Revolt of the Moderates*. New York: Harper & Brothers.

Ludwig, Emil. 1945. *The Moral Conquest of Germany*. Garden City, NY: Doubleday, Doran.

Luntz, Frank I. 2006. *Words That Work: It's Not What You Say, It's What People Hear*. New York: Hyperion.

Lustick, Ian S. 1993. *Unsettled States, Disputed Lands: Britain and Ireland, France and Algeria, Israel and the West Bank-Gaza*. Ithaca, NY: Cornell University Press.

2006. *Trapped in the War on Terror*. Philadelphia, PA: University of Pennsylvania Press.

Lüthi, Lorenz M. 2008. *The Sino-Soviet Split: Cold War in the Communist World*. Princeton, NJ: Princeton University Press.

Lynch, Cecelia. 1999a. *Beyond Appeasement: Interpreting Interwar Peace Movements in World Politics*. Ithaca, NY: Cornell University Press.

Lynch, Marc. 1999b. *State Interests and Public Spheres: The International Politics of Jordan's Identity*. New York: Columbia University Press.

2002. Why Engage? China and the Logic of Communicative Engagement. *European Journal of International Relations* 8(2): 187–230.

MacDonald, Callum A. 1986. *Korea: The War before Vietnam*. New York: Free Press.

MacDowall, David. 2004. *A Modern History of the Kurds*, 3rd edn. London: I. B. Tauris.

MacIntyre, Alasdair. 1981. *After Virtue: A Study in Moral Theory*. Notre Dame, IN: University of Notre Dame Press.

Mahoney, James. 2000. Path Dependence in Historical Sociology. *Theory and Society* 29(4): 507–548.

Mahoney, James and Dietrich Rueschemeyer (eds.). 2003. *Comparative Historical Analysis in the Social Sciences*. Cambridge University Press.

Mahoney, James and Kathleen Thelen (eds.). 2010. *Explaining Institutional Change: Ambiguity, Agency, and Power*. Cambridge, UK: Cambridge University Press.

Maney, Gregory M., Patrick G. Coy, and Lynne M. Woehrle. 2009. Pursuing Political Persuasion: War and Peace Frames in the United States after September 11th. *Social Movement Studies* 8(4): 299–322.

Manjikian, Mary. 2008. Diagnosis, Intervention, and Cure: The Illness Narrative in the Discourse of the Failed State. *Alternatives* 33(3): 335–357.

Mann, James. 2004. *Rise of the Vulcans: The History of Bush's War Cabinet*. New York: Viking.

Marshall, Will (ed.). 2006. *With All Our Might: A Progressive Strategy for Defeating Jihadism and Defending Liberty*. Lanham, MD: Rowman & Littlefield.

Massing, Michael. 2004. *Now They Tell Us: The American Press and Iraq*. New York: New York Review of Books.

Matloff, Maurice. 1986. Allied Strategy in Europe, 1939–1945, in *Makers of Modern Strategy: From Machiavelli to the Nuclear Age*, edited by Peter Paret. Princeton, NJ: Princeton University Press, pp. 677–702.

Matusow, Allen J. 1984. *The Unraveling of America: A History of Liberalism in the 1960s*. New York: Harper & Row.

May, Ernest R. 1962. The Nature of Foreign Policy: The Calculated versus the Axiomatic. *Daedalus* 91(4): 653–667.

Mayhew, David R. 2005. Wars and American Politics. *Perspectives on Politics* 3(3): 473–493.

McAlister, Melani. 2005. *Epic Encounters: Culture, Media, and U.S. Interests in the Middle East since 1945*, updated edn. Berkeley, CA: University of California Press.

McCartney, Paul T. 2004. American Nationalism and U.S. Foreign Policy from September 11 to the Iraq War. *Political Science Quarterly* 119(3): 399–423.

McDermott, Rose. 2004. *Political Psychology in International Relations*. Ann Arbor, MI: University of Michigan Press.

McDonald, Matt. 2010. "Lest We Forget": The Politics of Memory and Australian Military Intervention. *International Political Sociology* 4(3): 287–302.

McDonald, Matt and Matt Merefield. 2010. How was Howard's War Possible? Winning the War of Position over Iraq. *Australian Journal of International Affairs* 64(2): 186–204.

McDougall, Walter A. 1997. *Promised Land, Crusader State: The American Encounter with the World Since 1776*. New York: Houghton Mifflin.

McGee, Michael Calvin and John S. Nelson. 1985. Narrative Reason in Public Argument. *Journal of Communication* 35(4): 139–155.

McGinn, Bernard. 1994. *Antichrist: Two Thousand Years of the Human Fascination with Evil*. San Francisco, CA: HarperSanFrancisco.

McMahon, Robert J. 1999. Rationalizing Defeat: The Vietnam War in American Presidential Discourse, 1975–1995. *Rhetoric & Public Affairs* 2(4): 529–549.

Mearsheimer, John J. 1994/95. The False Promise of International Institutions. *International Security* 19(3): 5–49.

2001. *The Tragedy of Great Power Politics*. New York: W. W. Norton.

2002. Hearts and Minds. *National Interest* 69: 13–16.

2011. *Why Leaders Lie: The Truth About Lying in International Politics*. New York: Oxford University Press.

Mearsheimer, John J. and Stephen M. Walt. 2007. *The Israel Lobby and U.S. Foreign Policy*. New York: Farrar, Straus, & Giroux.

Medhurst, Martin J. 2000. Text and Context in the 1952 Presidential Campaign: Eisenhower's "I Shall Go to Korea" Speech. *Presidential Studies Quarterly* 30(3): 464–484.

(ed.). 2008. *Before the Rhetorical Presidency*. College Station, TX: Texas A&M University Press.

Merolla, Jennifer L. and Elizabeth J. Zechmeister. 2009. *Democracy at Risk: How Terrorist Threats Affect the Public*. Chicago, IL: University of Chicago Press.

Merritt, Richard L. 1995. *Democracy Imposed: U.S. Occupation Policy and the German Public, 1945–1949*. New Haven, CT: Yale University Press.

Meyer, Leo J. 1959. The Decision to Invade North Africa (TORCH) (1942), in *Command Decisions*, edited by Kent Roberts Greenfield. New York: Harcourt, Brace, pp. 129–153.

Meyers, David. 2007. *Dissenting Voices in America's Rise to Power*. Cambridge, UK: Cambridge University Press.

Miles, Michael W. 1980. *The Odyssey of the American Right*. New York: Oxford University Press.

Milkis, Sidney M. 1998. Franklin D. Roosevelt, Progressivism, and the Limits of Popular Leadership, in *Speaking to the People: The Rhetorical Presidency in Historical Perspective*, edited by Richard J. Ellis. Amherst: University of Massachusetts Press, pp. 182–211.

Miller, Benjamin. 2010a. Democracy Promotion: Offensive Liberalism versus the Rest (of IR Theory). *Millennium* 38(3): 561–591.

2010b. Explaining Changes in US Grand Strategy: 9/11, The Rise of Offensive Liberalism and the War in Iraq. *Security Studies* 19(1): 26–65.

Miller, Carolyn R. 1984. Genre as Social Action. *Quarterly Journal of Speech* 70(2): 151–167.

Miller, J. Hillis. 2004. "Taking up a Task": Moments of Decision in Ernesto Laclau's Thought, in *Laclau: A Critical Reader*, edited by Simon Critchley and Oliver Marchart. London: Routledge, pp. 217–225.

Mishler, Elliot G. 1995. Models of Narrative Analysis: A Typology. *Journal of Narrative and Life History* 5(2): 87–123.

Mitchell, Nancy. 2010. The Cold War and Jimmy Carter, in *The Cambridge History of the Cold War*, edited by Melvyn P. Leffler and Odd Arne Westad. Cambridge, UK: Cambridge University Press, pp. 66–88.

Mitchell, W. J. T. (ed.). 1981. *On Narrative*. University of Chicago Press.

Mitzen, Jennifer. 2006. Ontological Security in World Politics: State Identity and the Security Dilemma. *European Journal of International Relations* 12(3): 341–370.

Moffett, George. 1985. *The Limits of Victory: The Ratification of the Panama Canal Treaties*. Ithaca, NY: Cornell University Press.

Monten, Jonathan. 2005. The Roots of the Bush Doctrine: Power, Nationalism, and Democracy in U.S. Strategy. *International Security* 29(4): 112–156.

Moravcsik, Andrew. 1997. Taking Preferences Seriously: A Liberal Theory of International Politics. *International Organization* 51(4): 513–553.

Morgenthau, Hans. 1965. *Vietnam and the United States*. Washington, DC: Public Affairs Press.

1970. *Truth and Power: Essays of a Decade, 1960–70*. New York: Praeger.

Morgenthau Jr., Henry. 1945. *Germany is our Problem*. New York: Harper & Brothers.

Morris, Rebecca. 1994. Computerized Content Analysis in Management Research: A Demonstration of Advantages & Limitations. *Journal of Management* 20(4): 903–931.

Mueller, John E. 1971. Trends in Popular Support for the Wars in Korea and Vietnam. *American Political Science Review* 65(2): 358–375.

1973. *War, Presidents, and Public Opinion*. New York: Wiley.

2005. Simplicity and Spook: Terrorism and the Dynamics of Threat Exaggeration. *International Studies Perspectives* 6(2): 208–234.

2006. *Overblown: How Politicians, the Terrorism Industry, and Others Stoke National Security Fears*. New York: Free Press.

Mueller, John E. and Mark G. Stewart. 2012. The Terrorism Delusion: America's Overwrought Response to September 11. *International Security* 37(1): 81–110.

Müller, Harald. 2001. International Relations as Communicative Action, in *Constructing International Relations: The Next Generation*, edited by Karin M. Fierke and Knud Erik Jorgensen. Armonk, NY: M. E. Sharpe, pp. 160–179.

Murphy, Andrew R. 2009. Longing, Nostalgia, and Golden Age Politics: The American Jeremiad and the Power of the Past. *Perspectives on Politics* 7(1): 125–141.

Murphy, John M. 1990. "A Time of Shame and Sorrow": Robert F. Kennedy and the American Jeremiad. *Quarterly Journal of Speech* 76(4): 401–414.

    1992. Epideictic and Deliberative Strategies in Opposition to War: The Paradox of Honor and Expediency. *Communication Studies* 43(2): 65–78.

    2003. "Our Mission and Our Moment": George W. Bush and September 11th. *Rhetoric & Public Affairs* 6(4): 607–632.

Mutz, Diana C. 2006. *Hearing the Other Side: Deliberative Versus Participatory Democracy*. Cambridge, UK: Cambridge University Press.

Nabers, Dirk. 2009. Filling the Void of Meaning: Identity Construction in U.S. Foreign Policy After September 11, 2001. *Foreign Policy Analysis* 5(2): 191–214.

Nacos, Brigitte L., Yaeli Bloch-Elkon, and Robert Y. Shapiro. 2011. *Selling Fear: Counterterrorism, the Media, and Public Opinion*. Chicago, IL: University of Chicago Press.

Nahon, Karine and Jeff Hemsley. 2014. Homophily in the Guise of Cross-Linking Political Blogs and Content. *American Behavioral Scientist* 58(10): 1294–1313.

Naím, Moisés. 2013. *The End of Power: From Boardrooms to Battlefields and Churches to States, Why Being in Charge Isn't What it Used to Be*. New York: Basic Books.

Narizny, Kevin. 2007. *The Political Economy of Grand Strategy*. Ithaca, NY: Cornell University Press.

Nash, Christopher (ed.). 1990. *Narrative in Culture: The Uses of Storytelling in the Sciences, Philosophy, and Literature*. London: Routledge.

Nash, George H. 1976. *The Conservative Intellectual Movement in America since 1945*. New York: Basic Books.

Nash, Philip. 1997. *The Other Missiles of October: Eisenhower, Kennedy, and the Jupiters, 1957–1963*. Chapel Hill, NC: University of North Carolina Press.

Neuendorf, Kimberly A. 2004. Content Analysis – A Contrast and Complement to Discourse Analysis. *Qualitative Methods* 2(1): 33–36.

Neuman, W. Russell, Bruce Bimber, and Matthew Hindman. 2011. The Internet and Four Dimensions of Citizenship, in *Oxford Handbook of American Public Opinion and the Media*, edited by George C. Edwards, Lawrence R. Jacobs, and Robert Y. Shapiro. Oxford, UK: Oxford University Press, pp. 22–43.

Neumann, Iver B. 2002. Returning Practice to the Linguistic Turn: The Case of Diplomacy. *Millennium: Journal of International Studies* 31(3): 627–651.

Nexon, Daniel H. 2009. *The Struggle for Power in Early Modern Europe: Religious Conflict, Dynastic Empires, and International Change.* Princeton, NJ: Princeton University Press.

Nicholas, H. G. (ed.). 1981. *Washington Despatches, 1941–1945: Weekly Political Reports from the British Embassy.* Chicago, IL: University of Chicago Press.

Nixon, Richard. 1978. *RN: The Memoirs of Richard Nixon.* New York: Grosset & Dunlap.

Noelle-Neumann, Elisabeth. 1993. *The Spiral of Silence: Public Opinion – Our Social Skin*, 2nd edn. University of Chicago Press.

Nordlinger, Eric A. 1995. *Isolationism Reconfigured: American Foreign Policy For a New Century.* Princeton, NJ: Princeton University Press.

Novak, Michael. 1974. *Choosing Our King: Powerful Symbols in Presidential Politics.* New York: Macmillan.

O'Connor, Alice. 2008. Financing the Counterrevolution, in *Rightward Bound: Making America Conservative in the 1970s*, edited by Bruce J. Schulman and Julian E. Zelizer. Cambridge, MA: Harvard University Press, pp. 148–168.

Offenbach, Seth. 2010. The Other Side of Vietnam: The Conservative Movement and the Vietnam War. Ph.D. diss., Department of History, Stony Brook University.

2012. Defending Freedom in Vietnam: A Conservative Dilemma, in *The Right Side of the Sixties: Re-examining Conservatism's Decade of Transformation*, edited by Laura Jane Gifford and Daniel K. Williams. New York: Palgrave Macmillan, pp. 201–220.

Olick, Jeffrey K. 2005. *In the House of the Hangman: The Agonies of German Defeat, 1943–1949.* Chicago, IL: University of Chicago Press.

Olson, Lynne. 2013. *Those Angry Days: Roosevelt, Lindbergh, and America's Fight Over World War II, 1939–1941.* New York: Random House.

Onuf, Nicholas G. 1989. *World of Our Making: Rules and Rule in Social Theory and International Relations.* Columbia, SC: University of South Carolina Press.

Osgood, Robert E. 1953. *Ideals and Self-Interest in America's Foreign Relations*. Chicago, IL: University of Chicago Press.

Pach Jr., Chester J. 1987. Military Assistance and American Foreign Policy: The Role of Congress, in *Congress and United States Foreign Policy: Controlling the Use of Force in the Nuclear Age*, edited by Michael Barnhart. Albany, NY: State University of New York Press, pp. 137–153.

2006. The Reagan Doctrine: Principle, Pragmatism, and Policy. *Presidential Studies Quarterly* 36(1): 75–88.

Pach Jr., Chester J. and Elmo Richardson. 1991. *The Presidency of Dwight D. Eisenhower*. Lawrence, KS: University Press of Kansas.

Page, Benjamin I. and Lawrence R. Jacobs. 2009. *Class War? What Americans Really Think About Economic Inequality*. Chicago, IL: University of Chicago Press.

Page, Benjamin I. and Robert Y. Shapiro. 1985. Presidential Leadership through Public Opinion, in *The Presidency and Public Policy Making*, edited by George C. Edwards III, Steven A. Shull, and Norman C. Thomas. Pittsburgh, PA: University of Pittsburgh Press, pp. 22–36.

1992. *The Rational Public: Fifty Years of Trends in Americans' Policy Preferences*. Chicago, IL: University of Chicago Press.

Panke, Diana. 2010. Why Discourse Matters Only Sometimes: Effective Arguing Beyond the Nation-State. *Review of International Studies* 36(1): 145–168.

Paris, Roland. 2002. Kosovo and the Metaphor War. *Political Science Quarterly* 117(3): 423–450.

Pastor, Robert A. 1987. *Condemned to Repetition: The United States and Nicaragua*. Princeton, NJ: Princeton University Press.

Paterson, Thomas G. (ed.). 1971. *Cold War Critics: Alternatives to American Foreign Policy in the Truman Years*. Chicago, IL: Quadrangle Books.

Patterson, James T. 1972. *Mr. Republican: A Biography of Robert A. Taft*. Boston, MA: Houghton Mifflin.

Patterson, Molly and Kristen Renwick Monroe. 1998. Narrative in Political Science. *Annual Review of Political Science* 1: 315–331.

Payne, Rodger A. 2001. Persuasion, Frames and Norm Construction. *European Journal of International Relations* 7(1): 37–61.

Peake, Jeffrey S. and Matthew Eshbaugh-Soha. 2008. The Agenda-Setting Impact of Major Presidential TV Addresses. *Political Communication* 25(2): 113–137.

Peele, Gillian. 1984. *Revival and Reaction: The Right in Contemporary America*. Oxford: Clarendon Press.

Perelman, Chaïm. 1982. *The Realm of Rhetoric*. Notre Dame, IN: University of Notre Dame Press.

Perelman, Chaïm and Lucie Olbrechts-Tyteca. 1969 [1958]. *The New Rhetoric: A Treatise on Argumentation*. Translated by John Wilkinson and Purcell Weaver. Notre Dame, IN: University of Notre Dame Press.

Perkins, Serena A. and Elliot Turiel. 2007. To Lie or Not to Lie: To Whom and Under What Circumstances. *Child Development* 78(2): 609–621.

Perlovsky, Leonid. 2009. Language and Cognition. *Neural Networks* 22(3): 247–257.

Perret, Geoffrey. 1999. *Eisenhower*. New York: Random House.

Perrow, Charles. 1984. *Normal Accidents*. New York: Basic Books.

Pestritto, Ronald J. (ed.). 2005. *Woodrow Wilson: The Essential Political Writings*. Lanham, MD: Lexington Books.

Phillips, Kevin P. 1982. *Post-Conservative America: People, Politics, and Ideology in a Time of Crisis*. New York: Random House.

Pierson, Paul. 2004. *Politics in Time: History, Institutions, and Social Analysis*. Princeton, NJ: Princeton University Press.

Pillar, Paul R. 2001. *Terrorism and U.S. Foreign Policy*. Washington, DC: The Brookings Institution Press.

Poguntke, Thomas and Paul Webb (eds.) 2005. *The Presidentialization of Politics: A Comparative Study of Modern Democracies*. Oxford, UK: Oxford University Press.

Polkinghorne, Donald E. 1988. *Narrative Knowing and the Human Sciences*. Albany, NY: State University of New York Press.

Pollack, Kenneth M. 2002. *The Threatening Storm: The Case for Invading Iraq*. New York: Random House.

Posen, Barry R. 1984. *The Sources of Military Doctrine: France, Britain, and Germany Between the World Wars*. Ithaca, NY: Cornell University Press.

2014. *Restraint: A New Foundation for U.S. Grand Strategy*. Ithaca, NY: Cornell University Press.

Pouliot, Vincent. 2008. The Logic of Practicality: A Theory of Practice of Security Communities. *International Organization* 62(2): 257–288.

Powers, Richard Gid. 1995. *Not Without Honor: The History of American Anticommunism*. New York: Free Press.

Price, Richard M. 1998. Reversing the Gun Sights: Transnational Civil Society Targets Land Mines. *International Organization* 52(3): 613–644.

2003. Transnational Civil Society and Advocacy in World Politics. *World Politics* 55(4): 579–606.

Prior, Markus. 2007. *Post-Broadcast Democracy: How Media Choice Increases Inequality in Political Involvement and Polarizes Elections*. Cambridge University Press.

2013. Media and Political Polarization. *Annual Review of Political Science* 16: 101–127.

Quester, George. 1980. Consensus Lost. *Foreign Policy* 40: 18–32.

Radosh, Ronald. 1975. *Prophets on the Right: Profiles of Conservative Critics of American Globalism*. New York: Simon & Schuster.

Ragsdale, Lyn. 1984. The Politics of Presidential Speechmaking, 1949–1980. *American Political Science Review* 78(4): 971–984.

Rathbun, Brian C. 2008. A Rose by Any Other Name: Neoclassical Realism as the Logical and Necessary Extension of Structural Realism. *Security Studies* 17(2): 294–321.

2011. The "Magnificent Fraud": Trust, International Cooperation, and the Hidden Domestic Politics of American Multilateralism after World War II. *International Studies Quarterly* 55(1): 1–21.

2012. *Trust in International Cooperation: International Security Institutions, Domestic Politics and American Multilateralism*. Cambridge, UK: Cambridge University Press.

Reagan, Ronald W. 1990. *An American Life*. New York: Simon & Schuster.

Reichard, Gary W. 1975. *The Reaffirmation of Republicanism: Eisenhower and the Eighty-Third Congress*. Knoxville, TN: University of Tennessee Press.

Reinhard, David W. 1983. *The Republican Right since 1945*. Lexington, KY: University Press of Kentucky.

Reiter, Dan. 1996. *Crucible of Beliefs: Learning, Alliances, and World Wars*. Ithaca, NY: Cornell University Press.

2012. Democracy, Deception, and Entry into War. *Security Studies* 21(4): 594–623.

Reus-Smit, Christian. 2001. The Strange Death of Liberal International Relations Theory. *European Journal of International Law* 12(3): 573–593.

Rich, Frank. 2006. *The Greatest Story Ever Sold: The Decline and Fall of Truth in Bush's America*. New York: Penguin.

Ricks, Thomas E. 2006. *Fiasco: The American Military Adventure in Iraq, 2003 to 2005*. New York: Penguin.

2009. *The Gamble: General David Petraeus and the American Military Adventure in Iraq, 2006–2008*. New York: Penguin.

Ricoeur, Paul. 1984–1988. *Time and Narrative*. Chicago, IL: University of Chicago Press.

Riker, William H. 1986. *The Art of Political Manipulation*. New Haven, CT: Yale University Press.

1996. *The Strategy of Rhetoric: Campaigning for the American Constitution*. New Haven, CT: Yale University Press.

Ringmar, Erik. 1996. *Identity, Interest and Action: A Cultural Explanation of Sweden's Intervention in the Thirty Years War*. Cambridge University Press.

Risse, Thomas. 2000. "Let's Argue!": Communicative Action in World Politics. *International Organization* 54(1): 1–39.

Ritchie, Donald A. 2003. Advice and Dissent: Mike Mansfield and the Vietnam War, in *Vietnam and the American Political Tradition: The Politics of Dissent*, edited by Randall B. Woods. Cambridge, UK: Cambridge University Press, pp. 171–204.

Ritter, Kurt and David Henry. 1992. *Ronald Reagan: The Great Communicator*. New York: Greenwood Press.

Rodgers, Daniel T. 2011. *Age of Fracture*. Cambridge, MA: Harvard University Press.

Roe, Emery. 1994. *Narrative Policy Analysis: Theory and Practice*. Durham, NC: Duke University Press.

Rose, Norman. 1978. *Vansittart: Study of a Diplomat*. London: Heinemann.

Rosen, Stephen Peter. 1991. *Winning the Next War: Innovation and the Modern Military*. Ithaca, NY: Cornell University Press.

Rosenau, James N. 1963. *National Leadership and Foreign Policy: A Case Study in the Mobilization of Public Support*. Princeton, NJ: Princeton University Press.

Rosenman, Samuel I. (ed.) 1950. *The Public Papers and Addresses of Franklin D. Roosevelt: Humanity on the Defensive (1942)*, vol. 11. New York: Harper & Brothers.

1952. *Working with Roosevelt*. New York: Harper & Brothers.

Rossiter, Clinton. 1956. *The American Presidency*. New York: Harcourt, Brace.

Rothbard, Murray N. 2007. *The Betrayal of the American Right*. Auburn, AL: Ludwig von Mises Institute.

Rottinghaus, Brandon. 2010. *The Provisional Pulpit: Modern Presidential Leadership of Public Opinion*. College Station, TX: Texas A&M University Press.

Rushing, Janice Hocker. 1986. Ronald Reagan's "Star Wars" Address: Mythic Containment of Technical Reasoning. *Quarterly Journal of Speech* 72(4): 415–433.

Russett, Bruce M. 1972. *No Clear and Present Danger: A Skeptical View of the United States Entry into World War II*. New York: Harper & Row.

Russett, Bruce M. and Elizabeth C. Hanson. 1975. *Interest and Ideology: The Foreign Policy Beliefs of American Businessmen*. San Francisco, CA: W. H. Freeman.

Ryan, Halford R. 1988. *Franklin D. Roosevelt's Rhetorical Presidency*. New York: Greenwood Press.

Ryan, Marie-Laure. 2007. Toward a Definition of Narrative, in *The Cambridge Companion to Narrative*, edited by David Herman. Cambridge University Press, pp. 22–35.

Ryfe, David Michael. 2005. *Presidents in Culture: The Meaning of Presidential Communication*. New York: Peter Lang.

Saad, Lydia. 2001. *Americans Clearly Support a Military Response to Terrorist Assault*. Washington, DC: Gallup, Inc.

Saldin, Robert P. 2010. *War, the American State, and Politics since 1898*. Cambridge, UK: Cambridge University Press.

Samuels, Richard J. 2007. *Securing Japan: Tokyo's Grand Strategy and the Future of East Asia*. Ithaca, NY: Cornell University Press.

Sarles, Ruth. 2003. *A Story of America First: The Men and Women Who Opposed U.S. Intervention in World War II*. Westport, CT: Praeger.

Sawyer, R. Keith. 2001. *Creating Conversations: Improvisation in Everyday Discourse*. Cresskill, NJ: Hampton Press.

Scanlon, Sandra. 2009. The Conservative Lobby and Nixon's "Peace with Honor" in Vietnam. *Journal of American Studies* 43(2): 255–276.

Schank, Roger C. and Robert P. Abelson. 1995. Knowledge and Memory: The Real Story, in *Advances in Social Cognition*, vol. 8, edited by Robert S. Wyer Jr.. Hillsdale, OR: Lawrence Erlbaum, pp. 1–85.

Schank, Roger C. and Tamara R. Berman. 2002. The Pervasive Role of Stories in Knowledge and Action, in *Narrative Impact: Social and Cognitive Foundations*, edited by Melanie C. Greem, Jeffrey J. Strange, and Timothy C. Brock. Mahwah, NJ: Lawrence Erlbaum, pp. 287–314.

Schimmelfenig, Frank. 2001. The Community Trap: Liberal Norms, Rhetorical Action, and the Eastern Enlargement of the European Union. *International Organization* 55(1): 47–80.

Schlesinger Jr., Arthur M. 1958. *The Coming of the New Deal*. Boston, MA: Houghton Mifflin.

1992. *The Disuniting of America*. New York: W. W. Norton.

Schlozman, Kay Lehman, Sidney Verba, and Henry E. Brady. 2010. Weapon of the Strong? Participatory Inequality and the Internet. *Perspectives on Politics* 8(2): 487–509.

Schmitz, David F. 2001. *Henry L. Stimson: The First Wise Man*. Wilmington, DE: SR Books.

2003. Congress Must Draw the Line: Senator Frank Church and Opposition to the Vietnam War and the Imperial Presidency, in *Vietnam and the American Political Tradition: The Politics of Dissent*, edited by Randall B. Woods. Cambridge, UK: Cambridge University Press, pp. 121–148.

2006. *The United States and Right-Wing Dictatorships, 1965–1989*. Cambridge, UK: Cambridge University Press.

Schmitz, David F. and Natalie Fousekis. 1994. Frank Church, the Senate, and the Emergence of Dissent on the Vietnam War. *Pacific Historical Review* 63(4): 561–581.

Schneider, Gregory L. 2009. *The Conservative Century: From Reaction to Revolution.* Lanham, MD: Rowman & Littlefield.

Schneider, James C. 1989. *Should America Go to War? The Debate over Foreign Policy in Chicago, 1939–1941.* Chapel Hill, NC: University of North Carolina Press.

Scholes, Robert. 1980. Language, Narrative, and Anti-Narrative, in *On Narrative*, edited by W. J. T. Mitchell. Chicago, IL: University of Chicago Press, pp. 200–208.

Schrecker, Ellen. 1998. *Many are the Crimes: McCarthyism in America.* Boston, MA: Little, Brown.

Schroeder, Michael J. 2005. Bandits and Blanket Thieves, Communists, and Terrorists: The Politics of Naming Sandinistas in Nicaragua, 1927–36 and 1979–90. *Third World Quarterly* 26(1): 67–86.

Schudson, Michael. 2002. What's Unusual about Covering Politics as Usual, in *Journalism After September 11*, edited by Barbie Zelizer and Stuart Allan. London: Routledge, pp. 44–55.

Schuessler, John M. 2010. The Deception Dividend: FDR's Undeclared War. *International Security* 34(4): 133–165.

Schulzinger, Robert D. 1997. *A Time for War: The United States and Vietnam, 1941–1975.* New York: Oxford University Press.

2010. Détente in the Nixon–Ford years, 1969–1976, in *The Cambridge History of the Cold War*, vol. 2: *Crises and Détente*, edited by Melvyn P. Leffler and Odd Arne Westad. Cambridge, UK: Cambridge University Press, pp. 373–395.

Schweller, Randall L. 2006. *Unanswered Threats: Political Constraints on the Balance of Power.* Princeton University Press.

Scott, James C. 1985. *Weapons of the Weak: Everyday Forms of Peasant Resistance.* New Haven, CT: Yale University Press.

1990. *Domination and the Arts of Resistance: Hidden Transcripts.* New Haven, CT: Yale University Press.

Scott, James M. 1996. *Deciding to Intervene: The Reagan Doctrine and American Foreign Policy.* Durham, NC: Duke University Press.

Scraton, Phil (ed.). 2002. *Beyond September 11: An Anthology of Dissent.* London: Pluto Press.

See, Jennifer W. 2001. A Prophet without Honor: Hans Morgenthau and the War in Vietnam, 1955–1965. *Pacific Historical Review* 70(3): 419–447.

2002. An Uneasy Truce: John F. Kennedy and Soviet-American Détente, 1963. *Cold War History* 2(2): 161–194.

Selverstone, Marc J. 2009. *Constructing the Monolith: The United States, Great Britain, and International Commmunism, 1945–1950.* Cambridge, MA: Harvard University Press.

Senn, Martin and Christoph Elhardt. 2014. Bourdieu and the Bomb: Power, Language and the Doxic Battle over the Value of Nuclear Weapons. *European Journal of International Relations* 20(2): 316–340.

Sewell Jr., William H. 1996. Historical Events as Transformations of Structures: Inventing Revolution at the Bastille. *Theory and Society* 25(6): 841–881.

Seyranian, Viviane and Michelle C. Bligh. 2008. Presidential Charismatic Leadership: Exploring the Rhetoric of Social Change. *Leadership Quarterly* 19(1): 54–76.

Shamir, Boas, Michael B. Arthur, and Robert J. House. 1994. The Rhetoric of Charismatic Leadership: A Theoretical Extension, A Case Study, and Implications for Research. *Leadership Quarterly* 5(1): 25–42.

Shanahan, Elizabeth A., Michael D. Jones, and Mark K. McBeth. 2011. Policy Narratives and Policy Processes. *Policy Studies Journal* 39(3): 535–561.

Shanahan, Elizabeth A., Mark K. McBeth, and Paul L. Hathaway. 2011. Narrative Policy Framework: The Influence of Media Policy Narratives on Public Opinion. *Politics & Policy* 39(3): 373–400.

Shapiro, Michael J. 1981. *Language and Political Understanding: The Politics of Discursive Practices.* New Haven, CT: Yale University Press.

Shenhav, Shaul. 2005. Thin and Thick Narrative Analysis: On the Question of Defining and Analyzing Political Narratives. *Narrative Inquiry* 15(1): 75–99.

2006. Political Narratives and Political Reality. *International Political Science Review* 27(3): 245–262.

Sherry, Michael S. 1997. *In the Shadow of War: The United States since the 1930s.* New Haven, CT: Yale University Press.

Shulman, Marshall. 1973. Toward a Western Philosophy of Coexistence. *Foreign Affairs* 52(1): 35–58.

Silberstein, Laurence J. 1999. *The Postzionism Debates: Knowledge and Power in Israeli Culture.* New York: Routledge.

Silberstein, Sandra. 2004. *War of Words: Language, Politics and 9/11.* London: Routledge.

Simon, Dennis M. 2009. Public Expectations of the President, in *The Oxford Handbook of the American Presidency*, edited by George C. Edwards III and William G. Howell. Oxford, UK: Oxford University Press, pp. 135–159.

Singer, Peter. 2004. *The President of Good & Evil: The Ethics of George W. Bush.* New York: Dutton.

Skocpol, Theda, Ziad Munson, Andrew Karch, and Bayliss Camp 2002. Patriotic Partnerships: Why Great Wars Nourished American Civic Voluntarism, in *Shaped by War and Trade: International Influences on American Political Development*, edited by Ira Katznelson and Martin Shefter. Princeton, NJ: Princeton University Press, pp. 134–180.

Skowronek, Stephen. 1997. *The Politics Presidents Make: Leadership from John Adams to Bill Clinton*. Cambridge, MA: Belknap Press of Harvard University Press.

2008. *Presidential Leadership in Political Time: Reprise and Reappraisal*. Lawrence, KS: University Press of Kansas.

Smith, Barbara Herrnstein. 1981. Narrative Versions, Narrative Theories, in *On Narrative*, edited by W. J. T. Mitchell. Chicago, IL: University of Chicago Press, pp. 209–232.

Smith, Christian. 1996. *Resisting Reagan: The U.S. Central America Peace Movement*. Chicago, IL: University of Chicago Press.

Smith, Craig Allen. 2005a. President Bush's Enthymeme of Evil: The Amalgamation of 9/11, Iraq, and Moral Values. *American Behavioral Scientist* 49(1): 32–47.

Smith, Gaddis. 1986. *Morality, Reason, and Power: American Diplomacy in the Carter Years*. New York: Hill & Wang.

Smith, Geoffrey S. 1973. *To Save a Nation: American Countersubversives, the New Deal, and the Coming of World War II*. New York: Basic Books.

Smith, Jean Edward. 2007a. *FDR*. New York: Random House.

Smith, Mark A. 2007b. *The Right Talk: How Conservatives Transformed the Great Society into the Economic Society*. Princeton, NJ: Princeton University Press.

Smith, Philip. 2005b. *Why War? The Cultural Logic of Iraq, the Gulf War, and Suez*. Chicago, IL: University of Chicago Press.

Smith, Wayne S. 1987. Lies About Nicaragua. *Foreign Policy* 67: 87–103.

Snyder, Jack L. and Karen Ballentine. 1996. Nationalism and the Marketplace of Ideas. *International Security* 21(2): 5–40.

Snyder, Jack L. 1991. *Myths of Empire: Domestic Politics and International Ambition*. Ithaca, NY: Cornell University Press.

2015. Dueling Security Stories: Wilson and Lodge Talk Strategy. *Security Studies* 24(1): 171–197.

Sobel, Richard. 1993. Public Opinion about U.S. Intervention in Nicaragua, in *Public Opinion in U.S. Foreign Policy: The Controversy over Contra Aid*, edited by Richard Sobel. Lanham, MD: Rowman & Littlefield, pp. 49–58.

2001. *The Impact of Public Opinion on U.S. Foreign Policy since Vietnam*. New York: Oxford University Press.

Soifer, Hillel David. 2012. The Causal Logic of Critical Junctures. *Comparative Political Studies* 45(12): 1572–1597.

Somers, Margaret R. and Gloria D. Gibson. 1994. Reclaiming the Epistemological "Other": Narrative and the Social Construction of Identity, in *Social Theory and the Politics of Identity*, edited by Craig Calhoun. Oxford: Blackwell, pp. 37–99.

Somit, Albert and Steven Peterson. 1992. *The Dynamics of Evolution: The Punctuated Equilibrium Debate in the Natural and Social Sciences.* Ithaca, NY: Cornell University Press.

Sorensen, Theodore C. 1965. *Kennedy.* New York: Harper & Row.

Sorrentino, Richard M. and Christopher J. R. Roney. 2000. *The Uncertain Mind: Individual Differences in Facing the Unknown.* Philadelphia, PA: Psychology Press.

Sperber, Dan. 1990. The Epidemiology of Beliefs, in *The Social Psychological Study of Widespread Beliefs*, edited by Colin Fraser and George Gaskell. New York: Clarendon Press/Oxford University Press, pp. 25–44.

Spiegel, Steven L. 1985. *The Other Arab-Israeli Conflict: Making America's Middle East Policy, from Truman to Reagan.* Chicago, IL: University of Chicago Press.

Squires, James D. 1993. *Read All About It! The Corporate Takeover of America's Newspapers.* New York: Times Books.

Steel, Ronald. 1980. *Walter Lippmann and the American Century.* Boston, MA: Little, Brown.

Steele, Brent J. 2010. *Defacing Power: The Aesthetics of Insecurity in Global Politics.* Ann Arbor, MI: University of Michigan Press.

Steele, Richard W. 1973. *The First Offensive, 1942: Roosevelt, Marshall, and the Making of American Strategy.* Bloomington, IN: Indiana University Press.

 1974. The Pulse of the People: Franklin D. Roosevelt and the Gauging of American Public Opinion. *Journal of Contemporary History* 9(4): 195–216.

 1979. Franklin D. Roosevelt and his Foreign Policy Critics. *Political Science Quarterly* 94(1): 15–32.

 1984. The Great Debate: Roosevelt, the Media, and the Coming of the War, 1940–1941. *Journal of American History* 71(1): 69–92.

 1985. *Propaganda in an Open Society: The Roosevelt Administration and the Media, 1933–1941.* Westport, CT: Greenwood Press.

Stemler, Steven E. and Jessica Tsai. 2008. Best Practices in Interrater Reliability: Three Common Approaches, in *Best Practices in Quantitative Methods*, edited by Jason Osborne. Thousand Oaks, CA: Sage, pp. 29–49.

Stern, J. P. 1978. Nietzsche and the Idea of Metaphor, in *Nietzsche: Imagery and Thought*, edited by Malcolm Pasley. Berkeley, CA: University of California Press, pp. 64–82.

Stiglitz, Joseph E. and Linda J. Bilmes. 2008. *The Three Trillion Dollar War: The True Cost of the Iraq Conflict*. New York: W. W. Norton.

Stinchcombe, Arthur. 1965. Social Structure and Organizations, in *Handbook of Organizations*, edited by James G. March. Chicago, IL: Rand-McNally, pp. 142–193.

Stoler, Mark A. 2000. *Allies and Adversaries: The Joint Chiefs of Staff, the Grand Alliance, and U.S. Strategy in World War II*. Chapel Hill, NC: University of North Carolina Press.

Stoll, David. 2005. The Nicaraguan Contras: Were They Indios? *Latin American Politics and Society* 47(3): 145–157.

Stone, Lawrence. 1979. The Revival of Narrative: Reflections on a New Old History. *Past and Present* 85(1): 3–24.

Stone, Peter and Sherman Edwards. 1976 [1970]. *1776*. New York: Penguin Books.

Storrs, K. Larry and Nina Serafino. 1993. The Reagan Administration's Efforts to Gain Public Support for Contra Aid, in *Public Opinion in U.S. Foreign Policy: The Controversy over Contra Aid*, edited by Richard Sobel. Lanham, MD: Rowman & Littlefield, pp. 123–150.

Stritzel, Holger. 2007. Towards a Theory of Securitization: Copenhagen and Beyond. *European Journal of International Relations* 13(3): 357–383.

Strömbom, Lisa. 2014. Thick Recognition: Advancing Theory on Identity Change in Intractable Conflicts. *European Journal of International Relations* 20(1): 168–191.

Stromer, Marvin E. 1969. *The Making of a Political Leader: Kenneth S. Wherry and the United States Senate*. Lincoln, NE: University of Nebraska Press.

Stroud, Natalie Jomini. 2011. *Niche News: The Politics of News Choice*. New York: Oxford University Press.

Stuckey, Mary E. 1990. *Playing the Game: The Presidential Rhetoric of Ronald Reagan*. Westport, CT: Praeger.

1991. *The President as Interpreter-in-Chief*. Chatham, NJ: Chatham House.

2004. *Defining Americans: The Presidency and National Identity*. Lawrence, KS: University Press of Kansas.

Stueck, William. 1995. *The Korean War: An International History*. Princeton, NJ: Princeton University Press.

Suchman, Mark C. 1995. Managing Legitimacy: Strategic and Institutional Approaches. *The Academy of Management Review* 20(3): 571–610.

Suganami, Hidemi. 1996. *On the Causes of War*. Oxford: Clarendon Press.

1997a. Narratives of War Origins and Endings: A Note on the End of the Cold War. *Millennium* 26(3): 631–649.

1997b. Stories of War Origins: A Narrativist Theory of the Causes of War. *Review of International Studies* 23(4): 401–418.

1999. Agents, Structures, Narratives. *European Journal of International Relations* 5(3): 365–386.

Sunstein, Cass R. 2001. *Republic.com*. Princeton, NJ: Princeton University Press.

Suri, Jeremi. 2003. *Power and Protest: Global Revolution and the Rise of Détente*. Cambridge, MA: Harvard University Press.

2008. Détente and its Discontents, in *Rightward Bound: Making America Conservative in the 1970s*, edited by Bruce J. Schulman and Julian E. Zelizer. Cambridge, MA: Harvard University Press, pp. 227–245.

Swidler, Ann. 1986. Culture in Action: Symbols and Stategies. *American Sociological Review* 51(2): 273–286.

Talese, Gay. 1970. *The Kingdom and the Power*. New York: Bantam Books.

Taliaferro, Jeffrey W., Steven E. Lobell, and Norrin M. Ripsman. 2009. Introduction, in *Neoclassical Realism, the State, and Foreign Policy*, edited by Steven E. Lobell, Norrin Ripsman, and Jeffrey Taliaferro. Cambridge University Press, pp. 1–41.

Tananbaum, Duane. 1988. *The Bricker Amendment Controversy: A Test of Eisenhower's Political Leadership*. Ithaca, NY: Cornell University Press.

Tannenwald, Nina. 2007. *The Nuclear Taboo: The United States and the Non-Use of Nuclear Weapons since 1945*. Cambridge University Press.

Tarrow, Sidney. 1998. *Power in Movement: Social Movements and Contentious Politics*, 2nd edn. New York: Cambridge University Press.

Taylor, A. J. P. 1955. *Bismarck: The Man and the Statesman*. New York: Knopf.

Tetlock, Philip E. and Aaron Belkin (eds.). 1996. *Counterfactual Thought Experiments in World Politics: Logical, Methodological, and Psychological Perspectives*. Princeton, NJ: Princeton University Press.

Theiss-Morse, Elizabeth. 2009. *Who Counts as an American? The Boundaries of National Identity*. Cambridge, UK: Cambridge University Press.

Theoharis, Athan G. 1970. *The Yalta Myths: An Issue in U.S. Politics, 1945–1955*. Columbia, MO: University of Missouri Press.

1971. *Seeds of Repression: Harry S. Truman and the Origins of McCarthyism*. Chicago, IL: Quadrangle Books.

Tickner, J. Ann. 2001. *Gendering World Politics: Issues and Approaches in the Post-Cold War Era*. New York: Columbia University Press.

Tifft, Susan E. and Alex S. Jones. 1999. *The Trust: The Private and Powerful Family behind the New York Times*. Boston, MA: Little, Brown.

Tilly, Charles. 1998. International Communities, Secure or Otherwise, in *Security Communities*, edited by Emanuel Adler and Michael Barnett. Cambridge University Press, pp. 397–413.

Tjalve, Vibeke Schou and Michael C. Williams. 2015. Reviving the Rhetoric of Realism: Politics and Ethics in Grand Strategy. *Security Studies* 24(1): 37–60.

Too, Yun Lee. 2001. Epideictic Genre, in *Encyclopedia of Rhetoric*, edited by Thomas O. Sloane. Oxford University Press, pp. 251–257.

Torfing, Jacob. 2005. Discourse Theory: Achievements, Arguments, and Challenges, in *Discourse Theory in European Politics: Identity, Policy, and Governance*, edited by David Howarth and Jacob Torfing. Houndmills, Basingstoke: Palgrave Macmillan, pp. 1–31.

Trachtenberg, Marc. 1999. *A Constructed Peace: The Making of the European Settlement, 1945–1963*. Princeton, NJ: Princeton University Press.

2006. *The Craft of International History: A Guide to Method*. Princeton, NJ: Princeton University Press.

Trout, B. Thomas. 1975. Rhetoric Revisited: Political Legitimation and the Cold War. *International Studies Quarterly* 19(3): 251–284.

Trubowitz, Peter. 1998. *Defining the National Interest: Conflict and Change in American Foreign Policy*. Chicago, IL: University of Chicago Press.

2011. *Politics and Strategy: Partisan Ambition and American Statecraft*. Princeton, NJ: Princeton University Press.

Tucker, Robert W. 1988/1989. Reagan's Foreign Policy. *Foreign Affairs* 67(2): 1–27.

Tucker, Robert W. and David C. Hendrickson. 1992. *The Imperial Temptation: The New World Order and America's Purpose*. New York: New York University Press.

Tulis, Jeffrey K. 1987. *The Rhetorical Presidency*. Princeton, NJ: Princeton University Press.

Turiel, Elliot. 2002. *The Culture of Morality: Social Development, Context, and Conflict*. Cambridge University Press.

2015. Moral Development, in *Handbook of Child Psychology and Developmental Science*, vol. 1: *Theory and Method*, edited by Richard M. Lerner, Willis F. Overton, and Peter C. M. Molenaar. Hoboken, NJ: Wiley, chapter 13.

Turner, Victor. 1980. Social Dramas and Stories about Them. *Critical Inquiry* 7(1): 141–168.

Uebersax, John. 2013. Statistical Methods for Rater and Diagnostic Agreement. Available at www.john-uebersax.com/stat/agree.htm.

United States Senate, Committee on Foreign Relations. 1966. *The Vietnam Hearings*. New York: Random House.

United States, Office of War Information. 1942–1944. *American Attitudes toward World War II.* London and New York: Hutchinson & Co.

Vaïsse, Justin. 2010. *Neoconservatism: The Biography of a Movement.* Translated by Arthur Goldhammer. Cambridge, MA: Harvard University Press.

van Oudenaren, John. 1982. *U.S. Leadership Perceptions of the Soviet Problem Since 1945.* Santa Monica, CA: RAND.

Vanden Heuvel, Katrina (ed.). 2002. *A Just Response: The Nation on Terrorism, Democracy, and September 11, 2001.* New York: Thunder's Mouth Press/Nation Books.

Wagner, R. Harrison. 1993. What was Bipolarity? *International Organization* 47(1): 77–106.

Wagner, Wolfgang and Nicky Hayes. 2005. *Everyday Discourse and Common Sense: The Theory of Social Representations.* New York: Palgrave Macmillan.

Walter, Jochen and Jan Helmig. 2008. Discursive Metaphor Analysis: (De)construction(s) of Europe, in *Political Language and Metaphor: Interpreting and Changing the World*, edited by Terrell Carver and Jernej Pikalo. London: Routledge, pp. 119–131.

Wander, Philip. 1984. The Rhetoric of American Foreign Policy. *Quarterly Journal of Speech* 70(4): 339–361.

Wattenberg, Ben J. 1974. *The Real America: A Surprising Examination of the State of the Union.* Garden City, NY: Doubleday.

Weber, Katja and Paul A. Kowert. 2007. *Cultures of Order: Leadership, Language, and Social Reconstruction in Germany and Japan.* Albany, NY: State University of New York Press.

Webster, Donna M. and Arie W. Kruglanski. 1994. Individual Differences in Need for Cognitive Closure. *Journal of Personality and Social Psychology* 67(6): 1049–1062.

Wedeen, Lisa. 1999. *Ambiguities of Domination: Politics, Rhetoric, and Symbols in Contemporary Syria.* University of Chicago Press.

Wedeking, Justin. 2010. Supreme Court Litigants and Strategic Framing. *American Journal of Political Science* 54(3): 617–631.

Weisbrot, Robert. 2001. *Maximum Danger: Kennedy, the Missiles, and the Crisis of American Confidence.* Chicago, IL: Ivan R. Dee.

Weisiger, Alex. 2013. *Logics of War: Explanations for Limited and Unlimited Conflicts.* Ithaca, NY: Cornell University Press.

Welch, David A. 2005. *Painful Choices: A Theory of Foreign Policy Change.* Princeton, NJ: Princeton University Press.

Welch, William. 1970. *American Images of Soviet Foreign Policy: An Inquiry into Recent Appraisals from the Academic Community.* New Haven, CT: Yale University Press.

Weldes, Jutta. 1999. *Constructing National Interests: The United States and the Cuban Missile Crisis*. Minneapolis, MN: University of Minnesota Press.

Welles, Benjamin. 1997. *Sumner Welles: FDR's Global Strategist*. New York: St. Martin's Press.

Welles, Sumner. 1944. *The Time for Decision*. New York: Harper & Brothers. 1951. *Seven Decisions that Shaped History*. New York: Harper & Brothers.

Wendt, Lloyd. 1979. *Chicago Tribune: The Rise of a Great American Newspaper*. Chicago, IL: Rand McNally.

West, Mark D. (ed.). 2001. *Theory, Method, and Practice in Computer Content Analysis*. Westport, CT: Ablex.

Westbrook, Robert B. 2004. *Why We Fought: Forging American Obligations in World War II*. Washington, DC: Smithsonian Books.

Westerfield, H. Bradford. 1955. *Foreign Policy and Party Politics: Pearl Harbor to Korea*. New Haven, CT: Yale University Press.

Western, Jon. 2005. *Selling Intervention and War: The Presidency, the Media, and the American Public*. Baltimore, MD: The Johns Hopkins University Press.

White, Hayden. 1981. The Value of Narrativity, in *On Narrative*, edited by W. J. T. Mitchell. Chicago, IL: University of Chicago Press, pp. 1–23. 1987. *The Content of the Form: Narrative Discourse and Historical Representation*. Baltimore, MD: The Johns Hopkins University Press.

Widmaier, Wesley W. 2007. Constructing Foreign Policy Crises: Interpretive Leadership in the Cold War and War on Terrorism. *International Studies Quarterly* 51(4): 779–794.

Widmaier, Wesley W., Mark Blyth, and Leonard Seabrooke. 2007. Exogenous Shocks or Endogenous Constructions? The Meanings of Wars and Crises. *International Studies Quarterly* 51(4): 747–759.

Wildavsky, Aaron. 1966. The Two Presidencies. *Trans-Action* 4(2): 7–14. 1987. Choosing Preferences by Constructing Institutions: A Cultural Theory of Preference Formation. *American Political Science Review* 81(1): 3–22.

Wilentz, Sean. 2008. *The Age of Reagan: A History, 1974–2008*. New York: HarperCollins.

Williams, Bruce A. and Michael X. Delli Carpini. 2011. *After Broadcast News: Media Regimes, Democracy, and the New Information Environment*. New York: Cambridge University Press.

Williams, Michael C. 2007. *Culture and Security: Symbolic Power and the Politics of International Security*. Oxford: Routledge.

Williams, Raymond. 1977. *Marxism and Literature*. Oxford University Press.

Williamson, D. G. 2001. *Germany From Defeat to Partition, 1945–1963*. Harlow, UK: Pearson Education.

Winfield, Betty Houchin. 1990. *FDR and the News Media*. Urbana, IL: University of Illinois Press.

Winkler, Allan M. 1978. *The Politics of Propaganda: The Office of War Information, 1942–1945*. New Haven, CT: Yale University Press.

Winkler, Carol K. 2005. *In the Name of Terrorism: Presidents on Political Violence in the Post-World War II Era*. Albany, NY: State University of New York Press.

Wittkopf, Eugene R. 1986. On the Foreign Policy Beliefs of the American People: A Critique and Some Evidence. *International Studies Quarterly* 30(4): 425–445.

   1987. Elites and Masses: Another Look at Attitudes toward America's World Role. *International Studies Quarterly* 31(2): 131–159.

   1990. *Faces of Internationalism: Public Opinion and American Foreign Policy*. Durham, NC: Duke University Press.

Wittkopf, Eugene R. and Michael A. Maggiotto. 1983. The Two Faces of Internationalism: Public Attitudes toward American Foreign Policy in the 1970s – and Beyond? *Social Science Quarterly* 64(2): 288–304.

Wittkopf, Eugene R. and James M. McCormick. 1990. The Cold War Consensus: Did It Exist? *Polity* 22(4): 627–653.

Wolfe, Alan. 1979. *The Rise and Fall of the "Soviet Threat": Domestic Sources of the Cold War Consensus*. Washington, DC: Institute for Policy Studies.

Wolfers, Arnold. 1962. *Discord and Collaboration*. Baltimore, MD: Johns Hopkins University Press.

Wood, B. Dan. 2007. *The Politics of Economic Leadership: The Causes and Consequences of Presidential Rhetoric*. Princeton, NJ: Princeton University Press.

   2009a. Presidents and the Political Agenda, in *The Oxford Handbook of the American Presidency*, edited by George C. Edwards III and William G. Howell. Oxford University Press, pp. 108–132.

   2009b. *The Myth of Presidential Representation*. Cambridge, UK: Cambridge University Press.

Wood, B. Dan, and Arnold Vedlitz. 2007. Issue Definition, Information Processing, and the Politics of Global Warming. *American Journal of Political Science* 51(3): 552–568.

Woods, Randall Bennett. 1995. *Fulbright: A Biography*. Cambridge, UK: Cambridge University Press.

Woodward, Bob. 2003. *Bush at War*. New York: Simon & Schuster.

   2008. *The War Within: A Secret White House History, 2006–2008*. New York: Simon & Schuster.

Wunderlin, Clarence E. 2005. *Robert A. Taft: Ideas, Tradition, and Party in U.S. Foreign Policy*. Lanham, MD: Rowman & Littlefield.

2006. *The Papers of Robert A. Taft*, vol. 4: *(1949–1953)*. Kent, OH: Kent State University Press.

Yergin, Daniel. 1977. *Shattered Peace: The Origins of the Cold War and the National Security State*. Boston, MA: Houghton Mifflin.

Zagoria, Donald S. 1962. *The Sino-Soviet Conflict, 1956–1961*. Princeton, NJ: Princeton University Press.

Zakaria, Fareed. 1990. The Reagan Strategy of Containment. *Political Science Quarterly* 105(3): 373–395.

Zaller, John. 1992. *The Nature and Origins of Mass Opinion*. Cambridge, UK: Cambridge University Press.

1994. Strategic Politicians, Public Opinion, and the Gulf Crisis, in *Taken By Storm: The Media, Public Opinion, and U.S. Foreign Policy in the Gulf War*, edited by W. Lance Bennett and David L. Paletz. Chicago, IL: University of Chicago Press, pp. 250–274.

Zaller, John and Dennis Chiu. 1996. Government's Little Helper: U.S. Press Coverage of Foreign Policy Crises, 1945–1991. *Political Communication* 13(4): 385–405.

Zarefsky, David. 2009. History of Public Discourse Studies, in *The Sage Handbook of Rhetorical Studies*, edited by Andrea A. Lunsford. Los Angeles, CA: Sage, pp. 433–459.

Zaretsky, Natasha. 2011. Restraint or Retreat? The Debate over the Panama Canal Treaties and U.S. Nationalism after Vietnam. *Diplomatic History* 35(3): 535–562.

Zehfuss, Maja. 2007. *Wounds of Memory: The Politics of War in Germany*. Cambridge University Press.

Zelizer, Julian E. 2010. *Arsenal of Democracy: The Politics of National Security from World War II to the War on Terrorism*. New York: Basic Books.

Ziemke, Earl F. 1984. Improvising Stability and Change in Postwar Germany, in *Americans as Proconsuls: United States Military Government in Germany and Japan, 1944–1952*, edited by Robert Wolfe. Carbondale, IL: Southern Illinois University Press, pp. 52–66.

Index

Abrams, Elliott, 109–114
accommodationism, 220–225
Acheson, Dean, 40n.38, 225–233
action
  alternative narratives concerning
    September 11 and, 158–163
  in dominant narratives, 14–16
  erosion of non-interventionist
    narrative in face of, 75–83
  in national security narratives, 12–13
  in Terror narrative, 150–157
Afghanistan
  Soviet invasion of, 111–114, 265–269
  War on Terror and, 32–36, 269–275
agents and agency. *See also* authority;
    dramatic pentad
  in alternative narratives of September
    11, 161–163
  dynamics of contestation and, 41–48
  erosion of non-interventionist
    narrative in face of, 75–83
  narrative dominance and role of, 1–7
  in national security narratives, 7–16,
    276–279
  in Pearl Harbor narrative, 124–133,
    142–145
  in Reagan's Cold War rhetoric,
    119–121
  rhetorical skill as, 32–41
  Roosevelt's national security
    narrative and, 70–75
  in Terror narrative, 150–157
  United States hegemony and,
    148–149
age of fracture, national security
    narrative and, 276–279, 284–285
Alexander, Jeffrey, 14–16
Algeria, French policy failures in,
    265–269

Al Qaeda
  Iraq linked to, 32–36, 163–172
  responsibility for September 11
    attacks claimed by, 158–163
  Terror narrative and, 269–275,
    279–282
alternative narratives, 46–47
  to Cold War Consensus, 191–195
  dominant narrative marginalization
    of, 32–36, 46–47
  military success as advantage for,
    187–189
  nationalist narrative on Korean War,
    220–233,
  politics of national security and,
    183–189
  Reagan's Cold War narrative and,
    114–119
  rhetorical coercion concerning Iraq
    war and, 168–172
  to Roosevelt's Pearl Harbor
    narrative, 133–145,
  security narratives and, 22–24
  to Terror narrative, 158–163
America First Committee, 75–88,
American exceptionalism
  national security narrative and,
    13–14, 35–36
  post-Vietnam emergence of, 257–264
anti-war movement (Vietnam War)
  cautious rhetoric of, 251–257
  criticism of Vietnam War in,
    248–249
  delegitimation of, 245–246
argument. *See also* instrumental argu-
    ment; normative argument
  national security narratives and,
    279–285
  presidents' misuse of, 66–68

370

as rhetorical mode, 36–41
in Roosevelt's rhetoric, 79–83
Aristotle, 7–8, 31–32
Armitage, Richard, 148–149
arms control policy, 246–251
Aron, Raymond, 191–195
The Arrogance of Empire (Fulbright),
255–257
"Arsenal of Democracy" speech, 79–83
Ashcroft, John, 148–149
Atlantic Charter, 79–83
audience
legitimation of security narrative and,
14–16
response to security narrative and,
58–65
Austin, J. L., 22–24
authenticity
legitimation of security narrative and,
14–16
in Terror narrative, 161–163
authority. *See also* agents and agency
dominant narrative and, 25–26,
48–52
fragmentation of, 284–285
national security narratives and, 5–7,
31–32, 52–55, 279–282
in Roosevelt's Pearl Harbor
narrative, 133–142

Bacevich, Andrew, 269–275
Barthes, Roland, 8–9, 52–55
Basic National Security Policy (1962
draft), 236–245
battlefield performance. *See also* war
outcomes
Cold War consensus and, 219–220
erosion of dominant narrative and,
176–179
Korean War and, 225–233
politics of failure and, 179–183,
185–186, 225–233, 265–269
politics of national security narratives
and, 183–189, 282–285
success as support for narrative,
187–189
Bay of Pigs operation, 236–245
Berger, Thomas, 179–183
Berinsky, Adam, 91–96
Berlin, Isaiah, 138–142

Berlin Wall, as historical rupture,
148–149
Beschloss, Michael, 241–242
Betts, Richard, 191–195
Bially Mattern, Janice, 23n.98
bin Laden, Osama, 158–172,
Bismarck, Otto von, 17–18
Black, Edwin, 14–16
Blum, John Morton, 68–70
Bohlen, Charles, 233–236, 237–238
Bourdieu, Pierre, 8n.16
Bricker, John, 233–236
Brooks, David, 10–11, 12
Bruner, Jerome, 10–11, 36–41
Brzezinski, Zbigniew, 100–101,
155–156
bully pulpit
authority in dominant narrative and,
48–52
limits to, 66–68
Bundy, McGeorge, 187–189
Burke, Kenneth, 12–13, 52–55
Bush, George H. W.
Gulf War and, 169–170, 187–189
presidential narrative authority and,
50–52
rhetorical strategies of, 46–47
Bush, George W., 5–7, 38–39, 44–46
alternative narratives dismissed by,
158–163
Iraq setbacks and, 269–275
storytelling rhetoric of, 101–105
"surge" in Iraq and, 1
Terror narrative of, 122, 145–147,
150–157, 163–172, 279–282
Byrd, Robert, 169n.158

Callahan, William, 161
Cambodia, Vietnam War and
expansion into, 251–257
Cantril, Hadley, 128–133
Carroll, Lewis, 9
Carter, Jimmy, 99, 101–105, 114–115,
255–264,
case selection logic, 58–65
Casey, Steven, 128–133
Cato Institute, 155–156
causality, security narratives and,
20–24
Caute, David, 224

CAMBRIDGE STUDIES IN INTERNATIONAL RELATIONS